Light Basics Cookbook

Also by Martha Rose Shulman

Mexican Light

Provençal Light

Mediterranean Light

Entertaining Light

Fast Vegetarian Feasts

The Vegetarian Feast

Little Vegetarian Feasts

Feasts and Fêtes

The Classic Party Fare Cookbook

*Great Breads: Home-Baked Favorites from Europe,
the British Isles & North America*

Gourmet Vegetarian Feasts

The Spice of Vegetarian Cooking

Light Basics Cookbook

The Only Cookbook You'll Ever Need
If You Want to Cook Healthy

Martha Rose Shulman

William Morrow and Company, Inc.

NEW YORK

For Molly Friedrich

Library of Congress Cataloging-in-Publication Data

Shulman, Martha Rose.

Light basics cookbook / Martha Rose Shulman.—1st ed.

p.   cm.

Includes index.

ISBN 0-688-15549-9

1. Cookery.   2. Low-fat diet—Recipes.   I. Title.

TX714.S554   1999

641.5—dc21 98-17817

CIP

Printed in the United States of America

FIRST EDITION

1   2   3   4   5   6   7   8   9   10

BOOK DESIGN BY LAURA HAMMOND HOUGH

www.williammorrow.com

www.martha-rose-shulman.com

Contents

Acknowledgments

As always, thanks to my longtime agent, Molly Friedrich, who helped guide this project to a new editor. And thanks to that new editor, Pam Hoenig, who understood right away what I wanted to do with this book.

And as always, thanks to my husband, Bill Grantham, who is enthusiastic about everything I cook, even when he has to eat the same thing night after night until I get it right.

Thanks also to Clifford Wright and his children, Dyala, Seri, and Ali, for being such reliable and enthusiastic eaters.

Introduction

■

This is a book for people who want to learn to cook and eat well. By eating well, I mean eating food that is delicious and that makes you feel good, food that is vibrant and light but by no means ascetic. Some of you may already know something about cooking; you will use this book to retool your kitchen, refocus your menus, or simply add to your collection of recipes. But many of you know nothing or very little about preparing food; now it's time to learn. You will learn the basics here and develop a repertoire that will give you the confidence to feed yourself, your friends, and your family every day.

When I wanted to learn to cook—I was about seventeen years old—all I had to do was ask my mother to teach me. I wanted to learn the dishes we ate for dinner every night. Sometimes my mother would show me how to chop the onion, brown the meat, and make the spaghetti sauce. Other times she'd just hand me the cookbook with the recipe she used for the dish. With *Light Basics Cookbook* you will have both: somebody showing you how to chop the onion and a recipe to follow.

A number of you are more accustomed to eating food that has been prepared in a restaurant or take-out kitchen than to eating home cooking. Maybe your parents were too busy to cook when you were growing up or everybody in the family had so many activities that it was difficult to coordinate a sit-down meal. And then, as an adult, you found yourself too busy or too intimidated to cook. It may be difficult for you to envision where to begin, because you're used to picking up your dinner at the local supermarket salad bar. For you a good place to start might be with the tossed salad warm-up exercise on page 56, since that's what you like to eat every night. You might ask yourself, "Why bother?" since ready-made meals (what the supermarkets call "meal solutions") are so available at your local mega-supermarket or take-out place. My answer to that question is simple: you will eat better in every way if you prepare your own food. First of all, you will be in charge of the ingredients that go into the dishes you make, most important the fats. Cooking on an institutional scale, even fine cooking, always involves more fat, whether saturated or unsaturated, than you will use when you cook with the recipes in this book. You will also have more control over the flavor and quality of the produce, poultry, and fish that go into the dishes. Chicken dishes made with free-range chicken, the skin removed and fat trimmed, are going to contain less saturated fat and more flavor than dishes from even the most reputable carry-out chicken places. When you begin eating meals made with vegetables like tomatoes and peppers bought from local farmers at the farmers' markets and seasoned to your own taste, the prepared dishes you used to eat might begin to taste a little lifeless, heavy, or salty.

You will taste the difference, and you will notice more money in your wallet once you begin cooking for yourself. There is absolutely no comparison. You might think the trade-off is in time, and you may have a point. But if you care about enjoying food, and about your health, saving time will not be your highest priority.

In any case, cooking from this book won't be unduly time consuming—which is not to say that this is a "meals in minutes" cookbook. I think that cooking is fun, and I have tried to make it fun for you. I've minimized the number of ingredients wherever possible, and I've included many recipes that are made with ingredients you can keep on hand. Knowing how to market for both dry and fresh ingredients is half the battle when it comes to efficient, satisfying, healthy cooking and eating. Part I of this book will provide you with the necessary lists to get you going.

■ How to Use This Book ■

If you are a novice, or unconfident in the kitchen, begin at the beginning. Read through the first section of the book to get an understanding of how cooking works, starting with equipping your kitchen, pantry, and refrigerator and moving on to techniques. Go out and buy the food I tell you how to cut and chop starting on page 25 and practice. Then begin with "Warm-up Exercises" on pages 41–91. These are very detailed recipes that are designed to give you a basic cooking repertoire and teach you techniques at the same time. You can feed yourself and others if you master these dishes. After that, simply pick and choose the recipes that look appealing to you. The collection is designed with a broad range of tastes in mind—for Asian and Mexican food, Mediterranean and good old American. When you are preparing to cook one of the dishes and are not sure about a technique or ingredient, look it up in the index; I've tried to cover everything I ask you to do in the "How to Cook" chapter of the book, so refer back whenever you feel stumped.

If you have some cooking experience, just plunge in and cook the recipes that look appealing to you. If you feel you need to retool your kitchen for low-fat cooking, read through Part I to give you an idea about pantry shopping and equipment.

The dishes in this book not only taste good; they're light and fresh, suitable for everyday eating as well as for entertaining. But no healthy cuisine is worth your effort if it isn't enjoyable to eat. Learning to cook is not just about chopping, measuring, flipping food in a pan, knowing how to follow a recipe. It's about preparing food that tastes good. This means that you will have to taste it before you serve it. As you work through this book you will learn to make decisions about flavor—whether or not a dish needs more salt, garlic, pepper, or lemon juice. I hope you will pay attention to those recipe lines that read "Taste and adjust seasonings" and develop confidence in your own palate. The more you cook, the more sure of yourself you'll become; that's the ultimate goal of this book. Eventually I hope cooking will become so natural to you that you'll be able to cook without relying on recipes at all.

How to Cook

■

In many ways learning to cook is easier than learning other basic things, like riding a bicycle or swimming. You fall off a bike many more times than you ruin a dish. The way to learn to cook is to cook something, and often you'll get it right the first time if you follow the directions and have the right equipment. You may take a few spills along the way, but for the most part you'll have the satisfaction of succeeding and gradually you'll build a repertoire.

■ The Principles of Light Cooking ■

Learning to cook healthy, light food can be more difficult for the experienced cook, who must change techniques and approaches, than for the beginner. In fact, the principles of light cooking are very simple:

■ Include fresh, seasonal produce in every meal. Vegetables and fruits are the key to healthy cooking. Although this is not a vegetarian cookbook, the focus of this diet is largely plant based. Today's supermarkets and farmers' markets are stocked with an impressive array of produce, and if that's the focus of your diet, shopping becomes very exciting. What's in season? What looks good? I often plan meals for an entire week around a particularly good-looking pile of fresh green beans or asparagus or tomatoes that I've purchased at the farmers' market.

Although the recipes in this book are designed for one-stop supermarket shopping, I urge all of my readers to become acquainted with local farmers' markets. As good as all vegetables in a well-stocked supermarket might be, there is nothing better than produce freshly picked. Worlds of flavor will open up to you as you discover the taste of a really sweet pea, a vine-ripened tomato, a peach picked less than a day ago. You'll also become aware of the seasonality of things; it's a thrill when the first cherries come into Los Angeles markets in May, or the Blue Lake beans appear in these markets in the spring, or sweet corn arrives in the summer. It's difficult to think of cooking as a chore when you have seasonal produce to look forward to. If your city or town doesn't have farmers' markets, seek out greengrocers that stock fresh, seasonal fruits and vegetables.

I am not saying that an entire meal must be based on vegetables, all of which require preparation. But one fresh vegetable added to a pasta, even if it is made with prepared tomato sauce, will greatly increase the nutritional value—and the satisfaction—of your meal.

- Focus on animal protein low in saturated fat. This means fish, poultry, rabbit (popular in Europe but not so well thought of here). Some cuts of pork are also relatively low in saturated fat. Beef and lamb are high-fat meats, but they are being bred leaner. My focus, though, is on fish and poultry. Remove the skin from poultry and, if possible, buy free-range chicken since it is less fatty than mass-produced battery chicken that is confined to small enclosures and has not been shot up with hormones and antibiotics.

- Use nonfat yogurt, nonfat cottage cheese, and 1% or nonfat (skim) milk (I prefer 1%, nonfat being a bit watery).

- Cheeses: I do not recommend using nonfat cheese. This is manufactured stuff and has a rubbery texture and no flavor to speak of. Rather, use high-flavor cheeses like Parmesan, feta, and goat cheese in moderate amounts.

- Use monounsaturated oils like olive oil and canola oil, and use them sparingly. I am not an ascetic cook, and I don't believe you have to keep fats down to a teaspoon-size minimum for a recipe to be healthy. But generally, in a cooked dish I try to use no more than 1 to 2 tablespoons of oil for four to six people. For salad dressings you will have the choice of substituting nonfat yogurt or low-fat buttermilk for some of the oil, but I feel that a tablespoon of oil per person on a green salad is not unhealthy: a green salad is a very low-calorie dish, and an oil-based dressing does not increase its caloric bulk unduly, although it does increase the fat content.

- One dish can constitute a healthy, substantial meal. It can be a main-dish soup or salad, a stew, tacos, a stir-fry, or a pasta as long as there is variety and at least one fresh ingredient. I usually complement hot one-dish meals with a green salad, which is easily thrown together and gives me the crunch of lettuce or other raw vegetables that I crave at almost every meal.

- Do not underseason. One of the reasons that "light" cooking sometimes has the reputation of being bland is that too often it *is* bland. That's because cooks have become afraid of salt. Salt is essential, both for bringing out the flavors of foods and for bringing those flavors into balance. Food shouldn't have so much salt that it tastes "salty," but it should have enough to taste *good*. Garlic, pepper, fresh herbs and dried, lemon juice and zest are all important when it comes to seasoning. Low-fat food can have big flavors if you understand how to use them and bring them out.
- Keep your pantry and refrigerator stocked with the following ingredients so that good, healthy meals can be thrown together quickly.

If you are an experienced cook and want to convert recipes: Most recipes that call for large quantities of fat at the beginning, for sautéing the vegetables or browning the meat, can be converted to healthier dishes merely by cutting down on the fat. I find that 2 to 3 teaspoons (3 teaspoons=1 tablespoon) of oil is sufficient for sautéing one or two onions, or the equivalent volume of other vegetables, if you use a nonstick pan and keep the heat moderate. So look at the quantity of oil and first cut it in half. If it is still more than 2 tablespoons, try the recipe using just 2 tablespoons and see if that works.

▨ Marketing and the Light Basics Pantry ▨

The cuisine that I present in this book is meant to be not only delicious and healthy but convenient. My goal is for you to want to cook often, for yourself and your friends. This means having food on hand that can be transformed into a meal.

A healthy pantry extends from the cupboard to the refrigerator to the freezer. You don't need tons of space, but you need a cabinet large enough to hold a selection of cans, some bags of pasta, rice, and beans, and bottles of vinegar, oil, and spices. If your kitchen is a tiny apartment kitchen and the space isn't there, a shelf in a linen closet or coat closet is just as good. In Paris I had a "ladder kitchen," where I was forced to keep everything on a high shelf in a hallway. Though an inconvenience, climbing up on a ladder to reach a can of tomatoes took less time than running to the store.

You also need a bin or a bowl or a basket for onions and garlic, and one for potatoes. I like the stacked bins on casters that you can get at any hardware store or store specializing in storage furniture. My mother keeps her onions and garlic in a large basket on her countertop. When I had a very small kitchen in Austin, Texas, and I was catering, I hung tiered baskets from my ceiling for these ingredients.

You should be able to purchase all of the following ingredients in a supermarket. If something listed here is not in the supermarket, consider it nonessential.

MONTHLY PANTRY CHECKLIST
Canned and Bottled Goods

- Canned tomatoes: both 28-ounce and 14-ounce sizes. They can be whole or chopped, in juice ("recipe ready"), but *not* in puree.
- Prepared pasta sauce: Although you'll quickly find that your homemade sauce is better, there really are some good brands out there now. Check the labels for fat content, however, and buy the low-fat brands.
- Water-packed tuna: Don't get the no-salt variety unless you have a sodium problem, or the dishes you make won't taste as good.
- Canned beans: The ones I use most often are chickpeas, also called garbanzo beans. Next on the list are white beans and black beans. Red (or kidney) beans are nice added to chilies and salads. *Always rinse canned beans before using.* They will taste better and be more digestible.
- Canned or bottled roasted peppers: Great for quick salads, bruschetta, and pastas
- Bottled salsa (red or green)

Nonperishables

- Pasta: Several shapes and sizes, such as fusilli (corkscrews), penne, spaghetti, and farfalle (bow ties), macaroni and small shapes such as bite-size shells and orzi for soups; also buckwheat noodles (soba) for nourishing Asian soups and salads.
- Rice: Long-grain white rice is the most versatile; basmati rice is nice for pilafs and curries; Italian Arborio is essential if you plan to make risotto; brown rice is nourishing and has a nutty flavor and chewy texture—you can use it instead of white rice for stir-fries, stews, and side dishes, but remember, it takes twice as long to cook as white rice.
- Wild rice: Not really a rice but harvested from a kind of wild grass, wild rice is great for salads and side dishes and for pilafs.
- Couscous: A convenient food that we think of as a grain, couscous is really a pasta, made with semolina flour, the same type used for pasta. Instant couscous reconstitutes very quickly and has a nutty flavor and silken texture. Use it instead of rice to accompany stews and stir-fries and as the basis for main-dish salads.
- Bulgur: Bulgur is cracked wheat that has been cooked and dried. It can be reconstituted in hot water in 15 minutes, making it a convenient grain for

a salad or side dish, since it requires no cooking. It comes in fine, medium, and coarse grains. I recommend fine or medium.

- Dried beans: You don't have to fill your pantry with all of these beans, but this list will describe your options. If I had to choose two or three dried beans to keep on hand, I'd pick lentils, black beans, and chickpeas or black-eyed peas.

   1. Lentils: We often forget what a great dinner solution lentils can be. They cook quickly (30 to 45 minutes), require no soaking, and easily can be made into delicious high-protein soups and salads.

   2. Black beans are my standby for a great pot of beans (see page 204); I use them for Mexican dishes, for salads and soups, and in chilies.

   3. Chickpeas (also called *garbanzo beans*) are also important. These round, tawny beans have an earthy flavor and go into salads and soups, stews, and purees. They are the basis for hummus, the Middle Eastern chickpea puree. Canned chickpeas may be substituted for dried.

   4. Black-eyed peas are another quick-cooking bean (45 minutes) that requires no soaking. They have a marvelous flavor and make wonderful salads and soups.

   5. White beans are versatile for soups, salads, and stews. Dried can easily be replaced by canned. White beans are sold under various names: Great Northern, navy, small white beans. The sizes vary but not the flavor.

   6. Pinto beans make a good pot of beans and are great for chili.

   7. Red beans: Good for adding to chiles and vegetable stews.

   8. Split peas: For soups.

- Flour: Always have a small bag of unbleached all-purpose flour on hand. Even if you don't bake, there will be times when you'll need flour for one thing or another, such as thickening a sauce.

- Sugar: I don't use a lot of sugar, so I buy small boxes. But I need it all the time, especially the odd pinch that brings out the sweetness of tomatoes in my pasta sauces.

Oils, Vinegars, Condiments

- Olive oil: You don't have to buy the highest-priced olive oil to get good olive oil, but you do have to buy extra-virgin oil. I prefer the lighter tasting oils from France and Spain to the heavy, dark-green Tuscan oils that are all the rage but that, I think, can easily overpower a dish. For daily use, both in cooking and salad dressings, Colavita, available in supermarkets, is a good, reliable brand. Olive oil can be kept in a cool cupboard and does not require refrigeration.

- Canola oil: This is a monounsaturated oil that has virtually no flavor. For this reason it's good for certain dishes where food must be cooked in a small amount of oil but the flavor of the oil isn't intrinsic to the dish (such as stir-fries, curries, and Mexican dishes). Refrigerate after opening.
- Dark sesame oil: This Chinese oil is a condiment, really, used to season dressings, sauces, stir-fries, and noodle dishes. Buy in small bottles and keep in the refrigerator.
- Red wine vinegar or sherry vinegar
- Balsamic vinegar: This is an aged Italian vinegar with complex sweet and sour flavors and nuances resulting from the wooden barrels in which it is aged. There are very expensive, almost syrupy, balsamics that have been aged for many years and inexpensive brands that have little of the dimension of the high-quality brands. Sweetness is the dominating flavor in commercial, less expensive balsamic vinegars. However, for the purposes of the recipes in this book, where I use balsamic vinegar in combination with other vinegars and oils, the commercial supermarket brands are acceptable. To find better balsamics, choose vinegars that have been aged.
- Rice wine vinegar (for Asian dishes): This is a low-acid vinegar that also has a slightly sweet flavor. It is available in most supermarkets that sell Asian ingredients.
- Soy sauce: Regular or light: I recommend the Kikkoman brand.
- Capers: Refrigerate after opening.
- Dijon-style mustard: Refrigerate after opening.
- Bouillon cubes: Vegetable or chicken or both: Shop in a natural food store for a good-quality bouillon cube that is not loaded with salt, fat, and additives.
- Canned fat-free chicken broth
- Dried mushrooms: Both shiitake and dried porcini or cèpes. Keep in a tightly sealed jar.
- Harissa: A spicy condiment for couscous. A small tube or can will last for months. You can find harissa in imported food and Middle Eastern stores. Substitute Asian chile sauce or cayenne if you can't find it.
- Worcestershire sauce
- Anchovies
- Tabasco sauce

Liquor and Wine

- Dry sherry
- Dry white wine (such as sauvignon blanc or Pinot Grigio)
- Red wine (such as Merlot or Côtes-du-Rhône)
- Triple sec or Grand Marnier (for desserts)
- Kirsch (for desserts)

Vegetable Bins

- Onions: I use medium-size yellow onions for most cooking.
- Garlic: Have two heads at least; gets used up quickly.
- Potatoes: They will keep for a few weeks if they aren't new potatoes and they are removed from plastic bags. Keep them away from light, or their skins will begin to turn green. If you do notice green spots, cut them away with a paring knife before cooking. Keep garlic and onions away from potatoes in a separate bin.

Fruit (you can keep these in or out of the refrigerator)

- A few lemons
- Fresh fruit in season (never refrigerate bananas)
- Oranges

Refrigerator

- A block of imported Parmesan cheese: If you wrap it well in aluminum foil and place in a zippered plastic bag, you can keep a chunk of Parmesan in the refrigerator for a month or more. Save the rinds for flavoring soups.
- Imported black olives: The easiest to find are Kalamata, but I like Greek Amphissa and French Nyons even better. Have some green olives on hand as well, to serve with drinks and to use in certain dishes like the caponata on page 222.
- Fresh ginger: I find the best way to keep ginger once you've cut a piece off, is to put the root in a small jar and cover it with dry sherry.
- Eggs: According to the California Egg Commission, eggs will keep for five weeks after the "sell by" date on the package, provided they are bought from a case that is cold and stored in the original carton in the coldest (bottom) part of the refrigerator. Look for free-range eggs for the best flavor.

Freezer

- Frozen peas
- Boneless, skinless chicken breasts
- Whole-grain bread
- Corn tortillas
- Homemade chicken stock if possible

Putting Together a Spice Rack

I've moved a lot in the last four years, and one of the most expensive tasks I face each time I assemble my new kitchen is accumulating herbs and spices. Recently I discovered a catalog called Penzeys (PO Box 933, Muskego, WI 53150, 414-574-0277, fax 414-574-0278), which sells herbs and spices at very reasonable prices and in small and large quantities. Buying herbs and spices in small quantities is desirable since they don't have a very long shelf life. Natural food stores often stock herbs and spices in bulk or in small bags. Either the catalog or the natural food stores will almost certainly be a cheaper way to go than the supermarket spice shelf, and the quality will be just as good, if not better. Dried herbs and spices should be kept in a cool, dark cabinet and *not* near the stove; heat and light will rob them of their potency. The freezer is also a good place for them. I arrange mine alphabetically on stacked lazy susans for easy access.

Whole Spices Versus Ground

It's always better to use whole spices and grind them as you use them. In particular, there is absolutely no comparison between freshly ground pepper and pre-ground pepper, which develops a rancid flavor if it sits around already ground; and between freshly grated nutmeg and preground. Spices will have a much better, more vivid flavor when freshly ground. Use an electric spice mill for quick grinding. (You can always cheat and keep a jar of ground cumin as well as whole seeds or ground cinnamon as well as whole sticks on hand so that if you're feeling tired or lazy you'll still make a recipe that catches your eye.)

Here is a list of the dried herbs and spices that will come up in the recipes.

Herbs (only a few; mostly I call for fresh herbs)

- Bay leaves
- Oregano
- Sage (aka rubbed sage)
- Thyme
- Rosemary

Spices

- Caraway seeds
- Cayenne
- Cloves
- Whole dried red chiles
- Pure ground red chile
- Cinnamon
- Coriander seeds
- Cumin seeds
- Curry powder
- Fennel seeds
- Paprika
- Whole nutmeg
- Salt: I recommend sea salt. It really does taste better than regular table salt. Hain makes a good free-flowing sea salt that is sold in natural food

stores and in many supermarkets. I also recommend coarse sea salt, which has vivid flavor. I use it in sauces and soups when I have it on hand. It's expensive and not essential, but if you can afford it, you'll appreciate it. Kosher salt may be substituted.

- Black peppercorns: Grind pepper in a pepper mill or spice mill as you need it.
- Red pepper flakes

Shopping by the Week

I'm assuming that most of you, or many of you anyway, find grocery shopping an extreme pain and have little time for it. Cooking and eating well requires more organization than shopping hours. Many vegetables keep well in the refrigerator. If you eat fish, plan your fish menu for the day you shop, because fish is not a good keeper. Chicken breasts will keep for a couple of days in the coldest part of the refrigerator and can be frozen. The rest of the meals in this book are healthy combinations of vegetables and pasta or grains, beans, and main-dish soups and salads that will rely in part on the staples you have in your pantry.

Check your pantry before you go to the store. Replace the supplies that are getting low. Here are the foods that I buy once a week:

- Lemons
- Fruit (oranges, apples, bananas, and other fruit in season)
- Plain nonfat yogurt
- Nonfat cottage cheese
- 1% or nonfat (skim) milk (I prefer 1%)
- Two to four vegetables; 1 to 1½ pounds is usually sufficient for four servings. Use the scales in the produce section to weigh the vegetables. The best keepers are broccoli, green beans, sugar snap peas, zucchini, turnips, winter squash, beets with greens, carrots, and bell peppers.
- Flat-leaf (Italian) parsley, basil, and/or cilantro, also called *fresh coriander:* To keep fresh, cut about ½ inch off at the bottom of the stems. Wet a few paper towels and wrap around the stems, then seal in place with a piece of aluminum foil. Place in a zippered plastic bag, seal, and refrigerate. If the bunches are wet from supermarket produce section spraying, spin them dry and proceed as directed but wrap in paper towels before putting in the bag.
- Salad greens: The best keeper is romaine, followed by leaf lettuce or red leaf. Mesclun, or mixed baby field greens, is another type I buy often. The dryer the lettuce, the longer the shelf life. Supermarkets tend to spray their vegetables with water, which I find very annoying because it affects

their shelf life. When you get home, spin them dry and keep them in vegetable storage bags.

■ Scallions

Seasonal Produce

Certain things should be bought only in season. Then they should be bought all the time, because seasons are short. Although produce is now brought in from many places at all times of year, certain items are different foods altogether when you taste them in their natural season, freshly picked.

■ *Tomatoes:* The best place to buy tomatoes is at farmers' markets and local produce stands. They usually appear in June, but their best season is July through October. Learn what real tomatoes taste like. Live on tomato salads, fresh salsas, and uncooked pasta sauces during the season. Check tomatoes for soft spots when purchasing. They should be firm but ripe. Keep in a bowl or basket. *Do not refrigerate* or they'll lose their sweetness.

■ *Corn:* When I was growing up in Connecticut, we often devoted entire summer meals to corn and tomatoes. "It's a short season," we would say as we reached for our fourth ear. Steamed sweet corn, freshly picked, is sugary and needs no butter—a little salt and pepper if you wish. It is heavenly. Pull apart a couple of leaves when buying corn on the cob to make sure the kernels are whole and not diminished by a critter. Cook as soon after buying as possible.

■ *English peas:* When these are at their sweetest, I don't even like to cook them. They are like candy to me. All they need is a quick dip in boiling water or a 5-minute steam for sufficient cooking. If possible, open a pod to taste the peas to make sure they really are sweet.

■ *Asparagus:* Asparagus is another harbinger of spring. Choose thin stalks that don't look woody. Like peas, all they need is a dip in boiling water or a 5-minute steam.

■ *Cherries:* There is about a month every year, varying from state to state, from about mid-May to mid-June in California, June and July in the Midwest and East Coast, when sweet juicy cherries hit the market. Check cherries for bruises when selecting.

■ *Peaches, apricots, plums:* These are summer fruits that should give when you feel them and smell irresistible. They should have no bruises or soft spots. July and August are their season. Keep them out of the refrigerator unless very ripe.

■ *Strawberries:* Although you can get them year-round, local strawberries, which hit the markets in the spring in California and Florida and later in cooler climates, are much sweeter and juicier than those forced into existence at other times of year. Do not wash until you are ready to eat, because they keep better when dry. They can sit outside the refrigerator for a day.

- *Melon:* Smooth-skinned melons like Crenshaws will actually smell ripe if you put your nose up to them. Cantaloupes should not display too much green. Late spring through early fall is their time of year.

■ Equipment ■

You don't need to spend a lot of money on equipment to be a good cook, but a few items are indispensable to turning out successful, healthy meals easily. Note that some recipes specify "nonreactive" cookware. This encampasses most cookware, with the exception of aluminum and cast iron. Those metals will react with acids in fruits and leafy green vegetables and are best reserved for other foods.

Knives

Knives are the most important tool in any kitchen. Cooking with produce does require cutting and chopping almost every time you prepare a meal, and a sharp, sturdy knife will speed up this process immeasurably. A dull knife is much more dangerous than a sharp one, because you are forced to bear down hard on whatever you are cutting, and the knife can easily slip and cut your hand. You should have one all-purpose chef's knife, with a blade that is either 8 or 10 inches long, whichever is more comfortable in your hand. The knife should feel solid in your hand but not unwieldy. I am small and prefer an 8-inch chef's knife, whereas my bigger friends like longer, heavier knives. When shopping for a knife, ask the salesperson if you can hold a selection and choose the one that feels best in your hand. Stainless steel is the most convenient material. Carbon-steel knives keep a very sharp blade, but they can discolor food, and you have to remember to wipe them dry each time you use them.

In addition to your chef's knife you should have a couple of small, sharp stainless-steel paring knives for peeling and cutting smaller vegetables and fruits. Some cooks recommend a small serrated knife for cutting tomatoes, but I prefer my chef's knife. However, you should have a large serrated knife for cutting crusty bread.

For cutting really hard vegetables like winter squash, a cleaver can be very useful and also comes in handy when cutting apart a chicken.

Keeping Knives Sharp: Along with your chef's knife you should have a good sharpening stone or electric sharpener and a honing steel, which you

V-slicer

Mandoline-type grater

should use a few times each time you use the knife so that it holds its blade. If you don't feel confident about sharpening your knives yourself (many of today's sharpening tools make the task easy), have your knives sharpened professionally once every month or two. Sharpening services are listed in the yellow pages, and some markets and hardware stores also offer knife sharpening.

V-slicer: This is an inexpensive device with a flat surface and V-shaped blade. It's used to make thin, even slices and is particularly convenient for long vegetables like cucumbers. A more expensive version is called a *mandoline*.

Cutting Boards

You should have two, one for onions and other vegetables, one for fruit. The one you use for vegetables should be large and heavy. If it's small, it will be difficult to relax while you chop, and bits of food will fall off. Cutting boards can be wooden or plastic, but they should be heavy. For tomatoes I like a cutting board with a trough for catching the juice. Such a board is also useful for carving roast chicken, which will lose juice into the trough.

Nonstick Skillets, aka Frying Pans

The quality of nonstick cookware is excellent today, and every maker of pots and pans has a line. At restaurant supply stores you can find heavy nonstick pans of all sizes. Wearever makes a very good, reasonably priced line, with rubber covers for the handles, allowing for a solid grip. The more expensive Calphalon line is also excellent. You need one that is at least 12 inches wide. This may seem like quite a large pan for the inexperienced cook, but it will allow you to make everything in this book without any of it spilling out onto your stove. A pan this size is large enough for making a pasta sauce, then tossing the cooked pasta for four right in the pan to coat it with the sauce. For individual omelets, poaching eggs, and warming spices, I recommend a 7- or 8-inch heavy nonstick pan. I use the terms *frying pan* and *skillet* interchangeably.

Nonstick cookware scratches easily. If you stack your pans, put paper towels between them, or use the plastic lids from coffee cans so that the bottom of one pan doesn't scratch the nonstick surface of the other (I got that tip from *Cook's Illustrated* magazine).

A ridged, nonstick grill pan is very handy for grilling chicken breasts and fish on top of the stove.

Wooden Spoons and Spatulas

You need wooden spoons for stirring food in nonstick cookware. Metal will scratch the surface of the pan. Special plastic spoons and spatulas are also available, but I recommend wood, because they are sturdier and more heat-resistant. You should have at least three, and one should be wide. A spatula is necessary for making flat omelets, among other things.

Large, Heavy-Lidded Casserole, aka Dutch Oven

For beans, soups, and stews. It should hold at least 6 quarts. My favorite type is the enameled cast-iron Le Creuset. These are very heavy and hold the heat beautifully. They are expensive, but I've found more than one at garage sales, and now Le Creuset has some outlet stores. I often refer to a large lidded casserole as a *Dutch oven*.

Large, Lightweight Lidded Pot or Pasta Pot

The pasta pot with the basket that sits inside is convenient, but I got along without one for years. An inexpensive, lightweight large pot and a colander are just as efficient.

Steaming Basket

The metal type that folds up and will fit into any number of sizes of pots is what I use most often. For couscous or for the steamed chicken on page 109, a couscoussière (see page 18) or a tiered Chinese steamer is useful. Look for couscoussières in imported cookware shops; Asian markets sell tiered steamers. Some pasta pots have steamer inserts.

Saucepans

I find that I use saucepans most often for steaming and for heating water, so I don't spend a lot of money on them. I buy the light enameled or nonstick stacked pans I find in the supermarket. You should have a small one (for boiling the odd egg), a 1-quart pan, and a 2- or 3-quart pan. You should also have a lid that fits over all of them if they don't come with lids. A 1½-quart or 2-quart nonstick or heavy enameled saucepan is useful for cooking rice.

Baking Sheets

Either flat or jelly-roll pans. For roasting sweet potatoes, peppers, and tomatoes, baking cookies and breads. Look for nonstick brands.

Roasting Pan

For chicken and turkey.

Gratin

Baking Dishes

These can be Pyrex, earthenware, or enameled cast iron, square, oval, or round. You need them for baked dishes and desserts such as gratins, lasagnes, baked fish dishes, and fruit crumbles. You should have a 2- and a 3-quart size. A gratin is an oval baking dish; use interchangeably with baking dishes.

Tart or Pie Pans

These can be classic Pyrex pie pans that you can find in the supermarket or fancier fluted ceramic tart pans. It's useful to have more than one, because the crust recipes in this book make two crusts, so you can have one extra in the freezer, ready and waiting. Most of my recipes call for a 10-inch tart or pie pan.

Couscoussière

I mention this not because I think you need to go out and buy one but because I have one and mention it in a few recipes. A couscoussière is a large, lightweight metal pot with a steaming insert used for making couscous. The stew is cooked in the bottom part, and the couscous is steamed above it in the perforated lidded insert. It's very handy, but you can improvise with a steamer, a strainer, or a colander set into a large pot or casserole.

Utensils and Gadgets

Peelers: A potato peeler is a curved knife with a blade on the curve. It's good not only for peeling potatoes but for shaving off thin bits of Parmesan cheese, for peeling apples and other vegetables, and for removing wide strips of orange or lemon zest. A wider carrot peeler is also good for potatoes, as well as cucumbers and other vegetables.

Scissors: My kitchen scissors are one of the most important implements in my kitchen. I use them every day, primarily for cutting fresh herbs, but they're also very useful for trimming away chicken skin and fat (even poultry that has been skinned by the butcher still has a lot of fat on it). I sometimes use them to coarsely chop canned tomatoes right in the can.

Cheese Grater: I find that I use my small Mouli rotary grater the most, not just for grating Parmesan but for making bread crumbs from a hard piece of bread or toast. A box grater is fine too.

Lemon Zester: This allows you to scrape off thin strips of lemon and orange zest without scraping your knuckles, which always happens to me when I use a grater. You can scrape the zest off in strips, then finely chop it on a cutting board if the recipe calls for finely minced or grated zest.

Mouli grater

Two-pronged Meat Fork: This is helpful for carving roast chicken and turkey.

Wire Rack: For cooling tarts, cakes, and cookies.

Nutmeg Grater: There is simply no comparison between freshly grated nutmeg and preground. Buy whole nutmegs only. They often come with a little grater, but these aren't as easy to use as a classic nutmeg grater, which has a curved grating surface and an opening at the bottom for the grated nutmeg to fall through. I have a nifty grater that you can find in some specialty stores and catalogs, which shaves rather than grates the nutmeg; the nutmeg goes into a little cylinder, and you turn a handle to crank it down against the shaver.

Citrus Press: A hand press or an electric orange press. Lemon and lime juice are important flavorings in many cuisines, particularly low-fat cuisines. You can squeeze juice without this gadget, but you get more juice if you use one, and the seeds are strained out at the same time.

Garlic Press: Not necessary unless you can find a really good one with a deep cylinder and flat holes. Anything else isn't worth the effort, because it will crush rather than puree the garlic and you lose a lot in the process. However, I now use my mini-food processor almost as often as I use my garlic press.

E-Z-Rol Garlic Peeler: Not necessary unless you absolutely hate to peel garlic, but some people say this gadget has changed their lives. This is a rubber tube into which you put one or more unpeeled cloves of garlic. You roll your hands over the surface, and the peels are loosened.

Pepper Mill: Pepper should be bought only whole, as peppercorns, and freshly ground. Ground pepper quickly oxidizes and tastes bitter and even rancid compared to freshly milled pepper.

Whisks: A medium-size whisk is most useful (for beating eggs, making sauces, reconstituting thawed frozen soups), and I often use a very small whisk for making salad dressings.

Spatulas: A wooden one for cooking (particularly omelets, fish, and chicken breasts) and one or two rubber or plastic spatulas for other needs.

Tongs: Tongs are incredibly useful for cooking fish and chicken breasts in a grill pan or on a grill, for roasting peppers over a flame, for serving pasta, and for all sorts of grilling needs. Spring-loaded medium-length tongs are most useful. You can find them in restaurant supply stores.

Pastry Brush: For basting, oiling pans, brushing crusts with eggs, and more.

Ruler: Doesn't sound like a kitchen gadget, but recipes are always telling you how thick and thin things should be. A 1-foot straight edge might help you get an idea of what they mean.

Bowls: Work bowls are indispensable—the more the merrier. They stack, so they don't take up that much space. I like stainless steel. Have at least four—a 3-quart, 2-quart, 1-quart, and 1-pint. A very large stainless-steel bowl is also useful.

Large Colander: For draining larger quantities of food in the sink.

Strainers: A large medium-mesh strainer is most useful, and a small strainer will come in handy from time to time as well. I use my strainer to sift flour as well as for straining.

Salad Spinner: Indispensable. Before salad spinners, drying lettuce was tedious enough to prevent many of us from eating salads regularly. A spinner makes the chore of cleaning and drying lettuce and herbs a cinch.

Mortar and Pestle: A mortar and pestle is one of those tools you might not use too often, but there will be a time when you need one, for mashing garlic or for crushing spices.

Food Mill: Before there were blenders and food processors, there were food mills. Some cooks use them all the time, others hardly at all. A food mill is a simple, manual mill with blades (usually they come with medium, coarse, and fine blades) that lock in under a handle. You set the mill over a bowl, crank the handle, and out comes your puree. While it isn't indispensable, you might find that you prefer a food mill to any other gadget. Use it to puree soups and sauces. When you make tomato sauce and applesauce using a food mill, you don't even need to peel and seed or core the tomatoes or apples; just quarter them, cook them down, and then put them through the mill. The seeds and skins will be left behind.

Skewers: Either metal or bamboo. For kebabs; also handy for trussing a chicken.

Measuring Cups: You need two types of measuring cups:

- **Stacked measuring cups** for measuring dry ingredients; either stainless steel or plastic, these come in 2-cup, 1-cup, ½-cup, ⅓-cup, and ¼-cup sizes.
- **Pyrex measuring cups** for liquid measures. I recommend a quart size and a 2-cup size.

Measuring Spoons: I recommend having at least two sets, one for liquids and one for dry ingredients.

Table of Equivalents
1 tablespoon =
    3 teaspoons
1 cup = 16 tablespoons
1 pint = 2 cups
1 quart = 4 cups
1 pound = 16 ounces

Measuring Ingredients

The way you measure ingredients is particularly important when it comes to measuring dry ingredients for baking, since it is the weight, not the volume, that matters. A cup of flour can weigh anywhere from 4 to 6½ ounces, depending on the humidity and whether or not it has been stirred before measuring. Since flour settles in a bag, it becomes more dense, so it must be stirred before measuring.

Flour: Use calibrated straight-sided stainless-steel or plastic measuring cups (as opposed to Pyrex measures meant for measuring liquids). First stir the flour in the bag, or spoon it into a bowl, to aerate it. Then either spoon it into a measuring cup or scoop it using a quick sweeping motion (rather than a shoveling motion). Level it with the top of the measuring cup by running the blunt side of a knife across the top of the cup.

Baking powder and baking soda: Stir these ingredients before measuring as well. Sift baking soda, which tends to lump. Scoop with measuring spoons, then level off with the blunt edge of a knife.

Liquids: Use either a calibrated liquid measuring cup with a spout or the same type of cup you use for solids. When measuring in a liquid measuring cup, pour in the liquid and set the cup on a flat surface. The level should be dead even with the calibration on the cup.

Brown sugar: Pack tightly into the measure and level off as described for flour.

▪▪▪

Kitchen Twine: Mainly for tying together herbs to make a bouquet garni for soups.

Cheesecloth: For straining stocks and sandy mushroom-soaking broth; for tying together spices that will later be fished out of a soup or poached dessert.

Kitchen Scale: We aren't accustomed to having these useful items in our kitchen, but I urge you to invest in one. You don't need an expensive electronic model (I have both a mechanical and an electronic scale, and I use my mechanical one much more often). The important thing is that the scale have a large enough bowl for weighing ingredients. It is much easier to shop and cook by weight than by volume, and when trying to keep fats down, weighing items like cheese is important.

Meat Thermometer or Instant-Read Thermometer: For measuring the temperature of roast chicken and turkey to determine doneness.

Wraps, Etc.

Aluminum Foil: I use medium-weight foil for most purposes and heavy-duty foil for wrapping foods for the freezer.

Plastic Wrap

Wax Paper or Cooking Parchment

Zippered Plastic Bags: Have medium-size and large freezer bags as well as vegetable storage bags.

Electrical Appliances

Mini-Food Processor: I came to the miniature food processor, also called mini-prep and minichop, quite late in life—this year, in fact—and I use it all the time, particularly for mincing several cloves of garlic or a piece of fresh ginger. The small-bladed little food processor is quick and easy to clean, and I'm so glad I have one!

Food Processor: I don't use mine all that often (it is useless for chopping most vegetables, particularly onions, which it crushes rather than chops), but I couldn't be without it when it comes to making some of my favorite dishes, such as hummus and creamy pasta sauces. I also use it to crush tomatoes when making a sauce, which cuts chopping time down to nothing (because you no longer have to chop the tomatoes!).

Hand Blender: This blender blade on a stick takes all the trouble out of making pureed soups. No more transferring to a blender and worrying about splashing hot liquid on yourself. You submerge this inexpensive gadget directly into the soup to puree.

Blender: I use mine mostly for smoothies and for some salsas.

Spice Mill: This is the same as an electric coffee mill. However, you mustn't use your coffee mill for spices, because some spices leave a residue that your coffee beans will absorb.

Electric Stand Mixer: You don't *have* to have one. If you do, you'll use it for mixing batters, breads, and other doughs primarily. A less expensive **hand mixer** will come in handy for beating egg whites until stiff if you decide to make the meringue cookies on page 359.

■ Cooking Terms ■

Cooking techniques that rely on a great deal of oil (particularly deep-frying) aren't required in a healthy kitchen. Here are terms that will come up in the pages that follow.

Cook: My recipes often begin thus: "Heat the oil in a nonstick pan over medium heat. Add the onion and cook until tender, about 5 minutes. . . ." Where I might have once used the term *sauté*, now I use *cook*. To cook means to expose a food to heat and thereby change its nature. Food can be cooked by being exposed to dry heat, hot liquid, oil, or steam. My cooked dishes often begin by softening (or "cooking") vegetables or aromatics in a small amount of oil.

Sauté: In fact this term will come up rarely. *Sauté* is often misused by cooks: it means to cook quickly in a small amount of hot oil. The word comes from the French word for "to jump," because the food jumps around in the pan. I try to avoid using the word (it does slip into my recipes sometimes) in recipe instructions, because I use smaller quantities of oil that require slower, lower-temperature cooking.

Brown: This means to cook meat or vegetables, usually in a small amount of oil, until they take on a golden or brown color. In many recipes it is the first step. The trick to successful browning is to allow the golden color to develop but not to burn the food, which would transform the sweet flavors brought out by browning to bitter.

Steam: To steam is to cook a food by exposing it to steam produced by a boiling liquid (usually water). A steaming basket is placed above the liquid, and when the boil is reached, the food is added, the pot is covered tightly, and the heat is usually reduced to medium. Sometimes I put the food in the steaming basket in the pot before I bring the water to a boil. Vegetables cooked by steam lose very little in the way of vitamins, and if you are careful not to steam them for too long they retain a nice texture. Once vegetables are cooked as desired, they should be refreshed with cold water to stop the cooking. Either transfer immediately to a bowl of cold water and drain or drain and run a cold tap or spray over the vegetables until cool to the touch. In addition to vegetables, fish and chicken can be cooked by steam. Couscous is also traditionally steamed after being reconstituted, so that it swells and becomes truly tender.

Blanch: To blanch is to cook quickly, usually no more than a couple of minutes and often considerably less, in rapidly boiling salted water. Sometimes the purpose of blanching is merely to wilt a leafy green like spinach or beet greens, to soften a vegetable slightly before subjecting it to another type of cooking (like stir-frying or grilling), or to mellow the strong flavor of a vegetable (like cabbage). Blanching brings out the bright green and sweetness in vegetables like green beans and peas, and they retain a very agreeable texture when cooked this way. Vegetables should be transferred immediately to cold water after being blanched to stop the cooking.

Boil: To boil is to cook in boiling water, usually salted. Water is at a boil when it is bubbling rapidly. Pasta, hard-cooked eggs, and potatoes are cooked this way (potatoes can also be steamed, roasted, or baked). For cooking grains and soups, the liquid is often brought to a boil, then reduced to a simmer. Sometimes you will be asked to skim off foam when something comes to a boil (e.g., when you're making chicken stock or cooking beans). The foam contains bitter-tasting impurities. To do this, take a large spoon or a perforated skimmer and lift off the foam. I find it's easiest to get it off the spoon if I have a bowl of cold water next to the pot; I dip the spoon into the water, then continue skimming.

Simmer: To simmer is to cook in water or liquid that is just below the boil. The surface is ever so slightly bubbling. When it's at a bare simmer, it's just moving and not bubbling at all. Soups, beans, and stews are simmered after they reach the boiling point, or sometimes they're brought only to a simmer.

Poach: To poach is to cook gently in barely simmering water. Usually done with chicken, fish, and fruit.

Roast: To roast is to cook food in an oven (or over hot coals, but usually in the oven), often at high temperatures. Roasting brings out the natural sugars in sweet peppers and root vegetables like onions, beets, carrots, and parsnips, and in sweet potatoes. Roasting fish in a covered baking dish, with a small amount of moisture in the dish, is a great way to cook fish without creating any odor in the kitchen.

Roasting Tomatoes and Peppers: This is confusing, because you actually roast tomatoes, and sometimes peppers, under the broiler. Peppers are sometimes "roasted" over an open flame (see page 131), so, in fact, you're grilling them. Go figure. To roast tomatoes or peppers under the broiler, line a baking sheet with aluminum foil and place the tomatoes or peppers on top. Place under the broiler 2 to 3 inches from the heat (at the highest rack setting). Turn when the tomatoes or peppers have blackened and blistered, after 2 to 5 minutes, and repeat on the other side. Peppers might need to be turned a few times to get all the sides, but tomatoes will be done after roasting them top and bottom. Remove from the heat and transfer to a bowl. Allow to cool, then peel and proceed with the recipe. If you want the peppers to be softer, cover the bowl tightly with a plate and allow to cool. They will continue to steam.

Bake: Baking and roasting are effectively the same thing: cooking food in an oven. Baking is used in reference to breads and pastries but also casseroles, fish, and gratins.

Fry: To fry is to cook in oil. When I say to heat oil and cook an onion until tender, I am really asking you to fry it. But frying usually implies that more oil is used than the amount I call for in my recipes.

Stir-Fry: This is quick-frying, usually in vegetable oil. The food isn't added to the pan until the oil is quite hot, then it is quickly stirred in the pan or wok, usually for no more than a few minutes. Not as much oil is used in low-fat stir-frying as is used in traditional Asian stir-frying, and for this reason I sometimes blanch the vegetables first to make sure they're fully cooked.

Broil: To cook a food directly under a flame. Broiling is closely related to grilling, because the food is exposed directly to very high heat, but it doesn't result in a charcoal flavor the way grilling does.

Grill: To cook food directly above or on top of hot coals, either wood or charcoal. The heat is quite high, and the cooked food has an agreeable charred or smoky flavor.

▪ Chopping, Slicing, Dicing: ▪ "Knife Skills"

Knife skills sounds like quite a professional term, and it may make you nervous. My knife skills are not those of a trained chef; I'm slow and methodical. And I rarely cut myself. You don't have to be fast to have good knife skills, but you do have to have good, sharp knives.

How to Hold a Knife: Hold the handle in one hand (right hand if you are right-handed, left if you're left-handed). Steady the food that you are cutting with your other hand. Fold your fingertips in at the knuckles so that they aren't in the way of the knife. The most efficient way to cut or chop is to keep the tip of the knife steady on the cutting board while you move the body of the knife up and down. However, this won't work well if your knife isn't sharp.

The cell structures of fruits and vegetables are arranged in a definite pattern; you'll notice lengthwise lines in onions and a lengthwise cellular grain in green peppers. All vegetables are constructed this way, but it's more discernible in some than in others. You can dice vegetables easily if you cut first along the grain, then across it.

Preparing Onions

It might help if you take out a couple of onions and cut along with these explanations.

First, whether chopping, slicing, dicing, or mincing, look at the onion. Notice that there is a root end and a stem end. Cut the ends off, then cut the onion in half lengthwise, that is, down one of the lines that you see on the skin. Peel the skin and the first layer of the onion off each half and discard. Lay a half flat on your cutting surface. Steady it with one hand, folding your fingertips in at the knuckles so that they are protected from the blade of the knife.

A whole onion. Notice that there is a root end and a stem end.

Chop

This means to cut into small pieces. Most of my recipes tell you to chop an onion rather than to dice it. Dicing implies a more exact square, which isn't necessary for most of what you'll be cooking here. When a recipe calls for a chopped onion, this is what I want you to do: Cut off the ends, halve, and peel as just instructed. Slice from the edge toward the middle, along the lines. When you get to the middle, turn the onion around, holding on to the cut side, and work again from the other side toward the middle (this makes it easier to steady the onion without worrying about your fingers). Once the onion is sliced, turn it a quarter turn and cut across the slices at a right angle. The root end of the onion is solid and unlayered. Make sure to cut this away so that you don't end up with a big chunk of onion at one end. Repeat for the other half.

Make several parallel horizontal cuts across the onion half.

Dice

Here the vegetable is cut into exact squares. Before beginning the steps for chopping, lay a half onion on your work surface and make several parallel horizontal cuts across the onion half, about ¼ inch apart for finely diced onions, ½ inch for larger dice. Then follow the chopping instructions, slicing first along the lines, then across them.

Mince

I usually reserve this term for garlic, herbs, and ginger, but onions can be minced too. It is the finest cut. Follow the instructions for dicing and make very fine cuts. Then chop more finely by moving the knife up and down over the onions in a seesaw manner, holding the tip of the knife down with one hand.

Once the onion has been sliced along the lines, turn it a quarter turn and cut across the dices at a right angle.

Slice

For sliced onions, unless otherwise specified, cut the onion in half length-wise, then slice along the grain, as you would do in the first step for chop-ping onions, resulting in half-moon-shaped slices. Be sure to cut away the root end so the slices separate.

Rings

If a recipe instructs you to slice into rings, don't cut the onion in half. Cut the very ends off and remove the skin. If you have trouble peeling the onion, cut a lengthwise slit one layer deep down one side. You can then remove the layer of skin easily, taking with it a layer of onion. Slice rings across the grain, holding on to the onion carefully.

Rinsing Raw Onions

If you are not cooking the onion, once it has been chopped or sliced, rinse it with cold water. This removes many of the cells whose volatile juices stay with you long after you're eaten your meal. Either place the cut-up onion in a bowl of cold water, then drain, or place in a strainer and rinse thoroughly, or both.

Other Chopping Terms
(not often associated with onions)

Julienne

Julienne are thin strips, and the term is often used interchangeably with *matchsticks*. However, I think of julienne as thicker than matchsticks (and so does the julienne blade on my food processor). To make julienne, cut vegeta-bles into strips about ¼ inch wide and 1 inch long. For instance, if you are going to cut a zucchini into julienne, cut it into parallel lengthwise slices about ¼ inch thick. Pile a few slices on top of each other and cut into ¼-inch-wide strips, then cut the strips into 1-inch lengths. Make matchsticks the same way, but cut them about ⅛ inch thick. Or you can slice crosswise, stack several slices, and cut into thin strips.

Chiffonade

Chiffonade are thin crosswise strips. I associate chiffonade with leafy vegeta-bles, like lettuce, although the term is applied to other foods. To make chif-fonade of romaine lettuce leaves, stack several leaves, then roll up lengthwise. Cut very thin strips across the rolls.

Preparing Other Vegetables and Fruits

Garlic

Head of garlic with separate clove

A head of garlic is what you buy at the market. It consists of many cloves. To finely mince garlic cloves, finely slice off the hairy stem end, then peel (or peel first, then slice off the end). There are several ways to peel: hit the clove with the bottom of a jar or glass so that the skin splits; squeeze the clove between your thumb and fingers; put on a cutting board, place it under the flat side of a chef's knife, and lean on the knife; or put the cloves inside an E-Z-Rol Garlic Peeler (see page 19) and roll the tube under your hands. All of these methods loosen the skins. Lift off the skins and discard them. Cut the garlic cloves in half lengthwise, from the stem end to the tip. If there is a large green shoot down the middle, lift it out and discard it. It's sort of bitter. Lay a half clove down on its flat side and slice it thinly, then turn it a quarter turn and slice it thinly again to mince.

Green and Red Bell Peppers

Cut pepper into lengthwise strips.

To chop or dice, cut in half lengthwise and gently remove or cut away the stem, seeds, and membranes. You can see the cell structure on the inside of the pepper. I find that it's easiest to lay the pepper on its smooth side and cut on the inside. Proceed as for onions, cutting the pepper into lengthwise strips and then crosswise into dice. For rings, cut the top off crosswise and dig out the seeds with your fingers or with a small paring knife. Slice rings crosswise, against the grain.

Chile Peppers

First of all, to avoid irritating your hands and any other part of your body you touch with your hands after handling fresh chiles, wear rubber gloves or surgical gloves (you can buy them at the pharmacy). If you are not seeding the chile—i.e., you like things hot since the seeds contain lots of capsaicin, what makes hot peppers hot—cut away the stem, quarter lengthwise, and mince, using a quick up-and-down seesawing motion with your chef's knife. If you wish to remove the seeds, for a milder dish, quarter the chiles lengthwise and cut away the seed pod using a paring knife. For larger jalapeños, to seed, hold the chile by the stem and cut off the tip about ⅛ inch from the bottom. Stand on a cutting board on the cut end and, holding the pepper by the stem, slice off the sides. You'll be left with the stem, seeds, and inner membranes to discard in one piece. Slice or mince the chile as directed.

Tomatoes

See page 44, Warm-up Exercises.

Eggplant, Turnips, and Round Squash

Treat these and other roundish produce like onions and green peppers, even if you can't recognize the cell structure as easily. Cut in half lengthwise and lay a half cut side down on your cutting board. Dice, chop, and slice like onions.

Long Vegetables—Carrots, Zucchini, Celery, Cucumbers

This method of slicing applies to long vegetables to be sliced into crosswise medallions or on the diagonal. Cut straight across in parallel slices. Thin slices are about ¼ inch thick (very thin are thinner), thick slices are ½ inch thick. For long diagonal slices, cut at an angle. To cut several long vegetables at once, use a sharp, long knife, hold several vegetables side by side on your cutting surface, and slice several at once as if they were one item.

To chop carrots, quarter lengthwise or, if the carrot is quite large, cut into sixths or eighths lengthwise, then slice thinly across the cuts. To chop celery, make several lengthwise slices, then cut thinly across.

If your zucchini are huge, cut in half lengthwise and scoop out the seeds with a spoon or cut them out by cutting a trough down the middle using a paring knife.

Leeks

These have to be cleaned first, because there is usually sand or mud lurking between the layers. Cut away the dark green part of the leek and trim off the root end. Cut in half lengthwise. Place in a bowl of water for a few minutes, then run underneath the faucet, separating the layers with your thumbs and letting the water run between them to wash out sand. Slice or chop as directed.

Cut leeks in half lengthwise.

Scallions

Cut the root ends off and rinse. Remove the top layer of the onion. Slice crosswise. Discard the ends, where the green part loses its visual appeal. If instructed to chop, make several lengthwise cuts with the tip of your knife before slicing crosswise.

Mushrooms

First trim away the very end of the stem. Then rinse very briefly with cold water to remove sand. Wipe dry with paper towels. Cut up as directed. For portobello and shiitake mushrooms, wipe with a damp paper towel rather than rinse and cut away the entire stem, which is very tough.

Cabbage

To core and slice cabbage, first cut into quarters. Then cut away the thick stems. Discard outer leaves. Shredded cabbage is very thinly sliced. For coleslaw I thinly slice each quarter, then cut the slices into shorter pieces. You can also grate cabbage using a food processor, but I find it just as easy to shred with a knife.

Avocados

Cut three or four strips through to the avocado skin, but not through it. Then cut several strips crosswise for a dice. Scoop out the dice.

This eliminates the messy task of peeling. Cut the avocado in half lengthwise. Twist the two halves apart and remove the pit. Hold a half in one hand and, with a sharp knife, cut three or four strips lengthwise through to the skin but not through it; then cut several strips crosswise if you wish to dice the avocado. With a soupspoon, carefully scoop out the flesh. With this method, you can scoop out precut slices or dice and keep their edges smooth. If you are not using right away, toss the cut pieces with lemon juice to prevent discoloration. Wrap unused parts tightly in plastic wrap, so that cut sides will not discolor upon contact with air. Do not refrigerate hard avocados, or they won't ripen properly.

Cucumbers

To seed a cucumber, cut it in half lengthwise and scoop out the seeds with a spoon or cut in half lengthwise again so that you have spears. Run a sharp knife between the seeds and the cucumber pulp.

Corn on the Cob

Remove the kernels from the cob by standing the cob on end in a wide bowl and running a knife down between the kernels and the cob.

Spinach

Recipes for fresh spinach usually say *stemmed and rinsed*. For this somewhat tedious process I usually place the entire bunch (removed from its twisty if it's held together with one) in a sink or large bowl full of water, with the bottom of my salad spinner close by. Then I grasp each leaf in one hand and pull away the stem and discard with the other. Place the stemmed leaf in the bowl of your salad spinner (or in a large bowl). When all of the leaves are stemmed, fill the bowl with water and swish around vigorously to loosen sand. Lift from the water and discard the water. Repeat until no more sand remains.

To wilt, either blanch for a couple of seconds in a large pot of salted boiling water and transfer to a bowl of cold water, then drain. Or wilt in the water left on the leaves after washing: Heat a large nonstick skillet over high heat and add the spinach, in batches if necessary. It will begin to sizzle and wilt as soon as the water on the leaves comes to a boil. Stir until the spinach is wilted—this generally takes a couple of minutes—and transfer to a colander. Rinse with cold water. Squeeze out the water from the leaves, either by pressing in the colander, by squeezing in your hands, or, most effective, by wrapping in a clean kitchen towel and twisting the towel over the sink. The towel will get stained green, so it shouldn't be a precious one.

Asparagus

To trim, hold a spear in both hands and bend. It will break off where the woody part ends and the tender part begins.

Pineapples

To peel, hold the pineapple so that the place where the leafy top joins the fruit is flush with the edge of your table and the leaves extend over the edge. Hold on to the pineapple with one hand and push down on the leafy top with the other; it should break right off. To peel quickly and neatly, use a stainless-steel knife to cut the ends off; cut the pineapple in half lengthwise, then into quarters (quarters are easy to handle). Run a knife down between the skin and the outer edge of the flesh. Now run a knife down between the core and the flesh. For small chunks, cut the now neatly peeled quarters into halves or in thirds lengthwise, then dice crosswise.

Run a knife down between the pineapple skin and the outer edge of the flesh.

Peaches

If instructed to peel, bring a pot of water to a boil and drop in the peaches for 30 seconds or for a minute if the peaches are quite hard. Transfer to a bowl of cold water and remove the skins. Cut in half lengthwise (most peaches will have a lengthwise meridian; cut along this line) and gently pull away from the pit. Slice or dice as directed.

Plums

Cut in half lengthwise and gently pull away from the pit. If this is difficult, twist the two halves gently in opposite directions and pull away from the pit. Some plums are tightly bound to the pit. In this case, cut down each side of the pit as you would a mango.

Strawberries

To hull, use the point of a sharp paring knife to cut the hull—the stem—out in a wedge. Special strawberry hullers are available at cookware stores, but I think they're an unnecessary expense if you have a good paring knife.

Papaya

Cut in half lengthwise and scoop out the seeds with a spoon. Peel away the skin with a paring knife. If the papaya is quite large, cut in lengthwise pieces, then peel away the skin.

Melons

Cut in half lengthwise and remove the seeds. Slice in lengthwise strips; cut small crosswise sections down to the skin but not through it, the same way you do with an avocado (see page 30). Now run a knife along the inside edge of the rind and the pieces will fall right off.

Apples and Pears

There are two ways to core and slice apples and pears, which should be peeled first if a recipe so instructs. The classic way, for neat wedges, is to cut into quarters, then, using a paring knife, cut away the core of each quarter. A faster way, if you don't need neat wedges, is to cut the apple or pear straight down along each side of the core, making four cuts; the core will be removed. Then slice or dice each piece. To prevent discoloration, place in a bowl of water acidulated with the juice of half a lemon.

From the cut side of the mango, slice lengthwise, then crosswise, down to the skin but not through it.

Mangoes

Cut down the flat side of the pit on both sides so that you have two large, flat pieces with the peel on. Using a small, sharp knife, slice lengthwise from the cut side, down to the skin but not through it. Slice crosswise, down to the skin but not through it. Now press the skin side of the halves with your thumbs to turn inside out (it should look like the mango served in restaurants now). Slice off the little squares from the skin. For the rest of the mango, slice down the remaining sides of the pit and peel away the skin from these strips. There will still be some flesh adhering to the pit. Hold the mango over a bowl while you slice it off (or indulge: lean over the sink and eat what's left adhering to the pit).

Press the skin side of the scored mango half with your thumbs to turn inside out.

Oranges and Grapefruit

When you prepare oranges and grapefruit for most recipes, you will be removing the white pith just inside the rind as well as the rind. There are two ways to peel away both the pith and rind at the same time: (1) Beginning at the navel end of the orange, peel away the skin in a spiral, holding the knife at a slight angle so that you cut away the outside of the orange along with the skin. (2) Cut the ends off the orange. Place a flat cut end on a cutting board and cut down the sides in wide strips, cutting away the pith with the peel. You always lose a bit more of the orange than you'd like to doing it this way, but it's neat. Once the orange (or grapefruit) is peeled, you can either slice away the fruit by sawing between the section membranes or slice crosswise.

Herbs

The best way to chop herbs is to cut them with scissors. Put them in a wide jar or Pyrex measuring cup, point the scissors straight down into the jar, and cut. The herbs will not bruise if you use this method. If you chop herbs on a board, use quick, rapid strokes. Use a small, sharp knife; hold the handle in one hand and rest your other hand on top of the blade. Mince rapidly, pushing the herbs back to the center of your surface as they spread out.

Chopping Nuts

Nuts tend to fly all over the place if you work too quickly. Place nuts on a large cutting board. Use a large chef's knife or a cleaver and chop using a see-sawing motion, keeping the tip of the knife on the surface and moving the knife up and down. With your free hand, keep the nuts in place: cup it loosely over the nuts that aren't in contact with the knife and gently push them back toward the knife as they spread out on the board.

Removing Vanilla Seeds from a Vanilla Pod

If you are using vanilla seeds rather than pure vanilla extract for a recipe, cut the pod in half lengthwise using the tip of a sharp paring knife: lay the pod on a cutting board, set the point in the middle at one end, and cut down the length. Separate the pod into two long halves and scrape the seeds out using the tip of your knife. Don't throw away the pods: stick them in a jar of sugar, for aromatic vanilla sugar, which you can use for desserts.

Beating Egg Whites

Recipes that require beaten egg whites usually call for the whites to be beaten until they form soft or stiff peaks. To achieve this, you can use an electric beater (either a hand mixer or an electric stand mixer) or a large whisk (which requires more physical stamina but is not daunting). If you use a whisk, the egg whites will stiffen more quickly if you also use a copper bowl, because copper contains an acid that speeds up the process. Recipes often ask the cook to add a little cream of tartar (tartaric acid) or a drop of lemon juice to egg whites when they're going to be beaten. This acid has the same effect as a copper bowl. Make sure your bowl and beaters are thoroughly dry, since any moisture will interfere with the process. Begin beating or whisking. The egg whites will begin to foam quite quickly. Continue beating until they are white and thick. Now watch carefully, stopping the beating from time to time to lift some of the whites to see if they stand up on their own. When they have formed soft peaks, they will peak when you lift them and the peaks will bend over. The mixture will look smooth and silky. When they are stiff, the peaks will stand up straight. You don't want them to be dry, however; if they're dry, the mixture will break apart. Over-beating will cause this. Often, when you are beating several egg whites (four or more), there will be a pool at the bottom of the bowl after most of the mixture has stiffened. When this happens I usually transfer the stiffened mixture gently to another bowl and then beat the remaining whites.

Folding

Recipes often ask you to fold beaten egg whites into another mixture; and recipes for baked goods often have you folding dry ingredients into wet or vice versa. Folding is a gentle way to incorporate ingredients so that air bubbles necessary for the texture of the finished product are not broken. To fold in egg whites, place the egg whites in the center of the mixture or batter. Using a rubber spatula or a large spoon, scoop the egg whites down under the mixture in the bowl and toward the edge, then bring up the spatula or spoon at the edge of the bowl and fold the mixture over toward the center of the bowl. Turn the bowl a quarter turn and repeat. Work gently but briskly, scooping, folding over, and turning the bowl, until the mixture looks homogeneous. Use the same action to fold dry ingredients into wet. Some recipes will ask you to combine all the ingredients at once for folding, and others will ask you to add them a little at a time.

■ Safety in the Kitchen ■

By safety in the kitchen, I mean both the safety of the food you are dealing with and the physical safety of you and those around you.

Food Safety

Most cases of food poisoning come from meat, which can easily be contaminated by bacteria if not handled properly. Poultry is particularly susceptible to spoilage and is the main source of food-borne illness. But the risk of food poisoning from poultry and other meats is all but eliminated if it is stored and handled properly.

Here are some safety tips:

- Make sure your refrigerator is below 40°F and your freezer is at or below 0°F.
- Bring meats, fish, and poultry directly home from the market and refrigerate as soon after buying as possible. To avoid excess handling, leave them in their wrapping. Store in the coldest part of the refrigerator (the bottom).
- Wash your hands thoroughly after handling raw meat, poultry, or fish/shellfish. Use hot, soapy water and wash your fingertips well.
- Do not reuse kitchen towels that have come in contact with raw meat, poultry, or fish/shellfish before washing.
- Defrost frozen meat, poultry, and fish/shellfish in the refrigerator or microwave only. Defrosting at room temperature can cause bacterial contamination.
- Wash cutting boards, knives, and other utensils used to prepare meat, poultry, and fish/shellfish thoroughly in hot, soapy water before allowing them to come in contact with other foods. Do not use utensils you used for cooking meat for serving. Wash plates and bowls that have come in contact with raw meat before reusing.
- Marinate meat, poultry, and fish/shellfish in the refrigerator. Do not leave uncooked or cooked meat, poultry, or fish/shellfish at room temperature for more than an hour. Never use a marinade as a sauce unless it has been boiled for several minutes.
- Never eat raw meat, particularly poultry. Cook meat and poultry thoroughly.
- Use a separate "tasting spoon" to taste food when you are cooking. This should be a teaspoon or soupspoon, not the wooden spoon you are using to cook. Rinse it each time you taste.
- Wash fruits and vegetables thoroughly, *including* prewashed lettuces and precut vegetables.
- Never use eggs that have cracked shells. Cook eggs for at least 3 minutes or, if not cooking, make sure an acid like lemon juice or vinegar is included in the recipe; the acid will destroy bacteria. Wash utensils in hot, soapy water after working with raw eggs.

Physical Safety in the Kitchen

The kitchen, where you work with high heat and sharp blades, can be a dangerous place. Here are a few things to consider.

- Keep your stovetop safe by making sure that handles of pots and pans are not sticking out over the edge. This is especially important if children are around. It's easy to topple a hot pot of soup if the handle can be grabbed or knocked into.

- Keep hot pads or kitchen towels close to the stove; *remember* to use them to grab hot pots and pans so that you don't burn your hand. Put hot pots and pans down on trivets, hot pads, or towels.
- Dry knives and put them away after using. If you must drain them, make sure the points are facing down. Put away all knives and blades if children are around.
- Be careful of steam, especially in a small kitchen, where cabinets may be above stoves or kettles. Never reach directly above a boiling water kettle or pot. Steam burns are very painful; remember, steam is hotter than boiling water and can burn you deeper than contact with boiling water in the blink of an eye.
- When pureeing hot soups in a blender or food processor, puree in small batches to prevent splashing out and burning.
- Be very careful with food processor and minichop blades. *Never* get near them when the machine is running.
- Always double-check that you've turned off burners and the oven.

Kitchen Fires

Since we are not going to be doing any deep-fat frying here, the risk of an oil fire in the kitchen is minimal. However, it's important to know that water will not put out this kind of fire; it will only make it worse. You should have a small fire extinguisher in your kitchen, and if you don't, smother the fire with damp kitchen towels or blankets. The biggest causes of other types of kitchen fires are loose sleeves and the ends of kitchen towels. Always roll up your sleeves or change into short sleeves before cooking. Make sure paper towels, kitchen towels, and other fabrics are nowhere near flames; especially when you are using them as pot holders, make sure the ends of your kitchen towels are not dragging near the burners. If a pan of food flames, the flames will die out in the pan, so don't panic.

▪ How to Follow a Recipe ▪

Cooking schools teach cooks to prepare all ingredients ahead and arrange them in separate containers. This is called a *mise en place*, or *setup*. It's a good practice, particularly for beginning cooks. It makes it easier to be neat and precise as you cook, and you never panic because everything is there in front of you.

However, as you become more experienced and confident, you'll find that you might not need to prepare everything beforehand, that you can actually be measuring out an ingredient or preparing another while the onions are cooking or the water is coming to the boil. As my colleague Deborah Madison points out in her excellent book *Vegetarian Cooking for Everyone* (Broadway Books, 1997), cooking is not a linear activity. You begin boiling the pasta water first, although the pasta is the last thing you cook. But to understand the order and rhythm of things, you need some experience, and you need to be sure to read the recipe.

1. *Read the recipe all the way through first.* This is essential. You'll be able to visualize the dish, and you won't be hit with surprises while in the midst of cooking the food.
2. Get out the ingredients called for.
3. Get out the equipment that you'll need (steps 2 and 3 can be reversed).
4. Decide on serving dishes. Will you be serving directly from the pan or in separate serving dishes? Will you serve the plates in the kitchen or at the table?
5. Prepare ("prep") the ingredients as instructed. Measure out seasonings or have them at the ready with dry measuring spoons.
6. Read through the recipe again, then proceed step by step as directed.

▪ Tasting and Seasoning ▪

Following a recipe isn't all there is to cooking. If it were, everybody would be a good cook. *To succeed with a dish, you have to taste.* You are not finished making a dish until you have tasted and approved it. This is why you need the tasting spoon I mentioned earlier. Different cooks taste at different times. I usually taste toward the end of cooking (others taste constantly throughout). What I am looking for is *flavor.* Think of the best dishes you've ever eaten. Their flavors were vivid. This is how you want your food to taste. If you don't feel that the flavors linger long enough on your palate, that the ingredients are not in sharp enough focus or are out of balance, ask yourself first if there's enough salt. It's very common for dishes to be undersalted (it used to be the other way around, and in France and in many restaurants it often still is). You don't want the dish to taste salty, but you do want the salt to bring out the full flavor of the ingredients. Salt also brings flavors into balance. For example, a dish with chile peppers will be hot but not rounded out if there is not enough salt.

Sometimes it's a bit more garlic that's needed, or maybe another pinch of herbs or a bit of acid, like a sprinkle of lemon juice or rind. Or does it need a bit more heat? Cayenne, or more chile pepper? Remember that your clove of garlic may be smaller than mine, and the jalapeño I used to test a recipe might be hotter than yours. In the end, the flavors of your dish depend on your taste buds.

If you're not exactly sure what the recipe needs, ladle or spoon out a small amount into a bowl. Add a little bit of what you think it needs; for example, sprinkle on a little salt or a drop of lemon juice, give the mixture a stir, and taste. You will know when you've hit it right.

▪ How to Keep the Kitchen Clean ▪ While You're Cooking

Keeping the kitchen clean while preparing a meal can be a big challenge for beginning cooks. If you don't clean up as you go along, you may quickly become discouraged from ever cooking again. This is especially important in a small kitchen, where work space is at a premium. But a large kitchen full of equipment, pots, and pans all in need of a wash can be pretty depressing as well.

Every time you finish with an implement, give it a rinse and set it in the dish rack or put it directly into the dishwasher (do not, however, wash wooden spoons in the dishwasher). Try to keep your space as clear as possible. Have a kitchen towel or sponge at the ready for wiping down surfaces as you go along and a whisk broom for the floor (I do this at the end). It takes very little time to wash one tool, pot, pan, or bowl, whereas a pile of them can be quite overwhelming. The cleaning should be part of the rhythm of your cooking. While things are simmering on the stove, look around to see what can be washed up. I try to wash cooking pots, or at least fill them with soapy water, as soon as I've emptied them of food. Also, put food and containers away as soon as you've finished with them. Part of the chaos in a messy kitchen is the food left out.

Dealing with Scraps as You Prep: Onion peels, ends of zucchini, and tomato skins can quickly pile up on your work surface. For years I've used this method to keep them under control: when you begin to prep your vegetables, take out a bowl or a small bucket to use as a mini-trash-can on your work surface. I have a small red pail expressly for this. As I peel carrots, onions, etc., the scraps go directly into the bucket, which I empy into my trash can as it fills. This makes prep work go quickly as well, since I'm not always reaching for the trash can. Another way to deal with scraps is to put your cutting board on top of a big piece of newspaper and scrape the scraps onto the newspaper. Then just gather up the paper with the trash inside and throw away. There's also a plastic container for vegetable scraps you can buy that fits into the corner of your sink.

Other Tips to Make Cooking More Enjoyable and Easy

- Develop a small repertoire of dishes you feel confident making. The Warm-Up Exercises in the next chapter of this book are designed for this purpose.
- Rely on combinations of prepared and fresh foods to save time. I've already mentioned prepared tomato sauce, but foods like smoked turkey can be mixed into a delicious salad seasoned with prepared plum sauce (see page 151). Prepared Asian sauces can be tossed with steamed or stir-fried vegetables and rice for a quick meal. Ready-to-go salad greens require only a quick rinse.
- Work ahead if possible. Salad greens washed and dried ahead will take much of the time out of salad making. Cook twice the amount of rice or beans you need for one meal and use the leftovers for another. Have shredded cooked chicken (see page 97) on hand for quick tacos.
- Recycle leftovers. One night's roast chicken can be the next night's tacos or chicken salad. Cooked vegetables can be used for salads or pasta sauces. Beans can be used for salads, pastas, and tacos. Even stale bread can be the basis for a soup or salad.

A Few Recipes That Come Up in Several Places in This Book

Garlic Croutons

Speaking of stale bread, garlic croutons are something I make often for garnishing salads and soups. Here's how to make them: Toast thin slices of stale or fresh bread, preferably a rustic country bread, in a toaster or a medium oven. Remove from the toaster and rub both sides with the cut side of a clove of garlic (you can cut the garlic in half lengthwise or crosswise, and you don't have to peel it). Cut the croutons into small squares for salads; they can be larger for soups.

Advance preparation: **You can make these hours ahead of time, but the garlic tastes best if freshly applied.**

Pickled Broccoli Stems

Advance preparation:
These will keep for a couple of weeks in the refrigerator, but the color will fade.

PER SERVING:
1.8 gm total fat
.3 gm saturated fat
27.4 calories
2.4 gm carbohydrates
1.3 gm protein

Here's what to do with those big stems that you pay for and usually throw away. These make a great before-dinner nibble, and they're also good in salads.

3 to 4 broccoli stems
½ teaspoon salt
1 garlic clove, crushed, minced, or pressed
1 tablespoon wine vinegar, sherry vinegar, or apple cider vinegar
1 tablespoon olive oil

1. Peel the broccoli stems using a paring knife. The peels will pull away easily, especially if you work from the top toward the bottom of the stem. Slice thinly and place in a jar. Add the salt, cover the jar, and shake vigorously to distribute the salt. Refrigerate for several hours or overnight.
2. Drain out the water that has accumulated in the jar. Add the garlic, vinegar, and olive oil and shake again. Refrigerate for several hours. Serve with toothpicks or add to salads.

Drained Yogurt (or Yogurt Cheese)

Advance preparation:
This will last through the "sell by" date on your yogurt.

PER SERVING:
.1 gm total fat
.06 gm saturated fat
31.8 calories
4.4 gm carbohydrates
3.3 gm protein

Makes 1 cup

This is a staple in the Middle East. It's simple to make and to keep on hand and excellent made with nonfat yogurt. You can serve it plain or season it with herbs and/or garlic. Use as a spread, dip, sauce, or topping or sweeten with honey and use as a dessert topping or for dessert itself.

2 cups plain nonfat yogurt

Line a strainer with a double thickness of cheesecloth and set it over a bowl. Or you can use a large coffee filter such as a Melita, as long as your Melita doesn't smell too much of coffee. Place the yogurt in the strainer or filter and refrigerate for at least 1 hour and preferably 4. The water—about half the volume—will drain from the yogurt, which will now be very thick. Transfer the yogurt to a covered container and refrigerate.

Warm-up Exercises

■

The purpose of this chapter is to give you, right off the bat, a repertoire. If you're a true beginner, you will be walked through the
recipes step by step, and by the time you've cooked them all, you
will be confident about feeding yourself. If you already know something
about cooking, you'll just pick up ten good light recipes that will expand
your repertoire.

■ Five Light Easy Pieces ■

Don't worry: all the recipes in this book will not be long like the ones
here. Actually they just *look* long. That's because I'm assuming you know
nothing here; every detail is explained. Each recipe ends with a short version
for those in the know. The five recipes that follow will give you a small
repertoire: four main dishes and a salad that will go with any of them. Master these, and you'll be able to feed yourself, your friends, and your family.
The techniques you'll learn as you do these recipes will give you the confidence to go on and cook everything in the book.

Here's what you'll learn to do by making these dishes:

■ Pasta with Simple Tomato Sauce, made from fresh or canned tomatoes,
with variations for making it with ground turkey, turkey sausage, or
canned tuna: working with tomatoes, sautéing garlic, cooking pasta,
browning ground meat, cooking sausage.
■ Lemon and Garlic-Marinated Pan-Fried or Pan-Grilled Chicken Breasts
with Steamed Broccoli or Green Beans and Potatoes: marinating chicken

breasts, cooking chicken breasts, steaming green vegetables, cooking potatoes, cooking more than one dish for a meal.

- Tossed Green Salad with Classic Vinaigrette: washing and drying lettuce; making vinaigrette—you'll see that it takes only a minute to make a vinaigrette, and isn't it so much better than the bottled stuff?
- Grilled or Broiled Fish Steaks with Salsa served with steamed green beans or broccoli and new potatoes: cooking a piece of fish, timing the meal, making salsa if you aren't buying it.
- Asian-Style Stir-Fried Vegetables with Rice and variations with tofu and with lean pork: chopping vegetables, blanching vegetables, stir-frying, making an Asian sauce, cooking rice, working with tofu, browning meat.

■ Five More Light Easy Pieces ■

The purpose of these five recipes is twofold: to expand your repertoire and give you a dessert and to give you a few more basic dishes that you can cook quickly, after work. Some of the techniques you'll use in these recipes are ones you'll already have learned by making the first five.

- Ratatouille: If you can make a good ratatouille, you will understand what it means for vegetables to simmer in a little olive oil and their own juices over low heat and be transformed into a delicious, heady, Provençal vegetable stew. You can feed yourself on ratatouille for a week—you can toss it with pasta, eat it cold as a salad, blend it up as a soup, fill an omelet or a tart with it, top it with bread crumbs and Parmesan and bake it as a gratin, or take it to a picnic or a potluck.
- Roast Chicken: Every nonvegetarian cook should know how to roast a chicken, one of the easiest standby meals, particularly good if you've invited people over. Roast chicken per se is not low-fat, but without the skin the fat goes way down, and it's still a succulent main dish.
- Garlic Soup: One of my most frequent fast dinners, any vegetable can be added to it, and you can bulk it up with pasta, potatoes, rice, or stale bread.
- Mediterranean Tuna and Bean Salad: Another favorite pantry dinner. This is meant to introduce you to the concept of the main-dish salad. It's always good and always a possibility.
- Cherry Clafoutis: One of the easiest of impressive desserts, clafoutis is an often-overlooked dazzler. Clafoutis has everything people love about a fruit tart, without the hassle of a crust. Instead of cherries, you can

choose among a wide variety of fresh fruits in season and even canned or frozen fruit.

■ Five Light Easy Pieces ■

Pasta with Simple Tomato Sauce

■

Makes 4 servings

Lots of bottled sauces are good, but this is better. It has a cleaner, fresher, more vibrant flavor. You can make it with fresh or canned tomatoes, which makes it a summer or a winter sauce. Pasta isn't the only place for it: serve it with fish or chicken breasts or over crêpes or stuffed peppers, spread it on pizza dough, and spoon it over garlic-rubbed toasted bread. In this recipe you'll use it for pasta—and you'll learn to cook pasta while you're at it. Don't bother using fresh tomatoes if they aren't local, superripe, and sweet.

Pasta shouldn't be drowned in tomato sauce. The noodles should be bathed lightly in it. When you top the pasta with this, it might not look like enough to you at first, but once you toss the pasta, you'll see that all the great flavors of the sauce come through, balanced by the perfectly cooked—al dente—noodles.

1 tablespoon olive oil

2 to 3 large garlic cloves, to your taste, peeled and minced, or pressed

1¾ pounds tomatoes (7 medium-size fresh *ripe*) or one 28-ounce can tomatoes, drained (may use chopped *in juice* but *not* in puree; that's too thick here), if ripe tomatoes are not available

½ to ¾ teaspoon salt, to your taste, for the sauce, plus at least 1 tablespoon for the pasta water

⅛ teaspoon sugar

2 tablespoons slivered fresh basil leaves, ¾ teaspoon dried oregano or thyme, or a combination

Freshly ground black pepper to taste

¾ pound dried pasta (see page 48)

⅓ cup freshly grated Parmesan cheese

How to Mince Garlic

A *head* of garlic is what you buy in the market. It consists of many *cloves*. Separate two or three cloves (I recommend three, especially if they aren't very big) from the head. Using a sharp paring knife, slice off the hard stem

Get out the following equipment: kitchen scale if using; liquid measuring cup; measuring spoons; medium-size (2- to 3-quart) saucepan; deep-fry skimmer or slotted spoon if using; medium-size bowl; paring knife; chef's knife and cutting board; food processor if using; garlic press or minichop if using; large pot and colander or pasta pot; large, heavy nonstick skillet and wooden spoon; large, wide ceramic bowl if using; 2 large spoons, pasta servers, or tongs

PER SERVING:

7.4 *gm total fat*
1.8 *gm saturated fat*
423 *calories*
72.2 *gm carbohydrates*
15.60 *gm protein*

end. Peeling garlic is easy once you've loosened the skins. You have a few options for this:

1. Take a jar and hit the garlic with the bottom. Don't smash it, but hit it firmly so that the skin splits.
2. Put the garlic on a cutting board, place it under the flat side of a chef's knife, and lean on the knife.
3. Put the cloves inside an E-Z-Rol Garlic Peeler (page 19) and roll the tube under your hands.
4. Take each clove between your thumb and your forefinger and apply pressure; often you can get the skin to pop open this way.

All these methods loosen the skins. Lift off the skins and discard them. Cut the garlic cloves in half lengthwise, from the stem end to the tip. If there is a green shoot down the middle, lift it out and discard it; it's sort of bitter. If you're chopping the garlic, lay a half clove down on its flat side and slice it thinly, then turn it a quarter turn and slice it thinly again. Then, keeping the tip of your knife down—use a chef's knife for this—seesaw the knife up and down over the garlic, pushing it back toward the knife with your free hand every once in a while as it spreads out on the board. Chop the garlic until it is quite finely minced. Transfer to a little plate or dish.

How to Press Garlic

Cut the peeled cloves of garlic in half lengthwise and remove any green shoot. Cut the halves in half crosswise so they fit into the cylinder of your garlic press. Press one piece at a time into a little dish or onto a plate. When you open the press, lots of crushed garlic will be adhering to the plunger or piston of the press. Make sure to get that out. If it is just crushed but not pureed, send it through the press again. Scrape the garlic off the outside of the cylinder onto your plate. Immediately wash your garlic press or at least put it in a bowl or glass of water so that the garlic doesn't dry out and clog the holes.

How to Peel Tomatoes

If you're using fresh tomatoes, you'll have to peel them, then seed them. To peel tomatoes, all you have to do is drop them into boiling water for about 30 seconds, then rinse them with cold water and the skins come right off. You don't have to do this in a huge saucepan; you can do it in batches. On the other hand, if you want to get your pasta water hot ahead of time, use a great big pasta pot and drop the tomatoes in before you cook the pasta. I think, with seven tomatoes, it's easier to do this in batches, so that's what I'll advise here.

With a paring knife, cut out the stem and hull of the tomato by cutting a cone into the top. You have to do this eventually, and doing it now will make it easier to peel the tomatoes. Bring a medium-size or large saucepan of water to a rolling boil and drop in the tomatoes, about four at a time. While counting to thirty, fill a bowl full of cold water from the tap. Transfer the tomatoes from the boiling water to the cold water, using a deep-fry skimmer, slotted spoon, or just a plain old big spoon. Repeat with the remaining tomatoes, changing the cold water in the bowl with each batch, since the hot tomatoes will warm up the water. It's the shock of the cold after the boiling that loosens the skins so handily.

Drain the tomatoes and peel away the skins using your fingers.

■ If the skin doesn't pull away easily, either you didn't leave the tomato in the boiling water long enough, or your tomatoes aren't ripe enough (in which case use canned tomatoes, which are already peeled).

■ If you leave the tomatoes in the boiling water for too long, they'll begin to cook and you'll lose some of the pulp, which will adhere to the skins when you pull them off.

If you're using canned tomatoes, which are already peeled, pour off the juice. You might have to hull them and pull off any remaining bits of skin.

How to Seed Tomatoes

The seeds are bitter, so you want to get rid of them. You don't have to remove *every single seed*, but it's a good idea to rid the tomato of as many as you can in a single squeeze. If you want to save the juice in the tomatoes, seed them over a strainer set over a bowl. It's nice to add this to the tomato pulp when you cook the sauce. Cut the tomatoes in half, across the equator—i.e., halfway down from the stem end. Hold a tomato half with the rounded side against the inside of your hand. Hold it over the sink or over a bowl and squeeze, sort of gently (you don't want to crush the tomatoes); the seeds will come right out. If the tomato is very mealy, it will fall apart in your hand, a sign that it wasn't a very good tomato, but you can chop it up anyway.

If you're working with plum tomatoes, you may find it easier to cut them lengthwise and scoop out the seed pockets with your fingers. Try it both ways.

Canned tomatoes are usually plum tomatoes, but I usually halve them across the equator. They've been stewed a bit, so they're soft, and the seeds and juice will run right out. I usually do this right in the can.

Cut the tomato in half across the equator, halfway down from the stem end.

Crushing the Tomatoes in a Food Processor

If you have a food processor, save yourself a lot of time and transfer the seeded peeled tomatoes to the large bowl fitted with the steel blade. Pulse twenty to thirty times. The tomatoes should be crushed and pulpy, but *not* a smooth puree.

Chopping Tomatoes

If you don't have a food processor, get out your knife and cutting board. It's easy to chop the tomatoes, just more time consuming.

You might find it easier to use a serrated bread knife for this. I use my 8-inch chef's knife. Just be sure it's sharp. If you have a cutting board with a meat-cutting side that has a trough around the edge, use it because it's handy for catching the juice that tomatoes exude as you chop them. Lay a half tomato flat side down on your cutting board. Slice the tomato into thin strips. Turn your knife so that the flat side is parallel to your cutting board, steady the tomato by placing your free hand over the top, and cut through the length of the tomato. Now turn the half tomato a quarter turn and cut across the strips. You've now cut the tomato into small dice. For tomato sauce, you don't have to chop the tomatoes more finely than this since they'll break down further as they cook, but it won't hurt if you chop them finely, so why not get some practice? Hold the tip of your knife down with your free hand and seesaw the knife up and down quickly over the chopped tomatoes. They'll spread out, so push them back every once in a while with your free hand. Carefully transfer the chopped tomatoes to a bowl and rinse off your cutting board and your hands.

Another Way to Prepare Fresh Tomatoes

This is how many cooks in Greece and Spain do it. Try it if you think peeling tomatoes is a drag. Don't peel the tomatoes, just cut them in half across the equator and squeeze out the seeds. Place a grater over or in a wide bowl. Holding onto the skin side of the tomatoes, grate them on the large holes of your grater. When you get to the skin, stop! Don't grate it or your hand. Now the tomatoes are practically pureed.

And Another Way: With a food mill (see page 20), you don't have to bother with peeling and seeding at all. Quarter the tomatoes and cook the sauce as directed. When the sauce has cooked down, put through the medium blade of a food mill. The seeds and skin will be left behind.

How to Sliver Basil

First wash the leaves, then wrap them in paper towels to dry or spin them dry. Take several leaves and pile them on top of each other. Hold them together with one hand and use kitchen scissors to cut crosswise slivers with the other hand. Using the scissors is a gentle way to cut the basil; the leaves won't discolor because you don't bruise them as you might if you chop them with a knife.

Now measure out the remaining ingredients for the sauce.

Making the Sauce

Before you begin the sauce, if you want to get ahead, start the water boiling for the pasta (see below).

For the sauce you'll need a nonstick frying pan (also called a *nonstick skillet*) at least 12 inches wide. It should be heavy-bottomed, which means it shouldn't be really thin. You'll also need a wooden spoon or a plastic heat-resistant spoon made for stirring in nonstick cookware (metal scratches the finish).

This sauce cooks quickly. The tomatoes simmer at a good pace and cook down with the garlic into a thick, fragrant sauce.

Heat the nonstick frying pan over medium heat. Hold your hand *above* the pan; if you can feel heat coming off the pan, it's hot. Add the olive oil to the pan, wait a minute, and add the garlic. As soon as it begins to sizzle, stir constantly with a wooden or plastic heat-resistant spoon. Don't let the garlic turn hard or brown. It should become just translucent and fragrant, the color just slightly golden. *This should take about 30 seconds, a minute at most.* As soon as you observe these changes, add the tomatoes, salt, sugar, and dried herbs if you're using them. Turn the heat up just a little, to medium-high. Stir until the tomatoes begin to bubble. Cook, stirring often, for 15 to 25 minutes; the tomatoes should cook down and just begin to stick to the pan. The time this takes depends on how juicy the tomatoes are and how thin the bottom of your pan is. Remember to stir often. The sauce should smell wonderful. Stir in the fresh basil if you're using it. Taste the sauce with a teaspoon that you use just for tasting (called a *tasting spoon*; don't use the cooking spoon). Does it have enough salt? Add some if you don't think the sauce tastes vivid enough. Does it have enough garlic? Add another minced clove if you want it more pungent, and cook, stirring, for a few more minutes. Add a few turns of the pepper mill and remove from the heat.

At this point you can decide whether you want your sauce to have a smooth, uniform texture or if it's okay sort of chunky, as it is now. If you do want a smoother sauce, transfer it to a food processor fitted with the steel blade and blend or pulse for about 30 seconds, no more. Put it into a

Advance preparation: **The tomato sauce will keep, covered, for 5 days in the refrigerator and freezes well for several months.**

saucepan or back into the nonstick skillet. You'll heat it again just before serving.

How to Cook Pasta

You need a big pot for this. It shouldn't be too heavy, though, because you'll be filling it with water and lifting the whole pot to drain it (unless you have a pasta pot with a perforated basket insert that you lift right out, but these are expensive). Fill the pot three-quarters full with 4 to 5 quarts of water and bring the water to a rolling boil over high heat with the lid on. This takes time; that's why I suggest you start the water boiling at the same time you begin your sauce. You can always turn it off if it boils before you need it. Place a large colander in your sink. Get out a big ceramic bowl to serve the pasta in. Or you can toss and serve the pasta from the pan.

Have the pasta in a bowl or measuring cup. You can use any shape you want for the sauce. Twelve ounces is three quarters of most bags or boxes of pasta. Add a tablespoon of salt to the boiling water; the salt will cause the water to boil more rapidly and will add flavor to the pasta. Then, making sure the water is boiling hard, gradually add the pasta. The water will stop boiling momentarily when you add the pasta. Using a long-handled wooden spoon or pasta spoon, stir the pasta up from the bottom of the pot so that it doesn't stick. Put the lid back on the pot momentarily so that the water will come back to a boil more quickly. Once the pasta is moving around in the boiling water, you can mostly leave it alone, but every once in a while, give the bottom of the pot a scrape with the wooden spoon, just in case. Meanwhile, ladle a spoonful or two of the boiling water into your serving dish to warm it and reheat your sauce over low heat.

Sometimes the cooking time is written on the pasta box or bag, but often it isn't. Thin angel hair pasta cooks in a few minutes but most pastas take 7 to 12 minutes. With the exception of angel hair or capellini, I begin checking after about 7 minutes. Spoon out a piece of pasta or grab a piece with tongs. If it's spaghetti and it doesn't even bend much, don't bother for a few more minutes. Run the pasta under cold water so you don't burn your tongue, then bite into it. It shouldn't be hard in the middle, but it shouldn't be floppy or mushy either. *Al dente* (recipes are always instructing you to cook pasta *al dente*) means firm to the teeth, not mushy. Test again in a minute or two. When you test and it's cooked all the way through but still a bit firm in the middle—that is, it resists your teeth—you're ready to drain and serve.

Empty the water from the serving bowl, which should now be warm. Turn off the heat under your pot (it's easy to forget if you don't do it right away), and, using potholders, carefully bring your pot over to the sink. Slowly drain the pasta over the colander, being careful not to let the very hot

Measuring Pasta

Uh-oh, how do you figure out what ¾ pound of pasta is if you don't have a scale? I wish you did have a kitchen scale, because it comes in handy, *especially for pasta!* You can't measure pasta accurately since all pasta is shaped differently. Three quarters of a pound of, say, penne or fusilli is about 3½ cups. But how do you measure cups of spaghetti? A package of pasta usually weighs a pound, so use three quarters of the package. A 3-ounce serving of dry pasta is a substantial serving (although most restaurants will serve you 4 ounces). If you're trying to lose weight, try 2 or 2½ ounces instead.

water splash back on you and keeping your face and bare arms away from the very hot steam that will explode upward. The noodles don't have to be completely dry, but give the colander one shake, then pour the noodles into your warm serving dish. Immediately top with the sauce. Take it to the table or toss it in the kitchen. Toss, using two large spoons, salad servers, or tongs, until the pasta is coated evenly with the sauce. Don't spend too long doing this or it will cool off quite a bit. No matter how fast I do this, though, I can never get it to the table as hot as they do in restaurants. Serve and pass the cheese for people to sprinkle on. Alternatively, toss the pasta with the sauce in the pan.

Variations: Authentic Italian sauces that contain meat often contain very little. Meat was at one time scarce and very expensive in this once-poor country, and cooks were ingenious when it came to getting a lot of flavor out of a small amount of meat. A sauce that contains only 1 ounce of, say, beef or pancetta per person is not adding an undue amount of fat and cholesterol to your diet. However, it's easy today, in the United States, to find lower-fat meats like ground chicken and turkey and sausages made with poultry instead of higher-fat pork.

Tomato Sauce with Ground Turkey

To the tomato sauce recipe, add 6 ounces ground turkey. Prepare all of your ingredients for the sauce.

Before you make the tomato sauce, you need to cook the meat until all traces of pink disappear. Heat the olive oil over medium heat in your nonstick pan, the one you're going to use for the sauce, and add the ground turkey. Cook, stirring and breaking up the meat with a wooden spoon. When the meat is no longer pink anywhere, and bits of its surface are brown, remove the pan from the heat. Pour off any liquid, which is partially fat, from the pan. Season the meat with a few generous dashes of salt from the shaker. Return to the heat and add the garlic. Cook, stirring, until the garlic begins to color and smell fragrant, 30 seconds to a minute. Add the tomatoes and proceed with the recipe as directed, stirring often to make sure the meat is not sticking.

Tomato Sauce with Turkey or Chicken Sausage

To the tomato sauce recipe, add ¼ pound Italian-style turkey or chicken sausage—usually one sausage. Remove the sausage from its casing by tearing the casing away from the meat and crumble the meat.

Begin the recipe for tomato sauce as directed, by sautéing the garlic. As

PER SERVING:
11.6 gm total fat
2.9 gm saturated fat
498 calories
72.2 gm carbohydrates
24.3 gm protein

PER SERVING:
10.4 gm total fat
2.7 gm saturated fat
470 calories
72.3 gm carbohydrates
20.6 gm protein

soon as it begins to color, add the crumbled sausage. Cook gently, pressing the meat into the pan, until the meat is no longer pink, then stir in the tomatoes. Proceed as directed.

Tomato Sauce with Pancetta

To the tomato sauce recipe, add 2 ounces lean pancetta—about two ⅛-inch-thick slices. Dice the pancetta, then heat the olive oil over medium-low heat in the pan you are going to use for the sauce. Add the pancetta and cook, stirring, until it renders its fat and begins to color, 8 to 10 minutes. Pour off most of this fat and add the garlic. Proceed with the recipe as directed.

If You Like It Hot . . . Add to the olive oil 1 to 2 dried red peppers, crumbled, or ¼ teaspoon dried red pepper flakes along with the garlic and proceed.

Now that you're comfortable with . . .

- **peeling, seeding, and chopping tomatoes**
- **preparing garlic**
- **preparing fresh basil**
- **cooking pasta**

. . . you won't think twice about following a standard recipe for pasta with tomato sauce, which looks like this:

Pasta with Simple Tomato Sauce

Makes 4 servings

1 tablespoon olive oil
2 to 3 large garlic cloves, to your taste, peeled and minced or pressed
1¾ pounds tomatoes (7 medium-size fresh *ripe*) or one 28-ounce can tomatoes, drained (may use chopped in *juice* but *not* in puree; that's too thick here), if ripe tomatoes are not available
½ to ¾ teaspoon salt, to your taste, for the sauce, plus at least 1 tablespoon for the pasta water
⅛ teaspoon sugar
2 tablespoons slivered fresh basil leaves, ¾ teaspoon dried oregano or thyme, or a combination
Freshly ground black pepper to taste
¾ pound dried pasta (see page 48)
⅓ cup freshly grated Parmesan cheese

PER SERVING:
8.4 gm total fat
2.2 gm saturated fat
444.7 calories
72.4 gm carbohydrates
18.4 gm protein

1. Heat the oil in a large, heavy nonstick skillet over medium heat and add the garlic. When the garlic begins to color, add the tomatoes, salt, sugar, and dried herbs if using. Cook, stirring often, until the tomatoes are cooked down and beginning to stick to the pan, 15 to 25 minutes. Stir in the fresh basil if using, taste, and adjust for salt and garlic. Season with pepper and remove from the heat.
2. If you want your sauce to have a smooth, thick texture, transfer to a food processor and pulse or puree for 30 seconds. Return to the pan or to a saucepan and heat through before serving.
3. Bring a large pot of water to a rolling boil, then add the tablespoon salt and the pasta. Cook until the pasta is al dente, firm to the bite, and drain. Toss at once with the sauce and serve, passing the grated cheese.

Lemon- and Garlic-Marinated Pan-Fried or Pan-Grilled Chicken Breasts with Steamed Broccoli or Green Beans and Potatoes

Makes 4 servings

Terrific dinners can be thrown together quickly if you have chicken breasts on hand. The quality of the chicken is important, and in my estimation free-range chicken is worth the extra money. It's cheaper if you buy it on the bone, then ask the butcher to skin and bone it. Unfortunately, most supermarkets these days don't have in-house butchers who will do this. Instead, the chicken breasts are sold several to a package, often more than you need. This won't be a problem if you have a decent freezer. When you get the chicken breasts home, remove from the package those that you won't be using, wrap them tightly in plastic, then aluminum foil, and place in the freezer (see sidebar). They can be frozen for up to 3 months.

This is a homey, simple meal; the marinade of olive oil, lemon juice, garlic, and herbs provides wonderful Mediterranean flavors. The vegetables need no embellishment as far as I'm concerned, but if you want to, you can toss the potatoes with a bit of olive oil and sprinkle the broccoli with fresh lemon juice.

FOR THE CHICKEN BREASTS:

2 whole chicken breasts, split, boned, and skinned, or 4 half breasts

1 tablespoon olive oil

2 garlic cloves, peeled and minced or pressed

3 tablespoons fresh lemon juice

1 teaspoon chopped fresh rosemary and/or thyme leaves or ½ teaspoon dried rosemary and/or thyme

Salt and freshly ground black pepper to taste

Get out the following equipment: large bowl; fork, whisk, or wooden spoon; measuring spoons; chef's knife and cutting board; garlic press or minichop if using; vegetable brush; paring knife or potato peeler; steamer; 2- or 3-quart saucepan with lid; colander; large, heavy nonstick skillet or grill pan or well-seasoned cast-iron skillet or grill pan; spatula or tongs

Advance preparation: **This is all pretty last-minute, but you could marinate the chicken breasts before you go to work and cook them when you get home.**

PER SERVING:
7.0 gm total fat
1.4 gm saturated fat
454 calories
64.3 gm carbohydrates
35 gm protein

continued

Warm-up Exercises
51

1½ pounds small smooth-skinned ("waxy") potatoes, such as new potatoes, red potatoes, white creamers, or Yukon Gold (I love Yukon Gold)

1 medium-size head broccoli (about 1 pound) or 1 pound green beans

FOR GARNISH:

Fresh thyme or rosemary sprigs and/or lemon wedges

Buying and Preparing the Chicken

Try to buy the chicken at the butcher counter rather than from the precut, packaged meat cooler. Unless it's a huge package of precut chicken breasts, you'll probably get better value if you ask for whole chicken breasts and have the butcher split, bone, and skin them. If there's a great sale on precut boned and skinned chicken breasts, go ahead and get them. Try to get free-range; the next best thing is "natural" or "hormone-free" chicken.

When you unwrap the chicken, rinse it under cold running water and pat dry with paper towels.

You'll need a bowl large enough for the chicken breasts and a fork, whisk, or wooden spoon. Stir together the olive oil, garlic, lemon juice, herbs, salt, and pepper. Add the chicken and toss to coat it evenly with the marinade. Marinate for 15 to 30 minutes, in or out of the refrigerator, turning once or twice.

Meanwhile, prepare and cook the potatoes and the broccoli or green beans. Start with the potatoes, since they take longer to cook.

How to Clean Potatoes

You should have a vegetable brush for this. I never peel waxy potatoes, I just cut out any blemishes. I do give them a good scrub, though. Run them under cold water and scrub with the vegetable brush. If there are bumps where roots seem to be sprouting, or unappealing brown spots, cut them out with the tip of a paring knife or with the tip of a potato peeler.

If the potatoes are much bigger than golf balls, cut them into halves or into quarters so they cook more quickly.

How to Steam Potatoes

You'll need a steamer for this. The simplest is a stainless-steel collapsible steamer that fits into a saucepan. Put about an inch of water in a 2- or 3-quart saucepan and put in the steamer with the potatoes in it. Turn the heat on high, and when the water begins to boil, cover the pot and turn the heat down to medium. If you cook potatoes over too-high heat, they will fall apart. Golf-ball-size potatoes will take 15 to 20 minutes. If they're cut up, check them after 10 minutes. They're done when a knife is easily inserted all

Thawing Chicken Breasts

To thaw chicken breasts, use a microwave, following the manufacturer's instructions. For best results, if you can think ahead, thaw in the lower part of your refrigerator. It will take 2 to 3 days. Do not let them sit out on the counter at room temperature unless you want to flirt with salmonella.

the way through. Remove the potatoes from the heat when they're done. Drain out the water and take out the steamer, which you'll need for the broccoli. Put the potatoes back in the pan and put the lid back on (or, if you need this pan for the broccoli, transfer the potatoes to a bowl and put a plate over the top). They'll stay hot while you cook the chicken breasts.

How to Prepare Broccoli

Use a chef's knife for this. Get out a colander and a cutting board. Rinse the broccoli under cold water and drain in the colander.

Slice off the bottom of the stem and discard. Slice the top, flowery part away from the thick stems. You can use the stems or not; they're good to steam and also good to pickle (see page 40), so don't throw them away, but for now, set them aside. Break the top into little flowers (florets) by snapping off the little stems from the big stem. If some of the flowers are too big to snap, cut them off, then cut these flowers into halves or quarters. If using the stems, peel and dice.

How to Prepare Green Beans

Snap off the ends. If the beans have tough strings, remove them by snapping one end up in the direction of the string and pulling it back toward the other end so that the string comes away with it. Break the beans in half or into 2-inch lengths.

How to Steam Broccoli or Green Beans

You need the same kind of steaming arrangement you used for the potatoes and a colander in the sink. Put about an inch of water in a 2- or 3-quart saucepan and put in the steamer with the broccoli or green beans in it. Turn the heat on high, and when the water begins to boil, cover the pot and turn the heat to medium. Steam for 5 to 8 minutes; if you want the vegetables to be softer, steam for 10 minutes. Transfer to the colander and rinse with cold water to stop the cooking. (You can also put on a long oven mitt to protect your arm and hand, lift the steamer from the pot, transfer to the sink, and rinse with cold water.) Drain the water from the pan. Return the broccoli or beans to the pan and put the lid on to keep them warm while you cook the chicken breasts.

Or, for reheating, fill the saucepan with water and bring it to a simmer while you cook the chicken breasts. Just before you serve, place the steamed green vegetables in a strainer and dip into the simmering water to heat them through (this is what they do in restaurants).

Cooking the Chicken Breasts

You have a choice of pans here. Either use a heavy nonstick skillet large enough to accommodate all four breasts; a well-seasoned cast-iron skillet or grill pan with ridges; or a nonstick grill pan with ridges. You will also need a wooden or heat-resistant plastic spatula if you're using nonstick cookware; you can use metal if you're using cast iron. Or you can use tongs. You will also need a pastry brush for basting the breasts; in a pinch, you can use a spoon.

Get out serving plates or an attractive platter.

It's important that the pan be quite hot, especially if you're using a grill pan and want to have nice-looking grill stripes on the chicken breasts. Heat it for at least 5 minutes, longer if possible, over medium-high heat. Drop a bit of water on the pan. If it smokes and sizzles away on contact, the pan is hot enough. Toss the chicken breasts one more time so that they're well coated with the marinade and add them to the pan. Cook for 3 to 5 minutes. Lift one of the breasts; if cooking in a flat pan, it should be golden. If cooking in a ridged pan, it should have golden brown stripes across the surface.

Using a pastry brush, brush the top side of the breasts with the marinade before you turn them over. If you don't have a brush, spoon on some marinade and rub it over the surface with the back of the spoon. Flip the breasts over and cook until the second side is golden or striped, another 3 to 5 minutes. Transfer to plates or a platter. If there are any juices in the pan, pour them over the chicken breasts. *Throw out any remaining marinade and wash your pastry brush well with detergent and very hot water.*

If you want crisscross grill stripes: Halfway through the cooking on each side, slide the chicken breasts over a quarter turn. Now you'll have two sets of stripes crossing over each other.

Garnishing the Chicken

The meat needs a little color. Whether you're serving the breasts on a plate or a platter, lay a sprig of rosemary, parsley, or thyme across the breasts or on the side and set a small lemon wedge next to them. If you're serving them on a platter, surround them with herbs and lemon wedges. You can put the potatoes and green vegetables on the same platter.

Serve the chicken breasts with the potatoes and broccoli or green beans on the side. If the green vegetables have cooled too much, heat them for 20 to 30 seconds in a microwave or dip into simmering water as described earlier. If you want to, toss the warm potatoes with a teaspoon of olive oil before serving and sprinkle with salt and freshly ground pepper.

Now that you know how to . . .

- prepare and steam potatoes, broccoli, and green beans

- buy, marinate, and pan-fry or pan-grill chicken breasts

- serve them all together

. . . you won't think twice about following a standard recipe for lemon- and garlic-marinated pan-fried or pan-grilled chicken breasts, which looks like this:

Lemon- and Garlic-Marinated Pan-Fried or Pan-Grilled Chicken with Steamed Broccoli or Green Beans and Potatoes

■

Makes 4 servings

FOR THE CHICKEN BREASTS:
1 tablespoon olive oil
2 garlic cloves, peeled and minced or pressed
3 tablespoons fresh lemon juice
1 teaspoon chopped fresh rosemary and/or thyme leaves or $\frac{1}{2}$ teaspoon dried
    rosemary and/or thyme
Salt and freshly ground black pepper to taste
2 whole chicken breasts, split, boned, and skinned, or 4 half breasts

FOR THE POTATOES AND BROCCOLI OR GREEN BEANS:
$1\frac{1}{2}$ pounds small smooth-skinned ("waxy") potatoes, such as new potatoes,
    red potatoes, white creamers, or Yukon Gold (I love Yukon Gold)
1 medium-size head broccoli (about 1 pound) or 1 pound green beans

FOR GARNISH:
Fresh thyme or rosemary sprigs and/or lemon wedges

1. Stir together the olive oil, garlic, lemon juice, herbs, salt, and pepper in a large bowl. Add the chicken breasts and toss until well coated with the marinade. Marinate for 15 to 30 minutes, in or out of the refrigerator, turning once or twice.
2. Meanwhile, clean and steam the potatoes and broccoli or green beans in separate saucepans. Keep warm while you cook the chicken breasts.
3. Heat a nonstick skillet or ridged grill pan over medium-high heat. Drop a bit of water on the pan, and if it sizzles away on contact, the pan is hot enough. Toss the chicken breasts one more time so that they're well coated with the marinade, then add to the pan. Cook until golden, 3 to 5 minutes per side, basting the tops with the marinade before you flip them over. Remove from the heat and serve hot, with the potatoes and green vegetables, garnished with sprigs of rosemary or thyme and lemon wedges.

Tossed Green Salad with Classic Vinaigrette

■

Makes 4 servings

If you can make a simple salad, you can make any salad. And almost any food can become a salad once you know how to make a dressing. The simplest dressing—oil and vinegar or oil and lemon juice—takes no longer to assemble than it takes to shake and open a bottle of vastly inferior commercial dressing (that is filled with stabilizers and chemicals and doesn't taste like what dressing should taste like). Salads all over Italy and Greece are tossed with no more than these two ingredients (and salt and sometimes pepper). In France, home of the vinaigrette, mustard and perhaps garlic or shallot are added to the combination, which help to emulsify (thicken) it. Fresh or dried herbs are often added as well.

The other thing you have to know how to do is wash and dry lettuce. This used to be a pain in the neck before salad spinners came along. Now it's done quickly.

A good tossed green salad can contain one or several types of lettuce. The one lettuce I don't recommend is Iceberg; the leaves are too hard and slippery (not to mention flavorless), and they don't benefit from a nice dressing. Save Iceberg lettuce for shredding onto tacos. You can add other vegetables to a tossed salad for color, texture, and taste. My usual additions are sliced mushrooms and sliced red peppers (either fresh or marinated); I try to keep them on hand. I'll give you a number of suggestions for other additions after the recipe.

FOR THE SALAD:

½ pound salad greens, such as red leaf lettuce, romaine, Bibb lettuce, arugula, and/or mixed field greens like mesclun: about 1 small or ¾ medium-size head red leaf or ½ head romaine or 1 large or 2 small heads Bibb

2 to 3 tablespoons chopped fresh herbs, such as chives, parsley, basil, dill, and/or tarragon, to your taste

OPTIONAL:

2 to 3 mushrooms

3 scallions, both white and green parts

½ red bell pepper

½ medium-size regular cucumber or ¼ long European cucumber

2 or 3 ripe tomatoes or 8 cherry tomatoes

4 radishes

FOR THE VINAIGRETTE:

2 tablespoons good-quality red wine vinegar, sherry vinegar, or champagne vinegar *or* 1 tablespoon fresh lemon juice and 1 tablespoon vinegar of your choice

1 small garlic clove (optional), peeled and finely minced or pressed

$\frac{1}{8}$ to $\frac{1}{4}$ teaspoon salt, to your taste

1 teaspoon Dijon mustard

6 tablespoons extra-virgin olive oil

Freshly ground black pepper to taste

OR, FOR AN UTTERLY SIMPLE ITALIAN DRESSING:

$\frac{1}{8}$ to $\frac{1}{4}$ teaspoon salt, to your taste

2 tablespoons vinegar of your choice

6 tablespoons extra-virgin olive oil

OR, FOR AN UTTERLY SIMPLE GREEK DRESSING:

2 to 3 tablespoons fresh lemon juice

$\frac{1}{8}$ to $\frac{1}{4}$ teaspoon salt, to your taste

6 tablespoons extra-virgin olive oil

OR, FOR A LOW-FAT YOGURT OR BUTTERMILK VINAIGRETTE:

Substitute plain nonfat yogurt or buttermilk for all but 1 or 2 tablespoons of the olive oil

OR, FOR BALSAMIC VINAIGRETTE:

Substitute 1 to 3 teaspoons balsamic vinegar, to your taste, for the same amount of lemon juice or vinegar

How to Wash Salad Greens

Lettuce, even precut lettuce, is sandy, so lettuce must be washed before you make a salad. It's the main task in salad making.

For heads of lettuce: Fill the bottom part of a salad spinner, a large bowl, or half of a double sink with cold water. While you are running the water, break the leaves off the head and run each one under the water, turning them over once and rubbing the base of the leaf between your thumb and forefinger; the sand sticks in that curved bit at the base of the leaf. Place the leaves in the bowl or sinkful of water. Swish them around with your hands or, if your sink has a spray nozzle, run the spray into the water full blast to swish the leaves around and knock sand off the leaves. Put the top part of your salad spinner, or a colander, over a bowl or over the other half of your sink. Lift the leaves out of the water with your hands and trans-

Balsamic Vinegar

Balsamic vinegar, which is sweet, goes particularly well with mixed field greens and arugula, greens that have a bite to them. However, too much balsamic is too sweet, so it's best to use it in conjunction with lemon juice or vinegar.

fer to the colander or top of the spinner. Drain the sandy water out of the sink or bowl and rinse away all the sand. Fill again with water and submerge the lettuce again. Swish it around once more, lift from the water, and transfer again to the top of your spinner or to a colander set over a bowl or sink so water won't run all over your counter or floor. Now the lettuce is ready to dry.

For precut lettuces: These will be much less sandy, but the greens still need a swish. Fill your sink or bowl with cold water as directed. You don't have to rinse the leaves under running water. Put in the lettuces and swish around with your hands or with the spray nozzle. Lift from the water and drain. You don't have to repeat with most precut lettuces.

How to Dry Salad Greens

First of all, buy a **salad spinner**. They aren't very expensive. I especially like Copco spinners. Try them out in the store; you shouldn't have to use much force at all to turn the spinner. If it seems to stick, try another one. Don't crowd the spinner. Half a pound of lettuce shouldn't be too much for an average-size spinner, but if the lettuce seems stuffed into the basket, dry it in batches. Put the lettuce in the basket and the basket in the bowl. Cover and spin the lettuce vigorously for about 10 seconds and let the spinner come to a stop on its own. Take the top off, lift out the basket, and pour out the water that has accumulated in the bowl. Place the basket back in the bowl, replace the lid, and spin again. Take the lettuce out and transfer to a bowl if using right away. If not, wrap in a clean kitchen towel and place the towel in a plastic bag. Seal and refrigerate. Set your spinner upside down in your dish drainer so that it will be dry and ready to put away when you've finished dinner.

If you don't have a spinner, put a clean, dry kitchen towel on your counter. After you've washed the lettuce, shake each leaf (or, for precut lettuce, shake handfuls) over the sink and lay it on top of the towel in one layer. Place another towel on top and gently press down or roll the bottom towel up so that you have a roll of lettuce between two towels.

How to Wash and Chop Fresh Herbs

Herbs, like lettuces, are also sandy, particularly the leafy ones like parsley and cilantro that are sold in bunches. The sand lodges down in the stems and sticks to the leaves (even though you might not see it).

Chives, tarragon, dill: Hold the bunch in your hand and run under cold water or plunge several times into a bowl of cold water. Shake over the sink, then roll up in paper towels and let drain for a few minutes. Hold the stem end of the bunch, or a few sprigs of dill or tarragon, with one hand over the salad bowl and snip the other end into the bowl with kitchen scissors.

Parsley, oregano, marjoram: Stem, wash, and dry following the directions for lettuce. After you spin the herbs, wrap in paper towels for a few minutes to blot any remaining water. Place in a wide jar or a Pyrex measuring cup. Point the tips of a pair of kitchen scissors straight down in the jar. Cut the herbs with the scissors.

Cilantro: Fill a bowl or the bottom of your salad spinner with water. Hold the bunch, leaves facing down, and plunge into and out of the water several times. Drain the water and rinse out the bowl. Repeat until sand no longer accumulates in the water. Shake the cilantro over the sink, then spin a couple of times in the salad spinner, emptying out water from the bowl between spins. Wrap in a few layers of kitchen towels and let sit for a few minutes. To cut, with the cilantro still in a bunch, lay on a cutting board and, using a sharp chef's knife, cut across the leafy end of the bunch so that you are cutting slivers off the leaves. Don't worry if little bits of stem are mixed in.

Basil, mint, sage: Stem, wash, and dry following the directions for parsley. Stack leaves, three to six to a stack, and, using a sharp chef's knife, sliver crosswise or cut crosswise with scissors.

Rosemary: Wash and spin dry. Pull the spiky leaves from the tough center stem. Place on a cutting board and chop finely with a chef's knife; hold the tip of the knife down and move the body of the knife quickly up and down over the rosemary leaves. Rosemary can also be snipped with scissors.

Thyme: Pull the little leaves away from the stems; hold the top end of the stem in one hand and gently run your thumb and forefinger down toward the base, pulling away the leaves as you go.

Assembling the Salad

If the lettuce leaves are very large, tear them into halves or quarters. This is a matter of taste. In France, leaves are usually left whole and the cutting is left to the diner. But very large leaves, particularly romaine and leaf lettuce, can be unwieldy and result in salad dressing dripping on your shirt.

Place the lettuce in a large, wide salad bowl and sprinkle with the herbs and any optional ingredients. It's a mistake to use a small bowl, because when you toss the salad the leaves will fly all over the kitchen counter, the table, or the floor. You can toss your salad in a large stainless-steel bowl and transfer it to a prettier salad bowl, but of course this means you'll have one more bowl to wash. Or you can just serve it from the stainless-steel bowl. You don't have to have a wooden salad bowl, but you do have to have a large one.

Set the bowl aside, or in your refrigerator if it will be more than 30 minutes before you plan to serve it, and make your dressing. If the salad is to be refrigerated for more than 30 minutes, lay a dampened kitchen towel over the top so the lettuce won't dry out (refrigerators dry things out) or cover with plastic wrap.

How to Make Vinaigrette

A small glass jar is particularly useful for making salad dressing. You can shake the dressing in the jar and shake it again before you toss the salad. You can also mix the dressing, using a fork or small whisk, in a small bowl, a Pyrex measuring cup, or right in the salad bowl. Measure the vinegar or lemon juice and vinegar into your container. Add the garlic and salt. Using a fork, stir and mash the garlic and salt together. Add the mustard and stir with a fork to dissolve or, if you're using a jar, put the lid on tightly and shake the jar. Now the mixture will be quite thick. Add the olive oil and stir together with a fork or whisk or shake the jar again with the top on. Grind in pepper (or wait and add the pepper directly to the salad). Taste the dressing by dipping a piece of lettuce into it. Adjust salt to your taste.

If you like a more pungent dressing, add a bit more vinegar or lemon juice, teaspoon by teaspoon.

For Italian or Greek dressing, dissolve the salt in the vinegar or lemon juice, then stir in the olive oil—it won't really amalgamate, but when you give it a stir before you toss the salad it will be mixed well enough.

For low-fat vinaigrette, add the yogurt or buttermilk to the vinegar mixture and stir together before you add the olive oil. Thin out with a little water if desired.

Tossing the Salad

This is done just before you serve it. If you do it ahead of time, the lettuce will have wilted by the time you're ready to eat. The oil and salt in the vinaigrette cause the lettuce to wilt. Give the dressing another stir. Pour it on the lettuce. Using salad servers, two large spoons, or your hands, toss the salad by scooping under the greens and folding or flipping them over themselves. Do this at least ten times, even twenty. The leaves should be coated thoroughly and evenly with dressing. Serve at once.

Preparing the Optionals

Mushrooms: Slice off the bottom of the stem. Quickly rinse the mushrooms or, if they're hardly sandy at all, just wipe them with a damp paper towel. Wipe them dry with another paper towel. Slice the mushrooms using a sharp paring knife or chef's knife.

Scallions: Slice off the furry stem end. Rinse and remove the outer layer of the onion. Shake dry. Lay on a cutting board and trim about an inch off the green end. Slice thinly, both white and green parts.

Red bell pepper: Cut in half lengthwise, through the stem and down one of the indentations. Using your thumbs, pull out the seed pod under the stem and use your fingers to pull out the membranes along the cut side. Remove any other seeds, which is easy if you turn the pepper cut side down and tap it against your cutting board. Using a chef's knife or a paring knife (I prefer the larger knife), cut the pepper into thin lengthwise slices. If the pepper is very long and you want shorter pieces for your salad, cut the slices in half; hold them together in a bunch and cut all at once.

Cucumber: If the cucumber has thick bitter skin and big seeds, peel it with a vegetable peeler or a paring knife, cut it in half lengthwise, and scoop out the seeds with a spoon or a paring knife. If the seeds don't bother you, leave the cucumber whole. Slice thinly with a chef's knife. If you want prettier slices and the skin isn't bitter, score the cucumber with a fork: run the tines of the fork down the length of the cucumber on all sides and then slice.

Tomatoes: For larger tomatoes, cut out the core, then cut into wedges or cut in half and then slice each half. Eating a large cherry tomato is not dainty and not easy. Best to cut cherry tomatoes in half or small wedges; leave whole if very small.

Radishes: Wash and scrub any dirt off with a vegetable brush and trim it top and bottom. Slice crosswise or cut into thin wedges.

Now that you're comfortable with . . .

- **washing and drying lettuces and herbs**
- **making a vinaigrette**
- **preparing mushrooms, scallions, red pepper, cucumber, tomatoes, and radishes for a salad**

. . . you won't think twice about following a standard recipe for a tossed green salad with vinaigrette, which looks like this:

Tossed Green Salad

■

Makes 4 servings

FOR THE SALAD:

½ pound salad greens, such as red leaf lettuce, romaine, Bibb lettuce, arugula,
   or mixed field greens, washed, dried, and torn up if desired
2 to 3 tablespoons chopped fresh herbs, such as chives, parsley, basil, dill,
   and/or tarragon, to your taste

OPTIONAL:

2 to 3 mushrooms, trimmed and sliced
3 scallions, both white and green parts, trimmed and sliced
½ red bell pepper, seeded and thinly sliced into strips
½ medium-size regular cucumber or ¼ European cucumber, peeled and seeded
   if desired and sliced
2 or 3 ripe tomatoes, or 8 cherry tomatoes, cut into wedges or sliced if large
4 radishes, trimmed and sliced

FOR THE VINAIGRETTE:

2 tablespoons good-quality red wine vinegar, sherry vinegar, or champagne
   vinegar *or* 1 tablespoon fresh lemon juice and 1 tablespoon vinegar
1 small garlic clove (optional), peeled and finely minced or pressed
⅛ to ¼ teaspoon salt, to your taste
1 teaspoon Dijon mustard
6 tablespoons extra-virgin olive oil
Freshly ground black pepper to taste

1. Place the desired salad ingredients in a large, wide bowl.
2. Mix together the vinegar or lemon and vinegar with the garlic, salt, and mustard. Stir or whisk in the olive oil. Add pepper.
3. Just before serving, toss the salad with the dressing.

Grilled or Broiled Fish Steaks with Salsa

■

Makes 4 servings

A grilled or broiled piece of fish is one of the easiest and quickest of meals.
The quality of the meal depends, of course, on the quality of the fish, and
that will depend on the quality of the fish department in your supermarket
if you aren't lucky enough to live near a fish store. Fish is one of those foods
you really do need to cook the day you buy it, or no more than one day
later. Fish doesn't have good staying power, nor do I think it freezes well. If
you are doing your marketing once a week, why don't you make the day
you do your marketing the night you have fish?

One objection to fish cookery I've heard from people who live in small apartments is that the smell lingers in the kitchen long after the fish is cooked. If you broil rather than cook on top of the stove, this shouldn't be a problem. And broiling is a great method for firm-fleshed steaks like tuna, salmon, and swordfish, the types you're likely to find in supermarkets with fish counters.

Fresh fish actually needs little more in the way of condiments than lemon, salt, and pepper. But I'd never say no to salsa either, especially a nice salsa fresca. As for side dishes, serve steamed green vegetables in season—peas, asparagus, beans, broccoli—and potatoes or rice. Follow with a salad for a great meal.

FOR THE SALSA:

1 pound ripe fresh tomatoes

¼ small red onion, or more to taste

1 to 3 jalapeño or serrano chiles, to your taste

¼ cup chopped fresh cilantro, or more to taste

2 teaspoons red wine vinegar, balsamic vinegar, or fresh lime juice (optional)

Salt and freshly ground black pepper to taste

FOR THE FISH:

4 tuna, swordfish, salmon, or halibut steaks, about ¾ inch thick and weighing about 6 ounces each

1 tablespoon olive oil

Salt and freshly ground black pepper to taste

How to Buy Fish

The most important thing to consider when buying fish is the quality of the fish store. If, in the supermarket, the fish counter smells "fishy," forget about buying fish there. It won't be fresh enough. Ask the fishmonger if you can smell the fish if you have any doubts. The fish should be laid out in a case, not packaged with the meat, so choose another market if your usual supermarket doesn't have an actual fish department, where you can see the fish. Fish should look moist and glistening, with no dryness or yellowing at the edges. Salmon steaks should not be riddled with lots of visible white fat. Salmon is a fatty fish, but some farmed salmon is so fatty it doesn't taste good. You are shopping here for steaks, which are always bigger than what I consider a normal portion (particularly swordfish and tuna steaks). They are almost always cut at least 1 inch thick, which I find kind of excessive, but what can you do? I would prefer them ¾ inch thick. Ask the fishmonger if

Get out the following equipment: chef's knife and cutting board; 2 medium-size bowls; strainer; plastic or rubber gloves; paring knife; measuring spoons; 2- or 3-quart saucepan with lid and steamer; baking sheet covered with foil if broiling; large, heavy nonstick grill pan or skillet if pan-grilling; pastry brush; spatula or tongs

Advance preparation: The salsa will hold for a few hours in or out of the refrigerator. You can make it a day ahead of time, but know that it will become more watery and the pungency of the cilantro will fade.

PER SERVING:
5.2 gm total fat
0.8 gm saturated fat
211 calories
5.4 gm carbohydrates
33.6 gm protein

he'll cut the steaks into four equal pieces, or buy 1½ pounds and cut them when you go home (this is what I usually do; I buy two steaks, each one weighing about 12 ounces). When you get home, put the fish in the coldest part of the refrigerator until you're ready to make dinner.

Prepare the Salsa and the Vegetables

The fish doesn't need to be marinated, so get the rest of the meal out of the way first. If you're having a salad, throw it together (see page 56).

Preparing the salsa: The tomatoes don't need to be peeled or seeded, just chopped. You learned to do that when you made the pasta sauce (page 46).

Chopping the onion: Cut off the very ends of the onion, then cut the onion in half lengthwise, that is, along one of the lines. You need only a quarter of an onion here, and the onion should be small. Lay the onion down with the flat side on your cutting board. Remove the skin. Steadying the onion with your left hand if you're right-handed or with your right hand if you're left-handed, cut thin strips along the lines, from one side toward the center, i.e., toward your other hand. When you get to the center, stop and put away the uncut portion of the onion. Now turn the sliced quarter onion a quarter turn and cut across your slices, trying to make your strips as thin as possible so you get very small dice. Transfer your onion to a bowl and cover it with cold water, then strain and rinse again. You do this because you're eating the onion uncooked, and rinsing it will take away some of the volatile juices that can sour quickly, leaving that oniony taste in your mouth.

Mincing the chiles: It's a good idea to wear plastic gloves when you're working with chiles. Once you've handled the cut portions, your hands will be carrying the stuff that makes hot peppers hot, capsaicin. Rub your eye and you'll know what I'm talking about. I like surgical gloves, which you can get at a pharmacy or a medical supply store. They're thin and easy to work in. Cut the stem off the chile and cut it in half lengthwise. If you're using small serrano chiles and like things hot, you don't have to take the seeds and white ribs out, which contain more of the capsaicin. Jalapeños are larger, so even if you like things hot you might want to seed at least one of them. To seed the chiles, lift out the inner membrane, and the seeds will come with it in most cases. You can scrape them out with a knife or turn the chile over and tap it to remove the lingering seeds. Now lay the chile on its shiny side and cut long thin strips down the length. Cut across the strips for tiny dice. Or you can chop the chiles the way you would chop garlic or ginger. Lay them on the cutting board, hold the tip of a chef's knife against the cutting board, and saw up and down with rapid motions. Push the bits of chile back toward the center as they spread out.

Prepare the cilantro: See page 59 in the salad recipe.

Assemble the salsa: Mix together the tomatoes, red onion, chiles, cilantro, and vinegar or lime juice. Add salt and pepper. If not serving within the hour, refrigerate, but remove the salsa from the refrigerator at least a half hour before serving so that it isn't too cold.

Putting Together the Dinner and Cooking the Fish

You can actually be cooking the vegetables while you're preparing the salsa, but it's nice to get the salsa out of the way first. (Or maybe you bought prepared salsa so you didn't have to read the preceding directions.) Anyway, steam the potatoes and green vegetables as described on pages 51–55 for the chicken breast recipe. Have them done and warm before you begin the fish, because that's a last-minute operation.

Finally, cook the fish.

Broiling: Preheat your broiler. Place a rack 4 inches from the heat (probably the second to the highest setting). Cover a baking sheet with aluminum foil (it will be easier to clean afterward) and lightly oil the foil with olive oil. Brush the fish steaks on both sides with olive oil and lightly salt and pepper.

Timing: Fish cooks quickly, and once it overcooks it's like cotton, especially tuna. Measure the thickness of the fish steak. The rule of thumb for timing fish is 5 minutes total cooking time per ½ inch of thickness; however, the very high heat of a grill or broiler can cook faster, so if your steak is 1 inch thick, turn after 5 minutes, but check to see if it's done after it has cooked for 4 minutes on the other side. If it's ¾ inch thick, it will need about 4 minutes per side. *The exception here is tuna.* If you want the tuna to be pink in the middle, cook it for 3 minutes on each side. If you want it cooked through but still moist, cook it for 4 minutes. Place the steaks on the foil-covered baking sheet and set under the broiler. Close the door, or leave it cracked, and broil for 3 to 5 minutes, depending on the thickness of the steaks and the type of fish. Remove the baking sheet from the oven and flip the steaks over. The cooked side will be opaque now. Return to the oven and broil for another 3 to 5 minutes. Remove from the heat.

Pan-Grilling: This is just like pan-grilling chicken breasts, resulting in a nice grilled flavor, but the memory of your dinner will linger in the kitchen. Heat a nonstick skillet or ridged grill pan for at least 5 minutes and longer if possible over medium-high heat. Drop a bit of water on the pan, and if it smokes and sizzles away on contact, the pan is hot enough. Brush lightly with olive oil. Brush the fish steaks on both sides with olive oil and lightly salt and pepper. Cook for 3 to 5 minutes as directed. Flip over and cook for another 3 to 5 minutes.

If you want crisscross grill stripes: Halfway through the cooking on each side, slide the fish steak over a quarter turn. Now you'll have two sets of stripes crossing over each other.

Is the fish done? Test the piece that you will serve yourself. Take a fork or a knife and cut into it, then pull it apart gently to take a peek. White fish like swordfish or halibut should be opaque but not dry. Swordfish can be ever-so-slightly pinkish in the middle if you like fish on the underdone side. Salmon should be a lighter pink just about all the way through, though the middle should still be slightly more orange. Tuna should be slightly or very pink in the middle, depending on how you like it. It should *not* be cold in the middle.

Serve with the salsa partially spooned over the fish, partially on the side. The vegetables should still be warm. If they aren't, zap them for a few seconds in the microwave or dip them into simmering water.

Now that you know how to . . .

- **buy and cook fish steaks**

- **make salsa**

- **put a fish dinner together**

. . . you won't think twice about following a standard recipe for pan-grilled or broiled fish steaks with salsa, which looks like this:

Grilled or Broiled Fish Steaks with Salsa

■

Makes 4 servings

FOR THE SALSA:
1 pound ripe fresh tomatoes, chopped
¼ small red onion, peeled, minced, and rinsed with cold water
1 to 3 jalapeño or serrano chiles, to your taste, minced (and seeded for a
    milder salsa)
¼ cup chopped cilantro, or more to taste
2 teaspoons red wine vinegar, balsamic vinegar, or fresh lime juice (optional)
Salt and freshly ground black pepper to taste

FOR THE FISH:

4 tuna, swordfish, salmon, or halibut steaks, about ¾ inch thick if possible and weighing about 6 ounces each
Salt and freshly ground black pepper to taste
1 tablespoon olive oil

1. Mix together the tomatoes, onion, peppers, cilantro, and vinegar or lime juice and season with salt and pepper. If not serving within the hour, refrigerate, but remove the salsa from the refrigerator at least a half hour before serving so that it isn't too cold.
2. Rinse the fish steaks and pat dry with paper towels. Salt and pepper lightly and brush with olive oil.
3. Heat a nonstick skillet or ridged grill pan over high heat or preheat your broiler with the rack about 4 inches from the heat. Grill or broil tuna steaks for 3 to 4 minutes on each side. They should remain pink in the middle. Grill or broil swordfish, halibut, or salmon for 4 minutes on each side, or 5 minutes on one side, 4 to 5 minutes on the other if it's an inch thick. Transfer to a serving platter or plates and serve with the salsa.

Asian-Style Stir-Fried Vegetables with Rice

Makes 4 servings

Humble though this may be, it is one of my favorite dinners. It doesn't matter what vegetable or vegetables you have on hand; master the recipe, and you always have a good meal. The essentials are the seasonings—garlic, ginger, soy sauce, and vinegar. A nice and authentic-tasting variation adds Chinese sesame oil to the equation, for a rich nutty finish. But for the warm-up exercise I'd like to keep ingredients to a minimum (the list might already look long to you). You can make a stir-fry with a large assortment of vegetables or with just one. For this starter recipe, I'll give you two vegetables to work with, then I'll give you some variations.

The time-consuming part of this recipe is the preparation of the ingredients (and because I'm keeping it simple here, it won't take you all that much time). The actual cooking happens in a flash, which is why it's important to be organized and have everything prepared and measured before you begin the final cooking of the dish. I say *final* cooking because although this is a "stir-fry," some of the vegetables are cooked a little bit, either steamed or blanched (see page 23), before you quickly cook them in oil. That way you can cut way down on the traditional quantity of oil used for cooking the vegetables, because the vegetables are partially cooked when they hit the pan. As long as you follow the directions here, don't turn the heat too high, and keep stirring, your garlic and ginger, etc., won't burn. You can do this in a nonstick pan, or you can use a well-seasoned wok.

Get out the following equipment: **chef's knife and cutting board; paring knife; potato peeler if using; minichop if using or grater for ginger; garlic press if using; dry and liquid measuring cups; measuring spoons; small and medium-size bowls; 1- or 2-quart saucepan with lid; 2- or 3-quart saucepan with lid and steamer or large pot and deep-fry skimmer or slotted spoon; wok or large, heavy nonstick skillet; wooden paddle or spoon**

continued

FOR THE VEGETABLES:

1½ pounds broccoli *or* 1½ pounds snow peas or sugar snap peas *or* a
    combination

1 tablespoon peeled and finely minced fresh ginger

1 tablespoon finely minced garlic (2 large or 3 medium-size cloves)

¾ pound mushrooms, trimmed and thickly sliced

1 bunch scallions, white part and some of the green, trimmed and thinly
    sliced

1 to 2 tablespoons corn, canola, or peanut oil, as needed

FOR THE GLAZE:

½ cup defatted unsalted chicken stock (page 155), vegetable stock
    (page 156), canned low-sodium broth, or water

2 tablespoons soy sauce

1 tablespoon Japanese rice wine vinegar, distilled white vinegar, or cider
    vinegar

½ teaspoon sugar

1 tablespoon arrowroot or cornstarch

1½ tablespoons water

FOR THE RICE:

2 cups water

½ to ¾ teaspoon salt, to your taste

1 cup medium- or long-grain white or brown rice

How to Prepare Broccoli

Both the top flowery section of the broccoli (the florets) and the stems are
good to eat. But the stems must be peeled. Break or cut the florets from the
stem. To reduce the size of the really big florets, cut them lengthwise into
halves or quarters using a small knife. To prepare the stems, slice away the
bottom ends and discard. The skin of the stem is thick; you can see exactly
where it surrounds the stem, like tree bark. Take your small knife and place
it between the skin and the stem. Hold the stem steady with one hand and
flick the skin back with the knife. It peels off most easily if you work from
the top—the flower end—toward the bottom. If it doesn't peel off easily,
then steady the stem and just cut down the sides, between the skin and the
stem, to remove the skin. Now cut the stems in half lengthwise and slice
about ¼ inch thick.

How to Prepare Snow Peas or Sugar Snap Peas

The only thing you have to do here is remove the strings. Sometimes sugar snap peas don't even have strings, they're so young and tender. If there is a visible stem end, there is usually a string along the top. Snap off the stem by bending it back toward you and pull. Both stem and string should come away from the pod.

How to Mince Ginger

First of all, how much fresh ginger makes 1 tablespoon minced? About ¾ to 1 inch of the root, depending on how thick the root is. Cut that much away from the rest of the root and peel it using a paring knife or a potato peeler. You can mince ginger in a minichop or grate it using a fine grater or special ginger grater, but it's easy to mince it using a chef's knife. Place the ginger on a cutting board and slice crosswise as thin as you can. Stand the slices on top of each other and slice across them in thin strips. Lay them on the cutting board and, using an up-and-down seesaw motion with the tip end of your knife resting on the board and your free hand, knuckles curled, steadying the ginger, chop the strips of ginger very finely. The ginger will spread out on the board. Keep pushing it back to the center using your free hand.

How to Mince Garlic

This is explained in the recipe for Simple Tomato Sauce on page 43.

How to Prepare Mushrooms and Scallions

This was explained in the Tossed Green Salad recipe on pages 60–61. The only thing you must do differently here is keep the sliced scallion whites and greens separate.

Mixing Up the Glaze

In a measuring cup or a small bowl, stir together the stock or water, soy sauce, vinegar, and sugar. In a separate small bowl or measuring cup, dissolve the arrowroot or cornstarch in the water and set aside. Add this at the very end of cooking and give it another stir before you do.

How to Cook Rice

You should cook the rice before you cook the stir-fry, or the vegetables will be ready and the rice won't be cooked. Brown rice takes two to three times longer to cook than white rice, which gives you all the time you'll need to prepare everything else and set the table. The method for both is the same; the rice is simply cooked in simmering water.

Place the water in a 1- or 2-quart lidded saucepan and bring to a boil. Add the salt and rice. When the water comes back to a boil, *stir once and once only,* turn the heat down to low, and cover the pot tightly. Simmer white rice for 15 minutes. Remove the lid and look and listen. There will be holes in the mass of rice, into which you can peer to see if the water has evaporated. You will hear it as well. If you're really not sure, stick a chopstick, not a spoon, down to see if a small layer of rice is beginning to stick to the bottom of the pan. If it is, turn off the heat immediately, return the lid to the pan, and let the pan sit without touching it for 10 minutes (or longer). The rice will continue to steam and grow fluffy. If there is still water simmering, return the lid to the pan and check again every 5 minutes. The method for brown rice is exactly the same, except the rice takes 35 to 45 minutes. Check after 35 minutes.

Making the Stir-Fry

1. First steam the broccoli or the snow peas just until crisp-tender. Get out a lidded pot with a steamer basket. Put about 1 inch of water in the pot and set the steamer over the water. Set the broccoli or the snow peas in the basket. Bring to a boil over high heat and cover. Set the timer for 3 minutes, then quickly fill a bowl with ice water. As soon as the timer goes off, remove the vegetables from the heat and transfer to the cold water, then drain. They should be crisp-tender.

   You can also blanch the vegetables. I think steaming is simpler, but some cooks prefer the texture of the vegetables when they are quickly blanched and cooled in ice water. To do this, bring a large pot of water to a rolling boil over high heat. Meanwhile, fill a bowl with ice water. Add a tablespoon of salt to the pot of water when it comes to a boil, then drop in the vegetables. Boil for 30 seconds, counting from the time that the water comes back to a boil after you've added them. Remove from the water using a slotted spoon or deep-fry skimmer and transfer immediately to the ice water to stop the cooking. Drain and pat dry on paper towels.

2. Now you are ready to do the higher-heat, faster stir-fry cooking. Heat a wok or large, heavy nonstick skillet over high heat until hot enough to evaporate a drop of water on contact. Add 1 tablespoon of the oil, swirl to coat the wok, and reduce the heat to medium-high. Add the ginger and garlic and cook, stirring with a wooden paddle or spoon, until fragrant and beginning to color, 20 to 30 seconds. Add the mushrooms and the scallion whites and cook, stirring gently, for 2 minutes. Add the remaining tablespoon oil if the garlic and ginger are sticking and browning; add the broccoli or peas and cook, stirring constantly but gently, for 1 minute.

3. Stir the soy sauce mixture and add to the wok. Bring to a simmer and cook, stirring until the vegetables are just cooked through but still crisp, about 1 minute. Give the dissolved cornstarch a stir and add. Cook, stirring, until the sauce thickens and glazes the vegetables. Remove from the heat and sprinkle with the sliced scallion greens. Serve at once over the rice.

Asian Stir-Fried Vegetables with Tofu, Chicken, or Pork

To the recipe, add

PER SERVING (TOFU; CHICKEN; PORK):
13.8; 10.3; 14.2 gm total fat
1.9; 1.6; 3 gm saturated fat
414; 398; 428 calories
57.7; 55; 55 gm carbohydrates
19.7; 23.2; 22 gm protein

½ pound firm tofu plus 2 teaspoons soy sauce *or* ½ pound boneless pork loin *or* ½ pound boneless, skinless chicken breast *or* ½ pound shrimp, peeled and deveined (see page 299)
An additional 2 teaspoons corn, canola, or peanut oil

How to Prepare the Tofu: One-half pound of tofu is usually half of a block—they are usually sold in 1-pound pieces. Drain the tofu and pat dry with a kitchen towel. Cut into thin strips, about ¼ inch thick by 1 inch long, or into ½-inch dice. Toss with the soy sauce.

How to Prepare the Pork Loin: Cut into strips about ¼ inch thick and 2 inches long.

How to Prepare the Chicken Breast: Cut into strips about ¼ inch thick and 2 inches long.

1. Follow the recipe through step 1.
2. Heat your wok or nonstick skillet over medium-high heat until hot enough to evaporate a drop of water on contact. Add the additional 2 teaspoons oil and the tofu, meat, or shrimp. Cook, stirring all the while, until the meat is cooked through, the shrimp is pink, or the tofu is beginning to brown lightly on the edges, 2 to 3 minutes. The meat is cooked through when no traces of pink remain. Remove from the wok and transfer to a plate.
3. Proceed with step 2.
4. Return the meat, shrimp, or tofu to the pan and proceed with step 3.

Now that you know how to . . .

■ prepare ginger, garlic, broccoli, snow peas, sugar snap peas, and mushrooms for a stir-fry

- blanch or briefly steam green vegetables

- cook rice

- stir-fry vegetables

- prepare and cook strips of pork, chicken, tofu, or shrimp

. . . you won't think twice about following a standard recipe for stir-fried vegetables with variations, which looks like this:

Asian-Style Stir-Fried Vegetables with Rice

■

Makes 4 servings

1½ pounds broccoli, broken into florets, and stems peeled and chopped, *or*
    1½ pounds snow peas or sugar snap peas, ends and strings removed, *or* a
    combination

1 to 2 tablespoons corn, canola, or peanut oil, as needed

1 tablespoon peeled and finely minced ginger (a ¾- to 1-inch piece, depending
    on the thickness of the root)

1 tablespoon peeled and finely minced garlic (2 large or 3 medium-size
    cloves)

¾ pound mushrooms, trimmed and thickly sliced

1 bunch scallions, white part and some of the green, trimmed and thinly
    sliced, keeping the white and green parts separate

FOR THE GLAZE:

½ cup defatted unsalted chicken stock (page 155), vegetable stock
    (page 156), or canned low-sodium broth, or water

2 tablespoons soy sauce

1 tablespoon Japanese rice wine vinegar, distilled white vinegar, or cider
    vinegar

½ teaspoon sugar

1 tablespoon arrowroot or cornstarch dissolved in 1½ tablespoons water

1 cup medium- or long-grain white or brown rice, cooked

1. Steam the broccoli or the snow peas just until crisp-tender, about 3 minutes. Transfer immediately to a bowl of ice water, then drain and pat dry. Alternatively, blanch them by dropping them into a large pot of salted boiling water and boiling for 30 seconds, counting from the time that the water comes back to a boil after you've added them. Transfer immediately to the ice water to stop the cooking. Drain and pat dry on paper towels.

2. Heat a wok or large, heavy nonstick skillet over high heat until hot enough to evaporate a drop of water on contact. Add 1 tablespoon of the oil, swirl to coat the wok, and reduce the heat to medium-high. Add the ginger and garlic and cook, stirring with a wooden paddle or spoon, until fragrant and beginning to color, 20 to 30 seconds. Add the mushrooms and scallion whites and cook, stirring gently, for 2 minutes. Add the remaining tablespoon oil if the

garlic and ginger are sticking and browning; add the broccoli or peas and cook, stirring constantly but gently, for 1 minute.

3. Stir the soy sauce mixture and add to the wok. Bring to a simmer and cook, stirring, until the vegetables are just cooked through but still crisp, about 1 minute. Give the dissolved cornstarch a stir and add. Cook, stirring, until the sauce thickens and glazes the vegetables. Remove from the heat and sprinkle with the sliced scallion greens. Serve at once over the rice.

■ Five More Light Easy Pieces ■

Ratatouille

■

Makes 6 servings

I was so happy to hear National Public Radio commentator Daniel Pinkwater wax rhapsodic about the ratatouille that had helped him lose fifty pounds last year. He had discovered how versatile this dish is and, with no boredom or feelings of deprivation, had practically lived on the heady vegetable stew while losing weight.

I am giving you this recipe here in the Warm-up chapter not because it's a recipe for you to whip up as a quick dinner after work but because once you master this—and it isn't difficult—you will understand so much about cooking vegetables.

Ratatouille makes a great side dish with chicken or fish or other meat, it can start a meal, or it can be a meal. It keeps for 5 days to a week in the refrigerator, and it freezes well for several months.

I have sentimental feelings, too, about this Provençal vegetable dish, whose name comes from the French word *touiller,* meaning to stir or mix together. It was the first cooked vegetable dish that my mother taught me to make. My recipe has changed considerably since then; my first recipe called for ⅓ cup of olive oil, whereas this one calls for 2 tablespoons plus a teaspoon. I am always changing my recipe, and you no doubt have or will see many different approaches to the dish. But certain things about it remain constant, including its core ingredients: eggplant, onion, zucchini, garlic, peppers, and tomatoes. Herb choices vary, but I have always used thyme and/or oregano and added fresh basil at the end of cooking.

The method I'm using here is a very long, slow method of simmering the ratatouille. You don't have to work any harder, but you do need to be around for a few hours. That's why I recommend cooking up a batch of this on an evening or weekend and eating it during the week. Since it keeps so well, only getting better with time, you could plan to serve ratatouille at a weekend dinner party but make it one day or evening during the week.

Get out the following equipment: chef's knife, paring knife, and cutting board; baking sheet; measuring spoons; garlic press or minichop if using; medium-size saucepan and bowl; mortar and pestle; large, heavy casserole or Dutch oven with lid; large, heavy nonstick skillet and wooden spoon; colander and large bowl; small saucepan

Advance preparation: Ratatouille keeps for 5 days in the refrigerator and freezes well. It gets better overnight.

PER SERVING:
6.6 gm total fat
0.8 gm saturated fat
190 calories
30.2 gm carbohydrates
6.5 gm protein

continued

It's so annoying: you put the leftover tomato paste in the refrigerator, only to throw it out a few weeks later when mold appears. The best way to deal with this problem is to look for tomato paste in a tube, which unfortunately isn't always available. The other alternative is to freeze the remaining tomato paste in 1-tablespoon quantities. I spoon it out in mounds onto plastic, wrap them up, and freeze them in a zippered plastic bag. Then I pop them out and thaw them as needed.

To score eggplant, make an incision down the length of the cut side of each half.

2 pounds (2 large or 4 smallish) eggplant

2 tablespoons plus 1 teaspoon olive oil

2 large onions

6 large garlic cloves, peeled, 4 sliced or minced, 2 pressed or pureed with ¼ teaspoon salt

1 large red bell pepper

1 large green bell pepper

Salt to taste (at least ¾ teaspoon fine salt or 1½ teaspoons coarse sea salt)

1½ pounds (about 3 medium-size) zucchini

4 large or 6 medium-size ripe fresh tomatoes, peeled, seeded, and coarsely chopped

1 tablespoon tomato paste

1 bay leaf

2 teaspoons fresh thyme leaves or 1 teaspoon crumbled dried

2 teaspoons chopped fresh oregano leaves or 1 teaspoon crumbled dried

½ teaspoon coriander seeds, crushed

Freshly ground black pepper to taste

2 to 4 tablespoons slivered fresh basil, to your taste

How to Prepare Eggplant

Traditionally, eggplant is sliced and salted to draw out its bitter juices, then it's fried in oil. This doesn't work for the low-fat cook and, fat aside, I don't like the way the eggplant sucks up the oil like a sponge. So for twenty-five years I've been scoring or piercing and putting the eggplant into a very hot oven for 15 minutes or so. This quick roast has the same effect as the salting method; when it comes out of the hot oven and cools, it releases its juices. It also has a nice roasted flavor, and it isn't saturated with oil. Here's how you do it:

Preheat the oven to 450°F. Brush or rub a baking sheet with a teaspoon of olive oil. Using a chef's knife, cut the eggplant in half lengthwise, cutting right through the stem. Now take the tip of the knife, or the tip of a smaller knife, and make an incision down the length of the cut side of each half. *Do not allow the tip of the knife to go through the skin,* but get as close to it as you can. This is called *scoring* the eggplant. Place the eggplant halves on the baking sheet (or baking sheets if one isn't big enough) cut side down, rounded purple side up. Place in the oven and bake until the skins begin to shrivel and the edges against the pan are just beginning to brown, 15 to 20 minutes. Check after 15 minutes. Poke the purple skin with the tip of your finger, it should not resist. But the eggplant shouldn't be so cooked that it collapses either. Remove from the heat, transfer the eggplant to a colander, cut side down so they can drain, and allow to cool in the sink, where they will release some of their juice (meanwhile you can prepare the rest of the vegetables).

When the eggplant is cool enough to handle, cut the halves in half lengthwise along the score line. Peel away the skin if you wish (it doesn't bother me, but some people don't like it), and cut the eggplant into ¾-inch dice. To do this, cut lengthwise strips, then cut across the strips. Set aside.

How to Slice Onions

Using a sharp chef's knife, cut away the ends of the onion and remove the skin. This is facilitated by cutting a slit down the length of the onion, then unwrapping the skin, with maybe an outer layer of the onion. Cut the onion in half lengthwise, which means down one of the lines. Or you can cut the onion in half after cutting off the ends and lift the skin off each half. Now lay half an onion flat on your cutting board and cut strips along each line. Steady the onion with one hand while you cut toward that hand with your other hand. When you get very close to your fingertips or knuckles with the knife, turn the onion half around and cut toward the center from the outside again. Now cut off the solid bit at the root end that holds all the strips together. Scrape the sliced onions off the cutting board and into a bowl.

How to Mince or Press Garlic

See the instructions on pages 43–44.

How to Puree Garlic

You can do this in a mortar and pestle or with a small sharp knife. If using a mortar and pestle, put the cloves in the bowl and add the ¼ teaspoon salt (the salt helps to break down the garlic). Pound with the pestle until the garlic is mashed into a puree. Alternatively, put the clove on a cutting board and put the salt on the cutting board next to it. Steady the garlic clove with two fingers and scrape down the side of the clove, scooping up a little salt with the knife each time you scrape down. When you get too close to your fingers for comfort, mash together the salt and the rest of the garlic with the knife. You can also combine the garlic and salt in a saucer or shallow bowl and mash with a fork.

How to Slice Red and Green Peppers

Cut the pepper in half lengthwise, through the stem and down one of the indentations. Using your thumbs, pull out the seed pod under the stem and use your fingers or a small knife to pull out the membranes along the cut side. Remove any other seeds, which is easy if you turn the pepper cut side down and tap it against your cutting board or sink. Using a chef's knife or a paring knife (I prefer the larger knife), cut into strips about 1 inch wide by 2 inches long. Scrape into a bowl.

How to Prepare the Zucchini

Scrub the zucchini first, or wash it well and rub your hand up and down the vegetable under cold running water, then cut off the ends. With a large knife, halve the zucchini lengthwise. If the zucchini is quite large—you needed only two of them for 1½ pounds—then cut down the middle again so that you halve four lengthwise pieces. Now slice across the halves or quarters at ½-inch intervals. Scrape into a bowl or onto a plate.

How to Peel, Seed, and Chop Tomatoes

See the instructions on pages 44–46.

How to Pull Thyme Leaves Off Thyme Stems

If the thyme stems are very tender, then just chop them up with the leaves. If they're woody, you'll want to pull off the leaves. It's a bit tedious. Hold a stem in one hand, grasp the top end between the thumb and forefinger of your other hand, and slide this hand down toward the bottom of the stem, pulling the leaves back and off as you go.

What Do I Mean by Crumbled Dried Herbs?

When you are about to add the dried herbs to the stew, rub them between your thumb and first two fingers to extract more flavor.

How to Crush Coriander Seeds

Place them in a mortar and pestle and pound a few times. Or place them between sheets of wax paper and lean on them hard with the flat side of a knife or with the bottom of a heavy frying pan or a hammer.

How to Sliver Fresh Basil

See the instructions on page 47.

Making the Ratatouille

Prepare the eggplant as instructed. After you remove it from the oven, turn the heat down to 350°F. Oil a large, heavy lidded casserole (I like earthenware, but heavy enameled cast iron such as Le Creuset will work fine) with olive oil.

Heat 1 tablespoon of the olive oil in a large, heavy nonstick skillet over medium heat and add the sliced onions. Cook, stirring, until they have softened, about 5 minutes. They will be translucent and the slices will be flexible. Add half of the sliced or minced garlic and cook, stirring, until the onions have just begun to color, another 4 to 5 minutes. Remove from the heat and transfer the contents to the casserole.

Heat the remaining tablespoon oil in the skillet over medium heat and add the peppers. Stir for a couple of minutes and add about 1/4 teaspoon of the fine salt or 1/2 teaspoon of the coarse sea salt. Continue to cook, stirring often, until the peppers begin to soften, about 8 minutes. Add the zucchini slices and the remaining sliced or chopped garlic. Continue to cook, stirring, until the zucchini looks translucent, another 5 to 10 minutes. Transfer to the casserole containing the onions. Add the diced eggplant, half of the chopped tomatoes, and the tomato paste to the casserole. Stir in the bay leaf, thyme, oregano, crushed coriander seeds, and 1/2 teaspoon fine salt or 1 teaspoon coarse sea salt. Stir everything together, cover, and place in the oven. Set the timer for 30 minutes.

After 30 minutes, remove the casserole from the oven and give the mixture a good stir with a long-handled wooden spoon. Cover and return to the oven. Set the timer for 30 minutes.

When the timer goes off, remove the casserole from the oven and stir in the remaining tomatoes and the pressed or pureed garlic. Taste and adjust the salt. Add freshly ground pepper and return to the oven for another 30 minutes. Stir in the basil, cover, and return to the oven. Turn off the heat and leave the ratatouille in the oven for another hour. When the ratatouille is done, the vegetables should be extremely tender; the eggplant may even be falling apart, what I like to call "melting" consistency.

Place a colander over a bowl and dump the ratatouille into the colander. The juices will drain into the bowl. Transfer the juices to a small saucepan and return the ratatouille to the casserole. Heat the juices to a boil. Reduce by half over high heat; this means let the liquid evaporate until the volume has been reduced by half. Stir the reduced juices back into the ratatouille. Taste and adjust the seasonings. Serve hot or cold. For best results, cool and refrigerate overnight, then let come to room temperature, or heat, before serving the next day.

A faster method: It's still good, but the slow roasting brings out more of the sweetness of the vegetables. Instead of being baked in the oven, the stew can be cooked on top of the stove in 45 minutes to an hour. Follow the directions through step 3, then, instead of placing in a 350°F oven, cover and simmer over very low heat. Stir every now and again to make sure the ratatouille isn't sticking to the bottom of the pan and scorching. After 30 minutes, stir in the remaining tomatoes and the garlic and continue to cook until all the vegetables are tender and the mixture is fragrant, another 15 to 30 minutes. Proceed as directed.

Ways to Transform Leftover Ratatouille

It's great cold, plain or with a vinaigrette, served in lieu of salad on a bed of lettuce. But it also makes a great

- filling for omelets (see page 196)
- filling for a tart (see recipe, page 319)
- sauce for fish (see recipe, page 294)

Now that you know how to . . .

- prepare eggplant

- slice onions and bell peppers

- puree garlic

- prepare zucchini

- prepare thyme and crush coriander

. . . you won't think twice about following a standard recipe for ratatouille, which looks like this:

Ratatouille

■

Makes 6 servings

2 pounds (2 large or 4 smallish) eggplant
2 tablespoons plus 1 teaspoon olive oil
2 large onions, peeled and sliced
6 large garlic cloves, peeled, 4 sliced or minced, 2 pressed or pureed with
**   ¼ teaspoon salt**
1 large red bell pepper, seeded and cut into pieces about 1 by 2 inches
1 large green bell pepper, seeded and cut into pieces about 1 by 2 inches
Salt to taste (at least ¾ teaspoon fine salt or 1½ teaspoons coarse sea salt)
1½ pounds (about 3 medium-size) zucchini, cut in half lengthwise and sliced
**   about ½ inch thick (if the zucchini is very large, quarter it lengthwise**
**   before slicing)**
4 large or 6 medium-size ripe fresh tomatoes, peeled, seeded, and coarsely
**   chopped**
1 tablespoon tomato paste
1 bay leaf
2 teaspoons fresh thyme leaves or 1 teaspoon crumbled dried
2 teaspoons chopped fresh oregano leaves or 1 teaspoon crumbled dried
½ teaspoon coriander seeds, crushed
Freshly ground black pepper to taste
2 to 4 tablespoons slivered fresh basil leaves, to your taste

1. Preheat the oven to 450°F. Brush or rub a baking sheet with 1 teaspoon of the olive oil. Score the eggplant halves down to, but not through, the skin. Place on the baking sheet (or baking sheets if one isn't big enough) cut side down. Place in the oven and bake until the skins begin to shrivel and the edges against the sheet are browning, 15 to 20 minutes. Remove from the oven, transfer the eggplant to a colander cut side down so they can drain, and allow

to cool in the sink, where they will release some of their juice (meanwhile, you can prepare the rest of the vegetables). When the eggplant is cool enough to handle, cut the halves in half lengthwise along the score line. Peel away the skin if you wish and cut into ¾-inch dice. Set aside. Reduce the oven temperature to 350°F. Oil a large, heavy casserole with a lid, preferably earthenware, with olive oil.

2. Heat 1 tablespoon of the olive oil in a large, heavy nonstick skillet over medium heat and add the sliced onions. Cook, stirring, until softened, about 5 minutes. Add half the sliced or minced garlic and cook, stirring, until the onions have just begun to color, another 4 to 5 minutes. Remove from the heat and transfer the contents to the casserole.

3. Heat the remaining tablespoon olive oil in the skillet over medium heat and add the peppers. Stir for a couple of minutes and add about ¼ teaspoon of the fine salt or ½ teaspoon of the coarse sea salt. Continue to cook, stirring often, until the peppers begin to soften, about 5 minutes. Add the zucchini and the remaining sliced or chopped garlic. Continue to cook, stirring, until the zucchini looks translucent, another 5 to 10 minutes. Transfer to the casserole containing the onions. Add the diced eggplant, half the tomatoes, and the tomato paste to the casserole. Stir in the bay leaf, thyme, oregano, crushed coriander seeds, and ½ teaspoon fine salt or teaspoon coarse sea salt. Stir everything together, cover, and place in the oven. Set the timer for 30 minutes.

4. After 30 minutes, remove the casserole from the oven and give the mixture a good stir with a long-handled wooden spoon. Set the timer for 30 minutes.

5. When the timer goes off, remove the casserole from the oven and stir in the remaining tomatoes and the pressed or pureed garlic. Taste and adjust the salt. Add freshly ground pepper and return to the oven for another 30 minutes. Stir in the basil, cover, and return to the oven. Turn off the heat and leave the ratatouille in the oven for another hour.

6. Place a colander over a bowl and dump the ratatouille into the colander. Transfer the juices to a small saucepan and return the ratatouille to the casserole. Heat the juices to a boil. Reduce by half and stir back into the ratatouille. Taste and adjust seasonings. Serve hot or cold. For best results, cool and refrigerate overnight, then let come to room temperature, or heat, before serving the next day.

Roast Chicken

Makes 4 servings

There are many ways to roast a chicken. Master it, and you'll feel that you can invite anybody who isn't vegetarian to dinner, anytime. I always start with the oven high, then turn it down. This gives the chicken a nice crisp skin. However, other cooks keep the oven at one temperature for the entire time, high or medium. If you buy a meat thermometer, you'll be able to check to see if it's done the scientific way. I, however, learned to check to see if the chicken was done by piercing the thigh, which takes longest to cook, with a fork and seeing if the juice runs clear, with *no* sign of pinkness, then jiggling a leg to see if it moves freely. These two signs work well.

continued

I can't emphasize how important it is to buy a free-range organic chicken if you want to keep fats down. Chicken is roasted with the skin on, and it's fattier than you can imagine. I brought back many a chicken from the market while I was working on this recipe, and even the free-range birds required cutting away visible fat before I put the birds in the oven. I measured the fat that dripped into the baking dish after roasting a hormone-free, but not free-range chicken, and it was a full ⅔ cup! Free-range chickens move about, and they don't develop quite as much fat as battery (high-volume commercially raised) hens. They are fed grains, and they have more flavor. And they aren't chock full of hormones and antibiotics.

Even free-range chickens release a lot of fat when they roast. I find basting—brushing the chicken with its drippings as it roasts—unnecessary, because the skin doesn't seem to dry out since there's so much fat right underneath. So how do you get around this and still serve roast chicken? What I do is lift the chicken out of the roasting pan and onto a meat carving board, the kind that has a trough to catch the juices around the perimeter, and maybe inside the perimeter, once the chicken is done. It needs to rest for 5 to 10 minutes after it roasts so that its juices are reabsorbed into the meat, and there's no sense letting it sit in its fat in the pan. It's amazing how much fat you will leave behind in the pan (some of the liquid is juice, not fat), then on the board. I also remove the skin—not before I carve the chicken, but from the pieces as they're cut. Some people want the skin, so doing it this way allows for choice (I am not a martinet when it comes to low-fat eating). The skin lifts off easily, and you'll see how much fat is attached to it. Of course you might ask, what's the point of roasting a chicken if you're not going to eat the skin? But I think much of the flavor from the skin does get absorbed into the meat.

I usually season the chicken with garlic, lemon, and herbs, but a roast chicken needs nothing beyond salt and pepper to be good, provided you got a good free-range chicken to begin with. So I've made the garlic, lemon, and herbs optional for this warm-up lesson, but using them won't complicate the procedure unduly and does add a nice piquant dimension.

Serve the chicken with steamed or roasted potatoes (you can roast small potatoes right in the pan with the chicken—see note on page 83) or rice, or a steamed or roasted vegetable of your choice. Follow it with a nice green salad.

One 3½- to 4-pound free-range or "natural," hormone-free chicken
1 tablespoon plus 1 teaspoon olive oil
Salt and freshly ground black pepper to taste

OPTIONAL:

3 garlic cloves, peeled and crushed with the flat side of a knife

5 fresh rosemary sprigs

1 lemon, cut in half

How to Buy a Chicken

Buy a fresh, not frozen, chicken that is free-range or "natural" and hormone-free. I'm repeating myself here because it's that important. Just to confuse you, roasting chickens are usually called "fryers" or "broiler-fryers." Don't ask me why. I am always tentative when I ask for a fryer or a broiler that I know I'm going to roast or stew, but that's the chicken you want (I once bought a stewing hen for a stew, and it was tough as nails). If your supermarket has a butcher, you can get a good look at those chickens, which will not be wrapped in plastic. Wrapped or not, they should be plump and moist, with no visible blemishes. If the bird is packaged, there should be no red juice in the package; that's a sure sign that it has been frozen and thawed.

Breast side up

Sniff the chicken. Chicken can go off (so I learned, on Christmas when all the stores were closed and I was about to roast my chicken; we had to eat pasta!). If it has any hint of an off odor, tell the store manager.

Poultry is very perishable, so don't do a million errands after buying the chicken on a hot day. Take it home and put it in the bottom of the refrigerator. If you aren't going to cook it that night, unwrap it, set it on a plate, cover tightly with two layers of plastic wrap, and refrigerate.

Breast side down

How to Prepare a Chicken for Roasting

Before you get the chicken out of the refrigerator, begin preheating the oven to 450°F. It should preheat for 30 minutes so that it's nice and hot when you put in the bird.

Important: First reach inside the chicken's cavity and pull out the bag of giblets that the butcher has conveniently put there for you: it contains the liver, heart, and neck. You can cook up the livers for yourself (or your cats, as I do), discard them, freeze them, or use them for stock. We're not making gravy here—there is no such thing as a low-fat gravy—so you won't be using them for that. Save the neck for making stock, which you will do with the carcass of this bird (see page 155).

Trim away pieces of excess fat—they are loose pieces of yellow fatty skin—with a small knife or scissors and discard them. Now rinse the chicken inside and out under cold running water and blot dry, inside and out, with paper towels.

Oil the roasting pan with the teaspoon of olive oil and place the chicken in it. Drizzle the remaining tablespoon of olive oil over the chicken and rub it over the skin with your hands. Sprinkle with salt and pepper. Turn the chicken breast side down (you will be turning the bird over later, so don't worry if you've seen other recipes that say to put the bird in breast side up; that's how it finishes up).

If You Are Using the Optionals

Place the crushed garlic, three of the rosemary sprigs, and half of the lemon in the cavity of the chicken. Tuck the remaining sprigs of rosemary into the wings, close to the body of the chicken.

Roasting the Chicken

Place the chicken in the preheated 450°F oven and roast for 10 minutes. Turn the oven down to 350°F. Roast for 30 minutes, then turn the bird onto its back (breast up). To do this, put on oven mitts and clamp the chicken between a long two-pronged fork and a wooden spoon, or two long wooden spoons, or use tongs. Roast another 30 minutes.

Theoretically, the chicken needs about 20 minutes per pound. I always begin to check after 1 hour for a 3- to 3½-pound chicken. Test to see if the bird is done. First of all it should have a nice golden color. If it doesn't, roast for another 10 to 20 minutes. Take it from the oven and stick the point of a small sharp knife or a skewer into the thigh of the chicken. Stick the knife right down and pull it out. Juice will run out, and it should be clear. If it is slightly pink, you need to roast the chicken longer. Roast for 10 more minutes and check again. The other way to test is with an instant-read meat thermometer. Stick it into the thickest part of the thigh, making sure it doesn't touch bone. It should read at least 175°F.

Take the chicken from the oven and squeeze the other half of the optional lemon all over it. Transfer to a meat cutting board that has indentations cut into it to catch the juice and let it sit for 5 to 10 minutes (you can let it sit in the pan as well, but it will be sitting in its fat). This is important, because the juices settle back into the meat and the meat "relaxes," making the chicken juicy and tender. If you let the chicken rest in the pan, remove from the pan and transfer to a cutting board.

How to Carve a Roast Chicken

You'll need a sharp chef's knife, at least 8 inches long, a two-pronged fork, and a kitchen towel. Begin by removing the legs and thighs from the body of the bird. This bit of helpful instruction comes from my friend and colleague Elaine Corn (*Now You're Cooking*, Harlow and Ratner, 1994), who taught me to use a kitchen towel to pull off the legs and wings. Hold on to the end of a drumstick with the towel so that you don't burn yourself. Jiggle it and pull it back, away from the body of the chicken. You can pull the drumstick and thigh off together or cut them away by sticking the tip of your knife down into the now-exposed ball-and-socket joint and twisting the knife, while you steady the bird with a fork or with your towel-protected other hand. Remove to a platter or keep on the board if it's big enough. Then either pull or cut the drumstick from the thigh. This should be easy, because when you pulled back the drumstick, the bones cracked at the joint. Use the same method to remove the wings. Hold with a towel and pull from the side of the bird, twist, and cut away. Now carve the breast meat. You can slice across the grain, down the front of the bird, or slice down the sides. Place the sliced white meat on a platter and surround with the drumsticks, thighs, and wings or simply serve onto plates.

Note: To roast potatoes with the chicken, cut them into 1-inch pieces if they're large, keep whole if small, and add them to the pan when you turn the heat down to 350°F. My favorite roasting potatoes are Yukon Gold, which are moderately waxy. Stir when you turn the chicken over. Note that the potatoes will absorb chicken fat.

Now that you know how to buy, clean, and roast chicken, you won't think twice about following a standard recipe, which looks like this . . .

Roast Chicken

Makes 4 servings

One 3½-pound free-range, hormone-free chicken
1 tablespoon plus 1 teaspoon olive oil
Salt and freshly ground black pepper to taste

OPTIONAL:
3 garlic cloves, peeled and crushed with the flat side of a knife
5 fresh rosemary sprigs
1 lemon, cut in half

1. Preheat the oven to 450°F. Rinse the chicken inside and out under a cold tap and blot dry, inside and out, with paper towels. Oil a roasting pan with the teaspoon of olive oil and place the chicken in it. Drizzle the remaining tablespoon olive oil over the chicken and rub it over the skin with your hands. Sprinkle with salt and pepper. Place the crushed garlic, 3 of the rosemary sprigs, and half of the lemon in the cavity of the chicken. Tuck the remaining sprigs of rosemary into the wings, close to the body of the chicken. Turn the chicken breast side down in the pan.
2. Place the chicken in the preheated 450°F oven and roast for 10 minutes. Reduce the oven temperature to 350°F. Roast for 30 minutes, then turn the bird

onto its back (breast up). Roast until the skin is golden and the juices run clear when you cut into the thigh, about another 30 minutes.

3. Take the chicken from the oven and squeeze the other half of the optional lemon all over it. Let it sit in the pan for 5 to 10 minutes. Remove from the pan and transfer to a cutting board, preferably one with indentations to catch the juices. Carve and serve.

Garlic Soup

Makes 4 servings

Part of my confidence as a cook comes from the fact that I have certain dishes in my repertoire that require very little in the way of ingredients or forethought. I always have garlic, eggs, and bread in the house, so I always have the makings for this meal. This soup requires no real technique at all. Unlike the other warm-up recipes, you don't need an extended version to help you with the various steps. I'm including it in these warm-up exercises because it's so easy and satisfying, quickly achieved after a long day at work. You can add to the basic recipe any number of ingredients to vary the soup and make it more substantial—potatoes, pasta, green vegetables like broccoli or peas or green beans. The most important tool here will be your taste buds, which will tell you if there's sufficient salt and garlic. Although it's a garlic soup, the garlic loses its bite after it simmers for 15 minutes, and the soup ends up being quite comforting.

> 6 cups water
> 4 to 6 large garlic cloves, to your taste, peeled and minced or pressed, plus 1 garlic clove, cut in half
> 1½ to 2 teaspoons salt, to your taste
> 1 bay leaf
> ¼ to ½ teaspoon dried thyme, to your taste, a few sprigs of fresh, or 2 or 3 fresh sage leaves
> 4 thick slices country-style bread or French bread
> 2 large eggs, beaten
> 2 teaspoons olive oil (optional)
> Freshly ground black pepper to taste
> 2 tablespoons chopped fresh flat-leaf parsley leaves
> 2 to 3 tablespoons freshly grated Parmesan cheese, to your taste

1. Bring the water to a boil in a 3- or 4-quart saucepan or soup pot. Add the minced or pressed garlic, 1½ teaspoons of the salt, the bay leaf, and

Get out the following equipment: **chef's knife and cutting board; minichop or garlic press if using; liquid measuring cup and measuring spoons; small bowl and whisk or fork; 3-or 4-quart saucepan or soup pot; ladle; large pot and bowl if making the variation with wilted greens**

Advance preparation: **This is a last-minute soup.**

PER SERVING:
4.6 gm total fat
1.6 gm saturated fat
162 calories
21.6 gm carbohydrates
8.1 gm protein

the thyme or sage. Cover and simmer for 15 minutes. Taste: Does it taste good? Is there enough salt? Garlic? Make any adjustments.

2. *Make garlic croutons:* Toast the bread. As soon as it's done, rub both sides with the cut clove of garlic and set aside.

3. Beat together the eggs and optional olive oil. Spoon a ladleful of the hot soup into the eggs and stir together so the eggs don't curdle when you add them to the soup. Then turn off the heat under the soup and stir in the egg mixture. The eggs should cloud the soup, but they shouldn't scramble if the soup isn't boiling. Stir in the pepper and parsley.

4. Place a garlic crouton in each bowl. Ladle in the soup, sprinkle Parmesan over the top, and serve.

Garlic Soup with Pasta and Broccoli, Peas, Green Beans, or Sugar Snap Peas

Add ¼ pound (about 1½ cups) pasta such as fusilli, penne, or broken spaghetti and ½ pound broccoli florets or sugar snap peas or 1 cup fresh or thawed frozen peas to the soup at the end of step 1. Simmer until the pasta is cooked al dente, about 10 minutes. Meanwhile, make the croutons. Proceed with step 3.

Garlic Soup with Potatoes

At the *beginning* of step 1 add ½ pound waxy potatoes, such as Yukon Gold, white creamers, or red potatoes, scrubbed and sliced about ¼ inch thick. By the end of the 15 minutes they should be tender. If they are not, continue to simmer until they are and proceed with the recipe. You can also add broccoli florets or greens (spinach, beet greens, chard), about ½ pound. Add broccoli at the end of step 1 and simmer for 5 to 10 minutes before proceeding with the eggs. Wilt the greens separately and add along with eggs. To wilt greens, stem and wash thoroughly. Bring a large pot of water to a rolling boil and add 2 to 3 teaspoons salt and the greens. As soon as the water comes back to a simmer, drain and transfer immediately to a bowl of cold water. Drain and gently squeeze dry. Chop coarsely. Spinach and chard can also be wilted in a dry skillet, in just the water left on the leaves after washing. Other greens are a bit too tough for this. Stir over high heat until the spinach or chard wilts and turns bright green. Transfer to a bowl of cold water, drain, and proceed as directed.

Get out the following
equipment: **cutting
board and chef's knife;
colander or medium-
mesh strainer; medium-
size bowl; measuring
spoons and measuring
cup; garlic press or
minichop if using; 2- or
3-quart saucepan with
lid and steamer if using
optional steamed veg-
etables; salad bowl or
platter and servers**

Advance preparation:
**Without the optionals,
this is a great keeper.
You could do up a big
batch of this salad and
keep it for 5 days in the
refrigerator. Dinner will
be ready for you when
you get home.**

PER SERVING:
*17.3 gm total fat
2.1 gm saturated fat
438 calories
34.2 gm carbohydrates
35.9 gm protein*

Mediterranean Tuna and Bean Salad

Makes 2 servings as a one-dish meal

If you have a can of tuna and a can of beans in the cupboard, you have dinner. This pantry recipe requires little skill beyond the ability to use a can
opener. A simple high-protein combination with great flavor, this is eaten
widely throughout the Mediterranean. The authentic version would use
tuna packed in olive oil and would not include the optionals. But I don't
think the lower-fat water-packed tuna version loses much in the translation,
because of the delicious yogurt-based dressing. If you add any of the optionals, you'll have quite a substantial salad and be able to stretch this recipe
to feed three or four people. In any case, the recipe is easily doubled.

No new skills here—just a concept: in a light kitchen, dinner is often a
salad.

1 small red onion, peeled and very thinly sliced
Salt
1 tablespoon red or white wine vinegar
¼ cup water
One 6½-ounce can water-packed tuna, drained
¼ cup chopped fresh basil or flat-leaf parsley leaves or a combination
    (see Note)
1 to 2 teaspoons chopped or slivered fresh sage leaves (*not* dried), if
    available, to your taste
One 15-ounce can white beans, chickpeas, or borlotti beans

FOR THE DRESSING:
2 tablespoons fresh lemon juice
2 tablespoons red or white wine vinegar
Salt and freshly ground black pepper to taste
1 large garlic clove, or more to taste, peeled and minced or pressed
1 heaping teaspoon Dijon mustard
2 tablespoons olive oil
⅓ cup plain nonfat yogurt or 1½% buttermilk
¼ cup water, plus additional water as desired for thinning the dressing

OPTIONAL:
½ pound broccoli, broken into florets and steamed 5 minutes (page 53), or
    1 cup fresh peas, steamed 5 minutes
1 medium-size or large red bell pepper, seeded and chopped

2 cups baby field greens
Red and yellow cherry tomatoes

Sprinkle the onion slices with salt. Place half of them in a colander or strainer and the other half in a bowl with the vinegar and water. Set aside while you prepare the salad. This step eliminates much of the raw onion odor that otherwise lingers in your mouth for hours after eating.

Here's how you drain the tuna (you probably already know this and have since you were six years old): Take off the top with a can opener, then hold the can over the sink and press the top into the can with your thumbs while holding the can with your other fingers. Reverse the can over the sink to let all the water run out. Scrape the tuna into a large bowl. Break it up with a fork. Add the chopped fresh herbs. Rinse the salted half of the sliced onion thoroughly with water and toss with the tuna.

Drain the beans into a strainer held over the sink. Rinse with cold water. This gets rid of the canning liquid; it doesn't always taste so great. Some say rinsing makes the beans more digestible, too. Toss with the tuna.

Mix together the lemon juice and vinegar and season with salt and pepper. Add the garlic and mustard and whisk in the olive oil and yogurt or buttermilk. Thin out with a tablespoon or two of water if desired. Toss well with the tuna mixture. If you are including steamed broccoli or chopped pepper, toss with the mixture. Taste. Does it taste sharp and vivid? Add a little salt, or more lemon juice or garlic if desired.

If you wish, line a bowl or platter with the salad greens. Top with the tuna and beans. Drain the remaining onion slices and scatter over the top. Garnish with the optional cherry tomatoes and serve or chill and serve.

Note: Parsley is the easiest herb to keep on hand in the refrigerator. It should be on your once-a-week shopping list. Basil keeps well, too; see page 13. But it's not always easy to find, and sometimes it's expensive.

Cherry Clafoutis
Makes 8 servings

Most people have never even heard of a clafoutis (pronounced kla-foo-tee). It's a French dessert and has a very satisfying ratio of ease to impressiveness. It's as pleasing and pretty as a fruit tart, without the hassle of making the crust (not to mention the added calories), and as comforting as a pancake or a flan—which is what a clafoutis is, a kind of cross between a pancake and a flan with fruit in it. You can make it year-round with fruit in season. The cherry clafoutis is among my favorites; the cherries sweeten even more as they bake, and any dessert made during their short season is a treat. You'll find other clafoutis in the dessert chapter. When you make this you'll see that you don't have to be a pastry chef (and believe me, I'm not!) to make a winning dessert in no time.

One thing that may strike you as strange here is that I don't ask you to pit the cherries. That's because I learned to make this in France, where they never do; they'd lose too much juice as they bake, which would alter the texture of the clafoutis. This makes the preparation go very quickly indeed. *However, it's VITAL that you announce, upon serving this, that the cherries aren't pitted.* You'll find that the pits cause people to linger over this dessert, which is the best way to enjoy any food.

What distinguishes this clafoutis (and the other clafoutis in this book) from traditional clafoutis is that I use nonfat yogurt instead of whole milk or cream, which is what the French would use. This is a low-fat dessert but tastes rich.

> **1½ pounds fresh sweet cherries, such as Bing cherries, stems removed**
> **3 tablespoons kirsch (see Notes)**
> **6 tablespoons sugar**
> **3 large eggs**
> **1 vanilla bean or ½ teaspoon pure vanilla extract**
> **Pinch of salt**
> **⅔ cup sifted unbleached flour**
> **¾ cup plain nonfat yogurt**

How to Work with Vanilla Beans

Vanilla beans are quite expensive, but their tiny little seeds are incredibly delicious, and they look pretty in the batter. The "bean" is actually a long pod. Lay it on a cutting board and, with the tip of a small sharp knife, cut it in half down its length. Inside is a mass of sticky little seeds—that's where all the luscious vanilla flavor is. Using the tip of your knife, scrape down the inside to get the seeds out. Scrape them right into the bowl in which you are going to beat the eggs. Don't throw away the pods. Instead, allow them to dry out overnight, then stick them into a jar of sugar. Thus begins your vanilla sugar. After a few weeks the sugar will have a lovely vanilla scent. When recipes call for sugar and vanilla, use this sugar for added vanilla flavor.

How to Measure and Sift Flour

How much flour you actually get when you measure it depends on how you measure it. If it has been sitting in its bag or bin and you just dig it out, you will actually get more flour by weight than the recipe asks for, because it's packed. But if you stir the flour, then gingerly scoop it up, your measure will be more accurate. Sifting before measuring assures you that the flour will not be too packed. You don't need a fancy sifter for this, just a medium-mesh strainer. Place the strainer over a bowl. Use exact cup measures here, in this case a ⅓-cup measure. Give the flour a stir, scoop out a ⅓-cup measure, and, using a butter knife, level off the top by running the knife horizontally along the top ridge of the measure. Dump it into the strainer and scoop out another ⅓-cup measure in the same way. Now tap the strainer against the sides of the bowl or just shake it gently to sift the flour through. Remeasure the flour into another bowl, scooping it up from the bowl and leveling the top. Return any flour remaining in the bowl to the bag or bin.

Whisking

This recipe is so easy, I never bother with an electric mixer. The hand whisking goes quickly and is efficient. You'll need a medium-size wire whisk for this. Break your eggs into the bowl with the vanilla seeds; the bowl should be about a 3-quart mixing bowl, and if it has a lip, all the better for pouring the final batter. Using a wrist-flicking motion, beat the eggs with the whisk until the whites and yellows are amalgamated into a uniform mixture. It takes about ten to twelve revolutions of the whisk to get there. You're incorporating air into the eggs as you do this, and consequently the batter will be light. Now add the liquid from the cherries, the remaining sugar as directed, and the salt, and incorporate them into the eggs. Next you are asked to gradually whisk in the flour. This means don't dump in the flour all at once. Sprinkle in about a quarter of it and whisk it in, using the same wrist-flicking motion, until you no longer see flour, then repeat with another fraction, and so on until the flour is all incorporated. Now the batter will be pretty thick. Finally, whisk in the yogurt. Your goal here is a batter with a smooth texture.

Putting It All Together

This part is easy. You've buttered your baking dish, which is preferably a ceramic tart pan, and lined it with the cherries, and now you pour in the batter. Scrape every last bit of it out of the bowl with a rubber spatula. It will spread out and even out in the dish.

How Can You Tell When It's Done?

The edges and top should be beginning to brown. But the best way to tell is to use your fingers. Gently press on the top of it. It should resist.

Making the Clafoutis

Toss the cherries with the kirsch and 2 tablespoons of the sugar in a large bowl. Let sit for 30 minutes. Meanwhile, preheat the oven to 400°F. Butter a 10½-inch ceramic tart pan or round baking dish.

Beat the eggs with the seeds from the vanilla bean or the vanilla extract with an electric mixer or a whisk until smooth. Drain the liquid from the cherries into the eggs and add the remaining 4 tablespoons sugar and the salt. Beat together. Slowly beat in the flour a quarter at a time. Add the yogurt and mix together well.

Arrange the cherries in the baking dish. Pour the batter over them.

Bake in the preheated oven until the top is browned and the clafoutis is firm, about 25 minutes. Press gently on the top to see if it's firm. If it isn't, return to the oven for 2 to 5 minutes. Remove from the heat and cool on a wire rack. Serve warm or at room temperature.

Notes: Other fruits can be substituted for the cherries. See the pear clafoutis on page 350. Other favorites are peaches peeled, pitted, and sliced, and halved, pitted plums. Use 1½ to 2 pounds fruit, or enough to cover the bottom of the dish.

Kirsch is a cherry eau-de-vie. It's good to have a small bottle around for cooking.

Now that you're comfortable with . . .

■ **working with vanilla beans**

■ **sifting and measuring flour**

■ **whisking together a batter**

. . . you won't think twice about following a standard recipe for a clafoutis, which looks like this:

Cherry Clafoutis

Makes 8 servings

1½ **pounds fresh sweet cherries, such as Bing cherries, stems removed**
3 **tablespoons kirsch**
6 **tablespoons sugar**
3 **large eggs**
1 **vanilla bean or** ½ **teaspoon pure vanilla extract**
Pinch of salt
⅔ **cup sifted unbleached flour**
¾ **cup plain nonfat yogurt**

1. Toss the cherries with the kirsch and 2 tablespoons of the sugar in a large bowl. Let sit for 30 minutes. Meanwhile, preheat the oven to 400°F. Butter a 10½-inch ceramic tart pan or round baking dish.
2. Beat the eggs with the seeds from the vanilla bean or the vanilla extract in the bowl of an electric mixer or with a whisk until smooth. Drain the liquid from the cherries into the eggs and add the remaining 4 tablespoons sugar and the salt. Beat together. Slowly beat in the flour a quarter at a time. Add the yogurt and mix together well.
3. Arrange the cherries in the bottom of the tart pan or baking dish. Pour the batter over them.
4. Bake in the preheated oven until the top is browned and the clafoutis is firm, about 25 minutes. Press gently on the top to see if it's firm. If it isn't, return to the oven for another 2 to 5 minutes. Remove from the heat and cool on a wire rack. Serve warm or at room temperature.

The Recipes

Chicken and Turkey

■

This may seem like a strange place to begin (and if you're a vegetarian, go on to the next chapter). But if you can master chicken, you'll feel confident about feeding yourself, and you won't think twice about making the chicken salads in the next chapter or the chicken tacos in "Tacos, Quesadillas, and Accompanying Salsas." You'll also feel that you can give a dinner party because you've mastered Chicken with Two Heads of Garlic or Chicken with Mediterranean Flavors.

■ Light Chicken Basics ■

The most important thing to know about chicken and fat is that most of the fat is in the skin. If you eat chicken without the skin, you'll cut in half your intake of fat and saturated fat. As a matter of course, have the butcher skin your chicken (except when buying whole chicken to roast). If there is no butcher at your market, and all the chicken is packaged, stick with chicken breasts or pull off the skin yourself (it isn't difficult). You can take the skin off the chicken after cooking or before. It's easier afterward, but if the chicken is simmering with other ingredients, the fat will melt into the stew if you don't remove the skin beforehand. If you are roasting or steaming the chicken, you'll take the skin off after it is cooked. There's more fat in dark meat than in light, so skinless chicken breasts, which are light meat, are your best bet in any case. They are prepackaged in supermarket meat departments. Annoyingly, these packages often contain more chicken breasts than you want to buy at a given time, but they freeze well (see page 96).

It pays to buy hormone-free, free-range chicken.

Generally, I find the amount of fat on chickens appalling. Free-range chickens have been allowed to run around freely rather than sitting all day in a chicken coop, so they're leaner than battery chickens, which are confined to small spaces, although I still find myself trimming away lots of fat before I cook them. They taste better, too. They're also more expensive, but it's a worthwhile expense if you can afford it. The next best choice is "natural" or hormone-free chicken, which is now widely available in supermarkets.

■ Buying and Storing Chicken ■

Buy hormone-free, free-range chicken. If you're lucky enough to live near a butcher shop or a supermarket where there is an actual butcher (very rare these days), buy your chicken there. They won't be packaged, and you can be sure they'll be very fresh. Also, the butcher will do all the dirty work. You can buy whole chicken breasts and have him bone and skin them (cheaper than buying boneless skinless breasts) or buy whole chickens and have him cut them up and skin them.

If packaged chicken is your only option, check the "sell by" date carefully. Chicken is very perishable. The "sell by" date is seven to ten days after slaughter and the last date recommended for selling the chicken. You can store chicken in the bottom of your refrigerator for two to three days after the "sell by" date. Choose chickens that are moist and plump.

Chicken is extremely susceptible to bacterial contamination; that's why they keep it close to freezing in the supermarket. Don't go off to a baseball game after you've shopped without going home and putting the chicken in the refrigerator first. Keep it in its supermarket packaging and put it in the bottom of your refrigerator or the meat drawer. It should be cooked within three days. If you are freezing the chicken, unwrap it, rinse it, and pat dry with paper towels. Wrap tightly in aluminum foil or freezer wrap, making sure there are no air pockets. You can keep it frozen for up to a year.

Do not thaw chicken at room temperature. Bacteria can invade the first parts to thaw out before the entire piece has thawed. Thaw in the refrigerator or in the microwave, following the manufacturer's instructions, but in the microwave only if you are going to cook it right away. To thaw in the refrigerator, place the chicken pieces on a plate because they will drip. Allow about 6 hours per pound of meat (place in the refrigerator in the morning to thaw by dinner).

Keep chicken in the refrigerator until you are ready to cook it. Wash cutting boards, utensils you use for uncooked chicken, and your hands with hot, soapy water immediately after handling to avoid contaminating other foods. Wash the chicken with cold water and pat dry with paper towels. Trim away any visible pieces of fat. You'll be amazed by how much fat there is left to trim, even when the chicken has been skinned.

See page 79 for a roast chicken recipe.

■ A Basic Recipe ■

Shredded Poached Chicken Breast

■

Makes 1½ to 2 cups shredded chicken

Poaching skinned chicken breasts on the bone, then letting them cool in the broth, results in very moist meat and a light chicken broth, delivering two items for the price of one. You can freeze the broth for a later date if you don't need it right away (see Note). Shredded chicken is great to have on hand for salads, soups, tacos and quesadillas, pasta, and sandwiches. Here is a master recipe.

> 5 cups water
> 1 medium-size onion, peeled and quartered
> 2 garlic cloves, peeled and crushed
> 1 whole chicken breast with bone in, skinned and split
> ½ teaspoon dried thyme or oregano or a combination
> 1 to 1½ teaspoons salt, to your taste

1. Combine the water, quartered onion, and crushed garlic cloves in the saucepan and bring to a boil over medium heat. Add the chicken breasts and bring back to a simmer. Skim off any foam that rises, then add the dried herbs. Cover partially, reduce the heat to low, and simmer until the chicken is cooked through, 13 to 15 minutes. Add salt to taste. Allow the chicken to cool in the broth if there is time. Remove the chicken from the broth when cool enough to handle. Strain the broth for later use and refrigerate.

2. Once the breasts are cool enough to handle, shred them. Do this by tearing strips off the bone. You'll be amazed by how much meat you'll get. It's satisfying because the moist meat comes away from the bone so easily. If

Get out the following equipment: **chef's knife and cutting board; 3-quart lidded saucepan; skimmer or large spoon; strainer and medium-size bowl**

Advance preparation: **The cooked chicken will keep for about 3 days in the refrigerator.**

PER ½-CUP SERVING:
1.4 gm total fat
0.4 gm saturated fat
71.8 calories
0 gm carbohydrates
13.8 gm protein

you want a finer shred, just hold pieces in one hand and pull off shreds with the other. Store in a zippered plastic bag in the refrigerator until ready to use.

Notes: If you use skinned and boned chicken breasts, check carefully after 10 minutes since these cook faster than breasts on the bone. I cut them in half to see (since you're going to shred them anyway, it really doesn't matter).

The broth you will obtain here is a very light broth. As is, it's adequate for cooking rice or using for soups where you have the option of broth or water. If you want a richer broth, you can return the chicken bones to it and bring back to a boil. Reduce to a simmer and simmer, uncovered, until the liquid has reduced by a cup or two.

To freeze broth: Place first in the refrigerator in a bowl for several hours or overnight. Remove from the refrigerator and skim off fat from the surface of the broth. Transfer to one or more containers and freeze. Label the containers "Light Chicken Broth."

■ Another Basic Recipe ■

Poached Whole Chicken and Its Resulting Broth

■

Makes 4 to 6 servings of chicken and 3½ quarts broth

When you need a lot of chicken for a salad, soup, tacos, or whatever, the economical thing to do is simmer a whole bird, cut up, and make chicken broth at the same time. Of course, you should always have a couple of cans of broth or bouillon cubes around, but once you've tasted the homemade stuff, you'll see what a difference there is. Freeze what you don't eat (as a comforting chicken soup) right away in pint-size containers to pull out and thaw in the microwave as needed.

It's nice to have both the white and dark meat of the whole chicken. The chicken that you poach here can also be served on the bone, with a salsa or pesto or just about any sauce that tastes good to you.

The easiest way to get a low-fat chicken broth is to refrigerate it in a bowl overnight. The fat will float to the surface and solidify. Then you can just lift it off the top and proceed.

One 3- to 4-pound chicken, cut into 6 to 8 pieces and skinned (see Note)
2 cloves
2 medium-size or large onions, peeled and quartered
6 large garlic cloves, peeled (can be slightly crushed)
A few fresh flat-leaf parsley and thyme sprigs
1 bay leaf

Get out the following equipment: **kitchen scissors; very large stockpot or pasta pot, with at least an 8-quart capacity; large cooking spoon or skimmer; chef's knife and cutting board; kitchen twine; tongs; large colander or strainer; cheesecloth; large bowl**

Advance preparation: **Cooked chicken will keep for 5 days in the refrigerator. Cover it well or seal in plastic bags so that it doesn't dry out. Broth will keep for 3 to 4 days in the refrigerator and for 6 months in the freezer.**

PER SERVING:
9.6 gm total fat
2.6 gm saturated fat
274 calories
0 gm carbohydrates
44.1 gm protein

4 large carrots, peeled and thickly sliced

6 black peppercorns

4 quarts cold water

Salt (about 1 tablespoon, or more to taste)

1. Rinse the chicken pieces and place in the stockpot. Stick the cloves in two of the onion quarters. Place the onions and garlic in the pot. If you wish (but you don't have to), tie together the parsley and thyme sprigs and the bay leaf with kitchen twine. This is called, in cooking terms, a *bouquet garni*. Add the carrots and peppercorns to the pot and cover with the water.

2. Bring the mixture to a simmer over medium-high heat. When it gets to the simmering point, foam and scum (for lack of a better word) will appear on the surface. These are impurities that you need to skim off. Use a large spoon or a skimmer (it has holes, so you don't lose broth). Reduce the heat to low and skim off all the foam. Add the salt. Cover partially— that is, leave a little bit of space open on one side of the pot—and simmer gently for 25 minutes. Remove a piece of white meat (a breast piece) and cut into it to see if it is cooked through. If it isn't, simmer for another 5 minutes. Then remove all the pieces of white meat using tongs and place in a bowl. Continue to simmer until the dark meat is no longer ruddy and is just about falling off the bone, another 15 to 30 minutes. If you want very tender, falling-off-the-bone meat, you can simmer all the pieces together for an hour. Every once in a while, check the mixture and skim if necessary. Remove from the heat and uncover.

3. If you wish, allow the chicken to cool in the broth or remove from the broth using tongs. Set on a platter and, when cool enough to handle, shred if you need shredded chicken. Otherwise, serve warm with salsa or pesto or with lemon juice and a little olive oil.

4. Set the strainer or colander over a large bowl and line with cheesecloth. Carefully ladle the broth into the strainer. When all the broth has been strained, discard everything in the strainer. Cover the broth and refrigerate overnight.

5. In the morning, lift all the fat off the top of the broth and discard it. Then transfer the broth to freezer containers and freeze or use for soup or cooking rice. Remember to freeze some of it in small amounts; you don't always need enough for a soup.

Notes: Even when the chicken is skinned by the butcher, there will be a lot of fat left on and you should cut it away. The last time I brought a chicken home I cut away two extra cups of fat! Use a sharp pair of kitchen scissors for this. Just snip away the yellow fat wherever you see it. The wings won't be skinned, and there's lots of fat there, too. Take the scissors and cut away all the floppy bits of skin.

If you want a strong chicken broth, return the bones to the broth after shredding the chicken. Bring to a boil and cook down until a cup or two of liquid has evaporated.

Chicken Broth Using the Carcass of a Chicken: You don't have to buy a chicken every time you want to make broth. Chicken bones will do just fine. You can get chicken bones from your butcher. Or, every time you roast a chicken (or a turkey), use the carcass for broth. This has become a ritual for me; I feel wasteful if I throw it away. Use the preceding recipe, substituting the carcass for the meat, but simmer for 2 hours.

■ Six Ways of Looking at a Boneless, ■ Skinless Chicken Breast

If you've done the "Warm-up Exercises" (pages 41–91) you've cooked chicken breasts. These are the easiest part of the chicken to deal with, and the possibilities for seasonings go far beyond these six recipes.

Pan-Grilled Chicken Breasts with Salsa

■

Makes 4 servings

Any Mexican salsa works well here, and so, for that matter, do more exotic salsas like mango salsa. You can use prepared salsa, or you can quickly make your own. Of course I recommend the freshest possible salsa—i.e., home-made—for the best flavor. But if you have a ready-made salsa you love, go ahead and use it. Serve with corn tortillas as well as rice or potatoes.

1 to 1½ cups prepared or homemade salsa: salsa fresca (page 325), fresh
    tomatillo salsa (page 327), mango salsa (page 328), and peach salsa
    (page 328) are all good
2 whole chicken breasts, split, boned, and skinned (or 4 half breasts)
2 teaspoons olive oil
Salt to taste
1 lime, cut into wedges, for serving

1. Make the salsa if you are making it.
2. Brush the chicken breasts on both sides with the oil. Heat the skillet or grill pan over medium-high heat. Drop a bit of water on the skillet; if it

sizzles away at once, the skillet is hot enough. Cook the chicken breasts until golden, 3 to 5 minutes per side. Check one breast to make sure that it is cooked all the way through (it should no longer be pink in the middle). Remove from the heat and transfer to a platter or plates. Season with salt. Spoon on the salsa, with some of it over the chicken breast and some on the side. Serve with lime wedges.

Pan-Cooked Chicken Breasts with Ginger and Soy

Makes 4 servings

This easy marinade has pungent Asian flavors—garlic and ginger, soy and sesame. Serve the chicken breasts with steamed snow peas or sugar snap peas as well as rice or buckwheat noodles (soba).

1 tablespoon soy sauce

2 tablespoons water

½ teaspoon sugar

1 teaspoon peeled and grated or finely chopped fresh ginger

1 garlic clove, peeled and minced or pressed

1 tablespoon dry sherry

1 tablespoon dark sesame oil

2 whole chicken breasts, split, boned, and skinned (or 4 half breasts)

Chopped scallions, chives, or cilantro for serving

1. Stir together the soy sauce, water, sugar, ginger, garlic, sherry, and sesame oil. Toss with the chicken breasts in the bowl and marinate for 15 to 30 minutes at room temperature (any longer than that, put it in the refrigerator), turning at least once, while you prepare the rest of your dinner.

2. Heat the skillet or grill pan over medium-high heat. Drop a bit of water on the skillet; if it sizzles away at once, the skillet is hot enough. Toss the chicken breasts once more so that they're well coated with the marinade and add to the skillet. Cook until golden, 3 to 5 minutes per side; check one breast to make sure that it's cooked through (it should no longer be pink in the middle). Remove from the heat and serve hot, with chopped scallions, chives, or cilantro sprinkled over the top.

Get out the following equipment: chef's knife, small grater (unless you are chopping rather than grating the ginger); garlic press or minichop if using; bowl large enough for the chicken breasts; measuring spoons; whisk, wooden spoon, or fork; large nonstick skillet or grill pan; spatula or tongs

Advance preparation: This goes so quickly you hardly need to work in advance, but you can make up a batch of the marinade and keep it in the refrigerator for days. Come home from work, marinate your chicken breasts, and you have dinner.

PER SERVING:
6.5 gm total fat
1.4 gm saturated fat
183 calories
1.5 gm carbohydrates
27 gm protein

Makes 4 servings

You can cook the chicken breasts for this dish in the microwave or pan-grill them. Whichever way, the combination is quickly made. Serve with a steamed green vegetable like broccoli or green beans, plus steamed potatoes, rice, or pasta.

½ pound mushrooms, cleaned and stems trimmed

2 tablespoons olive oil if grilling, 1 tablespoon if microwaving

Salt to taste

3 to 4 large garlic cloves (to your taste), peeled and minced or pressed

1 teaspoon chopped fresh rosemary leaves or ½ teaspoon crumbled dried

½ teaspoon fresh thyme leaves or ¼ teaspoon dried thyme

½ cup dry white wine

1½ cups homemade or canned chicken or vegetable broth, or more as needed

Freshly ground black pepper to taste

2 whole chicken breasts, split, boned, and skinned (or 4 half breasts)

Chopped fresh parsley, rosemary, or thyme leaves for garnish

1. Make the mushroom topping. Slice the mushrooms or, if they're small, quarter them. Heat 1 tablespoon of the olive oil in the skillet over medium heat. Add the mushrooms and about ¼ teaspoon of the salt. In a couple of minutes they'll be sizzling and moist. They're releasing their own water, which will mostly evaporate. When most of the liquid has evaporated, add the garlic, rosemary, and thyme. Stir together for about half a minute, until you smell the garlic cooking. Add the wine and cook, stirring, until most of the wine has evaporated. Add 1¼ cups of the broth, reduce the heat, and simmer for 10 minutes, stirring occasionally. Taste. Is there enough flavor? Add more salt or garlic if not. Grind in some pepper and toss. The mushrooms should be glazed and the mixture shouldn't be watery; cook a few more minutes if it is. On the other hand, if it seems dry, add more broth. Keep warm while you cook the chicken breasts.

2. *To pan-cook:* Toss the chicken breasts with the remaining tablespoon of oil. Heat the grill pan or the skillet you used to cook the mushrooms after cleaning and drying it over medium-high heat. Drop a bit of water into the pan; if it sizzles away at once, the pan is hot enough. Add the chicken breasts to the pan. Cook until golden, 3 to 5 minutes per side. Check one breast to make sure that it's cooked all the way through (it should no longer be pink in the middle). Remove from the heat and transfer to plates

Get out the following equipment: chef's knife and cutting board; garlic press or minichop if using; measuring spoons; measuring cup; large nonstick skillet and wooden spoon; nonstick grill pan or microwaveable soufflé dish or ceramic tart pan that can turn in your microwave; spatula or tongs

Advance preparation: The mushroom topping will keep for a few days in the refrigerator. Reheat gently in a nonstick skillet or in the microwave before serving.

PER SERVING:
10.9 gm total fat
2.1 gm saturated fat
253 calories
4.3 gm carbohydrates
28.9 gm protein

or a platter. Spoon on the mushroom mixture, sprinkle with the parsley or other herbs, and serve.

To microwave: Place the cooked mushroom mixture in the soufflé dish or tart pan. Top with the chicken breasts, fanning them out in the dish. Cover tightly with plastic wrap, pierce the plastic in a couple of spots with the point of a knife, and microwave at 100 percent power for 8 minutes. Remove from the microwave using hot pads. Carefully remove the plastic, being careful not to let the steam burn your hands. Transfer to a platter or plates, spoon the mushrooms over the chicken, garnish with herbs, and serve.

Chicken Breasts with Thai Flavors

Makes 4 servings

The marinade here is a simplified version of a green curry. It's quite hot, accented with the marvelous flavors of ginger, cilantro, and mint or Thai basil (see Note).

½ teaspoon black peppercorns

¼ teaspoon coriander seeds

¼ teaspoon cumin seeds

1 garlic clove, peeled and minced

2 teaspoons peeled and grated or chopped fresh ginger

2 tablespoons chopped fresh cilantro leaves

2 tablespoons chopped fresh mint or Thai basil leaves

2 serrano or jalapeño chiles, seeded for a milder dish if desired and chopped

1 stalk lemongrass (see Note), tough outer layer removed and white part minced (omit if you can't find it)

1 teaspoon minced lime zest

Juice of 1 lime

¼ teaspoon salt, or more to taste

1 tablespoon canola oil

2 whole chicken breasts, split, boned, and skinned (or 4 half breasts)

1. Grind the peppercorns, coriander, and cumin seeds together in the spice mill. Combine with the garlic, ginger, cilantro, mint or basil, and chiles in the minichop or mortar and blend or mash together. Scrape into the bowl and stir in the lemongrass, lime zest and juice, salt, and canola oil. Toss together with the chicken breasts until coated and let sit for 15 minutes, either in the refrigerator or at room temperature, turning occasionally.

Get out the following equipment: **spice mill; chef's knife and cutting board; grater if using; measuring spoons; citrus zester if you have one or a sharp small knife; citrus press; minichop or a mortar and pestle; bowl for marinating the chicken breasts; large nonstick skillet or grill pan; spatula or tongs**

Advance preparation: **This marinade is best used within a few hours of making it, because the lime juice will cause the bright green of the herbs to dull to a drabber color. However, the flavors will still be fine after a day in the refrigerator.**

PER SERVING:
6.6 gm total fat
1.1 gm saturated fat
185 calories
2.8 gm carbohydrates
27 gm protein

continued

2. Heat the skillet or grill pan over medium-high heat. Drop a bit of water on the skillet; if it sizzles away at once, the skillet is hot enough. Toss the chicken breasts once more so that they're well coated with the marinade and add to the skillet. Cook until golden, 3 to 5 minutes per side. Check one breast to make sure that it's cooked through (it should no longer be pink in the middle). Remove from the heat and serve hot.

Note: Thai basil and lemongrass are available at Asian markets. Lemongrass is now sold in many supermarkets. Thai basil has small leaves and a distinct minty-peppery taste. Omit if you can't find the ingredients. The dish will still be good.

Microwaved or Pan-Cooked Chicken Breasts with Spicy Italian Sauce

Makes 4 servings

Pasta isn't the only vehicle for a good tomato sauce. This one is great with chicken breasts, fish, pizza, and pasta. I prefer the flavor of chicken breasts when they are pan-cooked or grilled, but the microwave is certainly an option here, especially if you have the sauce already made. You get home from work, put the sauce and chicken breasts in a dish, and dinner's ready after an 8-minute zap.

1 tablespoon plus 2 teaspoons olive oil if pan-cooking, 1 tablespoon if microwaving
2 to 3 large garlic cloves, to your taste, peeled and minced or pressed
1¾ pounds tomatoes (7 medium-size), peeled, seeded, and chopped, or one 28-ounce can, drained, seeded, and chopped (you can use recipe-ready chopped tomatoes; drain off the water)
Salt to taste
Scant ¼ teaspoon sugar
¼ teaspoon red pepper flakes, or more to taste
2 tablespoons slivered fresh basil leaves
2 whole chicken breasts, split, boned, and skinned (or 4 half breasts)

1. Heat 1 tablespoon of the oil in the large skillet over medium heat and add the garlic. When it begins to color, add the tomatoes, salt, sugar, and red pepper flakes. Cook, stirring often and crushing the tomatoes with the back of a wooden spoon, until the tomatoes are cooked down and beginning to stick to the skillet, 15 to 25 minutes. Stir in the basil, taste, and adjust the salt and garlic. Remove from the heat.

Get out the following equipment: chef's knife and cutting board; garlic press or minichop if using; measuring spoons; large, heavy nonstick skillet; wooden spoon; grill pan or second nonstick skillet, or microwaveable ceramic tart pan or soufflé dish that can turn in your microwave; pastry brush and spatula or tongs if pancooking the chicken

Advance preparation: The sauce will keep for a couple of days in the refrigerator and can be frozen for several months.

PER SERVING:
9.5 gm total fat
1.6 gm saturated fat
241 calories
8.6 gm carbohydrates
28.8 gm protein

2. *To pan-cook:* Brush the chicken breasts on both sides with the remaining 2 teaspoons oil. Heat the grill pan or skillet over medium-high heat. Drop a bit of water on the skillet and if it sizzles away at once, the skillet is hot enough. Cook the chicken breasts until golden, 3 to 5 minutes per side. Check one breast to make sure that it's cooked through (it should no longer be pink in the middle). Remove from the heat and transfer to a platter or plates. Spoon on the sauce and serve.

To microwave: Place the sauce in the tart pan or soufflé dish. Top with the chicken breasts, fanning them out in the dish. Cover tightly with plastic wrap, pierce the plastic in a couple of spots with the tip of a knife, and microwave at 100 percent power for 8 minutes. Remove from the microwave using hot pads. Carefully remove the plastic, being careful not to let the steam burn your hands. Transfer to a platter or plates. Spoon the sauce over the chicken and serve.

Kebabs with Vegetables and Chicken

Makes 4 servings

Kebabs are easily assembled and always pleasing. These have a distinctly Middle Eastern flavor. Serve these with bulgur, couscous, or basmati rice. The cardamom adds a marvelous aroma, but if you omit this expensive ingredient the dish will still be delicious.

1 pound boneless, skinless chicken breasts

2 medium-size red bell peppers, seeded and cut into ¾-inch squares

12 large mushrooms, cleaned and stems removed

2 small zucchini, trimmed and sliced ½ inch thick

2 small onions, preferably sweet red onions, quartered and the layers separated

2 large garlic cloves, peeled

¼ teaspoon salt, or more to taste

Seeds from 4 cardamom pods (optional)

½ teaspoon ground allspice

½ teaspoon ground cinnamon

¼ teaspoon freshly ground black pepper

1 teaspoon ground cumin, or more to taste

Juice of 2 large limes or lemons

2 tablespoons olive oil

½ cup plain nonfat yogurt

Plain nonfat yogurt and lemon or lime wedges for serving

Get out the following equipment: chef's knife and cutting board; measuring spoons and measuring cup; a spice mill; mortar and pestle; 2 large mixing bowls; grill or baking sheet; bamboo or stainless-steel skewers; tongs

Advance preparation: The chicken and vegetables can marinate in the refrigerator for up to a day.

PER SERVING:
10.6 gm total fat
1.8 gm saturated fat
292 calories
19.4 gm carbohydrates
31.5 gm protein

continued

1. Cut the chicken into 1-inch pieces and place in a bowl. Place the vegetables in another bowl.
2. Pound the garlic to a paste with the salt in the mortar. Grind the cardamom in the spice grinder or pound in the mortar and add to the garlic along with the other spices. Mix together with the lime or lemon juice, olive oil, and yogurt. Toss half of the sauce with the chicken, the rest with the vegetables. Refrigerate for 1 hour or longer, covered with plastic wrap, stirring every once in a while to coat again with the marinade.
3. If using them, soak the bamboo skewers in water for 30 minutes. Thread the chicken pieces onto skewers and the vegetables onto separate skewers, or you can alternate chicken and vegetables on the same skewers. I find that the vegetables can take a bit longer than the chicken, and for vegetarians the first way is more convenient, so that's what I do.
4. Prepare an outdoor grill, preheat your broiler, or preheat your oven to 400°F. Grill or broil the chicken pieces until cooked through, and the vegetables until crisp-tender and lightly charred, 5 to 10 minutes, turning halfway through, or bake for 10 to 15 minutes.
5. Serve with yogurt and lemon or lime wedges on the side, with grains.

■ Chicken Stews ■

Simmered chicken dishes are always a hit with company. These have Mediterranean flavors and get better over time. Serve them with rice, potatoes, pasta, or nothing more than bread.

Chicken with Mediterranean Flavors

■

Makes 4 to 6 servings

Wherever you go in the Mediterranean, you're bound to find a number of slow-simmered chicken dishes. Stewing and braising work beautifully with skinned chicken, keeping the meat moist and flavorful. This heady recipe is like a saucy chicken cacciatore. It's a no-fuss dish that's fancy enough for dinner parties and simple enough for a school night. If the saffron is too extravagant for you, don't worry about it. This is a great dish, with or without the saffron. Serve with rice, potatoes, or noodles.

One 3½- to 4-pound free-range or "natural," hormone-free chicken, cut into 6 to 8 pieces and skinned, or 3 to 3½ pounds skinned chicken pieces (breasts, thighs, legs) on the bone

Get out the following equipment: **chef's knife and cutting board; measuring spoons; measuring cup; large ovenproof heavy casserole or Dutch oven with a lid; large wooden spoon**

1 tablespoon olive oil

1 medium-size onion, peeled, halved, and thinly sliced

1 large red bell pepper, seeded and cut into ½-inch squares

4 to 6 garlic cloves, to your taste, peeled and minced or pressed

1¾ pounds tomatoes (7 medium-size), peeled, seeded, and chopped, or one
   28-ounce can tomatoes, drained, seeded, and chopped (you can use
   recipe-ready chopped tomatoes; drain off the water)

Salt to taste

½ cup dry white wine

2 teaspoons fresh thyme leaves or 1 teaspoon dried thyme

1 bay leaf

¼ teaspoon saffron threads (optional)

One 1-inch-wide piece orange zest

Freshly ground black pepper to taste

3 tablespoons chopped fresh flat-leaf parsley leaves

Advance preparation:
The finished dish, with-
out the parsley, can be
refrigerated for a cou-
ple of days. If you
make the dish the day
before, refrigerate it
overnight, then skim
off any fat that sits on
the top when you re-
move it from the refrig-
erator. This is a good
way to reduce the fat.

PER SERVING:
14.0 gm total fat
3.1 gm saturated fat
409 calories
16.3 gm carbohydrates
47.9 gm protein

1. Rinse the chicken pieces and pat dry with paper towels.

2. Heat the oil in the casserole or Dutch oven over medium-low heat. Add the onion and cook, stirring, until tender, about 5 minutes. Add the red pepper and cook, stirring, until the pepper softens, about 5 minutes. Add the garlic and stir together for about half a minute, until the garlic smells fragrant. Add the tomatoes and salt. Increase the heat to medium and cook, stirring often, until the tomatoes have cooked down some-what and the mixture smells very fragrant, about 10 minutes. Add the chicken and wine and stir together. Bring to a simmer. If there is foam on the surface, skim it off.

3. Add the thyme and bay leaf to the mixture and turn the heat down to low. Cover partially and simmer for 40 minutes, stirring and moving the chicken pieces around often. Add the saffron and orange zest and simmer until the chicken is just about falling off the bone, another 10 minutes. Taste. Does it need salt? Add salt if necessary and pepper to taste. Remove from the heat.

4. Just before serving, stir in the parsley.

Variation: If you want to cook a vegetable right in this stew for a great one-dish supper, add a medium-size zucchini—about ½ pound, cut in half lengthwise and sliced—to the mixture when you add the orange zest and saf-fron. Simmer until cooked through, about 10 minutes. Proceed with the recipe.

Chicken with Two Heads of Garlic

■

Makes 4 servings

This is a classic, called in its authentic version Chicken with Forty Cloves of Garlic. Don't worry, you don't have to peel all the garlic. It simmers with the chicken, becoming soft, sweet, and spreadable. The chicken is served with garlic croutons, which you can spread with the garlic. It's a luscious dish.

One 3½- to 4-pound free-range or "natural," hormone-free chicken, cut into 6 to 8 pieces and skinned, or 3 to 3½ pounds skinned chicken pieces (breasts, thighs, legs) with bone in

2 tablespoons olive oil

2 heads garlic, broken up into cloves, 1 clove cut in half

2 cups dry white wine

4 fresh thyme sprigs or ½ teaspoon dried thyme

2 fresh rosemary sprigs or ¼ teaspoon dried rosemary

½ teaspoon salt or more to taste

8 slices country bread

Chopped fresh flat-leaf parsley leaves for garnish

Freshly ground black pepper to taste

1. Preheat the oven to 375°F. Rinse the chicken pieces and pat dry with paper towels.
2. Heat 1 tablespoon of the oil in the skillet over medium-high heat. When it is hot, add the chicken pieces in a single layer (you may have to do this in 2 batches). Brown for 5 minutes, moving the pieces around a little with the wooden spoon or tongs to make sure they don't stick to the skillet. Turn the chicken pieces over and brown for another 5 minutes. Remove from the skillet and drain on a large plate or cutting board covered with paper towels. Repeat with the remaining chicken pieces if necessary. Remove the skillet from the stove.
3. Heat the remaining tablespoon olive oil in the casserole or Dutch oven. Add the garlic cloves (except the halved one) and cook, stirring, until their skins are colored slightly, 3 to 5 minutes. Add the browned chicken pieces to the casserole, placing them on top of the garlic cloves. Add the wine, thyme, rosemary, and salt and bring to a simmer. Cover the casserole and place in the preheated oven. Bake for 45 minutes.
4. While the chicken is baking, toast the slices of bread. Rub them with the cut clove of garlic as soon as you take them from the toaster. Distribute among four plates.

Get out the following equipment: chef's knife and cutting board; large plate; paper towels; measuring spoons; large, heavy nonstick skillet; large, heavy ovenproof casserole or Dutch oven with lid; large wooden spoon; tongs for turning the chicken; measuring cup

Advance preparation: This can be made a day ahead of time and reheated, but it's best made the day you're serving.

PER SERVING:
18.0 gm total fat
3.9 gm saturated fat
580 calories
33.2 gm carbohydrates
49.8 gm protein

5. Remove the chicken from the oven and check for doneness. It should be very tender, almost falling off the bone, and the garlic cloves should be spreadably soft. If it isn't done yet, bake for another 15 minutes. Transfer the chicken to a warm serving platter or distribute among the plates. Sprinkle with parsley.

6. Taste the sauce in the pot. Does it need salt? Add salt and pepper to taste. However if you'd like the sauce to be a little thicker, first place the casserole on a burner and bring the liquid to a boil. Reduce the sauce until thickened slightly, then check for salt.

7. Serve the chicken with the croutons, with the sauce and the garlic cloves spooned over the top. The garlic should be squeezed out of the skin onto the croutons. This is also good with potatoes or rice.

Moroccan Steamed Chicken

Makes 4 to 6 servings

This is an absolutely marvelous way to prepare chicken. Steam heat results in very moist meat, while the fat drips away into the steaming water below, and when the chicken is done, the skin comes off effortlessly, so it's a boon to the low-fat cook. The chicken is steamed under a fragrant bed of herbs, along with potatoes, carrots, and onions, making this a one-dish meal that needs no attention at all once it's steaming. It's stuffed with a delicious mixture of spiced parsley and cilantro, which takes on the quality of cooked greens after 1½ hours of steaming inside the chicken. The recipe is based on one by Fatéma Hal, from her beautiful book on the cuisine of Morocco, *Les Saveurs et les Gestes* (Paris: Editions Stock, 1995).

A *couscoussière* is a pot used in North Africa and France for making couscous; the couscous is steamed in the top part that sits on a big bottom pot. You don't need to have one for this, but you do need to have a steamer that will sit high enough up in a pot to allow 2 quarts of water to simmer below it. Pasta pots with a steamer insert will allow this.

FOR THE CHICKEN:
One 3½- to 4-pound free-range or "natural," hormone-free chicken
Salt
2 medium-size or large carrots, peeled and halved
1 medium-size onion, peeled and quartered
½ pound waxy potatoes, scrubbed
1 bunch cilantro
1 bunch fresh flat-leaf parsley leaves

Get out the following equipment: couscoussière or steamer big enough for the chicken and vegetables that will sit above 2 quarts water; vegetable peeler; chef's knife and cutting board; 2-quart mixing bowl; wooden spoon; measuring spoons; little dishes for the cumin and salt for serving

Advance preparation: **You can turn off the water and let the chicken sit in the steamer for an hour after it's done. It will remain moist and hot, but the cooking will have stopped.**

PER SERVING:
10.50 gm total fat
2.8 gm saturated fat
431 calories
34.30 gm carbohydrates
49.20 gm protein

Chicken and Turkey

2 quarts water

2 bay leaves

FOR THE STUFFING:

4 large garlic cloves, peeled and minced

2 cups chopped fresh flat-leaf parsley leaves (1½ to 2 bunches)

2 cups chopped fresh cilantro leaves (1½ to 2 bunches)

1 medium-size onion, peeled and chopped

1 teaspoon salt

1 teaspoon freshly ground black pepper

1 teaspoon freshly ground cumin seeds

1 teaspoon paprika

TO SERVE:

1 teaspoon freshly ground cumin seeds

1 teaspoon sea salt

1 or 2 lemons (optional), cut into wedges

1. Rinse the chicken inside and out and remove the bag of giblets if there is one. Set the giblets aside for another purpose or freeze (or cook them for your cats). Pat the chicken dry with paper towels and sprinkle with salt.

2. Mix together all of the ingredients for the stuffing. Fill the cavity of the chicken and sew it up with kitchen twine or truss it with a skewer or toothpicks (this is what I do). To do this, pull the edges of the cavity together and lace them together using the skewer or toothpicks. Place in the steamer or the top part of the couscoussière. Surround with the carrots, onion, and potatoes and cover with the herbs.

3. Place the water and bay leaves in the bottom of the steamer or couscoussière and set the steamer on top.

4. Bring the water to a boil, then reduce to a simmer. Cover the pot with aluminum foil or a lid, whichever allows a seal, and steam for 1½ hours. Test the chicken. The juice should run clear when the thigh is pierced with a knife.

5. Remove the lid or foil and, using tongs or meat forks, transfer the chicken to a meat-cutting board. Discard the herbs, but keep the vegetables. Cut the potatoes into halves or quarters and quarter the carrots. Remove the skin from the chicken by cutting down the length of the breast. It should pull away easily. Discard. Carve the chicken (see Warm-up Exercises, page 82).

6. Serve the chicken with the vegetables and a spoonful of the stuffing. Pass the cumin, sea salt, and lemon wedges for people to sprinkle on.

Tunisian Chicken with Olives

Makes 4 servings

The Tunisian way of making stews is very uncomplicated, yet the resulting flavors are complex and comforting at the same time. I think the trick here is to simmer the chicken for a very long time. A more authentic version might combine ground caraway seeds—about ½ teaspoon—with the cayenne or harissa, but I'm trying to keep this very simple. The flavors are big here. The spicy sauce reduces as the dish simmers away, and the chicken falls off the bone, succulent and fork-tender. Serve this spicy mixture with couscous (which you can steam above the chicken—see page 204) or rice.

One 3½- to 4-pound free-range or "natural," hormone-free chicken, cut into 6 to 8 pieces and skinned, or 3 to 3½ pounds skinned chicken pieces (breasts, thighs, wings) with bone in

1 tablespoon olive oil

1 medium-size onion, chopped

4 garlic cloves, minced or pressed

4 tablespoons tomato paste

½ teaspoon cayenne pepper or 1 tablespoon harissa, or more to taste

½ teaspoon caraway seeds (optional), ground

½ teaspoon freshly ground black pepper

3 cups water

Salt to taste

2 ounces (about ⅓ cup) imported green or black olives, pitted and cut in half lengthwise

Chopped fresh flat-leaf parsley leaves or cilantro for garnish

1. Rinse the chicken pieces and pat dry with paper towels. Set aside.
2. Heat the olive oil in the casserole or Dutch oven over medium heat. Add the onion and cook, stirring, until tender, about 5 minutes. Add the garlic and stir for about 30 seconds. Add 3 tablespoons of the tomato paste, the cayenne or harissa, the optional caraway, and the black pepper and stir together for a couple of minutes, until the mixture smells very fragrant.
3. Add the chicken pieces to the casserole and stir together for a couple of minutes, until coated with tomato paste and onion. Add the water, stir together, and bring to a simmer. Add the salt, cover, reduce the heat to low, and simmer for 40 minutes, stirring occasionally. Add the olives and simmer until the chicken is falling off the bone, another 20 minutes.

Get out the following equipment: chef's knife and cutting board; garlic press or minichop if using; measuring spoons; large, heavy ovenproof casserole or Dutch oven; wooden spoon

Advance preparation: **This can be made a day or two ahead of time. Reheat gently, then add the parsley or cilantro garnish.**

PER SERVING:
15.7 gm total fat
3.3 gm saturated fat
359 calories
7.4 gm carbohydrates
45.2 gm protein

4. Using tongs, remove the chicken pieces from the broth and place in a bowl. Add the remaining tablespoon tomato paste to the broth and turn up the heat so that the broth boils briskly. Reduce by about half, so that it's thick and fragrant. Taste and add salt and cayenne or harissa as desired. Return the chicken to the sauce, garnish with parsley or cilantro, and serve over couscous or rice.

■ Turkey ■

Turkey is the leanest of all meats; only 18 percent of the calories in the white meat without the skin are derived from fat, and if the dark meat is eaten without the skin, only 22 to 38 percent of its calories are derived from fat. Ground turkey makes a good substitute for high-cholesterol ground beef, but it does require more seasonings and moisture. I use it here for chili and for turkey burgers.

Roast turkey is one of those things that we think about only at holiday time, and if you've never roasted a turkey you might find the idea daunting. In fact it's incredibly easy—at least my recipe is. You just throw it in the oven and wait. Most turkeys weigh at least 10 pounds, making a very economical and convenient entree for a party (the last all-natural, delicious turkey I bought cost less than $2 per pound) since they are as good on a buffet, at room temperature, as they are warm. For a family meal a turkey will yield lots of leftovers for sandwiches and salads through the week.

As with chicken, the quality of the turkey is everything, especially for the low-fat cook. Butterball turkeys, the most popular turkeys sold in grocery stores, are infused with fat; that's why they're called Butterball. A free-range or all-natural, hormone-free turkey will be much leaner, and also much tastier. They are easily obtained from organic food stores and many poultry markets.

You can buy a whole turkey a day or two ahead of roasting it and keep it in the bottom of your refrigerator. Keep it in its tight wrapping, but put it in a plastic bag or overwrap it with aluminum foil so that any juices that leak out will not contaminate other foods in the refrigerator. Cut leftover turkey off the bone and store for up to 4 days in the refrigerator. Use the carcass to make stock (see page 155). Remove any leftover stuffing from the cavity and store in the refrigerator for up to 2 days.

Turkey cutlets, thinly sliced turkey breast, have become a popular lean meat, sold in packages in the grocery store. I find them a bit dry and tough, however. But if you're careful about not overcooking them—only 2 to 3 minutes per side—they're worth trying. Substitute them for chicken breasts in the recipes on pages 100–106, but reduce the cooking times. Use the same criteria to test for doneness: they should not be pink in the middle, and the surface should be nicely browned.

Roast Turkey

Makes 8 to 10 servings

There are many ways to roast a turkey, and some are more complicated than others. I've decided to give you the simplest method here; it involves no fiddling with or turning the big bird, just steady cooking at one temperature. To baste or not to baste? Some cooks insist on it to get an even sheen on the skin, while others insist that you'll get this anyway. I usually do baste, using a pastry brush rather than a baster. I simply dip the brush in the drippings in the pan from time to time and brush the turkey. Since I look for free-range or all-natural turkeys, which are not as fatty as the Butterballs sold in most supermarkets, I think the basting probably does contribute to a better-looking skin. However, being a low-fat eater, you may not wish to eat the skin anyway! So I leave the choice to you.

Make sure you know the weight of your turkey. It will be on the packaging or on your receipt from the grocery store. To be safe, make a note of it when you buy the turkey; the weight determines the roasting time. I give you a range for the roasting time. I have seen recipes that suggest as little as 10 minutes a pound and as much as 20 (which will result, in my opinion, in a very dry turkey). The bird must sit for 20 minutes before you can serve it and can sit for up to 50 minutes without cooling too much, so you have some leeway in your planning. The most important thing as far as safety is concerned is that the internal temperature of the turkey reach 165°F.

One 10- to 12-pound turkey, preferably free-range or "natural," hormone-free
1 recipe Corn Bread and Sage Stuffing (recipe follows)
Salt and freshly ground black pepper to taste
2 tablespoons olive oil

1. Preheat the oven to 375°F. Lightly oil the roasting pan. Set your oven rack low enough so the turkey will fit into your oven. Reach inside the cavity at either end of the turkey and pull out the giblets and neck that the butcher has placed there for you. Discard them or save them for making stock (if saving, wrap in plastic wrap and aluminum foil and refrigerate). Rinse the turkey and pat dry, inside and out, with paper towels. Cut away the big flap of fatty skin that flops over the hole at the drumstick end of the

Get out the following equipment: measuring spoons and large spoon for stuffing the turkey; large roasting pan; kitchen twine; pastry brush; meat or instant-read thermometer if using; chef's knife or carving knife and fork

PER SERVING:
16.30 gm total fat
4.8 gm saturated fat
375 calories
2.7 gm carbohydrates
50.80 gm protein

turkey. Fill the larger cavity, at the wing end, loosely with the stuffing; you can also stuff a bit into the other cavity. Salt and pepper the bird and rub with the olive oil. Tuck the wings under the thighs and tie the legs together with kitchen twine. Place in the roasting pan, breast side up. Roast for 11 to 15 minutes per pound (check after calculating the time for 11 minutes per pound), until it reaches an internal temperature of 165°F. Take the temperature at the thickest part of the thigh. Or use the old-fashioned test that I use: pierce the turkey with a serving fork or sharp knife at the fattest section of the thigh. If the juice runs clear, the turkey is done. If it is still pink, it needs more time in the oven. If basting, every 20 minutes take your pastry brush, dip it in the drippings in the pan, and brush over the surface of the turkey. The turkey skin should be browned all over, including the part just inside the wings and thighs. The flesh should feel firm and resilient when you press on it.

2. Remove from the heat and let rest, either in the roasting pan or on a carving board, for 20 minutes before carving. To carve, see instructions for roast chicken, page 82.

Corn Bread and Sage Stuffing

Makes enough for a 10- to 12-pound turkey; 8 to 10 servings

Everybody raves about this stuffing. It has a marvelous texture and depth of flavor, yet it's really very simple. It requires corn bread, which you can buy, but making it is awfully easy.

1 tablespoon olive oil

1 medium-size onion, peeled and finely chopped

2 garlic cloves, peeled and minced or pressed

3 celery ribs, chopped

4 to 5 cups crumbled corn bread (1 batch, recipe follows)

1 tablespoon chopped fresh sage or 1 teaspoon rubbed dried sage

1 tablespoon fresh thyme leaves or 1½ teaspoons crumbled dried thyme

½ cup chopped fresh flat-leaf parsley leaves

Salt and freshly ground black pepper to taste

3 tablespoons skim or 1% milk for moistening, or more as necessary

Heat the oil in the skillet over medium heat. Add the onion and cook, stirring, until just about tender, about 3 minutes. Add the garlic and celery and cook for 1 to 2 minutes, until the garlic is fragrant. Transfer to the bowl. Add all the remaining ingredients except the milk and stir together. Taste and adjust the sea-

Get out the following equipment: chef's knife and cutting board; garlic press or minichop if using; measuring spoons and measuring cup; large, heavy non-stick skillet and wooden spoon; large bowl

Advance preparation: You can make this up to 2 days ahead of time and keep in a covered bowl in the refrigerator. Moisten with the milk just before stuffing the turkey.

PER SERVING:
6.6 gm total fat
2.6 gm saturated fat
196 calories
27.60 gm carbohydrates
6.8 gm protein

sonings. Moisten with milk as needed. Use as a turkey stuffing or transfer to an oiled or buttered baking dish, cover with aluminum foil, and heat through in a preheated 325°F oven for 30 minutes.

Corn Bread

Makes 1 loaf; 8 to 10 servings

For a good corn bread stuffing, a good corn bread is essential. This one is a rich, moist corn bread with a grainy texture that I've been making for years. It's slightly sweet and goes beautifully with hearty soups, chilies, and stews. It's very quickly thrown together.

    1 cup stoneground yellow cornmeal
    ½ cup unbleached all-purpose or whole-wheat pastry flour
    ¾ teaspoon salt
    1 tablespoon baking powder
    ½ teaspoon baking soda
    1 cup plain nonfat yogurt
    ½ cup skim or 1% milk
    1 tablespoon mild honey, such as clover or acacia
    2 large eggs
    2 tablespoons unsalted butter

1. Preheat the oven to 425°F.
2. Place the cornmeal in a bowl and sift in the flour, salt, baking powder, and baking soda. Stir the mixture with a spoon or whisk to amalgamate. Beat together the yogurt, milk, honey, and eggs in the other bowl.
3. Put the butter in the baking dish or skillet and place it in the oven for about 3 minutes, until the butter melts. Remove from the heat, brush the butter over the sides and bottom of the dish, and pour the remaining melted butter into the yogurt-and-egg mixture. Stir together well, then fold the liquid mixture into the dry mixture (or vice versa). Do this quickly, being careful not to overwork the batter. A few lumps are okay.
4. Pour the batter into the hot, buttered pan, place it in the oven, and bake until the top is golden brown and a toothpick inserted in the center comes out clean, 30 to 40 minutes. Let the bread cool in the pan or serve it hot.

Get out the following equipment: **2 medium-size bowls; measuring cups (dry and liquid) and measuring spoons; sifter or strainer; whisk; rubber spatula; 9-inch-square or heavy 2-quart baking dish or 9-inch cast-iron skillet; pastry brush**

Advance preparation: **Although this is best served the day it's made, and it's so easy to throw together that it shouldn't pose a problem, it is also moist enough to keep for a day if wrapped in aluminum foil as soon as it cools. For stuffing you could easily make it a day or two ahead of time. As for leftovers, they will be good as long as they last, but keep the bread in the refrigerator after 2 days.**

PER SERVING:
4.8 gm total fat
2.4 gm saturated fat
168 calories
24.8 gm carbohydrates
6.2 gm protein

Turkey Burgers

Makes 4 servings

My father loved to make fabulous hamburgers, which we called "Gourmet Delight." They were made with chopped sirloin steak seasoned with Worcestershire sauce and items I never use today like MSG and garlic salt. Today I make a version of "Gourmet Delight" with turkey instead of high-cholesterol beef. There are many directions in which to take a turkey burger. You can make it like a hamburger, seasoned with onion, garlic, and parsley and topped with the usual garnishes. Or you can top it with plum sauce or hoisin sauce, which I prefer. You can give the burgers a further Asian ring by adding ginger and soy sauce to the mix, or flavor them with hot chiles and top with salsa for a Mexican approach.

1 small white onion, peeled and finely chopped (about ⅓ cup)

1 pound ground turkey (light meat)

1 to 2 large garlic cloves, to your taste, peeled and minced or pressed

2 tablespoons Worcestershire sauce

1 tablespoon cold water

Salt and freshly ground black pepper to taste

3 tablespoons finely chopped fresh flat-leaf parsley leaves

FOR SERVING:

Hamburger buns or pita bread

Ketchup, mustard, hoisin sauce, plum sauce, or salsa

Sliced onions, sliced red or green bell peppers, and/or tomatoes

FOR ASIAN STYLE, ADD:

2 tablespoons minced green or red bell pepper

2 to 3 teaspoons peeled and minced or grated fresh ginger, to your taste

1 tablespoon hoisin sauce or soy sauce

FOR MEXICAN STYLE, ADD:

1 to 2 serrano or jalapeño chiles, to your taste, seeded for a milder flavor and chopped

2 to 3 tablespoons chopped fresh cilantro leaves, to your taste

1. Rinse the onion with cold water and pat dry with paper towels. Mix with the ground turkey and remaining ingredients. Shape into 4 to 6 patties. Press them into ¾-inch-thick rounds.

2. Prepare the grill or heat the grill pan or skillet over medium-high heat until a drop of water evaporates immediately upon contact. Cook the burgers for 4 to 5 minutes per side. They should be just cooked through, not at all pink. Serve at once with the condiments and garnishes of your choice.

Turkey Chili

■

Makes 4 generous servings

There's something so satisfying about a good bowl of red. This one, made with ground dark-meat turkey, can be three-alarm or two-alarm, depending on the heat of the ground chile you use. It's important to use pure ground chile, which you can get at natural food stores that sell spices in bulk and at stores that sell Mexican and southwestern ingredients. Commercial blends are loaded with salt and other flavorings and don't have the pure chile taste. Serve this chili with corn bread, country bread, or corn tortillas.

1 pound ground turkey

2 tablespoons canola or olive oil

1 medium-size onion, peeled and chopped

1 large carrot, peeled and minced or grated (you can mince it in a minichop in batches)

1 medium-size or large red bell pepper, seeded and chopped

Salt to taste

¼ cup pure ground chile (mild or a mixture of mild and hot)

2 teaspoons ground cumin

2 garlic cloves, peeled and minced or pressed

1¼ cups water

One 28-ounce can crushed tomatoes

¾ teaspoon dried oregano

1½ cups cooked pinto or red beans (one 15-ounce can, drained and rinsed)

¼ teaspoon sugar (optional)

¼ cup chopped fresh cilantro leaves (optional)

1. Heat the skillet over medium-high heat and add the ground turkey. Cook, stirring and breaking up the meat, until it is browned, 8 to 10 minutes; there should be no sign of pink. Remove from the heat and pour off any liquid or fat from the skillet. Set aside.

2. Heat the oil in the casserole or Dutch oven over medium heat and add the onion. Cook, stirring often, until just about tender, 3 to 5 minutes. Add the carrot, bell pepper, and about ¼ teaspoon salt and cook, stirring often, until

Get out the following equipment: **large non-stick skillet and wooden spoon or spatula; chef's knife and cutting board; garlic press or minichop if using; measuring spoons; large, heavy ovenproof casserole or Dutch oven; saucepan for the variation with sausage**

Advance preparation: **The chili will keep for 3 days in the refrigerator and can be frozen. Make it a day ahead of time for the best flavor.**

PER SERVING:
16.9 gm total fat
3.1 gm saturated fat
383 calories
31.10 gm carbohydrates
30.20 gm protein

the vegetables are tender and fragrant, about 5 minutes. Add the ground chile and cumin and cook, stirring, until the mixture begins to stick to the pan, 2 to 3 minutes. Add the garlic, stir together for about 30 seconds, and add ¾ cup of the water. Stir together for a minute or two, until the mixture is thick. Stir in the browned turkey, then the tomatoes, oregano, and remaining ½ cup water. Add salt to taste, about 1½ teaspoons. Bring to a simmer, reduce the heat, cover, and simmer for 45 minutes to an hour. Stir often, because the chili tends to stick to the bottom of the pot. Stir in the beans, taste, and adjust the seasonings. If the chili tastes slightly bitter, stir in the sugar. If it is too hot, try adding a little more salt, which will balance out the spiciness. Set aside until ready to serve.

3. Just before serving, bring back to a simmer and stir in the cilantro if using.

Variation with Turkey Sausage: To the recipe, add ¼ to ½ pound spiced turkey (or turkey-and-chicken) sausage. Place the sausages in a large, heavy saucepan and add water to cover the sausages by about ½ inch. Bring to a simmer, reduce the heat to medium, cover, and simmer for 20 minutes, turning the sausages from time to time. Cut the sausages in half lengthwise and continue to simmer for 5 minutes. Pour off the cooking liquid, transfer the sausages to a cutting board, and cut into ¼-inch-thick slices. Stir into the chili at the end, heat through, and serve.

Salads

■

■ Light Salad Basics ■

One of the most important *Light Basics Cookbook* concepts is that a salad can be a meal. What makes a salad a salad? Dressing is the simple answer. What makes a salad a light salad? A dressing that isn't loaded with oil and a salad that isn't loaded with dressing. The dressings in this chapter differ from the classic vinaigrette in the "Warm-up Exercises" because most of the oil of a traditional dressing is replaced by yogurt or buttermilk.

Because I call for so little oil, it's important that what you use be of high quality and vivid flavor, so that you taste it. Even though extra-virgin olive oil is expensive, it's worth the investment here. You will be using it up slowly as you make your way through these salads. The same goes for nutty, rich-tasting walnut oil and dark sesame oil. When the flavor of the oil is going to be overwhelmed by spices or other seasonings, as in the grated carrot salad with curry-cumin dressing on page 146, canola oil is fine to use; you need it for the texture more than for the flavor.

What the dressing goes on can be cooked or raw, animal or vegetable, leaf or vegetable, grain or bean. And the simplest ingredients can be transformed into a main-dish salad. If I have a can of chickpeas, a head of broccoli, and an egg on hand, I have dinner provided I have the makings for a salad dressing. I'll steam the broccoli, soft-boil or hard-cook the egg, and whip up a low-fat yogurt vinaigrette in the time it takes the broccoli to cook. This is a favorite winter dinner, especially when my husband is away and I'm cooking for myself.

Leftovers in my refrigerator are almost always destined for the salad bowl. Chicken, fish, raw or cooked vegetables, grains and beans, and pasta will see their way into a salad with a tart and luscious dressing long before they're ready for the garbage. Today we have so many delicious lettuces available to us, and many of these have been prewashed, needing only a cursory rinse and a spin before they go into the salad bowl. They keep, sealed in a plastic bag, for a few days in the refrigerator, as long as they're not too wet (a supermarket practice that drives me crazy). Spin your lettuces before refrigerating them and keep them in perforated vegetable storage bags if they are wet. In any case, for best storage, keep them in perforated vegetable bags in the vegetable bin of your refrigerator.

TIPS FOR SUCCESSFUL SALADS

- Wash and dry lettuces, greens, and herbs thoroughly (see page 57).
- Tear lettuces gently to prevent bruising.
- Use scissors to cut fresh herbs.
- Add bright green vegetables and herbs to dressed salads shortly before serving unless instructed otherwise, because acids in salad dressings dull the green color.
- Toss leafy salads with enough dressing to coat the leaves just before serving—don't let the salad get soggy with dressing

■ A Quick Look at Lettuces ■

Mild "Lettucy" Lettuces

Red and green oak leaf: Red oak leaf, also called *red salad bowl,* has a soft texture and is harvested at both the baby and mature stages. Both the green and the red are very versatile, suitable for all kinds of salads.

Lollo rossa: Pretty loose-leaved lettuce with frilled red-tipped leaves. Good in all kinds of salads.

Bibb, Butter, Boston: Soft green round heads with a pale green heart. Good in all kinds of salads; also good for lettuce soup. Also comes in red variety.

Romaine: Long, crisp green leaves surrounding a more delicate heart of crisp green leaves. Also comes in red and ruby red varieties. Good in all kinds of salads, especially Caesar salad. Baby romaine is much more delicate than the mature version that we are most familiar with. An excellent keeper.

Tango: Curly, green leaves. Good in all kinds of salads.

Mâche: Dark green, tender, spoon-shaped leaves. Very mild and succulent, with a slightly nutty flavor. Vitamin-rich.

Spicy, Peppery Greens

These are all excellent sources of vitamins A and C, calcium, iron, and potassium.

Arugula (also called *rocket* or *roquette*): Peppery, nutty, dark green leaves

Baby red mustard: Mottled green-and-maroon leaves, with a distinct, mustardy flavor

Cress: Small dark green leaves with a strong, peppery flavor

Mizuna: Dark feathery leaves with a mild mustardy flavor

Tatsoi: Round, succulent dark green leaves with white rib, mild cabbage taste

Bitter Chicories

Belgian endive: These are elongated, tight, blanched heads. The leaves are crisp, with a bittersweet taste. They are good braised as well as raw. Red Belgian endive is also available.

Curly endive: The large, frilly, tough green outer leaves should be cooked. The blanched inner leaves can be eaten raw. This looks like frisée, another variety of chicory.

Dandelion greens: Dark, elongated, notched green leaves that become quite bitter and tough when older. Good in salads, soups, and braised or in tarts. This is the most nutritious of all the greens.

Escarole: The tough, broad, wavy outer leaves are best cooked. The blanched inner leaves are tender and very good in salads.

Frisée: These are frilly, lacy leaves that have a lot of texture and a delicate, slightly bitter flavor. Terrific in salads. They can take a tart dressing and are also very nice with baked goat cheese, or top with a poached egg.

Pan di zuchero (also called *sugar loaf chicory*): Looks a little like romaine. Broad, long green leaves can be used in salads and as wrappers for fillings.

Radicchio: Purple leaves with white ribs, formed into cabbagelike balls. This is great in salads but also grilled, braised, and in risotto.

Treviso radicchio: Purple with white ribs, like radicchio, but the leaves are shaped more like Belgian endive. Good in salads, grilled, and braised.

Sturdy Greens

These are all suitable for cooked greens salads. They have a spicy, mustardy/acidic flavor. All of these are high in vitamins A and C and calcium, and some are quite high in potassium.

Baby bok choy: Succulent chardlike flavor

Beet greens: Sharp tasting, slightly sour

Red and green chard: Sweet, spinachlike flavor

Collard greens: These leaves are tough but become sweet with long cooking. Cabbage flavor.

Kale: (Red Russian, white feathering, white flowering): Faint cabbage flavor. Good in slow-cooked stews, braised, or stir-fried.

Mustards: These have a tart, cabbage flavor.

Sorrel: Tart, slightly sour green leaves. Very good in soups and omelets.

Spinach: Young spinach is especially sweet and great in salads. Spinach need not be cooked.

■ A Quick Look at Fresh Herbs and ■ What They Go With

Sweet, Pungent, and Minty Herbs

Basil (sweet; Thai basil is minty): Tomato, lettuce, egg, and pasta salads

Chervil (sweet, delicate, slightly pungent): Grain, lettuce, egg, and chicken salads

Chives (sweet, oniony): Lettuce, potato, egg, chicken, grain, and bean salads

Cilantro (pungent citrusy): Curry, Asian, and Mexican salads

Dill (slightly sweet, pungent): Greek, lettuce, grain, potato, cucumber, and Middle Eastern salads

Fennel (sweet, anisy): Lettuce, Middle Eastern, potato, and egg salads

Mint (pennyroyal, peppermint, spearmint; minty, and peppermint is peppery): Middle Eastern, Moroccan, cucumber, fruit, lettuce, Greek, and tomato salads

Tarragon (sweet, pungent, slightly anisy): Lettuce, tomato, grain, chicken, and egg salads

Savory and Bitter Herbs

Lovage (celerylike): Lettuce, egg, and chicken salads

Marjoram (savory, bitter or sharp, pungent): Lettuce, potato, tomato, and tuna salads

Oregano (savory, bitter or sharp, pungent): Lettuce, potato, tomato, Greek, and cooked vegetable salads

Parsley (savory, bitter; flat-leaf—Italian—has more flavor than curly): Lettuce, potato, tomato, grain, bean, chicken, egg, carrot, cooked vegetable, and tuna salads

Rosemary (savory, pungent, astringent): Bean, pasta, cooked vegetable, and chicken salads

Sage (savory, pungent): Potato, chicken, bean, and tuna salads

Thyme and lemon thyme (savory, pungent, earthy; lemon thyme is lemony): Bean, pasta, cooked vegetable, chicken, lettuce, grain, and tuna salads

▪ How to Make a Salad Using Leftovers ▪

This is a conceptual exercise rather than one involving technique. Once you can make a dressing, you can make a salad with whatever might be on hand: a can of beans, last night's chicken, fish, or vegetables, those green beans you bought at the farmers' market that you need to use up—in fact, all vegetables that need using up.

Nothing goes to waste in my refrigerator until it shrivels up and dies. Everything is a potential salad, stale bread included (stale bread, sliced,

---

Good Salad Grains, Beans, and Pastas

Quick-cooking grains: **Bulgur, couscous, quinoa, basmati rice** *Longer-cooking grains:* **Rice (white and brown), wild rice, wheat berries** *Quick-cooking beans:* **Lentils, black-eyed peas** *Longer-cooking beans* **(you can substitute rinsed canned beans for any of these): Black beans, chickpeas, fava beans or giant white beans, pinto beans, white beans** *Pasta:* **Shapes such as fusilli, penne, orecchiette, farfalle, rigatoni, macaroni; Asian noodles like soba, rice vermicelli, cellophane noodles**

High-Protein Salads

Chicken salads (pages 148–151) Egg salad (page 183) Tuna salads Bean salads (pages 127–131, 139)

toasted, rubbed with garlic, and diced or broken into pieces, adds flavor and body to any salad, whether it's a main dish or part of a meal). This opens up all sorts of possibilities for dinner once the concept of salad-as-dinner is fixed in your brain and appetite.

TIPS FOR MAKING SALADS FROM LEFTOVERS

- For quantities, figure on at least ½ to 1 cup of salad per person.
- Cooked as well as raw vegetables can be the basis for a salad (think of potato salads). Roasted peppers are a favorite; when you see your bell peppers beginning to shrivel, roast them (see page 131). Some of the best salads from North Africa are made with cooked carrots (see page 144), cooked zucchini, and cooked eggplant. A cooked vegetable tossed with a simple vinaigrette—vinegar or lemon juice, olive oil, garlic, and salt—can be truly delicious. Included with the recipes for salad dressings are types of salads they go well with. Use this as a guide.
- Combine foods of different textures. For example, if you are going to make a salad of leftover fish, chicken, hard-cooked eggs, or beans, you will want to include something crunchy if you have it on hand. A diced pepper or cucumber or onion can be just the thing.
- For main-dish salads, add a high-protein item from the pantry or refrigerator—canned tuna, beans, eggs.
- If you have bits and pieces of vegetables like peppers and cucumbers in the refrigerator, or if you have herbs that you haven't used up, think of chopping them and combining them with quick-cooking grains like couscous, bulgur, or rice or with canned beans. And vice versa—if you have leftover grains or beans, toss them with a dressing and whatever bits you find in the refrigerator.

▪ Low-Fat Salad Dressings ▪

No matter how many low-fat salad dressings you find on supermarket shelves, none will be as good as the dressings you make at home. They can't be. The quality of a good dressing is a result of a freshly squeezed lemon or lime or a garlic clove that has been minced or pureed in the not-too-distant past. Bottled dressings have stale flavors that linger on the palate. Fresh dressings take minutes to prepare (see the utterly simple ones in the Tossed Green Salad warm-up exercise on page 56).

Look to the pantry and refrigerator to fill out a salad made from leftovers. Garnishes and additions include:

- **Canned roasted peppers**
- **Olives (particularly imported black olives)**
- **Capers**
- **Water-packed tuna**
- **Canned beans**
- **Rice, bulgur, couscous, pasta**
- **Parmesan cheese**
- **Goat cheese**
- **Walnuts, pecans, pine nuts**
- **Canned chipotle chiles**
- **Eggs**
- **Bread (fresh or stale, for croutons)**

Get out the following equipment: **lemon press; measuring spoons; measuring cup or medium-size jar; fork or small whisk; garlic press or chef's knife and cutting board**

Low-Fat Yogurt or Buttermilk Vinaigrette

Makes about ½ cup

2 tablespoons good-quality red wine vinegar, sherry vinegar, or champagne
   vinegar *or* 1 tablespoon fresh lemon juice and 1 tablespoon vinegar of
   your choice
1 small garlic clove, peeled and finely minced or pressed
⅛ to ¼ teaspoon salt, to your taste
1 teaspoon Dijon mustard
1 tablespoon extra-virgin olive oil
¼ cup plain nonfat yogurt or 5 tablespoons buttermilk
1 tablespoon water, or more to taste, if using yogurt
Freshly ground black pepper to taste

Mix together the vinegar or lemon juice and vinegar with the garlic, salt, and mustard using a fork or a small whisk. Stir in the olive oil and yogurt and water or buttermilk. Season with pepper. Thin out with more water as desired.

Low-Fat Lemon-Yogurt or Buttermilk Vinaigrette

Omit the vinegar and use 2 tablespoons lemon juice instead.

Note: This dressing, along with the variations that follow and the Asian Dressing and Lime Balsamic Vinaigrette (page 126), can also be made by placing all of the ingredients in a medium-size jar, screwing the lid on tightly, and shaking vigorously.

Low-Fat Walnut Vinaigrette

Substitute 1 tablespoon walnut oil for the olive oil.

Cumin Vinaigrette

Add ½ teaspoon ground cumin to Low-Fat Yogurt or Buttermilk Vinaigrette. Reduce mustard to ½ teaspoon.

Advance preparation:
Salad dressings will keep fine refrigerated for several days.

PER 2-TABLESPOON SERVING:
3.5 gm total fat
0.5 gm saturated fat
41 calories
1.8 gm carbohydrates
0.8 gm protein

PER SERVING:
3.5 gm total fat
0.5 gm saturated fat
42 calories
2.1 gm carbohydrates
1.0 gm protein

PER SERVING:
3.5 gm total fat
0.3 gm saturated fat
41 calories
1.8 gm carbohydrates
0.9 gm protein

PER SERVING:
3.5 gm total fat
0.5 gm saturated fat
42 calories
0.9 gm protein

Asian Dressing

Makes about ½ cup

The rice wine vinegar, soy sauce, hot chile oil, and sesame oil are available on the imported foods shelf of your supermarket.

1 tablespoon fresh lime juice

1 tablespoon rice wine vinegar or balsamic vinegar

1 small garlic clove, peeled and minced or pressed

1 to 2 teaspoons peeled and finely minced fresh ginger, to your taste

1 tablespoon soy sauce, preferably tamari or Kikkoman

½ teaspoon hot chile oil or a pinch of cayenne pepper (optional)

1 tablespoon dark sesame oil

¼ cup plain nonfat yogurt or 5 tablespoons buttermilk, to your taste

1 tablespoon water, or more to taste, if using yogurt

Salt and freshly ground black pepper to taste

Stir together the lime juice, vinegar, garlic, ginger, soy sauce, and chile oil or cayenne. Whisk in the sesame oil and yogurt and water or buttermilk. Thin out if desired with more water and season with salt and pepper.

Lime Balsamic Vinaigrette

Makes about ½ cup

1 tablespoon fresh lime juice

2 to 3 teaspoons balsamic vinegar, to your taste

Salt and freshly ground black pepper to taste

1 small garlic clove (optional), peeled and minced or pressed

¼ teaspoon Dijon mustard

1 tablespoon extra-virgin olive oil

¼ cup plain nonfat yogurt or 5 tablespoons low-fat buttermilk

1 tablespoon water, or more to taste, if using yogurt

Combine the lime juice, vinegar, salt, pepper, garlic, and mustard. Whisk in the olive oil and the yogurt and water or buttermilk. Thin the dressing, if desired, with more water.

This goes well with:

- Asian greens such as mizuna, tatsoi, and baby bok choy
- Buckwheat noodles or other Asian noodle salads
- Chicken and fish salads

PER 2-TABLESPOON SERVING:

3.4 gm total fat

0.5 gm saturated fat

44 calories

2.2 gm carbohydrates

1.1 gm protein

This goes well with:

- Spicy, peppery greens such as arugula and cress
- Baby field greens, which usually contain some of the peppery greens
- Bitter chicories like Belgian endive and escarole
- Sturdy greens like dandelion greens and beet greens
- Tomato salads

PER 2-TABLESPOON SERVING:

3.4 gm total fat

0.5 gm saturated fat

42 calories

2.2 gm carbohydrates

0.8 gm protein

Tomato Vinaigrette

■

Makes about 1¾ cups

This should only be made with tomatoes in season.

1 pound ripe tomatoes, peeled, seeded, and very finely chopped or crushed
   in a food processor
1 large garlic clove, peeled and minced or pressed
1 tablespoon balsamic vinegar
½ teaspoon salt, preferably coarse sea salt
Freshly ground black pepper to taste
1 tablespoon extra-virgin olive oil
2 tablespoons chopped fresh basil leaves

Stir together all the ingredients. Let sit for 10 to 15 minutes before using.

■ The Salads ■

Quick Broccoli and Chickpea Salad

■

Makes 4 servings

This is one of those salads that you really can make from pantry items. I think of it as a winter salad. I like it best warm, but serving it that way isn't essential.

1 pound broccoli, cut into florets and stems peeled and diced
One to two 15-ounce cans chickpeas, to your taste, drained and rinsed
2 large eggs
1 recipe Low-Fat Lemon-Yogurt or Buttermilk Vinaigrette (page 125)
Salt and freshly ground black pepper to taste
1 ounce Parmesan cheese, slivered or grated

1. Steam the broccoli (see page 53) until tender but not soft and still bright green, 5 to 8 minutes. Refresh with cold water, transfer to the salad bowl, and add the chickpeas.
2. Meanwhile soft-boil the eggs (4 minutes; see page 181), or you can boil them a little longer for harder yolks. Drain and run under cold water for several minutes.

continued

This goes well with:
■ **Pasta salads**
■ **Grain salads**

PER ¼-CUP SERVING:
1.1 gm total fat
0.1 grams saturated fat
17 calories
1.6 grams carbohydrates
0.4 grams protein

Get out the following equipment: steamer and lidded saucepan for the broccoli; saucepan for the eggs; measuring cup or jar and measuring spoons; chef's knife and cutting board; can opener; salad bowl and servers

Advance preparation: You can make the dressing a few hours ahead of time.

PER SERVING:
10.4 gm total fat
2.7 gm saturated fat
256 calories
24.9 gm carbohydrates
16.70 gm protein

3. Make the vinaigrette.
4. Carefully peel the eggs and cut them in half over the salad so the yolk runs out over the mixture, then slice the whites, or break in half over the salad bowl and scoop out each half. Salt and pepper them lightly. Break up the whites with your salad servers. Toss with the dressing and Parmesan and serve.

Note: You can also make this salad with leftover cooked broccoli or other green vegetables such as green beans or spinach. For a more substantial meal, add a drained can of water-packed tuna to the mixture.

A Main-Dish Salad of Chickpeas and Greens

Makes 4 servings

This is typical of many country salads from Provence, where greens, particularly chard and spinach, and chickpeas are abundant. I use a sturdy green like beet greens or chard for this dish. If I go to the farmers' market and buy beets with the greens still on, I'll use the beets for one salad and the greens for something else, like this (unless I make a beet and beet greens salad like the one on page 134). You can cook the greens as soon as you get them home and keep them in the refrigerator for up to five days so that the salad, if you use canned chickpeas, is put together in a flash. The greens and chickpeas can be warm or cold.

FOR THE SALAD:

4 to 5 quarts water

Salt to taste

1 pound fresh greens, such as chard, beet greens, or spinach, stemmed and well washed (page 57)

Two 15-ounce cans chickpeas, drained and rinsed, or 1½ cups dried chickpeas, cooked (page 205) and drained

½ cup chopped fresh flat-leaf parsley leaves

1 medium-size or large red bell pepper, seeded and diced

1 small red onion (optional), peeled, thinly sliced, and rinsed with cold water

FOR THE DRESSING:

3 tablespoons fresh lemon juice

1 tablespoon red wine vinegar or sherry vinegar

Salt and freshly ground black pepper to taste

1 large garlic clove, peeled and minced or pressed

Get out the following equipment: **chef's knife and cutting board; measuring cup or jar and measuring spoons; large pot for cooking the greens; deep-fry skimmer or slotted spoon; whisk or fork; garlic press if using; medium-size bowl; large salad bowl and servers**

Advance preparation: **The cooked greens and the chickpeas will keep for 5 days in the refrigerator. The salad can be assembled and held for up to a day in the refrigerator before being tossed with the dressing. Toss shortly before you serve it. The dressing will hold for a few hours.**

PER SERVING:
13.3 gm total fat
1.4 gm saturated fat
357 calories
46.3 gm carbohydrates
18.80 gm protein

1 tablespoon water

3 tablespoons olive oil

5 tablespoons plain nonfat yogurt or buttermilk

1. Bring the water to a rolling boil in the large pot and add a tablespoon or two of salt. Meanwhile, fill the bowl with ice water and set it next to the pot. Stir the greens into the boiling water and cook until soft but still bright green, 2 to 3 minutes. Transfer immediately to the bowl of cold water, using a deep-fry skimmer or a slotted spoon. Drain, squeeze out the water gently, and chop coarsely. Toss with the chickpeas, parsley, red pepper, and onion in the salad bowl.

2. Make the dressing. Stir together the lemon juice, vinegar, salt and pepper to taste, and the garlic. Whisk in the water, olive oil, and yogurt or buttermilk. Taste. Is there enough salt? Is it too sharp? Thin it out with a little water if it is. Toss with the salad and serve.

Lentil Salad, Warm or Cold

Makes 4 servings

My husband and friends talk about living for weeks on lentils during poor student days. I wonder if they were just cooking up a pot or if they had recipes for luscious salads like this. I really could eat this for a long time without getting tired of it. If you're going to live on lentils, try this salad.

FOR THE LENTILS:

1 pound dried lentils (about 2½ cups), washed and picked over

1 medium-size onion, peeled, cut in half, and each half stuck with a clove

2 large garlic cloves, peeled and cut in half

1 bay leaf

About 2 teaspoons salt, or more to your taste

FOR THE DRESSING:

¼ cup red wine vinegar

1 large garlic clove, peeled and minced or pressed

1 tablespoon Dijon mustard

Salt and freshly ground black pepper to taste

2 tablespoons extra-virgin olive oil

½ to 1 teaspoon ground cumin (optional), to your taste

¼ to ½ cup chopped fresh flat-leaf parsley leaves, to your taste, or a mixture of parsley and other herbs such as chives, tarragon, and thyme

Get out the following equipment: 3- or 4-quart heavy saucepan with lid; chef's knife and cutting board; strainer and bowl; measuring cup and measuring spoons; a small whisk or fork; salad bowl and servers

Advance preparation: This will keep for 3 days in the refrigerator, but it's best to add the parsley and/or herbs just before serving. To serve it warm, gently reheat it in a saucepan.

PER SERVING:
8.2 gm total fat
1.1 gm saturated fat
467 calories
69.80 gm carbohydrates
32.70 gm protein

continued

1. Place the lentils in the saucepan and cover with water by 1 inch. Add the onion halves, halved cloves of garlic, and bay leaf. Bring to a boil. Reduce the heat to medium-low, cover, and simmer for 30 minutes. Add the salt and simmer until the lentils are tender but not mushy, another 10 to 15 minutes. Remove from the heat and drain through the strainer set over a bowl, reserving the cooking water. Discard the onion, garlic, and bay leaf. Transfer the lentils to the salad bowl. Taste and adjust the salt.

2. Make the dressing. Mix together the vinegar, garlic, and Dijon mustard. Add a little salt and pepper and stir in the olive oil and about ½ cup mustard of the cooking liquid from the lentils. Add the cumin if using. Taste and adjust the salt. Stir into the lentils, along with the parsley or parsley and other herbs. Serve warm or cold.

Warm Lentil Salad with Goat Cheese

Make the salad as directed, to be served warm. Cut 3 ounces fresh goat cheese into rounds and top each portion of salad with a round of goat cheese before serving.

White Bean and Pesto Salad

Makes 4 servings

You can pull this together just by combining canned white beans, prepared pesto, and a few other ingredients; or you can cook the beans and make the pesto; or you can use canned beans and make the pesto, which is probably the best compromise. The optional green beans add a nice colorful and textural touch, but use only tender beans in season. In California I love the Blue Lake beans I get at farmers' markets in the spring and summer.

Two 15-ounce cans white beans, drained and rinsed, or 1½ cups dried white
    beans, cooked (page 205)
2 garlic cloves, peeled and halved lengthwise
¼ to ½ teaspoon salt, to your taste (more if using dried beans)
1½ cups fresh basil leaves, rinsed and dried
¼ cup extra-virgin olive oil
¼ cup bean-cooking liquid, plain nonfat yogurt, or low-fat buttermilk
¼ cup freshly grated Parmesan cheese
Freshly ground black pepper to taste
½ pound green beans (optional), trimmed, snapped in half, and steamed
    5 minutes (page 53)

PER SERVING:
12.7 gm total fat
4.2 gm saturated fat
524 calories
70 gm carbohydrates
36.6 gm protein

Get out the following equipment: **food processor fitted with the steel blade or mortar and pestle; spatula; measuring spoons and measuring cup; steamer if using the fresh green beans; salad bowl and servers**

Advance preparation: **This will keep for a couple of days in the refrigerator, but the garlic will grow more pungent.**

PER SERVING:
15.60 gm total fat
2.9 gm saturated fat
281 calories
24.00 gm carbohydrates
11.40 gm protein

Radishes or cherry tomatoes for garnish

Lettuce leaves for serving (optional)

1. If you are not using canned beans, cook the beans. Drain and retain ½ cup of the cooking liquid. If you are using canned beans, drain and rinse.
2. Turn on the food processor fitted with the steel blade and drop in the garlic cloves. When the chopped garlic adheres to the sides of the bowl, scrape down the sides of the bowl, add ¼ teaspoon of the salt and the basil and process until finely chopped. Scrape down the sides of the bowl. With the machine running, drizzle in the olive oil, then the liquid from the beans or the yogurt or buttermilk. Add the Parmesan and mix well. Season with pepper. Taste and adjust the salt.
3. Toss the pesto with the beans and green beans if using, garnish with radishes or cherry tomatoes, and serve over lettuce leaves if you wish.

Note: Pesto is wonderful if made in a mortar and pestle. Combine the garlic and salt in the mortar and grind to a paste. Add the basil leaves and grind to a puree, not by pounding but by crushing with the pestle as you rotate it around the sides of the bowl of the mortar. Drizzle in the olive oil a spoonful at a time, working it in with the pestle, then add the cheese and the cooking water from the beans or yogurt or buttermilk.

Roasted or Grilled Red Peppers

Makes 4 servings as a salad

Roasted red peppers are wonderful to have on hand, to eat as a salad or to add to salads made with other ingredients. You can either roast them in the oven or grill them over a gas burner, under a broiler, or over an outdoor grill. If you need one for a salad you are about to make and don't have any roasted peppers on hand, I suggest you grill the pepper since it goes more quickly. However, if you have several peppers to deal with, roasting in the oven is the most efficient method and has the advantage of giving you a lot of juice, which serves as a handy low-fat marinade for the peppers.

4 medium-size red bell peppers

Salt, preferably coarse sea salt, and freshly ground black pepper to taste

Get out the following equipment: baking sheet (if oven roasting); tongs; aluminum foil; 2 medium-size bowls with a plate that will cover one of them; chef's knife and cutting board; strainer

Advance preparation: Roasted peppers will keep, covered, for at least 5 days in the refrigerator. The oven-roasted peppers will be submerged in their own juice, and I recommend using the optional oil if you are keeping them for a few days, since it helps preserve the peppers.

Salads

131

continued

PER SERVING:
0.5 gm total fat
0 gm saturated fat
50 calories
10.70 gm carbohydrates
3.0 gm protein

OPTIONAL:

1 tablespoon extra-virgin olive oil

1 tablespoon red wine vinegar or balsamic vinegar

Minced or pressed garlic to taste

2 tablespoons slivered fresh basil or thyme leaves

Oven Roasting

Preheat the oven to 400°F. Cover the baking sheet with foil. Place the peppers on the baking sheet and bake in the hot oven until they are soft and the skins are brown and puffed, 30 to 45 minutes, turning the peppers with tongs every 10 minutes.

Grilling

Using a gas burner or a grill: This is the way to do it quickly in the kitchen. If you have a lot of peppers to grill it isn't so quick, but for one or two it's fine. It helps to have peppers that are not too crinkly but have straight, smooth sides.

Turn on the burner or light a grill (medium flame) and place the pepper directly over the flame. Grill, turning the peppers with tongs or two long spoons, until uniformly charred black.

Using the broiler: Preheat the broiler. Line a baking sheet with foil. Place the peppers under the broiler, 2 or 3 inches away from the heat (at the highest setting). Broil, watching the peppers and turning often, until uniformly charred.

To Finish the Salad

1. Remove the peppers from the heat and transfer to a bowl or a plastic bag. Cover the bowl with a plate or seal the bag and let sit for 30 minutes or longer. The peppers will continue to soften.
2. Carefully remove the skins and seeds from the peppers, holding them over the bowl so you don't lose any of the liquid. Rinse with cold water. Cut into wide or thin strips, as you wish. Toss with salt and pepper in another bowl and strain in the juice.
3. Add the olive oil, vinegar, and/or the garlic if you are using these ingredients and refrigerate until ready to serve.
4. Toss with the optional herb shortly before serving.

Arugula Salad with Beets

Makes 4 servings

This is one of my all-time favorite salads. I make it every week during the fall, winter, and early spring in Los Angeles, because every week I find beautiful beets at the farmers' markets. You get two dishes out of one item if you buy beets with the greens attached (see recipes for pasta with greens and for sautéed greens with garlic on pages 258 and 241). If you are doing one-stop shopping at the supermarket, you can make this easily with the beets you find there. In France we always bought our beets cooked—that's how they sold them—and I'm now finding cooked beets in my local supermarket produce section. That will speed things up, but it takes very little effort to roast them if you can't find them already cooked. And young beets, which is how you usually find them with their tops still on, are incredibly sweet and wonderful tasting.

FOR THE SALAD:

4 small to medium-size or 2 large beets, red, yellow, or a combination

6 ounces arugula, washed and dried

1 ounce Parmesan cheese, slivered, or goat cheese or blue cheese, crumbled (about ¼ cup) (optional)

FOR THE DRESSING:

2 teaspoons balsamic vinegar

1 tablespoon fresh lemon juice or sherry vinegar

Salt and freshly ground black pepper to taste

1 small garlic clove, peeled and minced or pressed

½ teaspoon Dijon mustard (optional)

¼ cup extra-virgin olive oil, or 2 tablespoons olive oil and 2 tablespoons plain nonfat yogurt or low-fat buttermilk

1. Roast the beets if they are uncooked. Preheat the oven to 425°F. Cut away the leaves by slicing across the top end, just below the stems (save the leaves for another purpose). Trim away the root and scrub the beets under warm water with a vegetable brush. Place in the baking dish and add about ¼ inch of water. Cover with a lid or foil and bake for 30 minutes to an hour, depending on the size of the beets. Medium-size beets take about 40 minutes, small ones 30, and really large ones an hour. Test for doneness by sticking a knife into the beet; it should slide right through. Remove from the oven and allow to cool.

Get out the following equipment: vegetable brush; cutting board and chef's knife; salad spinner; baking dish with a lid or aluminum foil; measuring cup or jar and measuring spoons; lemon press if using lemon; fork or small whisk; garlic press if using; salad bowl and servers

Advance preparation: The roasted beets will keep for several days in the refrigerator. I usually roast them as soon as I get them home from the market. Then I allow them to cool, put them in a zippered plastic bag, and refrigerate, peeled or unpeeled. The dressing can be made several hours ahead of time.

PER SERVING:
13.9 gm total fat
1.8 gm saturated fat
156 calories
7.6 gm carbohydrates
2.0 gm protein

continued

2. When the beets are cool, it will be easy to slip their skins off. Skin and cut in half lengthwise, then slice the beets very thin or cut into small wedges. Transfer to a salad bowl along with the arugula.

3. Stir together the balsamic vinegar, lemon juice or sherry vinegar, salt, pepper, garlic, and optional mustard. Whisk in the olive oil or olive oil and yogurt or buttermilk. Thin out the dressing if desired with about a tablespoon of water.

4. Just before serving, toss the arugula and beets with the dressing and the optional cheese.

Variation: This salad can be made with baby spinach or with mixed spring greens instead of arugula.

Beet and Beet Greens Salad

Makes 4 servings

Cooked greens are as good cold, served as a salad with lemon and olive oil, as they are hot, cooked with garlic and olive oil. This is a great way to use beets that you find in the farmers' market. You can use red or yellow beets for this.

1¾ to 2 pounds (1 good-size bunch or 2 smaller bunches) beets, with greens

1 tablespoon plus about ¼ teaspoon salt, or to your taste

2 teaspoons balsamic vinegar

2 tablespoons fresh lemon juice

1 garlic clove, peeled and minced or pressed

Salt and freshly ground black pepper to taste

3 tablespoons extra-virgin olive oil

1 tablespoon plain nonfat yogurt

Chopped white of 1 hard-cooked egg for garnish (optional)

1 tablespoon chopped fresh dill or flat-leaf parsley leaves

1. Cut away the greens from the beets and set aside. Trim the roots (cut off the long pointed strand at the end of the bulb).

2. Roast the beets. Preheat the oven to 425°F. Scrub the beets under warm water with a vegetable brush. Place in the baking dish and add about ¼ inch of water. Cover with a lid or foil and bake for 30 minutes to an hour, depending on the size of the beets. Medium-size beets take about 40 minutes, large beets an hour, and small ones about half an hour. Test for doneness by sticking a knife into the beet; it should slide right through. Remove from the oven and allow to cool.

Get out the following equipment: cutting board and knife; salad spinner or large bowl; baking dish with lid or aluminum foil; large pot (such as a pasta pot); slotted spoon or deep-fry skimmer; measuring spoons; measuring cup or jar; lemon press; fork or small whisk; garlic press if using; salad bowl and servers

Advance preparation: The roasted beets will keep for several days in the refrigerator. The cooked greens will also keep for a couple of days in the refrigerator, in a plastic bag or container.

3. While the beets are roasting, prepare the greens. Fill the pot with water and bring to a boil over high heat. Pull the leaves away from the stems and discard the stems. Place the leaves in the large bowl of cold water or the bottom of your salad spinner, and swish around to remove the sand. Lift from the water, change the water, and repeat. When the water on the stove comes to a boil, add 1 tablespoon of the salt and the greens. Meanwhile, fill the bowl you used for cleaning the greens with cold water and place it next to the pot. Cook the greens until tender, about 2 minutes, and transfer with a slotted spoon or skimmer to the bowl of cold water. Drain and gently squeeze out the water (you don't have to squeeze them dry).

4. When the beets are cool, it will be easy to slip or rub their skins off. Skin and cut in half lengthwise, then slice the beets very thin. Transfer to the salad bowl and toss with the vinegar. Add the greens to the bowl.

5. Stir together the lemon juice, garlic, salt, pepper, olive oil, and yogurt. Toss with the beets and their greens. Garnish with the chopped egg white if you wish and the dill or parsley and serve.

PER SERVING:
10.6 gm total fat
1.4 gm saturated fat
193 calories
22.50 gm carbohydrates
5.9 gm protein

Greek Salad

Makes 4 servings

Greek salad is probably the easiest, most straightforward salad in this book. Those of you who detest washing and drying lettuce will love it, since there is no lettuce. But you can make a Greek salad only if you can find luscious vine-ripened tomatoes; otherwise, it isn't worth the little bit of effort it requires. Greek salads are often dressed with nothing more than olive oil and a sprinkling of oregano. A combination of lemon juice and olive oil can be used. I like a bit of vinegar the best.

Get out the following equipment: large strainer or colander; chef's knife and cutting board; measuring spoons; salad bowl and servers

Advance preparation: This will hold for a couple of hours, but it will be juicier because the salt will draw out juice from the tomatoes and cucumbers.

PER SERVING:
12.30 gm total fat
2.4 gm saturated fat
177 calories
14.20 gm carbohydrates
3.9 gm protein

FOR THE SALAD:

¼ teaspoon salt, or more to your taste

1 large or 2 small red or sweet white onions, peeled and thinly sliced crosswise

3 large or 4 medium-size firm, ripe tomatoes, each cut into 6 to 8 wedges

1 medium-size regular cucumber or ½ long European cucumber, peeled, cut in half lengthwise, and sliced about ¼ inch thick

1 large green bell pepper, cut in half lengthwise, seeded, and sliced

8 Kalamata olives (optional), cut in half and pitted

1 tablespoon slivered fresh mint leaves (optional)

1 ounce feta cheese, crumbled

½ teaspoon crumbled dried oregano

Freshly ground black pepper to taste

continued

FOR THE DRESSING:

1 tablespoon red wine vinegar, sherry vinegar, or fresh lemon juice, or more
   to taste

3 tablespoons extra-virgin olive oil, or 1 tablespoon olive oil and 2
   tablespoons plain nonfat yogurt or low-fat buttermilk

1. Salt the onion slices and let sit in the strainer or colander in the sink
   while you prepare the other ingredients.
2. Prepare the other ingredients and place in the salad bowl. Rinse the salted
   onion rounds thoroughly and add to the bowl. Sprinkle on the oregano,
   black pepper, and some more salt. Toss with the vinegar or lemon juice
   and the olive oil or oil and yogurt or buttermilk. Taste. Is there enough
   salt? Vinegar or lemon? Adjust the seasoning and serve.

Tzatziki: Greek Cucumber and Yogurt Salad

Makes 6 servings

Tzatziki, a garlicky mixture of grated cucumbers and thickened yogurt, is
one of my favorite Greek dishes. Cucumbers keep well in the refrigerator, so
this salad should be a frequent possibility for you.

Salt to taste

1 long European cucumber, peeled and grated, or 2 medium-size regular
   cucumbers, peeled, seeded, and grated

1½ cups drained plain nonfat yogurt (about 3 cups undrained; see page 40)

2 to 3 garlic cloves, to your taste, peeled and minced, pressed, or pounded to
   a paste in a mortar and pestle with ¼ teaspoon salt

1 to 2 tablespoons chopped fresh mint or dill, to your taste

1 tablespoon red wine vinegar (optional)

1 tablespoon extra-virgin olive oil

Freshly ground black pepper to taste

1. Generously salt the grated cucumber, toss, and let sit in the strainer in the
   sink for 15 to 30 minutes. Rinse and squeeze out the water.
2. Toss the cucumber with the yogurt and the remaining ingredients in the
   salad bowl. Taste. Is there enough salt and garlic? Would it be better with
   more pepper? Adjust the seasonings. Refrigerate until ready to serve.

*Get out the following
equipment:* **grater or a
food processor fitted
with the grating blade;
chef's knife and cutting
board; vegetable peeler;
garlic press, minichop,
or mortar and pestle if
using any of these for
the garlic; medium or
large strainer; measur-
ing cup and measuring
spoons; salad bowl and
servers**

Advance preparation:
**This will hold for a few
hours, but the cucum-
ber will lose its texture
somewhat, and it will
continue to emit water,
so make sure to stir be-
fore serving.**

PER SERVING:
2.7 gm total fat
0.5 gm saturated fat
120 calories
14.80 gm carbohydrates
9.5 gm protein

Baby Spinach Salad with Mushrooms

Makes 4 to 6 servings

Now that already stemmed and washed spinach is so readily available in supermarkets, a spinach salad is easy to put together (in the "olden days" it took a long time to remove the sand from bulk spinach). Usually you can find packaged or bulk baby spinach; the tender, iron-rich leaves are just wonderful with mushrooms and a light, lemony vinaigrette.

4 to 6 large mushrooms, cleaned, trimmed, and thinly sliced

1 tablespoon fresh lemon juice

6 to 8 ounces tender baby spinach, rinsed and dried

2 tablespoons chopped fresh herbs, such as flat-leaf parsley, chives, tarragon, rosemary, and/or marjoram

1 recipe Low-Fat Yogurt or Buttermilk Vinaigrette using lemon juice and vinegar (page 125), or regular vinaigrette using lemon juice and vinegar (page 56)

1. Toss the mushrooms with the lemon juice in the salad bowl. Add the spinach and fresh herbs.
2. Make the vinaigrette and toss the salad with it just before serving.

Variations: You can add one or more of the following to the salad:

■ 2 tablespoons chopped walnuts
■ 1 ounce Gorgonzola or feta cheese, crumbled
■ 1 ounce Parmesan or Gruyère cheese, slivered or grated
■ 3 or 4 radishes, trimmed and thinly sliced
■ 1 small red onion, peeled, thinly sliced, and rinsed

Get out the following equipment: salad spinner; chef's knife and cutting board; garlic press if using; measuring spoons and measuring cup or jar; salad bowl and servers

Advance preparation: The spinach can be washed and dried hours ahead of time, then wrapped in a clean kitchen towel, sealed in a plastic bag, and refrigerated. The mushrooms can be sliced and tossed with the lemon juice a few hours ahead of time. The dressing will also hold for a few hours.

PER SERVING:
3.9 gm total fat
0.5 gm saturated fat
65 calories
6.1 gm carbohydrates
3.3 gm protein

Warm Potato and Goat Cheese Salad

Makes 4 servings

This makes a terrific dinner, easily made after work. Here's a great way to use those luscious new potatoes that you'll find in the spring in farmers' markets. However, you can also make it with older, larger waxy potatoes with equally delicious results.

Get out the following equipment: **steamer and saucepan with lid; chef's knife and cutting board; kitchen towel; measuring cup and measuring spoons; whisk or fork; garlic press if using; salad bowl and servers**

Advance preparation: **This salad will hold at room temperature for a few hours and makes a great picnic dish.**

PER SERVING:
11.70 gm total fat
4.10 gm saturated fat
403 calories
63.00 gm carbohydrates
10.90 gm protein

FOR THE SALAD:

1½ pounds (6 medium-size) new or Yukon Gold potatoes, scrubbed and cut into 1-inch dice (leave little new potatoes whole)

¼ cup dry white wine

Salt and freshly ground black pepper to taste

1 small red onion, peeled, thinly sliced, and rinsed with cold water

½ cup chopped fresh flat-leaf parsley leaves

3 ounces not-too-salty fresh goat cheese, crumbled or cut into pieces (about ⅓ cup)

FOR THE DRESSING:

3 tablespoons red wine vinegar or sherry vinegar

1 teaspoon Dijon mustard

1 garlic clove, peeled and minced or pressed

⅓ cup plain nonfat yogurt

2 tablespoons extra-virgin olive oil

TO FINISH THE SALAD:

2 tablespoons slivered fresh sage leaves, or more to taste

1. If the potatoes are small new potatoes, you can steam them whole. Place them in the steamer insert over an inch of water in the saucepan and bring the water to a boil. Reduce the heat to medium and cover. Steam the potatoes until tender, 10 to 15 minutes, or up to 20 minutes for whole potatoes. When they are tender, you should be able to pierce them with a fork or knife, but they shouldn't fall apart. Remove from the heat. If you have steamed whole new potatoes, using a kitchen towel to steady them without burning your fingers, cut them into quarters. Toss the hot potatoes at once with the wine, salt, and pepper. Add the onion, parsley, and goat cheese and toss together.

2. Mix together the vinegar, mustard, garlic, yogurt, and olive oil. Pour over the salad, add the sage, and toss together. Taste and adjust seasonings. Serve warm or at room temperature.

Main-Dish Potato and Green Bean Salad

Makes 4 servings

This salad is inspired by beautiful new potatoes and just-picked beans and sugar snap peas from the farmers' market, but you can easily shop for it at the supermarket. It's nice to use an assortment of pink and white potatoes and yellow and green beans, but you could also use one kind of potato and one kind of bean, or beans and sugar snap peas. The main thing is to make something fresh and glorious. The beans should be crisp and should snap when you bend them; they shouldn't be tired and floppy. This salad is great warm or cold.

FOR THE SALAD:

4 large eggs

1 pound waxy potatoes, preferably new potatoes, scrubbed and quartered if medium-size, cut into 1-inch pieces if large

¼ cup minced red or white onion, rinsed with cold water

1½ pounds fresh green beans, or an assortment of green and yellow wax beans, haricots verts, flat Italian beans, or green beans and sugar snap peas

2 to 3 tablespoons chopped fresh herbs, such as flat-leaf parsley, tarragon, basil, and chives, to your taste

1 ounce Parmesan cheese, shaved into thin slivers

FOR THE DRESSING:

2 tablespoons fresh lime juice

2 tablespoons vinegar of your choice: sherry, red wine, or white wine

1 large garlic clove, peeled and pounded into a paste with a little salt or pressed

Salt and freshly ground black pepper to taste

1 to 2 teaspoons Dijon mustard, to your taste

¼ cup extra-virgin olive oil

¼ cup plain nonfat yogurt or buttermilk

1. Hard-cook the eggs (see page 181). This should take about 7 minutes, but you can boil them longer. Drain and immediately run under cold water for a few minutes, then peel them. Cut in half and discard the yolks from two of the eggs. Dice the remaining whites and whole eggs together and set aside.

2. If the potatoes are small new potatoes, you can steam them whole. Place them in the steamer insert over an inch of water in the pot. When the wa-

Get out the following equipment: **chef's knife and cutting board; 1-quart saucepan; steamer and pot with lid or a large pot for boiling instead of steaming the beans; mortar and pestle or garlic press; lemon press; measuring cup or jar and measuring spoons; 2- or 3-quart bowl; vegetable peeler for the Parmesan; large salad bowl and servers**

Advance preparation: **All of the vegetables and the dressing can be prepared hours ahead of serving this salad, although it's awfully nice warm. Don't toss with the dressing until just before serving.**

PER SERVING:
11.7 gm total fat
4.90 gm saturated fat
471 calories
56.60 gm carbohydrates
17.20 gm protein

ter under the steamer comes to a boil, reduce the heat to medium and cover. Steam the potatoes until tender, 10 to 15 minutes, or up to 20 minutes for whole potatoes. When they are tender, you should be able to pierce them with a fork or knife, but they shouldn't fall apart. Remove from the heat.

3. While the eggs are boiling and the potatoes steaming, make the dressing. Combine the lime juice, vinegar, garlic, salt, and pepper in the jar or measuring cup. Whisk in the mustard, then the olive oil and the yogurt or buttermilk. Thin out if desired with a tablespoon or two of water.

4. If the potatoes are whole, use a kitchen towel to steady them with one hand and quarter them. Transfer the potatoes, whole or quartered, to the salad bowl and toss at once with half the dressing, salt, pepper, and the onion.

5. Steam the beans (or beans and sugar-snap peas) until crisp-tender, 5 to 8 minutes. Alternatively, bring a large pot of water to a boil and add about 2 teaspoons salt and the beans (or beans and peas). Boil for 1 minute and drain. Transfer immediately, whether steamed or blanched, to a bowl of cold water to stop the cooking and set the color, then drain.

6. Add the beans, chopped eggs, herbs, and Parmesan to the potatoes, toss with the remaining dressing, and serve.

Asian Noodle and Snow Pea Salad

Makes 4 main-dish servings or 6 starter servings

I like to use buckwheat noodles, called *soba* in Japanese, for this salad because they have such a marvelous nutty flavor. You can use other noodles if you can't get hold of soba—Japanese udon noodles or thin spaghetti. Buckwheat noodles cook more quickly than semolina noodles do. You can cook them ahead or when you make the salad. This salad can be served warm or cold.

1 recipe Asian Dressing (page 126)

Salt

½ pound soba (buckwheat noodles), cooked ahead (page 174) if desired

½ pound snow peas, strings trimmed

1 tablespoon dark sesame oil (available on the imported foods shelf of your supermarket)

1 bunch scallions, white and green parts, thinly sliced and kept separate

¼ pound firm tofu, sliced and tossed with 2 teaspoons soy sauce, *or* 1 cup shredded cooked chicken (optional; page 97)

Get out the following equipment: **large pot and colander or pasta pot; chef's knife and cutting board; measuring cup or jar and measuring spoons; garlic press or minichop if using for the ginger and garlic (do not use for the cilantro; use a knife or scissors); wide salad bowl or platter and servers or tongs**

¼ cup chopped fresh cilantro leaves

4 large radishes (optional), trimmed and thinly sliced

Lettuce leaves for the bowl or platter

2 teaspoons sesame seeds

Advance preparation: This will keep for a few hours in the refrigerator, but add the snow peas no more than an hour before tossing with the dressing, or they will lose their color. You could toss everything with the sesame oil and add the dressing closer to serving time. The salad makes a great leftover.

PER SERVING:
7.6 gm total fat
1.1 gm saturated fat
306 calories
49.90 gm carbohydrates
15.10 gm protein

1. Fill the pot with water and bring to a boil. While you're waiting for the water to boil, make the dressing. When the water reaches a rolling boil, add a generous amount of salt. Add the noodles, cook for 3 minutes, and add the snow peas. Cook for another 3 minutes and remove a strand of soba using the tongs. If it is still hard, cook for a few more minutes. Some soba noodles are thinner than others, so you'll have to check the noodles to determine the cooking time. When the soba is cooked al dente, drain, rinse with cold water, and toss in the salad bowl with the sesame oil, the scallion whites, tofu or chicken, and cilantro. Give the dressing a good stir and toss with the noodles, along with the optional radishes.

2. Line the salad bowl or a platter with lettuce leaves. Top with the noodles. Sprinkle the scallion greens and sesame seeds over the top of the salad. Serve warm, at room temperature, or chilled.

Note: If the noodles have been cooked ahead, steam the snow peas for 3 minutes or cook them in salted boiling water for 3 minutes. Drain and rinse with cold water.

Summer Tomato and Basil Salad

Makes 4 servings

There is only one time in the year to indulge in fresh tomatoes, and that's summer and early fall, when they are in season and coming into farmers' markets and produce stands. Today's farmers' markets offer a variety of tomatoes, and they feed me for at least one meal a day during their short sweet season. Use several kinds of tomatoes for this or just one type—but whatever you choose, they have to be vine ripened.

2 pounds firm, ripe tomatoes, cut into wedges

1 to 2 garlic cloves, to your taste, peeled and minced, pureed, or pressed

Salt, preferably coarse sea salt, and freshly ground black pepper to taste

1 tablespoon balsamic vinegar, or more to taste

1 tablespoon olive oil

¼ cup slivered fresh basil leaves

Get out the following equipment: chef's knife and cutting board; garlic press or minichop if using; measuring spoons; salad bowl and servers

Advance preparation: The salad can be made a few hours ahead, but add the basil shortly before serving.

PER SERVING:
4.2 gm total fat
0.5 gm saturated fat
86 calories
9.9 gm carbohydrates
2.4 gm protein

continued

Toss all the ingredients together. Taste. Is there enough salt? Garlic? Balsamic vinegar? If it tastes marvelous, serve. If it's just short of that, add whatever it needs.

Variations: You can add one of the following to the salad:

- A handful of imported black olives
- One small avocado, pitted, peeled, and diced
- 1 to 2 ounces crumbled feta (this is great with the olives, too)
- 2 ounces diced mozzarella
- 6 ounces pasta such as fusilli, penne, or orecchiette, cooked al dente (this also goes great with any of the above variations)

Couscous Salad

Makes 4 to 6 servings

This lemony salad is a sort of tabouli made with couscous instead of bulgur. Instant couscous (virtually all packaged couscous is instant) is one of the great convenience foods. It's important to chop the herbs and vegetables quite finely here.

1 cup couscous
½ cup fresh lemon juice (from 2 large lemons)
¾ cup water, or a little more, as needed
¾ teaspoon salt
½ teaspoon ground cumin
2 tablespoons olive oil
2 cups finely chopped fresh flat-leaf parsley leaves (1 large or 2 medium-size bunches)
¼ cup chopped fresh mint or cilantro leaves
4 scallions, white and green parts, chopped
1 medium-size or large red bell pepper, seeded and finely chopped
1 pound (4 medium-size) firm, ripe tomatoes, finely chopped
Small leaves of romaine lettuce for scoops

1. Place the couscous in the salad bowl. Mix together the lemon juice, water, salt, and cumin and pour evenly over the couscous. Let sit for 30 minutes, stirring the mixture with a wooden spoon or rubbing between your fingers and thumbs every so often to make sure it doesn't lump.

Get out the following equipment: **chef's knife and cutting board; measuring spoon and measuring cup; food processor fitted with steel blade if using to chop the parsley; salad bowl and servers; wooden spoon**

Advance preparation: **The salad will hold for several hours in the refrigerator.**

PER SERVING:
8.0 gm total fat
1.0 gm saturated fat
302 calories
49.10 gm carbohydrates
9.9 gm protein

2. Stir in the remaining ingredients except the lettuce leaves. Taste and adjust seasonings. Refrigerate until ready to serve. Garnish with the lettuce leaves, using them as scoops for the salad.

Wild Rice and Broccoli Salad

Makes 4 main-dish servings or 6 starter servings

I eat this salad as a main dish in the fall and winter, when broccoli is one of the easiest green vegetables to get ahold of, and wild rice fits the season. Sometimes I serve it as an opener for Thanksgiving dinner. In many stores broccoli crowns—the tops—are sold as well as whole bunches. If you use the stems for pickles (see page 40), you can buy the bunch and use just the crowns. Otherwise you won't be losing money if you buy the more expensive crowns.

The broccoli florets absorb the dressing in the most scrumptious way so that with each bite you get a rush of its tart, nutty essence. The red pepper is optional. It adds nice color and crunch, but if you don't want to chop one more thing the salad will be colorful enough without it. Walnut oil, which can be found at organic food stores and imported food stores, gives the salad a marvelous nutty flavor. I recommend French walnut oils for the best flavor. This salad is good warm or cold.

FOR THE SALAD:

3 cups water or broth (chicken or vegetable; may use canned)

1 cup wild rice, rinsed

¾ teaspoon salt (if using water or unsalted broth; ¼ to ½ teaspoon for salted broth), plus more for the dressing

1 pound broccoli crowns, broken into florets

⅓ cup broken walnuts or pecans

⅓ cup chopped fresh flat-leaf parsley leaves or a mixture of parsley and other fresh herbs such as thyme, sage, tarragon, or chives

1 small red bell pepper (optional), seeded and diced

FOR THE DRESSING:

2 tablespoons fresh lemon juice

1 tablespoon red wine vinegar or sherry vinegar

1 garlic clove, peeled and minced or pressed

Salt to taste

⅓ cup plain nonfat yogurt or buttermilk

3 tablespoons walnut oil

Freshly ground black pepper to taste

Get out the following equipment: 2- or 3-quart saucepan with lid; steamer and saucepan with lid; measuring cups; measuring spoons; chef's knife and cutting board; fork or small whisk; garlic press or minichop if using; salad bowl and servers

Advance preparation: You can prepare everything hours or even a day in advance, but don't toss the broccoli with the rice and dressing too far ahead of time or the green color will fade. It can hold with the dressing for about an hour.

PER SERVING:
16.90 gm total fat
1.4 gm saturated fat
339 calories
39.0 gm carbohydrates
12.6 gm protein

continued

1. Bring the water or broth to a boil in the saucepan and add the rice and salt. When the water comes back to a boil, reduce the heat to low, cover, and simmer until the rice is tender, about 45 minutes. Spoon out a few grains and rinse them with cold water. They should be splitting and tender to the bite, with no hardness in the shells. Drain off any remaining liquid.

2. While the rice is cooking, steam the broccoli until just tender, about 5 minutes (see page 53). Refresh with cold water (transfer to a colander and run it under cold water or transfer to a bowl of ice water and drain).

3. Combine the wild rice, broccoli, nuts, chopped herbs, and optional red pepper in the salad bowl. Mix together the lemon juice, vinegar, and garlic. Add salt. Stir in the yogurt or buttermilk and walnut oil and season with pepper. Combine well and taste. Adjust the salt. Toss with the salad until coated evenly and serve.

Cooked Carrot Salad with Cumin

Makes 4 servings

This is a Moroccan salad. In North Africa many salads are made with cooked vegetables. This one is seasoned with cumin. In Tunisia the same salad would be seasoned with caraway and perhaps harissa, a piquant chile paste.

1 pound carrots, peeled and thinly sliced
2 tablespoons extra-virgin olive oil
2 garlic cloves, peeled and minced or pressed
Salt to taste
½ teaspoon freshly ground black pepper
1 teaspoon ground cumin
¼ cup chopped fresh flat-leaf parsley leaves
3 to 4 tablespoons fresh lemon juice, to your taste
Black olives for garnish, pitted if desired (optional)

1. Bring about 1 inch of water to a boil in the saucepan. Place the carrots in the steamer, set in the saucepan, cover, and steam until tender, about 5 minutes. Drain and rinse with cold water.

2. Heat the oil in the skillet over medium heat and add the carrots, garlic, salt, pepper, and cumin. Stir together until the carrots are nicely coated with the mixture, about 5 minutes. Add the parsley, toss together, and transfer to the salad bowl. Toss with the lemon juice. Taste. Is there enough salt and cumin? Garnish with olives if you wish. Serve at room temperature.

Get out the following equipment: chef's knife and cutting board; garlic press or minichop if using; carrot peeler; steamer and medium-size lidded saucepan for cooking the carrots; measuring cup and measuring spoons; large nonstick skillet; wooden spoon; salad bowl

Advance preparation: **This will keep for a couple of days in the refrigerator, provided you don't add the lemon juice until shortly before serving. Allow to come to room temperature before serving.**

PER SERVING:
**7.1 gm total fat
1.0 gm saturated fat
119 calories
13.80 gm carbohydrates
1.6 gm protein**

Tunisian Carrot Salad

Substitute 1 teaspoon ground caraway seeds and about ¼ teaspoon harissa or ⅛ teaspoon cayenne pepper for the cumin. Garnish with sliced hard-cooked eggs and olives.

PER SERVING:
7 gm total fat
1 gm saturated fat
118 calories
13.8 gm carbohydrates
1.5 gm protein

■ Three Grated Carrot Salads ■

Carrots are marvelous in a grated carrot salad. Grating seems to make them even sweeter. I loved the grated carrot vinaigrettes I ate in France. Then I discovered an amazing Moroccan grated carrot salad, sweet with orange juice and orange flower water. Then I picked up a recipe for a grated carrot salad with a curry-flavored vinaigrette from a neighbor in the south of France. I love them all.

Carrot salads work best if the carrots are very finely grated. I have a mandoline-type grater, which is easy to manipulate and grates much more finely than my food processor; anyplace that sells V-slicers will probably sell these too, and they're worth looking for.

French-Style Grated Carrots in a Low-Fat Vinaigrette

■

Makes 4 servings

1 pound carrots
1 recipe Low-Fat Yogurt or Buttermilk Vinaigrette, using lemon juice and vinegar combination (page 125) and omitting the garlic if desired
¼ cup chopped fresh flat-leaf parsley leaves
Salt and freshly ground black pepper to taste

1. Peel the carrots and cut the tips off (if you're using a hand grater, leave the stem ends attached so that you can hold on to them as you grate). Grate on the fine holes of a grater or in the food processor. You should have about 4 cups. Transfer to the salad bowl.
2. Mix together the salad dressing and toss with the carrots and parsley. Taste and correct seasonings. Serve or chill and serve later.

Get out the following equipment: carrot peeler; grater with small holes or a food processor fitted with grating blade; lemon press; garlic press if using; chef's knife and cutting board; measuring cup or jar and measuring spoons; small whisk or fork; salad bowl and servers

Advance preparation: The carrots can be grated a day ahead of time, and the finished salad can be held for several hours.

PER SERVING:
3.8 gm total fat
0.5 gm saturated fat
94 calories
13.90 gm carbohydrates
2.4 gm protein

Grated Carrot Salad with Curry-Cumin Dressing

Makes 4 servings

FOR THE SALAD:

1 pound carrots, peeled and grated as described in step 1 on page 145

3 tablespoons capers, rinsed and chopped

¼ cup grated onion, rinsed with cold water

FOR THE DRESSING:

2 tablespoons fresh lemon juice

¼ teaspoon salt, or to your taste

1 small garlic clove (optional), peeled and minced or pressed

1 teaspoon good-quality curry powder

½ teaspoon ground cumin

Freshly ground black pepper to taste

2 tablespoons extra-virgin olive or canola oil

¼ cup plain nonfat yogurt or buttermilk

1. Toss together the grated carrots, capers, and onion in the salad bowl.
2. Stir together the lemon juice, salt, optional garlic, curry powder, cumin, and pepper. Whisk in the olive oil and yogurt or buttermilk. Taste and adjust salt. Toss with the carrots and serve or chill and serve.

Moroccan Carrot Salad

Makes 4 servings

This will work only if you squeeze the orange juice fresh; don't try it with the bottled stuff. Orange flower water is used widely in North African cooking. You can find it in Middle Eastern markets. It adds a special perfume to the salad. However, you can make this without the orange flavor water, and it will still be delicious.

2 tablespoons fresh lemon juice

½ cup fresh orange juice

1 teaspoon sugar

½ teaspoon ground cinnamon

1 tablespoon orange flower water (optional)

1 pound carrots, peeled and grated as described in step 1 on page 145

2 tablespoons slivered fresh mint leaves

Get out the following equipment: carrot peeler; grater with small holes or food processor fitted with grating blade; lemon press; garlic press if using; strainer; chef's knife and cutting board; measuring cup or jar and measuring spoons; small whisk or fork; salad bowl and servers

Advance preparation: The carrots can be grated a day ahead of time, and the finished salad will hold for several hours.

PER SERVING:
7.1 gm total fat
1.0 gm saturated fat
125 calories
14.50 gm carbohydrates
2.2 gm protein

Get out the following equipment: carrot peeler; grater with small holes or food processor fitted with grating blade; citrus press; chef's knife and cutting board; measuring cup and spoons; small whisk or fork; salad bowl and servers

Advance preparation: The carrots can be grated a day ahead of time.

PER SERVING:
0.3 gm total fat
0 gm saturated fat
70 calories
16.80 gm carbohydrates
1.5 gm protein
Light Basics Cookbook

Combine the lemon juice, orange juice, sugar, cinnamon, and orange flower water. Toss with the carrots in the salad bowl. Sprinkle on the mint and serve.

■ Four Chicken Salads and a ■ Turkey Salad

Chicken salads can take you around the world. Unfortunately the one most familiar to you may be our domestic mayonnaise-ridden version, served in a sandwich. Most popular Chinese chicken salads are also fat- and calorie-laden because they contain fried noodles and lots of oily dressing. But a great, flavorful chicken salad can be pulled off with a minimum of fat in the dressing. If you don't want to spend time poaching the chicken breasts, you can buy cooked skinless chickens (or discard the skin if cooked skinless chicken isn't available) and shred the meat. I often make one of these salads when I have leftover roast or steamed chicken.

Poached Chicken Breasts

■

Makes 4 servings

10 cups water

1 medium-size onion, peeled and quartered

2 garlic cloves, peeled and crushed

2 whole chicken breasts, skinned and split

½ teaspoon dried thyme or oregano or a combination

1 to 1½ teaspoons salt, to your taste

1. Combine the water, onion, and crushed garlic cloves in the saucepan and bring to a boil over medium heat. Add the chicken breasts and bring back to a simmer. Skim off any foam that rises, then add the dried herbs. Cover partially, reduce the heat to low, and simmer until the chicken is cooked through, 13 to 15 minutes. Add salt to taste. Allow the chicken to cool in the broth if there is time.

2. Remove the chicken from the broth when cool enough to handle. Remove from the bone and shred. Do this by pulling strips of the chicken away from the bone and pulling larger pieces apart. It pulls apart naturally into shreds. You should have 3 to 3½ cups of shredded chicken. Strain the chicken broth and set aside (see Note).

Note: You can use the broth for cooking rice and for soups (it will be a light broth), as well as for thinning out the dressings for the chicken salads that follow. Chill until ready to use and skim off any fat that settles on the surface.

Get out the following equipment: saucepan with lid (at least 3-quart capacity); chef's knife and cutting board; measuring spoons and measuring cup; strainer and bowl

PER SERVING:
1.4 gm total fat
.4 gm saturated fat
71.8 calories
0 gm carbohydrates
13.8 gm protein

Curried Chicken Salad

Makes 4 main-dish servings

Equipment for all of the salads: chef's knife and cutting board; medium-size or large bowl; measuring spoons and measuring cup or jar; salad bowl or platter and servers

Advance preparation: All of these salads will keep for a day in the refrigerator, but it's best to add the herbs closer to serving time so they retain their vivid color.

PER SERVING:
4.9 gm total fat
1.10 gm saturated fat
189 calories
5.7 gm carbohydrates
29.30 gm protein

FOR THE SALAD:

Poached Chicken Breasts (page 147)

1 bunch scallions, white and green parts, thinly sliced, or 1 small red onion, finely chopped and rinsed in cold water

1 small cucumber, peeled if waxy, seeded, and diced, or ½ long European cucumber, diced

2 to 4 tablespoons chopped fresh cilantro leaves, to your taste

FOR THE DRESSING:

1 tablespoon red wine vinegar

Salt and freshly ground black pepper to taste

1 teaspoon curry powder

1 teaspoon ground cumin

1 teaspoon Dijon mustard

4 teaspoons Best Foods or Hellmann's mayonnaise

¼ cup plain nonfat yogurt

Broth from poaching chicken for thinning dressing (optional)

TO FINISH THE SALAD:

1 bunch arugula or small head of lettuce (optional), preferably Boston, romaine, or a bitter lettuce like escarole or frisée leaves separated, washed, and dried

1. Combine the shredded poached chicken, scallions or onion, cucumber, and cilantro in the bowl.
2. Mix together the vinegar, ¼ to ½ teaspoon salt, pepper, curry powder, cumin, mustard, mayonnaise, and yogurt. Toss with the chicken mixture until coated evenly. Taste and adjust the seasonings. If you'd like a moister salad, add a few tablespoons of the broth from poaching chicken.
3. Line the salad bowl or platter with the arugula or lettuce leaves. Top with the salad and serve.

Asian Chicken Salad

Makes 4 main-dish servings

PER SERVING:
6.4 gm total fat
1.3 gm saturated fat
200 calories
4.90 gm carbohydrates
29.40 gm protein

Poached Chicken Breasts (page 147)

1 jalapeño or 2 serrano chiles (optional), seeded if desired and chopped

1 bunch scallions, white and green parts, thinly sliced and kept separate

1 small cucumber, peeled if waxy, seeded, and diced, or ½ long European cucumber, diced

¼ cup chopped fresh cilantro leaves

1 recipe Asian Dressing (page 126)

Broth from poaching chicken for thinning dressing (optional)

1 tablespoon toasted sesame seeds (optional)

1. Combine the shredded poached chicken, chiles, scallion whites, cucumber, and cilantro.
2. Make the dressing and mix well. Toss with the chicken mixture until coated evenly. Taste and adjust the seasoning. If you'd like a moister salad, add a few tablespoons of the broth from poaching chicken. Transfer to the platter or salad bowl. Sprinkle the top with the scallion greens and sesame seeds, if using, and serve.

Mexican Chicken Salad

Makes 4 main-dish servings

PER SERVING:
9.9 gm total fat
1.8 gm saturated fat
231 calories
5.0 gm carbohydrates
29.70 gm protein

FOR THE SALAD:

Poached Chicken Breasts (page 147)

4 large radishes, trimmed and chopped

½ cup fresh cilantro leaves, chopped

2 canned chipotle chiles, rinsed, seeded, and cut into thin strips

FOR THE DRESSING:

2 tablespoons fresh lime juice

3 tablespoons cider vinegar

1 garlic clove, peeled and minced or pressed

½ teaspoon ground cumin

¼ teaspoon salt, or more to taste

Freshly ground black pepper to taste

⅓ cup broth from poaching chicken

¼ cup plain nonfat yogurt

2 tablespoons extra-virgin olive oil

continued

TO SERVE THE SALAD:

1 small head romaine lettuce, leaves separated, washed, and dried

1. Combine the shredded poached chicken with the radishes, cilantro, and chipotles.
2. Mix together the lime juice, vinegar, garlic, cumin, salt, and pepper. Stir in the chicken broth and yogurt. Whisk in the olive oil. Toss with the chicken mixture until coated evenly. Taste and adjust the seasonings.
3. Line the platter or salad bowl with the lettuce leaves. Top with the salad and serve.

PER SERVING:
9.8 gm total fat
2.1 gm saturated fat
265 calories
11.00 gm carbohydrates
34.00 gm protein

Indonesian Chicken Salad with Spicy Peanut Dressing

Makes 4 main-dish servings

FOR THE SALAD:

Poached Chicken Breasts (page 147)

¼ cup slivered fresh mint leaves

¼ cup chopped fresh cilantro leaves

1 bunch scallions, white and green parts, thinly sliced and kept separate

1 medium-size or large red bell pepper, seeded and cut into very thin 1-inch-long strips

FOR THE DRESSING:

¼ cup fresh lime juice

2 teaspoons peeled and grated or finely chopped fresh ginger

1 garlic clove, peeled and minced or pressed

1 serrano chile, seeded for a milder salad if desired and coarsely chopped

2 tablespoons crunchy natural peanut butter

½ cup buttermilk or plain nonfat yogurt

Salt to taste

Broth from poaching chicken as needed

TO SERVE THE SALAD:

Small leaves from 1 head romaine lettuce

1 cup bean sprouts (optional)

2 tablespoons roasted peanuts, coarsely chopped

Fresh mint sprigs for garnish

1. Toss the shredded poached chicken with the mint, cilantro, scallion whites, and red pepper.

2. In a blender or a food processor, blend together the lime juice, ginger, garlic, chile, peanut butter, buttermilk or yogurt, and salt until smooth. Taste and adjust the salt. Thin out as desired with chicken broth.
3. Toss the chicken mixture with the dressing. Line the platter or bowl with the lettuce leaves and top with the chicken. Sprinkle optional bean sprouts, chopped peanuts, and scallion greens over the top. Garnish with mint sprigs and serve.

Asian Smoked Turkey and Cucumber Salad

Makes 4 servings

This cooling main-dish salad is easily thrown together. The flavor of the smoked turkey contrasts nicely with the refreshing cucumbers and mint, all of it tossed with a sweet and pungent dressing. Rice wine vinegar, sesame oil, and plum sauce are all available on the imported foods shelf of your supermarket and at Asian groceries.

1 long European cucumber, grated, or 2 medium-size regular cucumbers, peeled, seeded, and grated

Salt to taste

1 tablespoon rice wine vinegar or sherry vinegar, or more to taste

1 tablespoon dark sesame oil

1 teaspoon peeled and grated fresh ginger

2 tablespoons prepared plum sauce

6 ounces smoked turkey, cut into thin slivers

6 scallions, white and green parts, thinly sliced

2 tablespoons chopped or slivered fresh mint leaves

1 head Bibb lettuce for serving

Fresh mint leaves for garnish

1. Sprinkle the cucumber liberally with salt, toss, and let sit in the strainer set over a bowl or a colander set in the sink for 15 minutes. Rinse thoroughly and squeeze dry.
2. Stir together ¼ teaspoon salt and the vinegar. When the salt has dissolved, stir in the sesame oil, ginger, and 1 tablespoon of the plum sauce.
3. Toss the smoked turkey with the remaining tablespoon plum sauce.
4. In the salad bowl, combine the cucumber, vinegar mixture, turkey, scallions, and mint and toss together well. Taste. Is there enough vinegar? Salt? Add more if necessary. Chill until ready to serve. Serve on lettuce cups made with leaves of Bibb lettuce. Garnish with mint leaves.

Get out the following equipment: large grater or food processor fitted with grating blade; large strainer or colander; chef's knife and cutting board; measuring spoons; salad bowl and servers

Advance preparation: This will keep for a day in the refrigerator, although the colors will fade somewhat and the cucumbers will lose some of their crispness.

PER SERVING:
5.0 gm total fat
0.8 gm saturated fat
117 calories
10.50 gm carbohydrates
8.5 gm protein

Soups: Dinner in a Bowl

■

Soups make great light dinners because they're so filling. Not just the hearty soups like the delicious lentil soup with goat cheese on page 170 or the vegetable soup enriched with a light pesto on page 164, but even clear Asian soups, like those on pages 171–173, fill you up; it's all that nice hot, comforting liquid. And soups are easy. You don't have to mess around with time-consuming stocks here, although you are welcome to use them. You'll be surprised to see how tasty a soup made with vegetables, water, and aromatics can be. If you've done the Garlic Soup warm-up on page 84, you'll understand what I mean: garlic, water, salt, herbs, and an egg stirred in at the last minute are all you need for this remarkable potage.

In France, where I lived for 12 years, people make soups for dinner all the time. I think it's one of the reasons the French are in such good health. They may eat big lunches and lots of cheese and butter, but they eat simple, comforting vegetable soups for dinner. In Mexico as well, light soups often serve as the evening meal. I once literally lived on them in a Oaxaca village where I was weaving. My host family thought that gringos could digest only soups, so they fed me two soups a day for two months. I didn't complain. They were vegetable soups and chicken soups, made with a chicken or garlic broth and seasoned with lime and cilantro, or hearty bowls of beans; with corn tortillas they made terrific meals.

I make soups often for dinner parties, because I can get them done ahead of time, at least to a certain point. The selection that follows will give you a range of types of soup—hearty and thick, light and brothy, cold and hot—and flavors from around the world.

■ **Light Soup Basics** ■

- Aromatic vegetables are vegetables that add fragrance, sweetness, and flavor to a soup. They include onions, leeks, carrots, celery, and garlic. Mushrooms are also used to add flavor. Sometimes aromatic vegetables are the main ingredient of a soup.

- A bouquet garni is a bundle of herbs and aromatics added to the simmering broth and discarded at the end of cooking. It almost always contains a bay leaf and a few sprigs of fresh thyme and parsley, and mine sometimes includes a rind of Parmesan or the leafy part of a celery rib. These ingredients are tied together with kitchen string or tied up into a piece of cheesecloth.

- Sautéing aromatics isn't always necessary, and when it is you can use a minimum of oil or butter. One tablespoon suffices where fat is called for in these recipes. To keep the vegetables from sticking, use a heavy soup pot such as those from Le Creuset and keep the heat low. I have found, though, that it's often enough to throw everything into a pot, add water, and bring it to a simmer to get a fragrant pot of soup.

- "Cream" style soups don't need cream. I add potatoes or rice to vegetable soups and then puree the mixture to get a thick, creamy potage. Potatoes add body and flavor without overpowering the other vegetables. They also add nutrients. Rice has the same effect. When soups contain beans, the beans act as thickeners because of their starch. Even if the soup isn't supposed to be a puree, you can blend up a cupful for a more substantial broth. As for final enrichments, plain low-fat yogurt is usually my choice. I have also, and it's about the only time I do use it, used nonfat sour cream (for instance, with Hot or Cold Cream of Sorrel Soup, page 162). A little bit of grated Parmesan or Gruyère cheese won't hurt either if the soup calls for it. Asian soups don't need these final embellishments.

- Use Parmesan rinds to get a cheesy taste without adding more cheese. Simmer the hard rinds of Parmesan, those bits you usually throw away. You've paid for them, so here's a great way to use them. Add one or two rinds directly to the broth or wrap them in cheesecloth along with the bouquet garni or tie up with the bouquet garni, then remove at the end of cooking. They're great in bean and vegetable soups (see Hearty Vegetable Soup, page 164).

- Blender versus hand blender versus food processor: What I really recommend, what I use more than any other tool for my pureed soups, is the hand blender. You don't have to take the soup out of the pot, you don't make a mess, and the hot soup won't bounce out of the blender jar and burn you. It's just so simple. However, for blended cold soups like gazpacho, or if you want an exceptionally smooth texture, go with the blender. Food processors puree unevenly, which is okay if you're thickening something like a bean soup, where you're instructed to puree coarsely. But don't use a food processor for potato-thickened soups, because the potatoes become gummy against the large, fast-moving blades of the food processor. *Be sure to puree in batches if using the blender or food processor*; if you fill it more than half full, the hot soup will splash out and burn you.

▪ Freezing Soups ▪

Freeze soups in small containers so you can quickly thaw your dinner in a microwave. Label the containers.

SOUPS THAT FREEZE WELL

- Bean soups
- Hearty vegetable soups
- Cooked pureed vegetable soups: *However*, you must reblend the soup after you thaw it, because the starch in the potatoes or rice changes texture when the soup freezes. Don't be alarmed by the initial texture after thawing; reblend, then heat through, stirring with a whisk.

SOUPS THAT DON'T FREEZE WELL

- Uncooked fruit and vegetable soups
- Garlic soups with lightly cooked green vegetables
- Soups containing tofu
- Soups enriched at the last minute with egg (you can always omit the eggs, freeze the soups, and add them after heating through)
- Soups with noodles: These too can be made without the noodles, and the noodles added when you reheat them.

▪ Cooking Times ▪

Most of these soups are quickly made. Here are a few general ranges.

- Soups with hard vegetables like potatoes, carrots, turnips, and winter squash need to simmer for 30 to 45 minutes.
- Bean soups: Lentils, black-eyed peas, and split peas need only about 45 minutes. Black beans, chickpeas, and other beans that require soaking need up to 2 hours.

- Don't simmer the life and color out of bright green vegetables. Ten to 15 minutes is usually sufficient. If you're making a large batch, or making the soup for the freezer, steam or blanch the green vegetables separately and add them at the end of cooking to heat them through in the soup.
- Unless otherwise instructed, add fresh herbs just before serving.
- Add eggs and dairy products at the end of cooking, and do not boil or they'll curdle.

Chicken or Turkey Stock

Makes 10 cups

This is one of the pleasures of Thanksgiving and Christmas, and anytime I roast a chicken it's the stock I make afterward. I freeze it in small containers and have it on hand for months. You can make stock with fresh or cooked carcasses or with a whole chicken, skinned and cut up, or chicken pieces. The basic principle for a low-fat chicken stock is to make it a day before you wish to use it so that you can skim off the fat once the stock has cooled.

Fresh carcass of 1 chicken or turkey, carcass of 1 cooked chicken or turkey, or one 3- to 3½-pound chicken, skinned and cut into pieces

3 medium-size carrots, peeled and sliced

2 medium-size onions, peeled and quartered

1 leek, white and tender green parts, well washed and sliced

5 or 6 garlic cloves, to your taste, peeled and crushed

1 bouquet garni made with 1 bay leaf, 2 fresh thyme sprigs, and 2 fresh flat-leaf parsley or cilantro sprigs

1 teaspoon black peppercorns

Salt to taste (about 1 teaspoon per quart of water)

1. If you're using a fresh carcass, crack the bones slightly with a hammer. Combine all the ingredients in the soup pot and cover by 1 inch with water. Bring to a boil and skim off any foam that rises to the top. Reduce the heat to very low, cover partially, and simmer for 2 hours.
2. Strain through a cheesecloth-lined strainer into a large bowl or pot. Remove the bones or the chicken pieces from the strainer and place in a bowl. Allow to cool until you can handle them, then pick off the meat from the bones, and set aside for another purpose.
3. Cover the stock with plastic wrap and refrigerate overnight. The next day, lift off all of the fat that has accumulated on the top. Taste and correct the salt. Freeze in 1-quart and 2-cup containers if not using right away.

Get out the following equipment: **largest soup pot you own; chef's knife and cutting board; cheesecloth; measuring spoons and large measuring cup; large strainer and bowl**

Advance preparation: **This will keep for 3 or 4 days in the refrigerator and freezes well for up to 6 months.**

PER 1-CUP SERVING:
2.0 gm total fat
0 gm saturated fat
38 calories
5.0 gm carbohydrates
0 gm protein

■ Three Quick Vegetarian Stocks ■

When I work on soup recipes, I like to test them first with plain water to see how much inherent flavor the ingredients will bring to the broth. So most of the recipes in this chapter, unless specified, can be made with water. However, stock adds great dimension to a soup. Meat stocks are time consuming, but vegetable stocks are not, and do not require or yield little if any fat.

Vegetable Stock

■

Makes 7 cups

This one is mild, slightly sweet, and fragrant. It's a good all-purpose stock.

Get out the following equipment: **chef's knife and cutting board; vegetable peeler; kitchen string if desired; stockpot; measuring spoons and measuring cup; large strainer; large bowl**

Advance preparation: **This will keep for 4 days in the refrigerator and freezes well for several months.**

PER 1-CUP SERVING:
2.0 gm total fat
0 gm saturated fat
14 calories
3.0 gm carbohydrates
0 gm protein

1 bay leaf
A few fresh thyme sprigs
A few fresh flat-leaf parsley sprigs
2 quarts water
2 large onions, peeled and quartered
2 large carrots, peeled and thickly sliced
2 large leeks, white part only, well washed and sliced
3 large garlic cloves, peeled
2 celery ribs, with leaves, thickly sliced
½ pound (2 medium-size) waxy potatoes, scrubbed and diced
About 2 teaspoons salt, or more to your taste
1 teaspoon black peppercorns

1. If you wish, tie together the bay leaf and herb sprigs. They are tied together to facilitate fishing out at the end of cooking, but everything here is strained anyway, so it really isn't necessary.
2. Combine all the ingredients in the stockpot and bring to a boil. Reduce the heat to very low, cover, and simmer for 1 to 2 hours. Strain and discard the vegetables. Taste. Is there enough salt? Adjust the seasoning.

Ginger-Vegetable Stock

Add a 2-inch piece of fresh ginger, peeled and sliced, and 2 tablespoons soy sauce with the rest of the ingredients. Proceed as directed. This is a good stock for Asian soups.

Garlic Broth

Makes 7 cups

This is what I recommend as a vegetarian substitute for chicken stock. It has a rich, fragrant taste, sweet rather than pungent with long-simmered garlic.

    1 bay leaf
    A few fresh thyme sprigs
    A few fresh flat-leaf parsley sprigs
    2 quarts water
    2 heads garlic, cloves separated and peeled
    2 teaspoons salt, or to taste
    6 black peppercorns
    1 tablespoon olive oil

1. If you wish, tie together the bay leaf and herb sprigs. They are tied together to facilitate fishing out at the end of cooking, but everything here is strained anyway, so it really isn't necessary.
2. Combine all the ingredients in the stockpot and bring to a boil. Reduce the heat to very low, cover, and simmer for 1 to 2 hours. Strain and discard the garlic and herbs. Taste. Is there enough salt? Adjust the seasoning.

Get out the following equipment: **kitchen string if using; stockpot; measuring spoons and measuring cup; large strainer; large bowl**

Advance preparation: **This will keep for 4 days in the refrigerator and freezes well for several months.**

PER 1-CUP SERVING:
0 gm total fat
0 gm saturated fat
14 calories
3.0 gm carbohydrates
1.0 gm protein

Wild Mushroom Broth

Makes 6 cups

This is an intensely flavored broth that is made as a result of soaking dried wild mushrooms like porcini (cèpes). The flavor is meaty, and it's good for hearty vegetable soups that might traditionally be made with a meat stock. You can use the soaked mushrooms for salads, omelets, and other dishes, so don't throw them out. Some dried mushrooms like porcini are expensive and not always easy to locate. You can substitute dried Chinese mushrooms (shiitake), but the flavor will not be as intense.

    2 ounces (2 cups) dried porcini mushrooms or 3 ounces dried Chinese
        mushrooms or shiitake
    1 quart boiling water
    1 tablespoon soy sauce (optional)
    Salt and freshly ground black pepper to taste

Get out the following equipment: **2 medium-size bowls; strainer lined with cheesecloth; measuring cup and measuring spoons**

Advance preparation: **This keeps for 2 days in the refrigerator and can be frozen for several months.**

PER 1-CUP SERVING:
2.0 gm total fat
0 gm saturated fat
14 calories
3.0 gm carbohydrates
0 gm protein

continued

1. Place the mushrooms in a bowl and pour on the boiling water. Let sit for 30 minutes. Drain the soaking water through a cheesecloth-lined strainer into another bowl. Squeeze the mushrooms over the strainer to extract all the liquid. Add more water to the soaking liquid to measure 6 cups. Add the soy sauce if desired and season with salt and pepper.
2. Rinse the mushrooms in several changes of water. Squeeze dry and keep for another purpose.

▪ Thick Vegetable Soups ▪

When I learned to make soups twenty-odd years ago, I learned to thicken them using rich flour-and-butter combinations. The French still enrich their soups with cream. But I find that a potato or two or ¼ to ½ cup of rice does the trick for simple vegetable soups. Recipes vary, but say you had a couple of pounds of broccoli, cauliflower, or winter squash in your refrigerator and you wanted to make a very simple pureed soup. The formula that works best for me as far as texture is concerned is to use an equal volume of the vegetable in question and water, plus potatoes or rice for thickening and other aromatics (such as onion or garlic).

As for the blending, I find that nothing works more easily than a hand blender. There's literally no mess or sputtering. Definitely worth the investment. Here's how my formula works for broccoli:

Puree of Broccoli Soup

▪

Makes 4 servings

1 medium-size onion, chopped (about 1 cup)

2 garlic cloves, peeled and chopped or pressed

5 cups broccoli florets and chopped peeled stems (about 1½ pounds)

½ pound waxy potatoes (about 2 medium-size), peeled and diced, or
    ½ cup rice

5 cups water or chicken, vegetable, or garlic stock (pages 155–157) or
    canned low-sodium broth

1½ to 2 teaspoons salt and freshly ground black pepper to taste

1% milk, water, or stock as desired for thinning out

FOR GARNISH:

¼ cup freshly grated Parmesan or Gruyère cheese

Garlic Croutons (page 39)

Get out the following equipment: **chef's knife and cutting board; paring knife; potato peeler; garlic press or mini-chop if using; measuring spoons and large measuring cup; large, heavy soup pot or saucepan; cheese grater; blender, hand blender, or food mill fitted with the medium blade**

1. Combine everything except the milk and garnishes in the soup pot or saucepan and bring to a boil. Reduce the heat to low, cover, and simmer until the vegetables are tender and fragrant, 30 to 45 minutes.
2. Blend the soup, in batches if necessary. Don't blend too smooth; you want to retain some texture. Add milk, water, or stock to thin if desired. Return to the pot, taste and adjust the seasonings, heat through, and serve, topped with a sprinkling of cheese and a handful of garlic croutons.

Puree of Cauliflower

Substitute cauliflower florets and chopped peeled stems for the broccoli.

Seasoning ideas: 1 to 2 teaspoons curry powder or ground cumin (add at beginning); 1 to 2 teaspoons caraway seeds, lightly crushed (add at beginning); or ½ cup grated Gruyère cheese instead of Parmesan (stir in at the end, when heating through)

Puree of Winter Squash or Pumpkin

Substitute peeled and diced squash or pumpkin for the broccoli.

Seasoning ideas: 1 to 2 teaspoons fresh thyme leaves or ½ to 1 teaspoon dried (add at beginning); or 1 to 2 teaspoons slivered fresh sage leaves or ½ to 1 teaspoon dried (add at beginning)

Thick Carrot Soup with Fresh Mint

Makes 6 servings

This heavenly soup is pure carrot, set off with fresh mint, so the carrots have to be good—sweet and vivid. For me, this rules out the precut and miniature carrots now available in most supermarkets; these, in my experience, are bland. Taste them; if they're not sweet, just kind of bland and carrot textured, they'll be better off in a salad (like the ones on pages 144–147).

Butter is not unwelcome in light cuisine, but a little goes a long way. Here you need it to soften the onion—often referred to as "sweating" in culinary jargon—which helps to bring out the onion's sweetness. Don't overpuree this soup; it should be textured, not smooth. If you have a food mill, that's a good tool for pureeing, but you can use a blender or hand blender as long as you don't overdo it.

continued

Advance preparation: **These will all keep for 3 to 4 days in the refrigerator and can be frozen for several months. When you thaw them, however, you'll have to whisk or reblend to get the texture back.**

PER SERVING:
2.0 gm total fat
1.0 gm saturated fat
135 calories
24.0 gm carbohydrates
7.6 gm protein

Get out the following equipment: **chef's knife and cutting board; vegetable peeler; food processor fitted with steel blade if using; large, heavy soup pot; wooden spoon; measuring spoons and measuring cup; kitchen scissors for slivering the mint leaves; blender, hand blender, or food mill fitted with the medium blade**

1 tablespoon unsalted butter

1 small or ½ medium-size yellow onion or 4 to 5 shallots, peeled and minced (about ⅔ cup)

2½ pounds sweet carrots, peeled and finely chopped (can use a food processor for this; about 7 cups)

¼ cup rice

6 to 7 cups water or vegetable or defatted chicken stock (page 156 or 155) or canned broth as needed

Salt to taste

¼ teaspoon sugar (optional)

Freshly ground black pepper to taste

¼ cup slivered fresh mint leaves

1. Heat the butter in the soup pot over medium-low heat and add the onion. Cook, stirring, until very soft but not brown, 5 to 8 minutes. Add the carrots, rice, and water or stock. The amount of water or stock should be roughly equal to the volume of carrots and once in the pot should just cover the carrots by about ½ inch. Bring to a boil. Add about 1½ teaspoons salt, reduce the heat to low, cover, and simmer until the carrots are tender but not mushy, about 30 minutes.

2. Blend the soup coarsely however you choose. The rice should no longer be recognizable (it thickens the soup), but the soup should not be ultra-smooth. Return to the pot. Stir and taste. Is it vivid? Could it be sweeter? Does it have enough salt? If you think it could be a bit sweeter, stir in the sugar and taste. Season with pepper and heat through. Just before serving, stir in the mint. Serve hot.

Lettuce and Potato Soup

Makes 4 servings

Here's what to do with those lettuces that have been in the refrigerator a little too long. If you wish, add a little sorrel to this soup for a tangier flavor.

1 tablespoon olive oil

1 medium-size onion, peeled and chopped

4 garlic cloves, or more to taste, peeled and minced or pressed

1 pound waxy potatoes, peeled and diced

5 cups vegetable or defatted chicken stock (page 156 or 155) or canned low-sodium broth

1 bay leaf

½ teaspoon dried thyme

Salt to taste

1 pound Bibb or romaine lettuce, washed, stemmed, and leaves coarsely chopped

1 cup sorrel leaves (optional), stemmed and leaves coarsely chopped

½ cup 1% milk

Freshly ground black pepper to taste

Chopped fresh flat-leaf parsley leaves for garnish

Advance preparation:
This will keep for a few days in the refrigerator and can be served cold.

PER SERVING:
4.1 gm total fat
0.7 gm saturated fat
203 calories
37.4 gm carbohydrates
5.8 gm protein

1. Heat the olive oil in the soup pot or Dutch oven over medium heat and add the onion. Cook, stirring, until tender, 3 to 5 minutes. Add 1 clove of the garlic and stir together for about 30 seconds. Add the remaining garlic, the potatoes, stock, bay leaf, and thyme. Bring to a boil, season with salt, cover, reduce the heat to low, and simmer for 15 minutes. Add the lettuce and optional sorrel, stir together, cover, and simmer until the potatoes are thoroughly tender and falling apart, another 15 minutes. Remove from the heat.

2. Remove the bay leaf and puree the soup however you choose. Return to the pot, add the milk and lots of pepper, and heat through. Taste and adjust the seasonings, adding more salt or garlic if desired. Serve hot, garnished with chopped parsley.

Note: *This soup is also delicious served cold. To serve cold, allow to cool and chill for several hours. Serve garnished with a dollop of yogurt or nonfat sour cream and a sprinkling of parsley.*

Hot or Cold Cream of Sorrel Soup

Makes 4 servings

There are many popular versions of this soup found all over Europe but especially in Eastern Europe. It has a very tangy, acidic flavor. It always loses its bright green color when cooked. Sorrel is not so easily found in the supermarket, but should you run across it, this is the thing to do.

1 medium-size onion, peeled and chopped

1 large waxy potato, peeled and diced

1 quart vegetable or defatted chicken stock (page 156 or 155), water, or canned low-sodium broth

½ pound (about 6 cups) sorrel, stemmed and leaves coarsely chopped

2 tablespoons fresh dill

½ cup 1% or skim milk

Salt and freshly ground black pepper to taste

½ cup nonfat sour cream or plain yogurt for garnish

1. Combine the onion, potato, and stock in the soup pot or saucepan and bring to a boil. Reduce the heat to low, cover, and simmer until the vegetables are tender, about 30 minutes. Add the sorrel and dill and simmer for another 10 minutes. Stir in the milk, taste, and season with salt and pepper.
2. Puree the soup however you choose. Heat through, taste, and correct the salt.
3. Serve hot, or chill and serve cold, garnishing each bowl (whether hot or cold) with a generous dollop of sour cream or yogurt.

Sweet Potato and Butternut Squash Soup with Ginger

Makes 4 to 6 servings

This heavenly soup has a marvelous rich texture—though nothing in it is rich—and subtle flavor.

1 tablespoon canola oil

1 small onion, peeled and chopped

1 tablespoon peeled and grated or chopped fresh ginger

1 pound butternut squash, peeled and diced

1 pound sweet potatoes, peeled and diced

1 medium-size Yukon Gold or russet potato, peeled and diced

5 to 6 cups vegetable or defatted chicken stock (page 156 or 155), water, or
   canned broth, to your taste

Salt to taste

1 tablespoon dry or medium-dry sherry

FOR GARNISH:

1 to 2 teaspoons finely chopped or grated fresh ginger, to your taste

6 tablespoons plain nonfat yogurt

Advance preparation:
This will keep for
about 3 days in the re-
frigerator and can be
frozen for several
months.

PER SERVING:
3.9 gm total fat
0.4 gm saturated fat
277 calories
56.0 gm carbohydrates
5.9 gm protein

1. Heat the oil over medium-low heat in the soup pot or Dutch oven. Add
   the onion and cook, stirring, until tender, about 3 to 5 minutes. Add the
   tablespoon of ginger and cook, stirring, until it begins to smell fragrant,
   about 1 minute. Add the squash, sweet and white potatoes, 5 cups of the
   stock or water, and salt. Bring to a boil, cover, and reduce the heat to low.
   Simmer until all of the vegetables are thoroughly tender, about 30 minutes.

2. Puree the soup however you choose. Stir in the sherry. Stir together, reheat, and add the ginger garnish. Taste. Is there enough salt? Ginger?
   Adjust the seasonings. Thin out if desired with the additional cup of
   stock. Serve, garnishing each bowl with a tablespoon of yogurt.

Yellow Pepper Soup with Thyme

Makes 4 to 6 servings

The color alone is reason enough to make this luscious, savory soup that's as
good to eat cold as it is hot.

1 tablespoon olive oil

1 medium-size onion, peeled and chopped

1 medium carrot, chopped

3 large garlic cloves, peeled and minced or pressed

2 pounds (4 large) yellow bell peppers, seeded and cut into 1-inch pieces

Salt to taste

¼ teaspoon sugar

½ pound waxy potatoes, peeled and diced

1½ quarts garlic or defatted chicken stock (page 157 or 155), water
   (enriched with bouillon cube if desired; see Note), or canned broth

6 slices baguette or 3 slices country bread

1 garlic clove, halved

Freshly ground black pepper to taste

Leaves from 12 fresh thyme sprigs

Get out the following
equipment: **chef's knife**
and cutting board;
long-handled wooden
spoon; measuring
spoons; large measur-
ing cup and large,
heavy soup pot or
Dutch oven; blender or
hand blender

Advance preparation:
The soup will keep for
3 days in the refrigera-
tor and can be frozen
for several months.
Whisk or blend after
you thaw it to reamal-
gamate the ingredients.
The croutons must be
made the day you are
serving.

Soups: Dinner in a Bowl

continued

1. Heat the oil over medium heat in the soup pot or casserole. Add the onion and carrot and cook, stirring, until the onion is tender, about 5 minutes. Add the minced or pressed garlic, peppers, and about ½ teaspoon salt. Cook, stirring, until the peppers begin to soften, about 5 minutes. Add the sugar, potatoes, and stock or water, along with the bouillon cube if using. Bring to a boil, reduce the heat to low, cover, and simmer for 1 hour.

2. Meanwhile, toast the bread and rub each piece with the cut garlic. Cut into small squares for croutons.

3. Puree the soup however you choose. Season with pepper, heat through, and taste. Does the soup taste vivid? Does it need more salt or garlic? Adjust the seasonings.

4. Serve the soup, garnishing each bowl with a sprinkling of thyme leaves and a handful of croutons.

Note: One Morga vegetable bouillon cube and 6 cups water works deliciously.

Hearty Vegetable Soup

Makes 8 generous main dish servings

Sometimes, when I just don't know what else to serve for a dinner party, I make this incredibly delicious and filling vegetable soup. I season it with the tomato-basil pesto at the very end, and my guests think this is something I've worked on for hours. But it isn't; you just throw everything into the pot and let it simmer. Every repertoire needs a hearty vegetable soup, and here's one for you. It never fails to please.

½ pound green beans or half green beans and half yellow wax beans, trimmed and broken or cut into 1-inch pieces (2 cups)

2 medium-size zucchini, diced

1 large or 2 medium-size onions, peeled and chopped

6 large garlic cloves, peeled and minced or pressed

1 bay leaf

2 large carrots, peeled and chopped

2 celery ribs, chopped

2 leeks, white part only, well washed and sliced

2 medium-size turnips, peeled and diced

1 pound (4 medium-size) new or waxy potatoes, scrubbed and diced

1 pound (4 medium-size) firm, ripe tomatoes, peeled, seeded, and chopped, or one 14-ounce can tomatoes with juice

Get out the following equipment: kitchen string; largest soup pot you have; large measuring cup; chef's knife and cutting board; vegetable peeler; measuring spoons; garlic press or minichop if using

Advance preparation: This soup will hold for hours on top of the stove and can be cooked a day or two ahead of time, up to the adding of the reserved green beans, zucchini, and pasta. It makes a great leftover and freezes well for a few months, although the pasta will become very soggy.

3 quarts water

1 bouquet garni made with 1 bay leaf, a few fresh thyme sprigs, 1 Parmesan rind, and 1 fresh flat-leaf parsley sprig

Salt to taste

One 15-ounce can white beans, drained and rinsed

Freshly ground black pepper to taste

Tomato-Basil Pesto (recipe follows) or ½ cup chopped fresh basil leaves

¼ pound macaroni, fusilli, vermicelli, or broken spaghetti

½ cup freshly grated Parmesan cheese

PER SERVING:
4.3 gm total fat
1.3 gm saturated fat
294 calories
54.4 gm carbohydrates
11.3 gm protein

1. Set aside half the green beans and half the zucchini. Combine the rest of the fresh vegetables, the water, bouquet garni, and about 1 tablespoon salt in the soup pot and bring to a boil. Reduce the heat to low, cover, and simmer for 1½ hours. Stir in the white beans. Taste. Is there enough salt? Garlic? Adjust the seasoning and season with pepper.

2. While the soup is simmering, make the pesto if you are using that for the final enrichment.

3. Add the reserved green beans, zucchini, and pasta to the soup. Simmer until the pasta is cooked al dente and the vegetables are tender but still bright green, about 15 minutes.

4. Serve in wide soup bowls and top each serving with a tablespoon of the pesto, to be stirred into the soup, or a generous sprinkling of chopped basil. Pass the Parmesan at the table. (You can also stir all of the pesto into the soup, but it's more fun to let people do it themselves, and the flavor of the basil paste will be more intense when stirred directly into the individual servings.)

Note: You can omit the Parmesan from the pesto for an even lower-fat version. Use the Parmesan rind in the bouquet garni to get a cheesy flavor.

Variations: You can add other vegetables, like fresh peas, yellow squash, or greens to the soup.

Tomato-Basil Pesto

Makes ½ cup

2 cups tightly packed fresh basil leaves, washed and dried

¼ teaspoon salt

2 large garlic cloves, peeled

1 medium-size firm, ripe tomato, peeled, seeded, and cut into pieces

1 tablespoon olive oil

1 ounce Parmesan cheese (optional), grated (¼ cup)

Freshly ground black pepper to taste

Get out the following equipment: food processor fitted with steel blade; measuring cup and measuring spoons; chef's knife and cutting board

continued

Advance preparation:
This will keep for several days in the refrigerator.

PER 1-TABLESPOON
SERVING:
1.8 gm total fat
0.2 gm saturated fat
23 calories
1.4 gm carbohydrates
0.5 gm protein

Get out the following
equipment: chef's knife
and cutting board; garlic press or minichop if
using; large measuring
cup; large, heavy soup
pot or saucepan

Advance preparation:
The stock can be made
several days ahead of
serving. The soup itself
is a 10-minute operation.

PER SERVING:
11.0 gm total fat
0 gm saturated fat
163 calories
7.8 gm carbohydrates
9.3 gm protein

1. Place the basil and salt in the food processor and turn on the machine. Drop in the garlic cloves and let the processor run until the basil and garlic are finely chopped.
2. Turn off the machine, scrape the leaves down from the sides of the food processor, and turn on again. With the processor running, drop in the tomato and add the olive oil. Process until smooth.
3. Remove from the food processor and stir in the cheese and pepper. Taste and adjust the seasonings. Transfer to a serving bowl or to a covered jar and store in the refrigerator until shortly before serving.

Simple Mexican Soup with Tomato, Onion, and Cilantro

Makes 4 servings

I learned this recipe when I was working on my book *Mexican Light*. It's so easy and delicious that I can't bear to leave it out of this collection too. The flavors of the mint, lime, chile, and cilantro are wonderful, and the soup is thrown together in no time.

2 quarts good-quality defatted chicken or garlic stock (page 155 or 157)
2 fresh spearmint sprigs
1 medium-size white onion, peeled and finely chopped
1 garlic clove, peeled and minced or pressed
1 jalapeño chile, seeded if desired and finely chopped
1 pound firm, ripe tomatoes, peeled, seeded, and finely chopped
½ cup chopped fresh cilantro leaves
Salt to taste
1 small avocado, pitted, peeled, and finely chopped
2 limes, cut into wedges, for serving

1. Combine the stock, spearmint, onion, garlic, and chile in the soup pot or saucepan and bring to a boil. Boil for 5 minutes, then add the tomatoes and cilantro. Reduce the heat to low, simmer for another 5 minutes, and remove from the heat. Taste. Is there enough salt? Adjust the seasoning.
2. Place a spoonful of chopped avocado in each bowl, ladle in the soup, and serve, with lime wedges to be squeezed into the soup if people wish.

Variation: Crumble toasted tortillas into each bowl of soup just before serving.

Cold Turkish-Style Cucumber and Yogurt Soup

Makes 4 servings

This is a perfect summer soup, great for lunch or supper, and quickly made. There is a wait involved while the cucumbers drain, but you can be putting together a salad or having a drink during that time. I prefer the long European cucumbers or the Japanese cucumbers that I find in my farmers' market for this, because they don't require seeding. The better the quality of yogurt you use, the better this soup will be. Taste different brands to determine what you like the best. You will have a much more pungent soup if you pound the garlic in a mortar. If you don't have a mortar, puree it following the directions on page 75.

1 long European cucumber or 2 medium-size regular cucumbers, peeled

1 teaspoon salt, or more to your taste

2 garlic cloves, peeled

3 cups (1½ pounds) good-quality plain nonfat yogurt

¾ cup skim or 1% milk

2 tablespoons minced fresh dill or mint leaves

Freshly ground black pepper to taste (optional)

1 tablespoon olive oil

Fresh dill sprigs or mint leaves for garnish (optional)

Ice cubes for the bowls (optional)

1. If using regular cucumbers, remove the seeds: either quarter them lengthwise and run a knife between the seeds and the flesh of the cucumber or cut them in half lengthwise and scoop out the seeds with a small spoon. Cut the cucumber into very small dice (about ¼ inch). Transfer to a strainer set over a bowl or a colander set in the sink and toss with ¼ teaspoon of the salt. Allow to drain for 30 minutes. Squeeze the cucumber dice to remove more moisture.
2. Pound together the garlic and remaining ¾ teaspoon salt in a mortar and pestle until you have a smooth paste.
3. Place the yogurt in the large bowl and beat in the milk with a whisk or fork. Beat the yogurt until creamy, then stir in the pounded garlic and salt and the cucumber. Taste and add more salt if desired. Stir in the dill, pepper, and olive oil and refrigerate until ready to serve. Garnish each bowl with dill or mint. If you wish, add an ice cube to each bowl.

Get out the following equipment: chef's knife and cutting board; strainer or colander; large bowl; measuring spoons; mortar and pestle; whisk or fork

Advance preparation: This will keep for a few days in the refrigerator but is best freshly made. Stir together to smooth out the yogurt after it has sat, because the cucumbers will continue to release water.

PER SERVING:
4.0 gm total fat
0.8 gm saturated fat
163 calories
20.0 gm carbohydrates
12.5 gm protein

Gazpacho

■

Makes 6 servings

Gazpacho, the marvelous and refreshing cold vegetable soup from Spain, is like a salad in a bowl. Keep it in the refrigerator during tomato season for those hot summer nights when you don't want to cook. Here's the classic Mediterranean version, followed by a Mexican variation.

Get out the following equipment: small bowl; chef's knife and cutting board; large bowl; measuring spoons and large measuring cup; small bowls for garnishes; blender

Advance preparation: This will hold for a day in the refrigerator.

PER SERVING:
1.1 gm total fat
0 gm saturated fat
80 calories
14.9 gm carbohydrates
3.5 gm protein

FOR THE SOUP BASE:

4 thick slices stale French bread, crusts removed (about 1 ounce)

2 pounds (8 medium-size or 4 large) firm, ripe tomatoes, peeled and quartered

4 large garlic cloves, or more to taste, peeled

2 tablespoons red or white wine vinegar, or more to taste

About 1 teaspoon salt, or more to your taste

Freshly ground black pepper to taste

2 cups ice water

¼ cup chopped red or white onion, rinsed in cold water

FOR THE GARNISH AND TEXTURE:

1 small regular cucumber or ⅓ European cucumber, peeled, seeded, and minced

1 medium-size red or green bell pepper, seeded and minced

¾ pound firm, ripe tomatoes, diced

Slivered fresh basil or parsley leaves

1. Soak the bread in water to cover in the small bowl until soft, 5 to 10 minutes. Squeeze out the water.
2. Blend the bread together with the remaining soup base ingredients in the blender until smooth. Taste and adjust the seasonings. Chill for several hours in the large bowl.
3. Toss together the cucumber, green pepper, and tomatoes or pass in separate bowls. Ladle the soup into each bowl, then top with the garnishes. Decorate with slivered basil or parsley and serve.

Mexican Gazpacho

TO THE SOUP BASE, ADD:

2 jalapeño or 4 serrano peppers, seeded for a milder soup

1 teaspoon crushed cumin seeds

TO THE GARNISHES, ADD:

1 to 3 serrano or jalapeño peppers to your taste, seeded for a milder soup
   and minced

¼ cup chopped fresh cilantro leaves

Black-Eyed Pea Soup with Cumin and Cilantro

Makes 6 servings

Black-eyed peas cook quickly and have a comforting, earthy flavor. Cumin and cilantro are marvelous seasonings; the origin of this soup could be the Middle East or Mexico.

1 pound (2 heaped cups) dried black-eyed peas, washed and picked over

1 medium-size onion, peeled and chopped

2 to 4 large garlic cloves, to your taste, peeled and minced or pressed

2 quarts water

1 bay leaf

1 to 2 teaspoons ground cumin, to your taste

Salt to taste

Freshly ground black pepper to taste

Additional water or 1% milk, to taste for thinning the soup

Leaves from 1 bunch cilantro, chopped

1 medium-size red bell pepper, seeded and chopped

½ cup plain nonfat yogurt, drained (page 40) if desired

1. Combine the black-eyed peas, onion, half the garlic, the water, and the bay leaf in the soup pot and bring to a boil. Reduce the heat to low, cover, and simmer for 30 minutes. Add the cumin, salt, the remaining garlic, and black pepper and simmer until the beans are thoroughly tender and fragrant, another 30 minutes.

2. Puree the soup however you choose. If it is very thick, thin out with water or milk. Heat through and taste. Is there enough salt, garlic, and cumin? Stir in half the cilantro and half the red peppers.

3. Serve the soup, garnishing each bowl with a spoonful of yogurt, a sprinkling of red pepper, and a sprinkling of cilantro.

Get out the following equipment: chef's knife and cutting board; measuring spoons and measuring cup; garlic press or minichop if using; large, heavy soup pot; blender, hand blender, or food processor fitted with steel blade

Advance preparation: This will keep in the refrigerator, without the red pepper or cilantro, for 5 days. It can also be frozen for several months.

PER SERVING:
1.0 gm total fat
0.2 gm saturated fat
183 calories
32.8 gm carbohydrates
12.1 gm protein

Lentil Soup with Goat Cheese Garnish

Makes 4 servings

This savory lentil soup has a scrumptious, creamy goat cheese enrichment that is stirred in just before serving.

2 teaspoons olive oil

1 medium-size onion, peeled and chopped

4 garlic cloves, peeled and minced or pressed

2 cups dried brown lentils, washed and picked over

7 cups water

1 bay leaf

Salt to taste

1/3 cup plain nonfat yogurt

3 ounces not-too-salty goat cheese, crumbled (about 1/3 cup)

Freshly ground black pepper to taste

1/4 cup chopped fresh flat-leaf parsley leaves

1. Heat the oil in the soup pot over medium heat. Add the onion and cook, stirring, until softened, 3 to 5 minutes. Add 2 of the garlic cloves and stir together. Add the lentils, water, and bay leaf and bring to a boil. Reduce the heat to low, cover, and simmer for 30 minutes. Add the remaining 2 garlic cloves and 1 to 2 teaspoons or more salt. Cover and simmer for another 15 minutes.

2. Meanwhile, blend together the yogurt and the goat cheese until smooth, using a fork or a food processor.

3. Remove the soup from the heat and remove the bay leaf. Puree the soup coarsely in batches however you choose. Return to the pot, season with pepper, taste, and adjust the salt. Heat through gently and stir in the parsley. Serve, topping each bowl with a generous dollop of the yogurt-and-goat cheese mixture, which diners should stir into their soup.

■ Asian Soup Broths ■

Japanese broths for noodle soups and for miso soups are very quickly made. The first two require a trip to a Japanese market for ingredients that you can keep on hand in your pantry. If no such market exists in your community, you can still make the Japanese soups that follow. Just use vegetable stock (page 156), mushroom broth (page 172), or Very Quick, Very Simple Bouillon with Soy Sauce (page 173).

The first ingredient is packaged dashi, a Japanese soup stock made primarily from dried bonito flakes (bonito, widely used in Japanese cooking, is a fish, a member of the mackerel family, that is dried and shaved into flakes), usually with some added seaweed, salt, and often MSG, but usually not too much of that. It comes in teabag-type pouches that smell quite fishy. But the actual stock is milder than the pouches lead you to believe it will be. Sometimes it tastes a little bitter to my palate, but that's nothing that a teaspoon of sugar won't fix. The dashi sack is simmered for about 10 minutes, according to the directions on the package, then discarded. I find that one dashi bag is sufficient for twice the amount of water called for on the package. The one I've been using calls for 3 cups water, and I make a good stock using 4 to 6 cups with one bag.

The other ingredient is mirin, a sweet Japanese wine; sweet sherry can be substituted. It sweetens the broth slightly, which is what you want if the dashi is bitter. Traditional Japanese broth also calls for a seaweed called *kombu*, which you steep for only about 5 minutes. I've decided that, for our purposes, you can get a perfectly delicious broth without the kombu, so I'm not calling for it. One less thing to buy.

So here are a few stocks for you to use for the Japanese Meals-in-a-Bowl recipes that follow.

Get out the following equipment: **large saucepan; large measuring cup; measuring spoons; tongs; strainer and small bowl for the recipe with the dried mushrooms**

Advance preparation: **All of these stocks will keep in the refrigerator for 3 days and can be frozen for a few months.**

Plain Dashi

■

Makes 3 to 6 cups

1 dashi bag

3 to 6 cups water

1 teaspoon soy sauce

½ to 1 teaspoon sugar, to your taste

Simmer the dashi bag in the water in the saucepan over low heat, following the instructions on the packet. Discard the bag and add the soy sauce. Taste. Is it bitter? Add sugar if necessary.

PER **1**- TO **2**-CUP SERVING:
0 gm total fat
0 gm saturated fat
5 calories
1.2 gm carbohydrates
0.1 gm protein

Dashi Broth with Mirin

Makes 5 cups

This is based on a recipe by Linda Burum, from her book *Asian Pasta* (Aris Books, Berkeley, 1985).

PER 1-CUP SERVING:
0 gm total fat
0 gm saturated fat
19 calories
2.3 gm carbohydrates
0.2 gm protein

   5 cups water
   1 dashi bag
   1 teaspoon sugar
   3 tablespoons mirin or sweet sherry
   1 tablespoon soy sauce, or more to taste

Bring the water to a simmer in the saucepan and add the dashi bag. Cover and simmer for 10 minutes or follow the directions on the packet. Discard the bag. Add the remaining ingredients and bring to a simmer. Cover and simmer for another 10 minutes. Taste and add more soy sauce if desired.

Mushroom Broth

Makes 5 cups

PER SERVING:
0 gm total fat
0 gm saturated fat
4 calories
0.6 gm carbohydrates
0.4 gm protein

   5 cups water, defatted chicken stock (page 155), vegetable stock (page 156),
      or dashi broth (page 171) (may use canned broth)
   10 dried shiitake mushrooms
   2 tablespoons soy sauce

Place the mushrooms in the measuring cup. Bring the water or stock to a boil in the saucepan and pour it over the mushrooms. Let sit for 30 minutes. Drain (through a cheesecloth-lined strainer if the mushrooms are sandy). Squeeze the mushrooms over the broth and then seal them in a zippered plastic bag and refrigerate to add to soups and stir-fries. Return the broth to the pot and add the soy sauce. Taste and add more soy sauce if desired.

Mushroom Dashi

■

Makes 6 cups

1 quart plain dashi (page 171)
2 cups mushroom broth (page 172) made with water

Combine the two stocks and use for Japanese soups.

PER 1-CUP SERVING:
0 gm total fat
0 gm saturated fat
3 calories
0.6 gm carbohydrates
0.2 gm protein

Very Quick, Very Simple Bouillon with Soy Sauce

■

Makes 5 cups

This stock requires no work at all, just good-quality bouillon cubes, such as the Swiss Morga bouillon. Organic food stores stock these.

5 cups water
1 vegetable bouillon cube
¼ cup soy sauce, preferably Kikkoman or tamari
Salt to taste (only if using unsalted bouillon)
8 dried shiitake mushrooms (optional)

Bring the water to a boil in the saucepan, add the bouillon cube, and, when it is dissolved, stir in the soy sauce. Taste and add salt as desired. If using the mushrooms, simmer them in the stock for 30 minutes, then drain through a fine strainer, lined with cheesecloth if the mushrooms are sandy.

PER 1-CUP SERVING:
0 gm total fat
0 gm saturated fat
10 calories
1.4 gm carbohydrates
0.8 gm protein

■ Three Japanese Meals-in-a-Bowl ■

These soups are inspired by one of my favorite restaurants in the Bay Area, O Chame. My favorite meals at this beautiful, quiet Berkeley restaurant were called "Meal-in-a-Bowl." A large ceramic bowl contains a fragrant Japanese broth, with noodles (either soba or udon) and a vegetable and protein combination, such as spinach and tofu or salmon, daikon, and chicken, smoked trout and bean sprouts. It really was a meal in a bowl, comforting and filling, yet light. Now that I no longer live in Berkeley, I'll just have to make do with these renditions.

In Japan noodles are cooked separately, using a method called the "add-water" method. They are then added to soups or stir-fries as needed. The directions for this follow, but I'm also giving you the option of cooking the noodles right in the stock, which will mean one less pot to wash but will make it harder to get them evenly distributed among the bowls. You can always cook noodles ahead and keep them in the refrigerator to add to soups or to use as the basis for another dish.

Cooking Asian Noodles

Bring 3 to 4 quarts of water to a boil in a large pot. Add the noodles gradually, so that the water remains at a boil, and stir with a long-handled wooden spoon to be sure they don't stick together. When all the noodles have been added and the water comes back to a rolling boil, add 1 cup cold tap water. Let the water come back to a rolling boil and add another cup of water. Bring back to a boil again. Repeat one more time. By the time the water comes to a boil after the third cup of water is added, the noodles should be done. Take one with a pair of tongs, rinse it with cold water, and taste to see if it is cooked al dente. When the noodles are cooked al dente, drain and rinse with cold water. If not using right away, transfer to a zippered plastic bag or a tightly covered bowl and refrigerate.

These soups are best served in wide soup bowls or in quite large deep ones. You can arrange each type of food side by side or pile them on top of each other. I prefer the side-by-side look, with the broth spooned over all.

Note: Some packages of soba have the noodles wrapped in individual bundles. This is convenient because each bundle weighs 1.5 ounces, which is one portion.

Tofu and Spinach Meal-in-a-Bowl

Makes 4 servings

5 to 6 cups Japanese stock of choice (pages 171–173)

6 ounces soba, udon, or spaghettini, preferably cooked (see above)

½ pound fresh spinach, stemmed and leaves well washed

¾ pound firm tofu, cut into 1-inch cubes

1 bunch scallions, white part and about ⅓ green part, thinly sliced and kept
separate

1. Bring the stock to a simmer. Use 5 cups if you have already cooked the noodles, 6 cups if you are cooking the noodles in the stock. Add the noodles if they have not been cooked, and simmer until cooked al dente, 5 to 7 minutes. Add the spinach, tofu, and scallion whites. Simmer for 2 minutes and turn off the heat.

Advance preparation:
For all three of the meals-in-a-bowl, the stock and noodles can be prepared up to 3 days ahead. The spinach can be stemmed and washed, then dried, a couple of days ahead.

Get out the following equipment: **chef's knife and cutting board; heavy soup pot; pasta pot if cooking the noodles separately; kitchen scale; large measuring cup; tongs; ladle**

PER SERVING:
8.0 gm total fat
1.2 gm saturated fat
288 calories
39.2 gm carbohydrates
21.9 gm protein

2. Distribute the noodles, spinach, and tofu among 4 bowls. Ladle in the broth, top with the scallion greens, and serve.

Note: If you cook the noodles in the broth, they will absorb liquid, and you will have less of it for the bowl. This is why I call for 6 cups if cooking the noodles in it. You could add a bit more water if you want more broth in your bowl.

Meal-in-a-Bowl with Bean Sprouts or Spinach (or both!) and Salmon

PER SERVING:
7.82 gm total fat
1.2 gm saturated fat
326 calories
35.6 gm carbohydrates
31.0 gm protein

Makes 4 servings

5 to 6 cups Japanese stock of your choice (pages 171–173)
1 thin slice fresh ginger, peeled
6 ounces soba, udon, or spaghettini, preferably cooked (page 174)
1 pound salmon fillet, trimmed of fat and skin and cut into 4 equal pieces
½ pound fresh spinach, stemmed and well washed, or 2 cups mung bean sprouts
1 bunch scallions, white part and about ⅓ of the green part, thinly sliced and kept separate

1. Combine the stock and ginger in a saucepan or soup pot and bring to a simmer. Use 5 cups of the stock if you have already cooked the noodles, 6 if you're cooking them in the stock. If you are cooking the noodles in the stock, add them and cook until al dente, 5 to 7 minutes.
2. Add the salmon, spinach if using, and the scallion whites, cover, and turn off the heat. Let sit without removing the cover for 5 to 8 minutes. The salmon should be just cooked through and the spinach wilted.
3. Divide the salmon, noodles, and spinach and/or sprouts evenly among 4 bowls. Ladle in the broth. Sprinkle on the scallion greens and serve.

Smoked Trout and Spinach or Daikon Radish

Makes 4 servings

Daikon radishes are long white radishes, used extensively in Japanese and Chinese cooking. They have a mild flavor and pleasing texture. They are available wherever Asian vegetables are sold.

continued

5 to to 6 cups Japanese stock of your choice (pages 171–173)

6 ounces soba, udon, or spaghettini, preferably cooked (page 174)

½ pound fresh spinach, stemmed and well washed, or 2 cups grated daikon radish, or both

½ pound smoked trout (four 2-ounce fillets), skin removed

1 bunch scallions, white part and about ⅓ of the green part, thinly sliced and kept separate

1. Bring the stock to a simmer. Use 5 cups if you have already cooked the noodles, 6 cups if you are cooking the noodles in the stock. Add the noodles if they have not been cooked and simmer until cooked al dente, 5 to 7 minutes. Add the spinach if using, the trout, and scallion whites. Cover, turn off the heat, and let sit until the spinach wilts, about 3 minutes.

2. Distribute the trout, noodles, spinach, and/or daikon radish among 4 bowls. Ladle in the stock, sprinkle on the scallion greens, and serve.

Chinese Cabbage Soup with Tofu or Chicken

Makes 4 to 6 servings

Chinese cabbage, also called Napa cabbage, keeps very well in the refrigerator, so you can buy one when you do your weekly marketing and use it in stir-fries, salads, and this soup through the week.

6 cups Ginger-Vegetable Stock (page 156) or Very Quick, Very Simple Bouillon with Soy Sauce (with 1 cup water added to the recipe, page 173)

½ medium-size head Chinese or Napa cabbage, cored, halved lengthwise, and sliced crosswise into strips about 1 inch wide (about 4 cups)

2 to 3 teaspoons peeled and minced or grated fresh ginger, to your taste

1 bunch scallions, both white and green parts, thinly sliced and kept separate

½ pound medium or firm tofu, diced, or 1 whole chicken breast, poached (page 147) and shredded (1½ to 1¾ cups)

Salt to taste

¼ cup chopped fresh cilantro leaves

Bring the stock to a simmer in the soup pot and add the cabbage, ginger, and scallion whites. Allow to simmer over low heat until the cabbage is just wilted, about 3 minutes. Stir in the tofu or chicken and simmer for another minute. Taste. Is there enough salt? Stir in the cilantro and serve.

Noodle Soup with Tofu or Chicken,
Dried Mushrooms, and Peas

■

Makes 6 servings

This is a quick soup you can play around with. You can use shredded chicken breast or tofu, snow peas or regular peas (frozen or fresh), buckwheat noodles (soba) or vermicelli or angel hair pasta. Whatever vegetables go into it, it will be light and delicious and nourishing, pungent with ginger and cilantro, with a broth that is almost meaty.

> ½ ounce (½ cup) dried shiitake mushrooms (about 8)
>
> 2 cups boiling water
>
> 1 quart Very Quick, Very Simple Bouillon with Soy Sauce (page 173),
> defatted chicken stock (page 155) or canned broth, or vegetable stock
> (page 156)
>
> 2 tablespoons soy sauce, preferably Kikkoman or tamari (omit if using Very
> Quick, Very Simple Bouillon with Soy Sauce)
>
> 2 teaspoons peeled and chopped or grated fresh ginger
>
> 6 ounces buckwheat noodles (soba), vermicelli, or angel hair pasta, already
> cooked if desired (see Note)
>
> ½ pound medium or firm tofu, diced, or 1 whole chicken breast, poached
> (page 000) and shredded (1½ to 1¾ cups)
>
> 1½ cups fresh or thawed frozen peas or ¼ pound (2 cups) snow peas, trimmed
> Salt to taste
>
> 6 tablespoons chopped fresh cilantro leaves

1. Place the dried mushrooms in the bowl and pour on the boiling water. Let sit until the mushrooms have softened, 15 to 30 minutes. Strain through a cheesecloth-lined strainer set over a bowl and squeeze the mushrooms to extract as much fragrant liquid as possible. Rinse the mushrooms in several changes of water to remove all grit.

2. Transfer the soaking water to a measuring cup and add water to measure 2 cups. Combine this with the stock in the soup pot. Slice the mushroom caps (discard the tough stems) and add to the stock, along with the additional soy sauce, if using, and the ginger. Bring to a boil, stir in the noodles, tofu or chicken, and peas or snow peas, and simmer until the noodles are cooked al dente, about 5 minutes. Taste and add salt if needed. Stir in the cilantro and serve.

Note: You can cook the noodles ahead, following the instructions on page 174. If you do this, simply divide the cooked noodles among soup bowls and ladle the soup over them.

Get out the following equipment: bowl for soaking the mushrooms; strainer (lined with cheesecloth if mushrooms are very sandy); measuring cup and measuring spoons; garlic press or mini-chop if using; chef's knife and cutting board; heavy soup pot; long-handled wooden spoon

Advance preparation: The stock and the mushroom broth will hold for a few days in the refrigerator, as will cooked noodles. If using poached chicken, the cooked chicken will also hold for a few days in the refrigerator. The soup should be made just before serving.

PER SERVING:
2.2 gm total fat
0.3 gm saturated fat
168 calories
30.2 gm carbohydrates
9.9 gm protein

Clear Soup with Lemongrass and Shrimp

Makes 4 main-dish servings or 6 starter servings

This is a delightful soup with Thai flavors. You might think shelling shrimp is a pain, but once you taste this incredibly easy stock you can make just by simmering the shells, you'll decide it's worth it. You can make this more or less hot depending on how many chiles you use and whether or not you seed them. Lemongrass, a citrusy-pungent bulb, can be found wherever Asian produce is sold. It gives this soup its Thai flavor.

Advance preparation: The shrimp shell stock will keep for a day in the refrigerator, and you can also freeze it for a few months. However, the peeled shrimp won't keep for more than a day in the refrigerator. You can make the soup up to the addition of the tomatoes and lemongrass, then hold it for several hours before bringing it back to a simmer and adding the shrimp.

PER SERVING:
2.6 gm total fat
0.4 gm saturated fat
172 calories
10.9 gm carbohydrates
24.8 gm protein

1 pound fresh medium-size shrimp, with shells on

6 cups water

Salt to taste

2 fresh spearmint sprigs

1 medium-size white onion, peeled and finely chopped

2 hot green chiles (serrano, jalapeño, or Thai), or more to taste, seeded for a milder soup if desired and finely chopped

1 pound firm, ripe tomatoes, peeled, seeded, and finely chopped

2 stalks fresh lemongrass, bottom white part only, hard outer layer discarded, and the rest very thinly sliced

1 to 2 tablespoons fresh lime juice, to your taste

½ cup chopped fresh cilantro leaves

1 small avocado (optional), pitted, peeled, and finely chopped

2 limes, cut into wedges

1. Peel and devein the shrimp, saving the shells (see page 299).
2. Bring the water to a boil in the soup pot and add the shrimp shells. Skim off any foam that rises to the top and reduce the heat to a simmer. Cover and simmer for 30 minutes. Strain into a bowl through a cheesecloth-lined strainer. Discard the shrimp shells. Measure and add water if necessary to measure 6 cups. Return to the soup pot and add salt, beginning with about 1½ teaspoons.
3. Add the spearmint, onion, and chiles to the pot and bring to a boil. Boil for 5 minutes, then add the tomatoes and lemongrass. When the liquid comes back to a boil, reduce the heat to low and simmer for another 5 minutes. Stir in the shrimp and simmer until they turn pink, 3 to 5 minutes. Stir in the lime juice and cilantro and remove from the heat. Taste. Is there enough salt? (I usually add a bit more.) Lime juice?
4. Place a spoonful of chopped avocado in each bowl if you wish, ladle in the soup, and serve, passing lime wedges.

Eggs

∎

Why Eggs Have a Place in My Low-Fat Repertoire

Eggs are not a particularly high-fat food; they're just a high-cholesterol food. They've gotten a bad rap ever since we began to become concerned about cholesterol. But it turns out that saturated fat, the kind found in red meat and full-fat dairy products, has more of an effect on blood cholesterol than dietary cholesterol does.

I think eggs are wonderful. They're an inexpensive and low-calorie source of perfect protein (a perfect protein supplies all the amino acids in the right balance and is the most efficient type of protein for your body to use), and they're loaded with vitamins and minerals. They also taste great, cook quickly, and are the basis for some of the most appealing dishes, as you'll see in the pages that follow.

The American Heart Association recommends no more than four eggs a week for healthy people. That's an easy range to stick with here. With the exception of scrambled eggs (page 197), none of my egg dishes contains even two whole eggs per serving. And many of them give you the option of substituting egg whites for some of the yolks.

Which brings me to the next lesson:

How to Separate Eggs

Different cooks do it different ways. It helps if you don't mind getting egg on your hands. Then you can just break an egg into a bowl and gently lift out the yolk, or you can break the egg and let the yolk rest in your hand as you let the white slip between your fingers into a bowl.

The "pro" way is to crack the egg deftly at the equator against the surface of your bowl and separate it into two equal halves. The yolk will be in one half. Holding the egg over your bowl, pass the yolk carefully from one half to the other, letting the white run into the bowl. Discard the yolk or transfer it to another bowl (and cook it up for your dog or cat). When separating more than one egg, transfer the whites to a bowl as you do each egg, so that if you louse up and break the yolk on, say, the third egg, you won't lose all the whites (this matters only if you have to beat egg whites until stiff for a recipe). You can also invest in an egg separator. I've never had one myself.

Whichever way you choose to separate eggs, they will separate more easily if they are cold. So if a recipe calls for separated eggs at room temperature, separate them while cold, then let them come to room temperature.

Buying and Storing Eggs: Egg Safety

Salmonella has been in the headlines a lot. People can become infected by uncooked or soft-cooked eggs. In actual fact, the risk is very slim: two in 10,000 eggs were contaminated at the last survey, and these were battery eggs, raised on huge poultry farms where the chickens have no room to move around. I think that the best prevention against infected eggs is to buy free-range eggs, which are produced by smaller egg farmers. But the *best* reason to buy free-range eggs is that they taste at least ten times better than battery eggs. The yolk is a much deeper yellow color, the whites and the shells are firmer, they make fluffier everything, they have real flavor. I can't emphasize enough what a difference there is between the two. Since you aren't going to be eating that many eggs, they ought to taste and look good!

Be sure to keep the eggs at the top of your shopping bag when you go grocery shopping. When you get home, don't take them out of the carton. Throw away those egg holders in your refrigerator. Eggs absorb flavors through their thin shells, and the door is not the coldest part of the fridge. Put them in a cool part of the refrigerator, in their container.

Hard-Cooked Eggs

∎

There is more than one way to hard-cook an egg. You can boil it (so it can be accurately called "hard-boiled"), or you can bring it to a boil, then off the heat, and let it sit with the lid tightly on the pot for 20 minutes. I frankly haven't found that one method is superior to the other, but some cooks say that with the latter method you don't get that dark separating line between the yolk and the white. You don't get it when you don't boil the eggs too hard for too long either. So you decide.

1. Place eggs in a saucepan that is big enough to hold them in a single layer and to cover them by about an inch of water. Cover with cold water. (It's important to put the eggs in the saucepan *first*, then add the water. If you drop them into the water, they may break when they hit the bottom of the pan.)
2. Place the pan over medium-high heat and bring to a boil.
   Method 1: Turn the heat down to a simmer or a very slow boil and cook for 10 minutes.
   Method 2: Cover the pot with a tight-fitting lid or a plate and remove from the heat. Let sit for 20 minutes for large eggs, 17 for medium.
3. *Important:* Drain the eggs and run under cold water for several minutes—either in a colander or in a bowl or in the pot in which they cooked, after you tip the hot water out. If you don't cool the eggs down like this, right away, they'll be difficult to peel. If you do this, the white membrane between the whites of the eggs and the shell will come away easily from the eggs so that you can peel off the shell neatly, which will be important if you aren't chopping the eggs.
4. Crack the eggs by tapping them gently and turning them on your counter or cutting board. Then peel away the shell and the thin membrane between the shell and the egg.

Soft-Boiled Eggs

∎

Soft-boiled eggs are luxurious in the way that poached eggs are. It's that soft, runny yolk, which should be the bright yellow-orange of a good free-range egg. It coats the bits of toast that I dip into it in the most satisfying way. Who needs butter? This is the egg I make when I want an egg in the morning. If you get hooked on these, you'll want to treat yourself to a few egg cups (although you can just as easily scoop the soft-boiled egg into a bowl). The process of making soft-boiled eggs is different from hard-cooked. Timing is

Advance preparation:
Hard-cooked eggs will last for a week in the refrigerator. Mark them with an X so you don't confuse them with the uncooked eggs.

PER SERVING:
5.3 gm total fat
1.6 gm saturated fat
78 calories
0.6 gm carbohydrates
6.3 gm protein

PER SERVING:
5.0 gm total fat
1.6 gm saturated fat
75 calories
0.6 gm carbohydrates
6.2 gm protein

everything here, so you have to put them directly into boiling water and begin the countdown right away. If you don't prick the eggs with a pin first, they will crack when you put them into the hot water. A pinprick gives the expanding air that would have broken the eggshell an escape hatch. A pushpin works well. I also submerge the eggs in warm to hot tap water before I spoon them into the boiling water to try to minimize the thermal shock. The size of the eggs will determine the timing: a large egg will be perfect, with a runny yolk and a solid white, in 4 minutes. A medium-size egg will overcook in that time and needs 3 to 3½ minutes. A jumbo egg needs 4½ minutes.

1. Bring a pot of water large enough to hold your eggs in one layer to a rolling boil.
2. While you're waiting for the water to boil, transfer the eggs from their carton to a bowl of warm water. Using a pushpin, prick the bottom of the wide end of each egg. Make sure you aren't squeezing the egg with the hand you're holding it in, or it will shatter all over the place when the pin goes in. Set the timer for 4 minutes for large eggs, 3½ for medium, 3 for small, and 4½ for jumbo.
3. Turn the heat down until the water is at a medium boil. Put an egg in a spoon and gently lower it into the water. Repeat with the remaining eggs. Start the timer as soon as the first egg goes into the water.
4. When the timer goes off, immediately drain the eggs and transfer to a bowl of cold water. Run cold water over the eggs for about a minute, then serve with salt, pepper, and toast.

To serve: If you have egg cups, then set the eggs in the cups and serve. If you don't, then serve them in bowls. You can serve them in the shell or scoop them out. Break them around the middle using a knife to crack the shell, then pull the halves apart and scoop out the egg into the bowl.

Soft-Boiled Eggs on a Salad

Run the eggs under the cold water for a couple of minutes after the timer goes off. Then carefully peel the egg and set it on the salad. Or break in half and scoop out onto the salad.

Egg Salad

■

Makes enough for 4 main-dish servings or 8 sandwiches

Egg salad doesn't have to be all about whole eggs and mayonnaise. A delicious salad can be made with a lower-fat dressing, and you can leave out some of the yolks and never miss them. Fresh herbs make this vivid. This is an egg salad with texture, which can be increased by adding the optional bell pepper.

8 large eggs
Salt and freshly ground black pepper to taste
¼ to ½ cup chopped fresh herbs, to your taste, such as flat-leaf parsley, tarragon, basil, or dill
2 celery ribs, finely chopped
1 small red onion, peeled, finely chopped, and rinsed
1 medium-size green or red bell pepper (optional), seeded and finely chopped
1 tablespoon red wine vinegar
1 teaspoon Dijon mustard
4 teaspoons Best Foods or Hellmann's mayonnaise (these are the only brands that are not sweet and taste like what, in my opinion, mayonnaise should taste like)
¼ cup plain nonfat yogurt
Lettuce leaves or arugula for the platter or bowl (optional)
Radishes or cherry tomatoes for garnish (optional)

1. Hard-cook the eggs, following the instructions on page 181. Peel and cut in half. Remove and discard the yolks from 4 of the eggs (or more if you wish). Chop the eggs and egg whites together finely and transfer to the mixing bowl. Sprinkle with salt and pepper. Add the herbs, celery, onion, and optional bell pepper.
2. Stir together the vinegar, mustard, mayonnaise, and yogurt. Season with salt and pepper. Toss with the egg mixture until combined evenly. Taste. Is there enough salt and pepper? Could it use more herbs or onion?
3. Transfer to the salad bowl or platter, lined with lettuce leaves or arugula and garnished with radishes or cherry tomatoes if you wish, and serve, or chill and serve later. Or use for sandwiches.

Get out the following equipment: **a pot for cooking the eggs; chef's knife and cutting board; measuring cup or jar and measuring spoons; whisk or fork; medium-size mixing bowl; salad bowl or platter and servers**

Advance preparation: **This will keep for a few days in the refrigerator, but the herbs will fade out a bit.**

PER SERVING:
13.9 gm total fat
3.7 gm saturated fat
206 calories
5.8 gm carbohydrates
14.0 gm protein

Egg Salad with Cumin or Curry

Stir ½ to 1 teaspoon ground cumin or curry powder, or ½ to 1 teaspoon of each, to your taste, into the dressing, and proceed as directed

To Serve as an Hors d'Oeuvre

Cut squares of red bell pepper and toast slices of baguette or pita triangles, top with spoonfuls of the egg salad, and serve on a platter.

Stuffed Hard-Cooked Eggs

Makes 12 halves; 6 hors d'oeuvre servings

There's no hard-and-fast rule that a stuffed (or "deviled") hard-cooked egg has to be filled with egg yolks made even more caloric and high-fat with mayonnaise. Hard-cooked egg whites make such convenient boats for fillings. They can be cut into quarters once they're filled, for smaller, daintier hors d'oeuvres.

6 large eggs

SMOKED SALMON OR TROUT FILLING:

3 ounces smoked salmon or trout (about ½ cup chopped)

2 tablespoons plain nonfat yogurt

1 tablespoon fresh lemon juice, or more to taste

½ to 1 teaspoon Dijon mustard (optional), to your taste

Salt to taste

Chopped fresh dill for garnish

Get out the following equipment: saucepan for cooking the eggs; food processor fitted with steel blade; spatula; measuring spoons; chef's knife and cutting board or scissors for the dill; spoon or pastry bag; platter

PER SERVING:
2.3 gm total fat
0.7 gm saturated fat
56 calories
1.0 gm carbohydrates
7.3 gm protein

1. Hard-cook the eggs as described on page 181. Peel and cut in half lengthwise. Carefully lift out the yolks. Discard all but two.
2. Place the salmon or trout in the food processor and pulse until finely chopped. Add the hard-cooked egg yolks and process until well blended. Add the yogurt, lemon juice, and optional mustard and process until smooth. Season with salt.
3. Pipe or spoon the filling into the halved egg whites. If you wish, cut these in half lengthwise, for quarters. Place on the platter, sprinkle with dill, and serve.

EGG SALAD FILLING:

Fill the egg white halves with ½ cup of the egg salad, preferably the version with cumin or curry powder.

MASHED POTATO AND PESTO FILLING:

¼ pound waxy potatoes, such as Yukon Gold or red potatoes, peeled

2 to 4 tablespoons milk, as needed

Salt to taste

3 tablespoons prepared pesto

Freshly ground black pepper to taste

Slivered fresh basil leaves or small basil leaves for garnish

1. Steam or boil the potatoes until tender, 15 to 20 minutes (see page 52). Drain and mash with the fork or potato masher. Add the milk, season with salt, and mash together until the mixture is smooth. Stir in the pesto. Taste and adjust the seasoning with salt and pepper.

2. Pipe or spoon into the egg white halves, sprinkle with pepper, garnish with basil, and serve.

Poached Eggs (Elaine Corn's Method)

Makes 4 eggs

One of the things I love about my work is that, after 25 years, I'm always finding better, easier ways to do things. Back in the seventies I spent a week mastering poached eggs, and until recently I had pretty much stuck to the method I learned then. But when I was working on this chapter, I came across a method for poaching eggs in *Cook's Illustrated* magazine, in an article by my friend and colleague Elaine Corn. It took only one try for me to be converted. Using this method, there is very little of the "feathering" of the egg whites that I used to get poaching eggs in a saucepan. The tops of the yolks are nicely enrobed in their whites, as they should be, and the method is easy.

I love poached eggs; a deep yellow, free-range egg, poached just until the white sets over the yolk, then served on top of a piece of toast, is about as fine a breakfast as I can think of. But breakfast is far from the only place for poached eggs; they're great atop a salad, and when added to a bowl of soup the soup becomes a main-dish meal. They also make a heavenly topping for vegetables like asparagus or spinach (see the recipes that follow); the yolk runs out over the vegetables, resulting in a luxurious sauce.

Get out the following equipment: saucepan for cooking the eggs; the equipment needed for the egg salad (page 183); spoon; platter

Get out the following equipment: saucepan or steamer for cooking the potatoes; potato masher or fork; measuring spoons; spoon or pastry bag

Advance preparation: All the fillings and hard-cooked eggs will hold for a few days in the refrigerator. Fill the eggs the day you are serving them. They will hold for a few hours.

PER SERVING:
3.8 gm total fat
0.7 gm saturated fat
75 calories
5.1 gm carbohydrates
4.8 gm protein

Get out the following equipment: 8- or 10-inch nonstick skillet; lid or a plate that will fit snugly over the top of the skillet; 4 teacups or coffee cups with handles; measuring spoons; slotted spoon, skimmer, or spatula; medium-size bowl; kitchen towel

Advance preparation: Will keep for 3 days in a bowl of water in the refrigerator. To reheat, bring a pan of water to a boil, carefully transfer the eggs to the pan, turn off the heat, cover, and leave for 30 seconds.

Eggs
185

continued

PER SERVING:
5.0 gm total fat
1.6 gm saturated fat
75 calories
0.6 gm carbohydrates
6.2 gm protein

Having a nonstick skillet is essential for this method. It eliminates the need for buttering the bottom of a saucepan, and the recipe goes quickly because it doesn't require as much time as it does for water to come to a boil in a saucepan. Vinegar is added to the water for a reason: it lowers the pH of the water, which in turn lowers the temperature at which the yolks and whites set. This means that the water doesn't have to be at a rolling boil, which can cause the whites to spread about and require trimming later (that's what I meant by feathering). I use the same pan that I use for omelets, an 8-inch heavy nonstick skillet. You can poach two or four eggs at a time in a pan this size. Before you begin, make sure you have a lid or plate that will fit snugly over the skillet, because it must be covered tightly for the eggs to cook once you've turned off the heat.

4 medium-size, large, or jumbo eggs
½ teaspoon salt
1 tablespoon vinegar

1. Fill the skillet with water, up to about ½ inch shy of the rim. Bring to a boil.
2. Meanwhile, break an egg into each cup.
3. When the water comes to a boil, add the salt and vinegar. Set the timer for 3½ minutes for medium eggs, 4 minutes for large eggs, and 4½ minutes for jumbo eggs. Turn the heat down to medium so the water isn't bubbling furiously, because your hands will come close to it for a few seconds. Take a cup in each hand, lower the bottom gently into the water, then turn the lips into the water and tip the eggs in. Turn off the heat and cover the pan (if cooking on an electric stove, remove the pan from the burner). Start the timer. Fill the bowl with cold water.
4. When the timer goes off, carefully scoop up the eggs, one at a time, in the slotted spoon or skimmer or with a spatula. Transfer to the bowl of cold water to stop the cooking, then lift the eggs from the water, using the slotted spoon or gently in the palm of your hand, and drain briefly on a folded towel. Return the pan to the burner and repeat the process with the other 2 eggs. If you wish, you can tip 2 eggs into the water, then immediately tip the next 2 eggs into the water, and cook all four together. Serve on toast or in a bowl.

Italian-Style Asparagus with Poached Eggs and Parmesan

Makes 4 servings

This is a delicious one-pot light supper that can be put together quickly after work. It's served all over Italy when asparagus is in season. In the authentic dish, the eggs are usually fried, but why mess up another pan? You can cook the asparagus, then poach the eggs in the same pan. The idea here is to swish the asparagus spears around in the egg and Parmesan, which make an instant and nourishing sauce.

2 pounds asparagus
1 tablespoon vinegar
Salt to taste
4 large eggs
Freshly ground black pepper to taste
¼ cup freshly grated Parmesan cheese

1. Trim the ends off the asparagus by bending the tough ends back until they snap off. Rinse. Place the steamer above 1 inch of water in the non-stick pan and bring to a boil. When the water comes to a boil, cover and steam until tender, 5 to 8 minutes. Remove the steamer from the pan and fill the pan with water to within about ½ inch of the rim. Wrap the asparagus in a kitchen towel to keep warm.
2. Warm the plates in the microwave or a 200°F oven.
3. Bring the water to a boil. Add the vinegar and ½ teaspoon salt. Set the timer for 4 minutes. Turn the heat down to medium so the water isn't bubbling furiously. Break the eggs into the teacups. Start the timer and slip each one into the water. Poach as instructed on page 185. Fill a bowl with cold water. When the timer goes off, carefully scoop up the eggs, one at a time, in the slotted spoon or skimmer. Transfer to the bowl to stop the cooking. Drain on a folded kitchen towel.
4. Meanwhile, distribute the asparagus among the warm plates. Place a poached egg on top of the asparagus on each place. Sprinkle with salt, pepper, and the Parmesan cheese and serve at once.

Get out the following equipment: **lidded non-stick pan large enough to cook the asparagus; steamer; 4 teacups or coffee cups with handles; grater; slotted spoon or skimmer; 4 plates; kitchen towel**

Advance preparation: **The asparagus could already be cooked and will hold for a few days in the refrigerator. To reheat it, dip it into simmering water for 30 seconds before you poach the eggs.**

PER SERVING:
6.9 gm total fat
2.6 gm saturated fat
143 calories
9.8 gm carbohydrates
12.9 gm protein

Get out the following equipment: cutting board; bread knife and chef's knife; large pot; medium-size bowl filled with cold water; 8- or 10-inch nonstick skillet; toaster; 4 teacups or coffee cups with handles; 4 plates

Advance preparation: The poached eggs and cooked spinach will hold separately for 3 days in the refrigerator. To reheat, dip into simmering water for 30 seconds and remove with a slotted spoon.

PER SERVING:
6.9 gm total fat
1.9 gm saturated fat
229 calories
28.4 gm carbohydrates
16.1 gm protein

Spinach with Poached Eggs

Makes 4 servings

A much more elaborate French version of this dish has you creaming the spinach and covering the spinach and poached eggs with a soufflé mixture. Why work so hard? This light version has the essentials that I love: cooked fresh spinach, bathed with the sauce of a poached egg yolk.

4 thick slices country bread
1 large garlic clove, cut in half
1 tablespoon plus ½ teaspoon salt
2 pounds spinach, stemmed and leaves washed
1 tablespoon vinegar
Freshly ground black pepper to taste
4 large eggs
2 tablespoons freshly grated Parmesan cheese (optional)

1. Toast the bread and rub with the cut side of the garlic clove as soon as it is cool enough to handle. Divide among the plates.
2. Fill the pot with water, bring to a boil, and add 1 tablespoon of the salt and the spinach. As soon as the water comes back to a boil, remove the spinach from the water with a slotted spoon and transfer to the bowl of cold water. Drain and gently squeeze the spinach. Chop the spinach coarsely and season to taste with salt and pepper. Divide into 4 portions and place on top of the croutons.
3. Set the timer to 4 minutes. Fill the skillet with water and bring to a boil. Turn down the heat to medium so the water isn't boiling furiously. Break the eggs into the teacups, then slip each into the water. Start the timer and poach as instructed on page 185. Drain and place a poached egg on top of each spinach portion. Sprinkle with salt, pepper, and the Parmesan, if using, and serve hot.

Poached Huevos Rancheros

Makes 4 servings

This is a lighter version of a classic. Poaching the eggs not only absolves you of using oil for frying but allows you to cook the eggs ahead if you're doing this for a brunch, so you can sleep a little later. Mexican queso fresco is a crumbly, light white cheese that can be found in supermarkets that sell Mexican ingredients. You can substitute Feta cheese if you can't find it.

Get out the following
equipment: **chef's knife
and cutting board;
blender; large heavy
nonstick skillet and
wooden spoon; 8- or
10-inch nonstick skil-
let; 4 teacups or coffee
cups with handles; slot-
ted spoon or skimmer;
medium-size bowl; 4
plates**

Advance preparation:
**The sauce can be made
and the eggs poached a
day or two ahead of
time. The rest is a last-
minute operation.**

PER SERVING:
*9.4 gm total fat
2.0 gm saturated fat
266 calories
34.5 gm carbohydrates
11.6 gm protein*

FOR THE SAUCE:

2 pounds (8 medium-size or 4 large) ripe tomatoes or one 28-ounce can
   tomatoes, peeled, seeded, and coarsely chopped

2 to 3 serrano chiles or 1 to 2 jalapeño chiles, to your taste, seeded for a
   milder sauce and chopped

2 garlic cloves, peeled

2 teaspoons olive or canola oil

½ small onion, peeled and chopped

About ½ teaspoon salt, to your taste

FOR THE TORTILLAS AND EGGS:

8 corn tortillas, plus additional tortillas to pass at the table

1 tablespoon vinegar

Salt

4 large eggs

Freshly ground black pepper to taste

1 tablespoon chopped fresh cilantro leaves

2 tablespoons crumbled Mexican queso fresco (optional)

1. Make the sauce. Place the tomatoes, chiles, and garlic in a blender and
   puree, retaining a bit of texture.

2. Heat the oil in the large nonstick skillet over medium heat. Add the onion
   and cook, stirring, until tender, about 3 to 5 minutes. Add the tomato
   puree (it should sizzle at once) and cook, stirring, until the sauce thickens
   and begins to stick to the skillet, about 10 to 15 minutes. Taste and season with salt. Keep warm while you heat the tortillas and poach the eggs.
   (If you have sauce already made, bring to a simmer in a saucepan.) If the
   sauce is too thick to spoon easily over tortillas, thin out as desired with
   water.

3. Heat the tortillas in one of the following ways: wrap in aluminum foil and
   heat through in a 350°F oven for 15 minutes; heat 1 or 2 at a time in a
   dry nonstick skillet over medium-high heat until flexible; wrap in a clean
   kitchen towel and steam for 1 minute, then allow to sit, covered, for 10
   minutes; wrap in wax paper and heat in a microwave for a minute.

4. Have the plates ready. Fill the skillet with water and bring to a boil. Turn
   the heat down so it won't bubble furiously. Add the vinegar and a little
   salt. Break the eggs into the teacups and slip into the water. Turn off the
   heat, cover, and poach for 4 minutes. Meanwhile, fill the bowl with cold
   water. Carefully scoop up the eggs one at a time with a slotted spoon or
   skimmer. Transfer to the bowl to stop the cooking. Drain on a folded
   kitchen towel.

continued

5. Place 2 warm tortillas, overlapping, on each plate. Spoon some sauce over the tortillas, then top with a poached egg. Spoon some more sauce over the eggs, then sprinkle on salt, pepper, the cilantro, and cheese if using. Serve at once, passing additional tortillas at the table.

Large Frittata

Makes 6 main-dish servings, 10 to 12 hors d'oeuvre servings

These large *frittate* (singular: *frittata*), flat omelets, are endlessly versatile, always beautiful, and please everybody. They're very convenient because they keep well in the refrigerator, and they're good cold. You can make them up for a party, or even for dinner, a few days ahead of time; then, when you come home from work, toss a salad together and your meal is ready!

Made in a nonstick pan (I use a heavy-duty 15-inch pan), these omelets require only a tablespoon of olive oil. If you wish, you can substitute whites for some of the egg yolks. The method for making them is the same no matter what filling you use. You make up the filling first, then stir it into the beaten egg mixture, heat the pan, and cook. Here's the master recipe.

Filling of your choice (recipes follow)
10 large eggs
Salt to taste (about ½ teaspoon) and a generous amount of freshly ground
    black pepper
3 tablespoons low-fat milk
1 tablespoon olive oil

1. Make the filling according to the recipe.
2. Beat the eggs in the mixing bowl. Stir in the salt, pepper, milk, and filling.
3. Heat the olive oil in the skillet over medium-high heat. Hold your hand above it; it should feel hot. Drop a bit of egg into the skillet; if it sizzles and cooks at once, the skillet is ready. (The reason it *must* be hot is that you want the eggs to form a cooked surface on the bottom of the skillet immediately. You will be lifting this gently with a spatula and tilting the skillet so that the uncooked eggs run underneath, and the omelet cooks layer by layer.)
4. Pour in the egg mixture. Swirl the skillet to distribute the eggs and filling evenly over the surface. Shake the skillet gently, tilting it slightly with one hand while lifting up the edges of the frittata with the spatula, in your other hand, to let the eggs run underneath during the few minutes of cooking. Turn the heat down to low, cover (use a pizza pan if you don't have a lid that will fit your skillet), and cook for 10 minutes, shaking the skillet gently every once in a while. From time to time remove the lid and

loosen the bottom of the frittata with a wooden spatula, tilting the skillet so that the bottom doesn't burn. It will, however, turn a deep golden brown. This is fine. The eggs should be just about set; cook a few minutes longer if they're not. Meanwhile, preheat the broiler.

5. Finish the frittata under the broiler for 2 to 3 minutes, watching very carefully to make sure the top doesn't burn (it should brown slightly, and it will puff under the broiler). Remove from the heat, shake the skillet to make sure the frittata isn't sticking (it will slide around a bit in the non-stick skillet), and allow to cool for at least 5 minutes and up to 15. Loosen the edges with a wooden or plastic spatula. Carefully slide from the skillet onto the platter. If serving the next day, allow to cool to room temperature, cover with plastic wrap, then aluminum foil, and refrigerate. Serve hot, at room temperature, or cold. As a main dish, cut into wedges, like a pie. For hors d'oeuvres, cut into diamond shapes. To do this, cut the frittata into strips 1 to 1½ inches wide. Turn the platter and cut strips on the diagonal to make diamond shapes. This makes great picnic fare.

Substituting Egg Whites for Some of the Yolks: Instead of 10 whole eggs, use 6 whole eggs and 10 egg whites.

Frittata with Sweet Red Pepper and Peas

PER SERVING:
13.1 gm total fat
3.2 gm saturated fat
212 calories
10.6 gm carbohydrates
13.3 gm protein

1 tablespoon olive oil
1 medium-size onion, peeled and chopped
1 large red bell pepper, seeded and diced
Salt to taste
1 to 2 garlic cloves, to your taste, minced or pressed
1½ pounds fresh peas in the pod, shelled, or 1½ cups frozen peas, thawed
2 to 3 tablespoons chopped fresh parsley or basil leaves or a combination, to
    your taste

1. Heat the oil in a large, heavy nonstick skillet (or your omelet pan) over medium heat and add the onion. When it begins to soften, after about 3 minutes, add the red pepper and a little salt. Stir together and cook, stirring often, until the onion and pepper are tender, 5 to 8 minutes. Stir in the garlic, cook for another minute, and remove from the heat. Transfer to a bowl and rinse and dry your skillet if using it for the frittata.

2. If using fresh peas, steam until tender, 5 to 8 minutes, and refresh under cold water. Thaw frozen peas by covering with boiling water for 2 minutes and draining.

3. Beat the eggs as directed, stir in the filling (the onion and pepper, the peas, and herbs), and proceed with the recipe.

PER SERVING (SALMON OR
TROUT):
12.2 gm total fat
3.3 gm saturated fat
207 calories
4.4 gm carbohydrates
19.2 gm protein

PER SERVING:
13.3 gm total fat
3.3 gm saturated fat
214 calories
11.4 gm carbohydrates
13.3 gm protein

Asparagus (and Smoked Salmon or Smoked Trout) Frittata

1 pound asparagus, trimmed and cut into ½-inch lengths

3 tablespoons chopped fresh chives or dill

½ pound smoked trout, crumbled, or smoked salmon, crumbled or chopped
   (optional)

1. Steam the asparagus until tender and still bright green, 5 to 8 minutes. Drain and refresh under cold water. Shake dry.
2. Beat the eggs as directed, stir in the asparagus, herbs, and trout or salmon, if you wish, and proceed with the recipe.

Red Pepper and Zucchini Frittata

1 tablespoon olive oil

1 large onion, peeled and chopped

1 large red bell pepper, seeded and diced

¼ teaspoon salt

1½ pounds zucchini, trimmed, cut into ¼-inch dice, or cut with the julienne
   blade of your food processor

2 large garlic cloves, peeled and minced or pressed

Freshly ground black pepper to taste

2 to 3 tablespoons chopped fresh flat-leaf parsley or basil leaves, or a
   combination, to your taste

1. Heat the olive oil in a large, heavy nonstick skillet (or your omelet pan) over medium heat and add the onion. Cook, stirring, until it begins to soften, about 3 minutes, and add the red pepper and salt. Cook, stirring, for a few minutes, until the pepper begins to soften, then add the zucchini, garlic, and pepper. Cook, stirring, until the zucchini is tender but still bright green, 5 to 10 minutes. Remove from the heat and transfer to a bowl. Rinse and dry your pan if using it for the frittata.
2. Beat the eggs as directed, stir in the filling (the zucchini mixture and the herbs), and proceed with the recipe.

Middle Eastern Fresh Herb Frittata

PER SERVING:
10.9 gm total fat
3 gm saturated fat
157.8 calories
3.2 gm carbohydrates
11.6 gm protein

2 cups coarsely chopped fresh flat-leaf parsley leaves

1 cup chopped fresh dill

½ cup chopped fresh cilantro leaves

½ cup chopped fresh chives or scallions, both white and green parts

Beat the eggs as directed and stir in the herbs. Proceed with the recipe.

Mushroom Frittata

PER SERVING:
13.5 gm total fat
3.3 gm saturated fat
213.6 calories
9.3 gm carbohydrates
13.5 gm protein

1 tablespoon olive oil

1 medium-size onion, peeled and chopped

1½ pounds mushrooms or 1 pound wild mushrooms such as portobello, shiitake, cremini, or oyster mushrooms and ½ pound cultivated mushrooms, trimmed or stemmed, cleaned, and thickly sliced

3 large garlic cloves, peeled and minced or pressed

Salt to taste

¼ cup dry white wine

½ teaspoon crumbled dried thyme

1 teaspoon chopped fresh rosemary leaves or ½ teaspoon crumbled dried (optional)

Freshly ground black pepper to taste

1. Heat the oil in a large, heavy nonstick skillet over medium heat and add the onion. Cook, stirring, until tender and beginning to brown, about 8 minutes. Add the mushrooms, garlic, and about ¼ teaspoon salt and continue to cook, stirring often, until the mushrooms have released their liquid and the liquid has just about evaporated (the mushrooms shouldn't be dry but shouldn't be swimming in liquid either), 10 to 15 minutes. If there is still a lot of liquid in the skillet after this time, turn up the heat to medium-high so that it cooks off more rapidly. Stir in the wine, thyme, and rosemary and cook, stirring, until the liquid in the skillet has thickened and glazed the mushrooms, 5 to 10 minutes. Season with salt and pepper and remove from the heat.

2. Beat the eggs as directed, stir in the filling, and proceed with the recipe.

Potato and Onion Frittata

1½ pounds waxy potatoes, such as Yukon Gold or red new potatoes,
    scrubbed and sliced about ¼ inch thick
1 tablespoon olive oil
1 medium-size onion, peeled and chopped
Salt and freshly ground black pepper to taste
½ teaspoon crumbled dried thyme, or 1 teaspoon fresh thyme leaves

1. Steam the sliced potatoes until just tender, 8 to 10 minutes. Remove from the heat.
2. Heat the oil in a large, heavy nonstick skillet over medium heat and add the onion. Cook, stirring, until it is tender and just beginning to color, 5 to 8 minutes. Stir in the potatoes and toss together (don't worry if some of the slices break apart). Add the salt, pepper, and thyme and remove from the heat.
3. Beat the eggs as directed. Stir in the onion and potatoes and proceed with the recipe.

Ready-Made Fillings: A number of canned, jarred, and frozen foods make delicious, quick fillings. Here are some suggestions:

- Marinated roasted red peppers (jarred or canned): Drain and dice. Mix with minced garlic if you wish and stir into the eggs. Use 4 peppers or more to taste.
- Artichoke hearts (jarred or canned): Drain and dice. Mix with minced garlic if you wish and stir into the eggs. Use 6 artichoke hearts or more to taste.
- Prepared tomato sauce: Stir 1 cup, or more if desired, into the eggs for a beautiful salmon-pink color. You can also add 2 to 4 tablespoons grated Parmesan to this variation.

Quick Individual Omelets, Flat or Folded

Makes 1 serving

Get out the following equipment: small or medium-size mixing bowl, whisk or fork, measuring spoons; 8-inch heavy nonstick skillet; spatula; plate

An omelet for one or two can be made in a flash. It requires very little oil or butter in a nonstick pan and certainly not the three eggs you may associate with restaurant omelets. A handful of chopped herbs and some garlic, cooked spinach or greens, chopped tomatoes, tomato sauce, sautéed mushrooms, and scallions all make make great fillings that require little work or forethought. I got into the habit of using olive oil for my omelets when I lived in the south of France. If you prefer butter, the small amount called for here won't hurt.

These go so quickly that they can be made in quick succession if you're feeding more than just yourself. They are the type of omelets you are bound to get in southern France or Italy.

PER SERVING:
15.7 gm total fat
3.9 gm saturated fat
201 calories
1.5 gm carbohydrates
12.7 gm protein

2 large eggs, or 1 large egg and 2 large egg whites
Salt and freshly ground black pepper to taste
1 teaspoon low-fat milk
Filling of your choice (see recipes that follow)
1 to 1½ teaspoons olive oil or unsalted butter, to your taste

1. Beat the eggs or egg and egg whites together in a small bowl using a whisk or a fork. The whites and yolks should be amalgamated nicely. Add the salt, pepper, milk, and the filling of your choice.

2. Heat the olive oil or butter in the skillet over medium-high heat. Hold your hand over the skillet; it should feel hot. Drizzle in a bit of egg, and if it sizzles and cooks at once, the skillet is ready. (The skillet *must* be hot so that the eggs form a cooked surface on the bottom immediately, which you will lift to allow uncooked egg to run underneath to cook.)

3. Pour in the egg mixture and tilt and swirl the skillet to coat the bottom evenly. Gently lift the edges of the layer of eggs that has set and tilt the skillet to let more egg run underneath. Shake the skillet constantly but gently and continue to lift the skillet and tilt it to allow uncooked egg to run underneath the cooked egg. When the top of the omelet is just about set, slide it out onto a plate and serve. The egg will continue to cook, so the omelet won't be runny. If you want it completely set, fold it over (easy in a nonstick skillet) and flip it back and forth for another half minute or so, then slide it out onto a plate.

The other way to cook the top side is a bit unwieldy, but this is how the Italians do it: slide the omelet out onto a plate when the bottom is set but the top is still runny. Reverse the skillet over the plate and, holding the plate against the pan, flip the plate over so that the uncooked side of the omelet is now on the surface of the skillet. Cook for another 30 seconds to a minute and slide onto the plate.

You can keep the omelets warm in a very low oven while you make more of them. Or serve at once.

Scallion and Herb Omelet

PER SERVING:
20.3 gm total fat
4.5 gm saturated fat
247 calories
2.9 gm carbohydrates
13.1 gm protein

FOR EACH OMELET:

1 teaspoon olive oil

2 to 3 scallions, to your taste, both white and green parts, chopped

1 to 2 tablespoons chopped fresh herbs, such as flat-leaf parsley, dill, basil, thyme, or tarragon, to your taste

Heat the olive oil over medium heat in the skillet in which you will cook the omelet. Add the scallions and cook, stirring, until the white part is translucent, about 3 minutes. Remove from the heat. Stir into the eggs along with the herbs and proceed with the recipe.

Swiss Chard or Spinach Omelet

PER SERVING:
16.4 gm total fat
4.0 gm saturated fat
369 calories
36.3 gm carbohydrates
28.1 gm protein

FOR EACH OMELET:

½ pound Swiss chard or spinach, stemmed and leaves washed

1 to 2 garlic cloves, to your taste, peeled and minced or pressed

Wilt the chard or spinach in the water left on the leaves after washing over high heat in a dry skillet. Remove from the heat, rinse briefly with cold water, and squeeze dry. Chop coarsely. Add to the eggs along with the garlic and proceed with the recipe.

Asparagus and Parmesan Omelet

PER SERVING:
16.8 gm total fat
4.5 gm saturated fat
227 calories
3.2 gm carbohydrates
15.6 gm protein

FOR EACH OMELET:

3 to 4 stalks asparagus, trimmed and cut into ½-inch-thick slices

2 teaspoons freshly grated Parmesan cheese

1 to 2 teaspoons chopped fresh chives or flat-leaf parsley leaves, to your taste

Steam the asparagus until tender, 5 to 8 minutes. Stir into the eggs with the Parmesan and herbs and proceed with the recipe.

Tomato Omelet

PER SERVING:
17.8 gm total fat
4.1 gm saturated fat
240 calories
5.6 gm carbohydrates
13.8 gm protein

FOR EACH OMELET:

3 to 4 tablespoons Simple Tomato Sauce (page 53)

1 teaspoon slivered fresh basil leaves

Prepare the tomato sauce as directed, stir into the eggs along with the basil, and proceed with the recipe.

Wild Mushroom Omelet

PER SERVING:
20.7 gm total fat
4.6 gm saturated fat
276 calories
8.2 gm carbohydrates
15.4 gm protein

FOR EACH OMELET:

¼ pound wild mushrooms, such as cremini, portobello, shiitake, oyster, or chanterelles, stemmed or trimmed and sliced ½ inch thick

Salt to taste

1 teaspoon olive oil

1 large garlic clove, minced or pressed

Freshly ground black pepper to taste

Heat the mushrooms with the salt over medium-high heat in a heavy non-stick skillet until they begin to exude water. Stir until the water evaporates, then add the olive oil and garlic. Cook, stirring, for about 1 minute, until the garlic and mushrooms are fragrant. Season with pepper and remove from the heat. Allow to cool slightly before stirring into the eggs and proceeding with the recipe.

Scrambled Eggs

Makes 4 servings

This may be the first thing you ever learned to cook. It is for me. But when I learned to cook it, there was a lot of butter in the equation. With today's nonstick cookware, all that butter isn't necessary—just a little for flavor. Scrambled eggs will always be an important late-night dinner in our home, the kind of meal you can rustle up when you come home, starving, from the theater or a party. The key to success is to scramble them very, very slowly over very low heat. Then they'll be buttery without the butter.

8 large eggs, or 4 large eggs and 7 large egg whites

¼ to ½ teaspoon salt, to your taste

Get out the following equipment: **large mixing bowl for beating the eggs; 10-inch heavy nonstick skillet; measuring spoons; whisk or fork**

continued

PER SERVING:
12.1 gm total fat
4.48 gm saturated fat
168 calories
1.3 gm carbohydrates
12.6 gm protein

Freshly ground black pepper to taste

2 teaspoons low-fat milk

2 teaspoons unsalted butter

1. Beat the eggs or eggs and egg whites together in the bowl until amalgamated. Add the salt, pepper, and milk and beat together.

2. Heat the skillet over low heat and melt the butter. When it has melted, add the eggs. Stir them slowly and constantly with a wooden spoon or a plastic spatula. Nothing will happen for the first few minutes, but eventually flat, wide curds will begin to form on the bottom of the skillet. Keep stirring them up, allowing the uncooked egg on the top to get to the bottom of the pan. It will take at least 10 minutes of gentle stirring over low heat for the eggs to set. They should be creamy rather than hard. If you want larger, harder curds, cook the eggs over medium heat.

3. Distribute the eggs among plates and serve at once, with toast and more salt and pepper.

Additions:

- *Smoked salmon:* When the eggs have just about set, stir in about 4 ounces chopped smoked salmon.

- *Herbs:* Stir about ¼ cup chopped fresh herbs, such as chives, flat-leaf parsley, or tarragon, into the eggs before you add them to the skillet.

- *Salsa:* For huevos Mexicanos, heat ½ to 1 cup cooked tomato salsa, ready-made or homemade (page 326), in the skillet, then add the beaten eggs to it.

- *Onion:* Cook 1 medium-size onion, peeled and chopped, in 2 teaspoons olive oil over medium heat until tender, 5 to 8 minutes, and stir them into the eggs before adding them to the skillet.

- *Fresh garlic:* When fresh green garlic is in season, slice up 3 or 4 cloves and cook gently in 2 teaspoons olive oil over medium heat until fragrant but not colored, about 1 minute. Remove from the heat and stir into the beaten eggs before adding them to the skillet.

Zucchini "Soufflé"

Makes 4 servings

This isn't a soufflé in the traditional sense; it's much lighter, with no rich sauce, very little cheese, and fewer eggs than a classic soufflé. However, it does puff up when you bake it (and then fall) like a soufflé. It makes a wonderful light supper with a green salad and bread.

1½ pounds zucchini, ends trimmed

1¼ to 1½ teaspoons salt, to your taste

2 teaspoons olive oil

½ medium-size onion, peeled and finely chopped

4 large eggs

½ cup nonfat cottage cheese

2 ounces Gruyère cheese, grated (½ cup)

2 tablespoons chopped fresh flat-leaf parsley leaves

½ cup fresh bread crumbs (white or whole wheat)

Freshly ground black pepper to taste

2 large egg whites

1. Preheat the oven to 375°F. Oil the soufflé dish.
2. Grate the zucchini and toss in the colander with 1 teaspoon of the salt. Set in the sink and let sit for 20 minutes.
3. Meanwhile, heat the oil in the skillet over medium heat. Add the onion and cook, stirring, until tender, about 3 minutes. Remove from the heat.
4. Combine the whole eggs and cottage cheese in the food processor and process until smooth. Transfer to the large bowl and stir in the onion, Gruyère, parsley, and bread crumbs.
5. Squeeze out the excess water from the zucchini and rinse well. Squeeze dry in a clean kitchen towel, then stir into the egg mixture. Season with salt and pepper as desired. Beat the egg whites until they form stiff but not dry peaks and gently fold into the zucchini mixture (see page 33 for tips on beating egg whites and folding). Spoon into the prepared soufflé dish.
6. Bake until puffed and browned, 40 to 45 minutes, and serve.

Get out the following equipment: **grater; colander; 2-quart soufflé dish; measuring spoons; medium-size heavy nonstick skillet; wooden or plastic spoon; food processor fitted with steel blade; medium-size bowl and whisk or electric mixer; spatula; measuring cups; large bowl**

Advance preparation: **The mixture can be assembled up to the folding in of the beaten egg whites and held in the refrigerator for several hours. Bring to room temperature and stir before proceeding with the egg whites and baking.**

PER SERVING:
12.3 gm total fat
4.6 gm saturated fat
227 calories
10.9 gm carbohydrates
18.6 gm protein

Grains, Beans, Vegetables, and Tofu

I could have devoted this entire book to grains, beans, and vegetables; they are at the heart of healthy cooking. If you are vegetarian, you probably already know how important these foods are; and if you are not, they should still constitute a greater portion of a *Light Basics* diet than meat does.

There are so many theories about what people should eat to maintain proper weight and good health, and diet fashions come and go. My feeling about what constitutes a good diet is quite simple: I think that no matter what else we eat, we should be eating a variety of fresh fruits, vegetables, and other plant-based foods, i.e., grains and beans. And we shouldn't overeat. What's great about fresh produce, grains, and beans is that it's very difficult to eat too much of them. What's even better is that they taste so good and offer us the full gamut of vitamins and minerals.

Today's farmers' markets present an exciting array of seasonal produce. Even the supermarket produce section reflects our renewed interest in vegetables: look at the number of different greens and lettuces, fresh herbs, and varieties of potatoes now available in your local store. You should be able to find anything called for in these pages.

This chapter includes recipes for main dishes as well as simple vegetable side dishes. The hearty grain dishes like the risottos, the bean dishes, stir-fries, and many of the gratins are nourishing main dishes. Gratins can also serve as side dishes. Basic vegetable preparations like steamed artichokes and oven-roasted potatoes are designed to give you a repertoire for dealing with these vegetables. The chart on pages 224–225 should also help; refer to it when you come home with a vegetable you've never cooked before and can't find a recipe for it. Remember, too, that you can make a meal of simply steamed, roasted, or pan-cooked vegetables with grains. When vegetables are at the height of their flavor, why not put them at the center of your plate?

▪ Grains Basics ▪

I'm not going to cover all the grains here, just the ones that you will be most likely to cook—fast-cooking grains that are easy to find in a supermarket. These include regular white rice, brown rice, basmati rice, wild rice, bulgur, and couscous. Grains are often the most important food on the plate, the bulk of the meal. When you serve stir-fried vegetables with rice, or vegetable couscous, the rice and couscous are not just accompaniments but integral parts of the dish. But grains can also be a side dish, with meat, poultry, or fish.

How to Cook Rice

There are a few ways to cook rice. The two that you will use for the recipes in this book are steamed rice and Mexican- or pilaf-style rice.

Steamed Rice

A very simple method, used for stir-fries and simple rice side dishes. Use 1 part long-grain or medium-grain white rice and 2 parts water. One cup rice will feed four people as a side dish. Place the water in a 1-or 2-quart saucepan with a lid and bring to a boil. Add salt—½ to ¾ teaspoon per cup of rice (to your taste)—and the rice. When the water comes back to a boil, stir *once and once only*, reduce the heat to low, and cover the pot tightly. Simmer white rice for 15 minutes. Remove the lid and look and listen. There will be holes in the mass of rice, into which you can peer to see if the water has evaporated. You will hear it as well. If you're really not sure, stick a chopstick or a spoon down into it to see if a small layer of rice is beginning to stick to the bottom of the pan. If it is, turn off the heat immediately, return the lid to the pan, and let the pan sit without touching it for 10 minutes (or longer). The rice will continue to steam and grow fluffy. If there is still water simmering, return the lid to the pan and check again in 5 minutes. For brown rice, use the same method, but use 2¼ parts water to 1 part rice. (Note: There is some variation among different brands of brown rice. If you buy it packaged in the supermarket, check the back of the package for instructions; some will call for 2 parts water to 1 part rice, others for 2½ parts water to 1 part rice.) Steam for 35 minutes and check. Brown rice takes 35 to 45 minutes to cook.

Mexican- or Pilaf-Style Rice

Use 1 part white rice, 2 parts water or broth (chicken or vegetable), ¼ to ¾ teaspoon salt (depending on the saltiness of the broth if using), and 1 tablespoon oil or butter. Bring the liquid to a bare simmer in a saucepan and add the salt. Taste to make sure there is enough salt (it should taste fairly salty). Heat the oil over medium heat in a heavy 1½ or 2-quart saucepan and add to the rice (and other aromatics if called for). Cook, stirring, until the grains of rice are separate, a few minutes. Stir in the simmering stock. Bring the mixture to a boil, stir down the sides of the pan, reduce the heat to low, cover, and simmer, as for steamed rice, until the water is absorbed, 15 to 20 minutes. Remove the saucepan from the heat. If you wish, place a clean kitchen towel or a double layer of paper towels between the lid and the pan. The towel will absorb moisture, and the rice will be fluffier. With or without the toweling, let sit, covered, for 5 to 10 minutes. The grains should be tender and separate.

Basmati Rice

Basmati rice is a fragrant, delicate rice from the Middle East, Pakistan, and India. It's particularly nice with curries and in pilafs. The grain is long and fragrant, with a nutty aroma. Domestic basmati rice is called texmati. You can cook basmati rice in the same way you cook Mexican- or pilaf-style rice above, but first you must wash it in several rinses of water. Washing removes starch that clings to the rice grains and could make the cooked rice sticky. Place the rice in a bowl and fill with water. Pour through a strainer, rinse, and return to the bowl. Repeat this process until the water runs clear. If you want longer grains, soak the rice for 30 minutes before cooking. Another way to cook basmati rice is to boil it in a large pot of water. Clean the rice as instructed. Bring a large pot of water to a boil, add ¼ teaspoon salt per cup of rice, then the rice. Stir until the water comes back to the boil. Boil for 5 minutes and test for doneness. If the rice is cooked through, drain through a strainer or colander. Shake the rice and serve.

Wild Rice

This is not technically rice; rather it is a grain with a nutty, rich flavor. Use 1 part wild rice and 3 parts water or broth. Wild rice tends to be a bit dusty and should be washed. Wash the rice in several changes of water, until the water runs clear. Bring the liquid to a boil in a 2-quart saucepan and add ½ to ¾ teaspoon salt per cup of wild rice (depending on the saltiness of the broth) and the rice. Bring back to the boil, cover, and reduce the heat to low. Simmer until the rice is tender and the outer shells have split, about 40 to 45 minutes. Drain through a colander or strainer if there is still liquid in the pot. Return to the pot and cover until ready to serve.

How to Cook Bulgur

Bulgur is wheat that has been steamed, dried, and cracked. It has a marvelous nutty flavor and chewy texture, and it's an easy, quick-cooking grain to work with. It makes a great pilaf and goes well with all vegetable dishes. It comes in fine, medium, and coarse grinds; I recommend medium grind as the most versatile. Fine bulgur, however, is excellent for tabouli salads. To cook, place the bulgur in a bowl and stir in ¼ to ½ teaspoon salt per cup of bulgur (to your taste). For 1 cup of bulgur, bring 2 cups water or broth to a boil and pour over the bulgur. Cover the bowl with a plate and let sit until the bulgur is tender, 15 to 25 minutes. If water remains in the bowl, drain through a strainer and press the bulgur gently to extrude more water.

How to Cook Couscous

Couscous is not really a grain. It's pasta in granular form, made from semolina (hard durum wheat) and water. Couscous is served in all kinds of ways. Sometimes it is piled onto a serving plate or a large conical serving dish called a *tagine* and topped with a stew. Other times the couscous is spooned into wide bowls and the stew liquid and vegetables are ladled over it, with meat or fish served on the side. In Paris, where going out for couscous is the equivalent of going out for Mexican food in the American Southwest, diners season their couscous to taste with harissa, a fiery hot chile paste. But in many Tunisian dishes the harissa is added to the stew that goes over the couscous.

Today couscous has become a popular food, because instant couscous is available in supermarkets and takes very little time to cook. There are strong feelings in the food world about instant couscous (and noninstant *is* available in organic food stores). Many of my colleagues consider instant couscous stale tasting and nothing like the silky, nutty-tasting noninstant product. I am not in their camp. That is, I agree that traditional couscous probably tastes better than boxed instant. But I don't find the instant product objectionable, and I appreciate its convenience. However, I do agree that couscous, in most cases (the salad on page 142 excepted), should be steamed after it is reconstituted. But steaming can take place in a covered dish in the oven as well as on top of the stove. Here's how to prepare couscous:

Quantities of couscous are slightly greater per person than for other grains. I usually use about 1½ cups of couscous for four people. In North Africa virtually all of the cooks have a pot called a *couscoussière*, which is like a steamer, with a perforated top portion for steaming the couscous. These are very handy, although they are far from necessary. You can always use a large strainer or a colander set above a pot for steaming the couscous.

For Precooked Couscous Place the couscous in a bowl. Add ½ to 1 teaspoon salt (to your taste) per cup of couscous. Cover the couscous with warm or hot water or broth, using ½ cup more liquid than the volume of couscous (e.g., for 1½ cups couscous, use 2 cups liquid). Let soak for 20 minutes, stirring from time to time, with a wooden spoon or, more effective, rubbing the couscous between your moistened thumbs and forefingers to keep it from lumping.

To Steam the Couscous Place the precooked couscous in the top part of a *couscoussière* if you have one or in a strainer or colander that fits snugly over a pot. If you are serving the couscous with a stew, steam above the stew for the best flavor. Otherwise, steam above boiling water, making sure the couscous does not touch the water. If there is a big space between the edge of the colander or strainer and the pot, wrap a kitchen towel between the edge of the strainer or colander and the pot so that no steam will escape. Cover the strainer with a lid. Steam the couscous for 15 minutes and transfer to a serving dish.

To heat through in an oven Place the precooked couscous in a lightly oiled casserole and drizzle a tablespoon of olive oil over the top. Cover with aluminum foil and place in a preheated 350°F oven until hot and steamy, 15 to 20 minutes.

A Great Pot of Beans

Makes 6 servings

A great pot of beans has a rich, fragrant broth, the result of the beans themselves, onion, garlic, and herbs. Different beans take different herbs. My favorite pot of beans is a pot of black beans, so let's start with that. Pinto beans are cooked in the same way.

To drain or not to drain: Most beans must first be soaked so that they will absorb water and swell. Otherwise, cooking takes hours (for a slow cooker, soaking is not required). We used to be instructed to pour off the soaking water and cook the beans in fresh water. This was thought to eliminate some · of the gases that cause flatulence. Now cooks rarely throw out the soaking water; conventional wisdom has changed in regard to its digestibility, and most beans cooked in their soaking water are more flavorful. With black beans and pintos, you get a richer, darker broth, and probably more nutri-

Get out the following equipment: **large bowl; measuring cup; chef's knife and cutting board; garlic press or minichop if using; measuring spoons; large, heavy bean pot, casserole, or Dutch oven**

Advance preparation: **Beans will keep in the refrigerator for about 4 days. They get better overnight. They also freeze well.**

PER SERVING:
1.1 gm total fat
0.3 gm saturated fat
271 calories
50.0 gm carbohydrates
16.8 gm protein

ents, if you cook the beans in their soaking water. However, with white beans and chickpeas I usually drain the soaking water because I don't like the taste of it.

> 1 pound (2 heaped cups) dried black or pinto beans, washed and picked over (to make sure there are no stones mixed in)
> 2 quarts water
> 1 medium-size onion, peeled and chopped
> 4 large garlic cloves, peeled and minced or pressed
> About 2 teaspoons salt, or more to your taste
> 2 tablespoons chopped fresh cilantro leaves

1. Soak the beans in 7 cups of the water in the bowl for at least 6 hours.
2. Transfer the beans and their soaking water to the bean pot, casserole, or Dutch oven. Bring to a boil and skim off any foam that rises. Add the onion and half the garlic. Make sure the beans are covered by at least 1 inch of water (add the remaining cup water if they aren't), reduce the heat to low, cover, and simmer for 1 hour.
3. Add the salt, remaining garlic, and cilantro. Continue to simmer until the beans are quite soft and the broth is thick and fragrant, about another hour. Taste. Is there enough salt? Add if necessary. Let sit overnight in the refrigerator for the best flavor.

White Beans, Navy Beans, Giant White Beans: After soaking, drain the beans. Place in the bean pot and cover by an inch with fresh water. Omit the cilantro. Add 1 large bay leaf along with the onion and first 2 cloves of garlic. Cook as above. Check to make sure they are not getting mushy after 1½ hours of cooking.

Chickpeas: These need no aromatics, just salt. Soak, then drain, place in the bean pot, and cover by an inch with fresh water. Cook as instructed, adding nothing but the salt during the last hour of cooking.

Black-Eyed Peas: These cook quickly and require no soaking. Wash and pick over for stones. Combine with 2 quarts water and bring to a boil. Skim off any foam that rises. Add the onion, half the garlic, and a bay leaf. Reduce the heat to low, cover, and simmer for 30 minutes. Add salt to taste and the remaining garlic. Simmer until soft but not mushy, another 15 to 30 minutes. Taste and adjust seasonings.

Lentils: Like black-eyed peas, these require no soaking. Follow the instructions for black-eyed peas.

Get out the following equipment: chef's knife and cutting board; measuring spoons and measuring cup; mortar and pestle; garlic press or minichop if using; small skillet and bowl; large, heavy nonstick skillet and wooden spoon or spatula

Advance preparation: **This dish keeps well. It can sit on top of the stove for several hours, and it will keep in the refrigerator for at least 3 days. However, for the most vivid herb flavor, stir in the fresh herbs just before serving.**

PER SERVING:
11.4 gm total fat
1.3 gm saturated fat
355 calories
51.1 gm carbohydrates
15.0 gm protein

Turkish Chickpea Stew

Makes 4 generous main-dish servings

This dish has wonderful complex flavors, yet it's very easily made. You can cook the chickpeas ahead or use canned chickpeas. This is adapted from a recipe in *Classic Turkish Cooking* by Ghillie Bassan (St. Martin's Press, New York, 1997). Pomegranate molasses is used in Middle Eastern cooking and can be found in Middle Eastern markets. Serve this stew with rice or bulgur.

½ teaspoon red pepper flakes

2 tablespoons olive oil

2 medium-size onions, peeled and thinly sliced

4 garlic cloves, peeled and minced or pressed

1 teaspoon cumin seeds, crushed in a mortar and pestle

1 teaspoon fennel seeds, crushed in a mortar and pestle

1 teaspoon brown sugar or 2 teaspoons pomegranate molasses

1 tablespoon white wine vinegar, sherry vinegar, or fresh lemon juice

1½ to 1¾ pounds firm, ripe tomatoes, peeled, seeded, and chopped, or one
    28-ounce can tomatoes, drained, seeded, and chopped

Salt to taste

½ pound dried chickpeas, cooked (page 205) and drained, or two 15-ounce
    cans, drained and rinsed (about 3 cups)

¼ pound fresh spinach, well washed and stemmed

A handful each fresh flat-leaf parsley, dill, and mint leaves, chopped (about
    ¼ cup each)

Lemon wedges and plain nonfat yogurt for serving

1. Heat the small skillet over medium heat and add the red pepper flakes. Shake the skillet and toast the flakes just until they begin to smell a bit toasty. Immediately transfer to a plate or small bowl and set aside.

2. Heat the oil in the large skillet over medium heat and add the onions. Cook, stirring, until tender, about 5 minutes, then add the garlic, cumin, and fennel. Continue to cook until the onions have colored slightly, 5 to 8 minutes. Add the sugar or pomegranate molasses and stir together for a minute, then stir in the vinegar or lemon juice, tomatoes, about ½ teaspoon salt, and the toasted red pepper flakes. Cook, stirring, until the tomatoes have cooked down and are beginning to stick to the skillet, about 10 minutes. Stir in the chickpeas and spinach. Add enough water so that the vegetables are covered partially and the dish can simmer. Simmer, uncovered, over medium heat, stirring often, for 20 to 25 minutes. The

dish should be saucy but not watery. Taste. Is there enough salt? The salt should even out the pungency of the spices. Add salt to taste and stir in the herbs. Serve with lemon wedges and yogurt.

Tomato and Bean Gratin

Makes 6 servings

My husband calls this delicious dish the best baked beans he's ever tasted. Make it in the wintertime with dried beans and canned tomatoes and in summer with fresh tomatoes and, if you can find them, fresh borlotti beans. You can also use a mixture of dried beans, say, pintos and white beans, for a pretty variation.

1 pound (2 heaping cups) dried white, navy, Great Northern, or pinto beans, washed, picked over, and soaked for 6 hours (see Note); or 3 pounds unshelled fresh borlotti or cranberry beans, shelled (4 heaping cups)

2 quarts water

2 medium-size onions, peeled and 1 stuck with a clove, the other chopped

6 large garlic cloves, peeled and minced or pressed

1 bay leaf

Salt to taste

2 tablespoons olive oil

2 pounds fresh or canned tomatoes, peeled, seeded, and chopped

⅛ teaspoon sugar

2 teaspoons fresh thyme leaves or 1 teaspoon dried thyme

Freshly ground black pepper to taste

3 tablespoons slivered fresh basil leaves, or more to taste, if available

¼ cup fresh or dry bread crumbs

1 ounce Parmesan cheese, grated (¼ cup)

1. *For dried beans:* Drain the soaked beans and combine with the water, the whole onion stuck with the clove, 2 of the garlic cloves, and the bay leaf in the soup pot, casserole, or Dutch oven. Bring to a boil, skim off any foam that rises, reduce the heat to low, and simmer for 45 minutes. Add 2 teaspoons salt, or more to taste, and continue to simmer until the beans are tender but not mushy, 45 to 60 minutes. Remove from the heat and drain over a bowl. Taste the broth and add salt if necessary.

   For fresh beans: Combine the water, clove-stuck onion, 2 garlic cloves, and the bay leaf in the pot and bring to a boil. Add beans and 2 teaspoons salt. Reduce the heat to medium and cook until the beans are tender and the broth

Get out the following equipment: **chef's knife and cutting board; garlic press or minichop if using; large soup pot, heavy casserole, or Dutch oven; measuring spoons; colander or large strainer and bowl; 3-quart gratin or baking dish; large, heavy nonstick skillet or casserole and wooden spoon**

Advance preparation: **The beans, tomato sauce, and the bean-and-tomato stew will all keep for 3 to 4 days in the refrigerator. Then all you have to do is turn the mixture into the gratin dish, sprinkle on the bread crumbs and Parmesan, and bake. The assembled gratin will hold for several hours in or out of the refrigerator before baking.**

PER SERVING:
7.3 gm total fat
1.7 gm saturated fat
376 calories
57.7 gm carbohydrates
22.1 gm protein

Grains, Beans, Vegetables, and Tofu
207

fragrant, 30 to 45 minutes. Remove from the heat and drain over a bowl.

2. Preheat the oven to 425°F. Oil the gratin or baking dish. Heat 1 tablespoon of the oil in the skillet or casserole over medium-low heat. Add the chopped onion and cook, stirring, until tender, 5 to 8 minutes. Add half the remaining garlic and cook, stirring, for about 30 seconds, until the garlic begins to color. Add the tomatoes, the rest of the garlic, a generous pinch of salt, and the sugar, and increase the heat to medium. Cook, stirring often, until the tomatoes have cooked down a bit and smell fragrant, about 10 minutes.

3. Stir the beans, 2 cups of their broth, and the thyme into the tomatoes. Bring to a simmer, taste, adjust the salt, and season with pepper. Reduce the heat to medium-low and simmer until the mixture is thick and fragrant, 15 to 30 minutes. Stir often to prevent the mixture from sticking to the pan. Stir in the basil if using.

4. Spoon the tomato-bean mixture into the oiled gratin dish. Mix together the bread crumbs and Parmesan and sprinkle over the top in an even layer. Drizzle on the remaining tablespoon olive oil. Bake until the top has browned, 20 to 30 minutes. Serve hot.

Note: Draining the beans is optional. Some people find it harder to digest beans that have not been drained of soaking water. But some of the flavor goes out with the soaking water. If you do not drain the beans, measure the soaking water and add more water if necessary to make 2 quarts.

Winter Vegetable Couscous

Makes 4 very generous servings

There are many versions of vegetable couscous, and I love them all. I especially appreciate the use of root vegetables like turnips and vitamin-rich vegetables such as pumpkin. Also, you'll note that no fat is called for here. Everything is simmered together, and all the flavor comes from the vegetables and spices.

1 cup dried chickpeas, washed, picked over, soaked overnight or for several
    hours in 3 cups water, then drained.

2 quarts water

2 medium-size or large onions, peeled and sliced

1 leek, white part only, washed well and sliced

2 large carrots, peeled and thickly sliced

2 medium-size turnips, peeled and cut into wedges

4 large garlic cloves, peeled and minced or pressed

Get out the following equipment: dry and liquid measuring cups; chef's knife and cutting board; garlic press or minichop if using; large stockpot, Dutch oven, or couscoussière; measuring spoons; second stockpot for blanching the greens; large strainer or colander

1 bay leaf

2 to 3 teaspoons salt, to your taste, for the stew, plus 1 tablespoon for blanching the greens

1 teaspoon dried thyme

¼ teaspoon powdered saffron or saffron threads

½ teaspoon ground cinnamon

1 pound pumpkin or winter squash, peeled and cut into large cubes

1 teaspoon harissa or ¼ teaspoon cayenne pepper, plus more to your taste for serving

Freshly ground black pepper to taste

1 bunch greens (¾ to 1 pound), such as Swiss chard, beet or turnip greens, kale or spinach, washed well and stemmed

2 cups instant couscous

¼ cup chopped fresh cilantro or flat-leaf parsley leaves

Advance preparation: **The vegetable stew will keep for 3 days in the refrigerator. Do not stir in the parsley or cilantro until you re-heat and serve. The couscous can be recon-stituted hours before serving and then steamed or heated in the oven.**

PER SERVING:
4.4 gm total fat
0.6 gm saturated fat
711 calories
142.0 gm carbohydrates
31.5 gm protein

1. Combine the drained chickpeas, water, onions, leek, carrots, turnips, 2 garlic cloves, and the bay leaf in a stockpot or Dutch oven or in the bottom part of a couscoussière. Bring to a boil, reduce the heat to low, cover, and simmer for 1 hour. Add the salt, remaining 2 garlic cloves, thyme, saffron, cinnamon, pumpkin or winter squash, and harissa or cayenne, and simmer for another 30 minutes to an hour, until the chickpeas are tender. Taste and adjust the salt and cayenne or harissa. Add a generous amount of pepper.

2. While the stew is simmering, bring a large pot of water to a boil, add a tablespoon of salt, and blanch the greens (see page 23). Drain, rinse with cold water, squeeze gently, and chop coarsely. Stir into the vegetable stew.

3. Place the couscous in a bowl. Strain off 2½ cups of the cooking liquid from the vegetables and pour it over the couscous. Let sit for 20 minutes, until the liquid is absorbed. Stir every 5 minutes with a wooden spoon or rub the couscous between your moistened thumbs and fingers so that the couscous doesn't lump. The couscous will now be soft; fluff it with a fork or with your hands. Taste the couscous and add salt if necessary.

4. Place the couscous in a colander, sieve, or the top part of a couscoussière and set it over the vegetable mixture, making sure that the bottom of the colander does not touch the liquid (remove some of the liquid if it does). Place a lid over it and steam for 15 minutes. (Alternatively, warm the couscous in a covered casserole in a preheated 350°F oven for 20 minutes.) Transfer the couscous to a serving bowl. Stir the cilantro or parsley into the vegetable/broth mixture.

5. To serve, spoon the couscous into warmed wide soup bowls and ladle on a generous helping of the broth and vegetables. Pass harissa or cayenne for those who want to spice up their couscous.

■ How to Make Risotto ■

I debated with myself about including risotto in a basic cookbook. Risotto won. I have never found it difficult to make, even when I was a beginner. And it's a great, substantial, impressive, and delicious dish for the low-fat cook. It intimidates some because it requires tending, but it isn't really finicky—you just have to stir it a lot. Risotto is a creamy, savory rice dish made with short-grain Italian Arborio rice, which has a roundish, chewy grain. It can be very simple—rice, stock, a little onion, and Parmesan—or it can contain vegetables, seafood, and other seasonings like saffron and herbs. It's a great dish for putting vegetables like asparagus, peas, mushrooms, or green beans to use. And it is incredibly versatile—I have made it with pumpkin, fennel, sweet peppers, radicchio, greens, favas, and fish.

Risotto is made by cooking rice slowly in a fragrant broth. First you cook the rice, often with a bit of onion and perhaps some garlic, in a little butter or olive oil (a lot, in traditional recipes) to separate the grains. Then you add a bit of wine, which adds great flavor to the rice. When the rice has absorbed the wine, you add a ladleful or two of simmering stock, just enough to barely cover the rice, and stir the rice until it has absorbed most of the stock. You keep adding stock gradually in this way until the rice is cooked al dente, firm to the bite, which takes about 25 minutes. Then you add one last ladleful and any final enrichments, like Parmesan or a beaten egg, and serve the creamy dish. For most vegetable risottos I usually add the vegetables about halfway through and cook them in the simmering stock along with the rice.

Basic Risotto

■

Makes 4 side-dish servings or 2 very generous main-dish servings

About 4 cups vegetable, garlic, or defatted chicken stock (pages 155–157), or
  canned broth, as needed

1 tablespoon olive oil or unsalted butter

½ small onion, peeled and minced (about ¼ cup)

1 cup Arborio rice

¼ cup dry white wine

Salt to taste

1 large egg (optional), beaten

1 ounce Parmesan cheese, grated (¼ cup)

Freshly ground black pepper to taste

Get out the following equipment: chef's knife and cutting board; measuring spoons; dry and liquid measuring cups; grater; 2-quart saucepan; ladle; large, heavy nonstick skillet and wooden spoon; small bowl and fork or whisk if using

1. Have the stock simmering over low heat in the saucepan.
2. Heat the oil or butter over medium heat in the skillet and add the onion. Cook, stirring, until the onion begins to soften, about 3 minutes. Add the rice and cook, stirring, until the grains of rice are separate and beginning to crackle, 1 to 2 minutes.
3. Stir in the wine and cook over medium heat, stirring constantly. The wine should bubble, but not too quickly—you want some of the flavor to cook into the rice before it evaporates. When the wine has just about evaporated, stir in a ladleful or two of the simmering stock, enough to just cover the rice. The stock should bubble slowly. Cook, stirring often, until it is just about absorbed. Add another ladleful of the stock and continue to cook in this fashion, not too fast and not too slowly, adding more stock when the rice is almost dry, for 20 to 25 minutes. Taste a bit of the rice. Is it cooked through? It should taste chewy but not hard in the middle—and definitely not soft like steamed rice. If it is still hard in the middle, you need to add another ladleful of stock and cook for another 5 minutes or so. Now is the time to ascertain if there is enough salt. Add if necessary.
4. Add another small ladleful of stock to the rice. Beat together the optional egg and the Parmesan, stir into the rice, and immediately remove from the heat (if not using the egg, just stir in the Parmesan with the last ladleful of stock). Season with pepper, taste one last time, and adjust the salt. The rice should be creamy. Stir for a couple of seconds and serve.

Variation: You can add 1 to 2 garlic cloves, minced or pressed, after cooking the onion for 3 minutes, along with the rice.

Lemon Risotto

Add 2 to 3 tablespoons (to your taste) fresh lemon juice and the finely chopped zest of ½ lemon at the end, with the final ladleful of stock, the egg, and the Parmesan.

Advance preparation: **I've experimented with cooking risotto halfway through, then returning to the dish and finishing it just before serving, with good results. Several hours before serving, you can begin the risotto and cook halfway through step 3, that is, for about 15 minutes. The rice should still be hard when you remove it from the heat. Fifteen minutes before serving, resume cooking as instructed.**

PER SERVING:
5.8 gm total fat
1.9 gm saturated fat
292 calories
49.0 gm carbohydrates
7.2 gm protein

PER SERVING:
5.8 gm total fat
1.9 gm saturated fat
295 calories
49.9 gm carbohydrates
7.3 gm protein

Asparagus and Saffron Risotto

■

Makes 4 to 6 servings

I usually serve this luscious risotto as a main dish or as a dinner party first course. The golden saffron-colored rice against the bright green asparagus is stunning.

Get out the following equipment: chef's knife and cutting board; garlic press or minichop if using; dry and liquid measuring cups; 2-quart saucepan; ladle; lemon zester and lemon press; grater if using; large, heavy nonstick skillet and wooden spoon

Advance preparation: The dish can be prepared through step 3 a few hours before serving. Finish just before serving.

PER SERVING:
5.3 gm total fat
0.8 gm saturated fat
435 calories
82.5 gm carbohydrates
10.6 gm protein

6 to 7 cups vegetable, garlic, defatted chicken stock (pages 155–157), or
   canned broth, as needed
1 tablespoon plus 1 teaspoon olive oil
1 small onion or shallot, peeled and minced
2 to 3 garlic cloves, to your taste, peeled and minced or pressed
Salt to taste
1½ cups Arborio rice
½ cup dry white wine
½ teaspoon saffron threads, crushed by rubbing between your fingers
1½ pounds asparagus, bottoms trimmed and cut into 1-inch pieces
1 ounce Parmesan cheese (optional), grated (¼ cup)
¼ cup chopped flat-leaf parsley leaves
1 tablespoon fresh lemon juice
1 teaspoon grated lemon zest
Freshly ground black pepper to taste

1. Have the stock simmering over low heat in the saucepan.
2. Heat 1 tablespoon of the oil in the skillet over medium heat. Add the onion or shallot and cook, stirring, until tender and beginning to color, about 5 minutes. Add the garlic and a little salt and cook for another 30 seconds, until the garlic begins to color. Add the remaining teaspoon of oil and the rice and continue to cook, stirring, until all the grains are separate, 1 to 2 minutes.
3. Stir in the wine and cook, stirring constantly. The wine should bubble, but not too quickly—you want some of the flavor to cook into the rice before it evaporates. When the wine has just about evaporated, stir in a ladleful or two of the simmering stock, enough to just cover the rice, and the saffron. The stock should bubble slowly. Cook, stirring often, until it is just about absorbed. Add another ladleful of the stock and continue to cook in this fashion, not too fast and not too slowly, adding more stock when the rice is almost dry, for 15 minutes.
4. Add the asparagus and continue adding stock and stirring the rice as you have been doing for another 10 to 15 minutes. Taste a bit of the rice. Is it

cooked through? It should taste chewy but not hard in the middle—and definitely not soft like steamed rice. If it is still hard in the middle, you need to add another ladleful of stock and cook for another 5 minutes or so. The asparagus should be tender. Now is the time to ascertain if there is enough salt. Add if necessary.

5. Add another ladleful of stock to the rice and stir in the Parmesan, parsley, lemon juice, lemon zest, and pepper. Remove from the heat. Taste and adjust the seasonings. The rice should be creamy. Stir for a couple of seconds and serve.

Risotto with Mushrooms and Green Beans

Makes 2 to 3 very generous main-dish servings or 4 starter or side-dish servings

Mushrooms lend a meatiness, and green beans add color and texture to this luscious risotto, which I usually serve as a one-dish meal. Think of this when you have mushrooms in the refrigerator that are just a little too old for a salad but not ready to be thrown out.

4 to 5 cups vegetable, garlic, defatted chicken stock (pages 155–157), or
  canned broth, as needed
2 tablespoons olive oil
½ small onion, peeled and minced (about ¼ cup)
½ pound mushrooms, cleaned, stems trimmed, and sliced
Salt to taste
2 large garlic cloves, peeled and minced or pressed
1 cup Arborio rice
½ cup dry white wine
6 ounces green beans, trimmed and broken in half (about 1½ cups)
1 ounce Parmesan cheese, grated (¼ cup)
Freshly ground black pepper to taste

1. Have the stock simmering over low heat in the saucepan.
2. Heat 1 tablespoon of the oil in the skillet over medium heat. Add the onion and cook, stirring, until it begins to soften, about 3 minutes. Add the mushrooms and about ¼ teaspoon salt and cook, stirring, until the mushrooms release liquid. Continue to cook, stirring, until the liquid is just about evaporated, about 5 minutes. Stir in the remaining tablespoon olive oil, the garlic, and the rice. Cook, stirring, until the grains of rice are separate and beginning to crackle slightly, 1 to 2 minutes.

Get out the following equipment: **chef's knife and cutting board; garlic press or minichop if using; dry and liquid measuring cups; grater; 2-quart saucepan; ladle; large, heavy nonstick skillet and wooden spoon**

Advance preparation: **You can begin the risotto several hours before serving and cook halfway through step 3, that is, for about 15 minutes. The rice should still be hard when you remove it from the heat. Fifteen minutes before serving, resume the cooking as instructed.**

PER SERVING:
19.0 gm total fat
4.8 9 gm saturated fat
731 calories
112.0 gm carbohydrates
18.8 gm protein

Grains, Beans, Vegetables, and Tofu

continued

3. Stir in the wine and cook, stirring. The wine should bubble, but not too quickly—you want some of the flavor to cook into the rice before it evaporates. When the wine has just about evaporated, stir in a ladleful or two of the simmering stock, enough to just cover the rice. The stock should bubble slowly. Cook, stirring often, until it is just about absorbed. Add another ladleful or two of the stock and continue to cook in this fashion, not too fast and not too slowly, adding more stock when the rice is almost dry, for 10 minutes. Add the green beans and continue adding stock as before for another 10 to 15 minutes. Taste a bit of the rice. Is it cooked through? It should taste chewy but not hard in the middle—and definitely not soft like steamed rice. If it is still hard in the middle, you need to add another ladleful of stock and cook for another 5 minutes or so. Now is the time to ascertain if there is enough salt. Add if necessary.

4. Add another ladleful of stock to the rice. Stir in the Parmesan and remove from the heat. Season with pepper, taste one last time, and adjust the salt. The rice should be creamy. Stir for a couple of seconds and serve.

Alternative method: If you want the green beans to retain a brighter green color, blanch them before adding to the risotto and add to the risotto later than indicated here. Blanch them either directly in the stock or in a pot of boiling water. Bring the water or stock to a boil and add a teaspoon or more of salt if using water and the beans. Cook until bright green and just tender, 3 to 5 minutes. Remove from the stock with a slotted spoon or skimmer or drain if blanching in water. Refresh with cold water and set aside. Add to the risotto 5 minutes before the end of cooking.

▪ Stir-Fries ▪

Spicy Stir-Fried Tofu and Asparagus with Rice

Makes 4 servings

This glistening green-and-white stir-fry, like most stir-fries, is quickly accomplished and makes a delicious supper. If you don't like tofu, make it with chicken breasts (see the variation). Green garlic is young, tender, sweet-tasting garlic that comes into farmers' markets in the spring. The bulbs look a bit like leeks.

1 pound asparagus, bottoms trimmed and cut into 1-inch pieces on the
   diagonal
2 tablespoons soy sauce
1 teaspoon white wine vinegar or sherry vinegar
½ teaspoon sugar

Advance preparation: **All of the ingredients can be prepared hours ahead of time, and the rice can be cooked ahead and reheated, but the cooking is done at the last minute.**

PER SERVING:
14.9 gm total fat
1.7 gm saturated fat
396 calories
49.7 gm carbohydrates
19.9 gm protein

¼ cup water

2 teaspoons arrowroot or cornstarch

2 tablespoons canola or peanut oil

1 tablespoon peeled and chopped fresh ginger

1 to 2 dried red chiles, to your taste, crumbled

2 garlic cloves (omit if using green garlic), peeled and minced or pressed

½ cup chopped scallions, both white and green parts, or green garlic, bulbs only

12 ounces firm tofu, cut into small dice

2 tablespoons chopped fresh cilantro leaves

1 cup rice, cooked (page 201)

1. Bring a small amount of water to a boil in a saucepan or wok. Place the asparagus in the steamer over the water, cover, and steam for 3 minutes. Remove from the heat and rinse abundantly with cold water, or transfer to a bowl of ice water. Set aside.
2. Mix together the soy sauce, vinegar, sugar, water, and arrowroot or cornstarch in the measuring cup.
3. Heat your wok or skillet over medium-high heat until hot enough to evaporate a drop of water on contact. Add 1 tablespoon of the oil, then add the ginger, chiles, and garlic cloves if using. Cook, stirring, until they color and become fragrant, about 30 seconds. Add the scallions or green garlic and cook, stirring, for a minute, then add the remaining tablespoon oil and stir in the tofu. Cook, stirring and tossing, until the tofu just begins to color, 2 to 3 minutes. Stir in the asparagus and toss together.
4. Give the soy sauce mixture a stir and add to the vegetables. Cook, stirring, until the sauce glazes the tofu and vegetables, which will happen very quickly Stir in the cilantro, remove from the heat, and serve with the rice.

Spicy Stir-Fried Chicken and Asparagus

PER SERVING:
9.0 gm total fat
1.1 gm saturated fat
348 calories
46.0 gm carbohydrates
20.1 gm protein

Substitute 8 to 10 ounces boneless, skinless chicken breasts for the tofu. Cut the chicken breasts into strips about ¼ inch thick and 2 inches long. Follow the recipe through step 2. Heat your wok or skillet over medium-high heat until hot enough to evaporate a drop of water on contact. Add 1 tablespoon of the oil and the chicken. Cook, stirring, until the chicken is cooked through and there are no longer any traces of pink, 2 to 3 minutes. Remove from the wok and transfer to a plate. Add the remaining tablespoon oil to the wok and continue from step 3. Add the cooked chicken back to the wok after you add the asparagus.

Get out the following equipment: chef's knife and cutting board; garlic press or minichop if using; measuring spoons and measuring cup; large pot; medium bowl of ice water; large, heavy nonstick skillet or well-seasoned wok; wooden spoon or spatula

Advance preparation: All of the ingredients can be prepared and ready to cook, and the sugar snap peas can be blanched hours ahead of time. The stir-frying is a last-minute operation.

PER SERVING:
17.1 gm total fat
2.0 gm saturated fat
435 calories
52.5 gm carbohydrates
20.5 gm protein

Stir-Fried Tofu and Sugar Snap Peas with Rice

Makes 4 servings

This simple stir-fry is quickly made. Sugar snap peas are marvelously sweet, and their flavor and crunch are set off by the soft, gingery tofu.

2 teaspoons salt

1 pound sugar snap peas, strings removed

2 tablespoons soy sauce

1 teaspoon white wine vinegar or sherry vinegar

½ teaspoon sugar

¼ cup water

2 teaspoons arrowroot or cornstarch

2 tablespoons canola or peanut oil

1 tablespoon peeled and chopped fresh ginger

2 garlic cloves, peeled and minced or pressed

12 ounces firm tofu, cut into small dice

2 tablespoons dark sesame oil

1 cup rice, cooked (page 201)

1. Bring a pot of water to a boil. Add the salt and sugar snap peas, boil for 2 minutes, and transfer to the bowl of ice water to stop the cooking. Drain and set aside.

2. Mix together 1 tablespoon of the soy sauce, the vinegar, sugar, water, and arrowroot or cornstarch in a small measuring cup or bowl.

3. Heat the wok or skillet over medium-high heat until a drop of water evaporates on contact. Add the oil, then add the ginger and garlic. Cook, stirring, until they color and become fragrant, about 30 seconds. Add the tofu and the remaining tablespoon soy sauce. Cook, stirring and tossing, until the tofu just begins to color, 2 to 3 minutes. Stir in the sugar snap peas and toss together.

4. Give the soy sauce mixture a stir and add to the vegetables. Stir together until the sauce glazes the tofu and vegetables, which will happen very quickly (almost instantly). Immediately remove from the heat and stir in the sesame oil. Serve with the rice.

Spicy Stir-Fried Tofu with Chinese Greens and Daikon

Makes 4 servings

This is a spicy, brothy stir-fry with meaty dried Chinese mushrooms and tofu. If you want a thicker glaze, use the optional cornstarch or arrowroot mixture. Daikon are long, fat white radishes used widely in China and Japan. If you have trouble finding daikon in your supermarket, substitute ½ pound turnips. Peel them, cut in half, and slice paper-thin.

½ ounce (about 5 large) dried shiitake mushrooms

Boiling water as needed

1 pound Chinese greens, such as baby bok choy, Chinese broccoli, or Napa cabbage

1 tablespoon peeled and finely minced fresh ginger

1 tablespoon peeled and finely minced or pressed garlic

½ teaspoon salt, preferably kosher salt or sea salt

½ to ¾ teaspoon dried red pepper flakes, to your taste

2 tablespoons soy sauce

¼ cup sake or dry sherry

1 to 2 tablespoons canola oil, as needed

¾ pound firm tofu, cut into ¾-inch cubes

½ pound daikon radish, peeled and sliced into paper-thin rounds

2 teaspoons cornstarch or arrowroot dissolved in 1½ tablespoons water (optional)

1 cup rice, cooked (page 201), or ½ pound soba, cooked (page 174)

1. Place the dried mushrooms in a bowl and pour over boiling water to cover. Let sit for 15 minutes while you prepare the remaining ingredients. When thoroughly softened, drain over another bowl through the strainer (lined with cheesecloth if the mushrooms are sandy), squeeze out more moisture over the strainer, and rinse well to remove sand. Set the soaking water aside. Cut away the tough stems and discard and slice the caps ½ inch thick.

2. While the mushrooms are soaking, prepare the greens. Wash thoroughly. Cut off at the base and slice the leaves and stems about 1 inch thick. For cabbage, cut larger leaves in half lengthwise first. If the broccoli stems are thick, blanch in a large pot of boiling water for 10 seconds, then submerge in cold water to stop the cooking and drain.

Get out the following equipment: 2 small or medium-size bowls; chef's knife and cutting board; garlic press or minichop if using; vegetable peeler; fine-mesh strainer lined with cheesecloth; measuring cups and measuring spoons; well-seasoned wok or large, heavy nonstick skillet and wooden spoon or spatula

Advance preparation: The mushrooms can be soaked, greens blanched, and all the ingredients prepared hours ahead of time. The cooking is last-minute.

PER SERVING:
13.3 gm total fat
1.6 gm saturated fat
405 calories
50.1 gm carbohydrates
20.3 gm protein

Advance preparation:
The mushrooms can be soaked, greens blanched, and all the ingredients prepared hours ahead of time. The cooking is last-minute.

PER SERVING:
14.9 gm total fat
2.1 gm saturated fat
433 calories
58.2 gm carbohydrates
19.8 gm protein

3. Combine the ginger, garlic, salt, and pepper flakes in a bowl and mash together with a fork. Cover and set aside.

4. Combine the soy sauce, sake or sherry, and ⅓ cup of the strained soaking water from the mushrooms in another bowl, cover, and set aside.

5. Heat the wok or skillet over medium-high heat until a drop of water evaporates on contact. Add 1 tablespoon of the oil and the garlic mixture and cook, stirring, until fragrant and beginning to color, about 30 seconds. Add the sliced mushrooms and tofu and cook, stirring gently but constantly, for 2 minutes. Add a teaspoon of the remaining oil or as needed to prevent sticking. Add the daikon and toss for another 30 seconds to a minute, until just beginning to soften. Add the greens and toss for another 30 seconds to a minute, until beginning to wilt.

6. Stir the soy sauce mixture and add to the wok. Bring to a boil, cover the wok, and reduce the heat to low. Simmer for 30 seconds to a minute, until the greens are just wilted and the stems crisp-tender. If you want a thicker sauce, stir the cornstarch mixture and add. Stir until the sauce glazes the tofu and vegetable mixture. Remove from the heat and serve at once over rice or noodles.

Spicy Stir-Fried Tofu with Zucchini and Carrots

Makes 4 servings

This is a piquant, multicolored stir-fry. I like it with rice or with noodles. Both carrots and zucchini are good keepers, so think of this dish when you find them in the drawer of your refrigerator and you're wondering what to eat.

Get out the following equipment: chef's knife and cutting board; minichop if using; 2 medium-size bowls; measuring cup and measuring spoons; large pot or saucepan; bowl of ice water; well-seasoned wok or large, heavy nonstick skillet and wooden spoon or spatula

Advance preparation:
The vegetables can be prepared and blanched hours before you make this. The ingredients for the sauce can also be mixed. It's best if you serve this dish right away, but it does reheat well.

1 tablespoon peeled and finely minced fresh ginger

1 tablespoon peeled and finely minced garlic

½ teaspoon salt, preferably kosher or sea salt

½ to ¾ teaspoon red pepper flakes, to your taste

½ cup unsalted vegetable or defatted chicken stock (page 156 or 155), canned broth, or water

2 tablespoons soy sauce

2 tablespoons rice wine vinegar or distilled white vinegar

½ teaspoon sugar

¾ pound carrots, peeled and cut on the diagonal into ⅛-inch-thick rounds

1 pound zucchini, cut on the diagonal into ¼-inch-thick rounds

2 tablespoons corn, canola, or peanut oil

¾ pound firm tofu, cut into ¾-inch cubes

1 tablespoon cornstarch or arrowroot dissolved in 1½ tablespoons cold
    water or stock
2 scallions, both white and green parts, cut on the diagonal, for garnish
1 cup rice, cooked (page 201) or ½ pound soba, cooked (page 174)

PER SERVING:
15 gm total fat
2.1 gm saturated fat
433 calories
58.2 gm carbohydrates
19.8 gm protein

1. Combine the ginger, garlic, salt, and pepper flakes in a bowl and mash together with a fork. Cover and set aside.
2. Combine the stock, broth, or water, soy sauce, vinegar, and sugar in another bowl, cover, and set aside.
3. Bring a pot of water to a boil and add the carrots. Blanch for 15 seconds
   (once the water returns to the boil), remove from the water, and transfer
   to the bowl of ice water to stop the cooking. Drain and set aside. Return
   the water to a boil and add the zucchini. Blanch for 15 seconds, remove
   from the water, and transfer to the ice water to stop the cooking. Drain
   and set aside.
4. Heat the wok or skillet over medium-high heat until a drop of water
   evaporates on contact. Add 1 tablespoon of the oil, swirl to coat the wok,
   and reduce the heat to medium-high. Add the ginger mixture and cook,
   stirring, until fragrant and beginning to color, about 30 seconds. Add the
   tofu and cook, stirring gently, for 2 minutes. Add the remaining tablespoon oil and the carrots and cook, stirring constantly but gently, for 1
   minute. Add the zucchini and cook, stirring constantly but gently, for another minute.
5. Stir the soy sauce mixture and add to the wok. Bring to a simmer, cover,
   and cook until the vegetables are just cooked through but still crisp,
   about 1 minute. Give the cornstarch mixture a stir and add. Cook, stirring, until the sauce thickens and glazes the tofu and vegetables (this happens almost immediately). Remove from the heat and sprinkle with the
   sliced scallions. Serve at once over rice or noodles.

Fried Rice and Vegetables

Makes 4 servings

Fried rice is a great dish for using up leftovers—meat, tofu, vegetables, and,
of course, rice. It can be simple or elaborate. If you have nothing in the
fridge but a carrot or a bunch of broccoli, fine, as long as you have garlic,
ginger, soy sauce, and eggs.

continued

2 teaspoons salt

1 bunch broccoli, broken into florets and stems peeled and chopped

2 tablespoons canola, peanut, or safflower oil

1 medium-size onion, peeled and chopped, or 1 bunch scallions, both white and green parts, sliced and kept separate

2 large garlic cloves, peeled and minced or pressed

2 teaspoons peeled and minced or grated fresh ginger

2 large eggs, beaten

3 cups cooked white or brown rice (page 201)

1 to 2 tablespoons soy sauce, to your taste

2 to 3 tablespoons chopped fresh cilantro leaves, to your taste

1. Bring a pot of water to a boil, add the salt, and drop in the broccoli. Blanch for 3 minutes and transfer to the ice water. Drain and set aside.
2. Heat the wok or skillet over medium-high heat until a drop of water evaporates on contact. Add the oil and the onion or the scallion whites. Stir until translucent, 2 to 3 minutes, then add the garlic and ginger. Stir for about 30 seconds, until fragrant and starting to color, then add the broccoli. Stir together for a minute, then add the beaten eggs. As soon as you see them beginning to set, stir in the rice and soy sauce. Toss together for a couple of minutes, until the rice is heated through and the eggs are dispersed through the rice. Remove from the heat, stir in the cilantro and scallion greens, taste and adjust the soy sauce, and serve.

■ Vegetable Dishes ■

Steamed Artichokes

■

Makes 4 servings

A steamed artichoke, hot or cold, can make a light supper or a terrific starter. Sometimes they're so large that one will be sufficient for two people. I love the leisure of eating artichokes, leaf by leaf, until you get to the treasured heart. As for dips, I use a lemony vinaigrette or a garlicky yogurt dip, and never give butter a thought.

2 large or 4 medium-size artichokes

½ lemon

How to Prepare Artichokes: Artichokes take a bit of work before you cook them—not much, but you should trim away the thorny ends of the leaves. This is when you'll really be glad that you bought those kitchen scissors. First, lay the artichoke on a cutting board and, using a sharp chef's knife, cut away the entire top quarter of the artichoke in one slice. Now cut across the thorny end of each of the leaves with scissors. This goes faster than you think. Cut the stems so that the artichoke will stand upright, and rinse thoroughly under cold water. Rub the cut surfaces with the cut side of your lemon to prevent discoloring.

Bring about 1 inch of water to a boil in the bottom of a saucepan, wok, or steamer. Place the artichokes on a steaming rack upside down or, if the rack is too high and the lid won't fit over the artichokes, place them right in the water upside down. Cover, reduce the heat to medium, and steam for 30 to 40 minutes, depending on the size of the artichokes. Check from time to time to make sure the water hasn't all evaporated. Test for doneness by pulling a leaf away; it should not resist. Remove from the heat and serve, or rinse with cold water, allow to cool, and serve cold or at room temperature.

Yogurt Dip with Mint or Dill

Makes about ¾ cup

This is not only good with artichokes. Try it with crudités, steamed vegetables, or baked potatoes.

> ¾ cup plain nonfat yogurt or drained nonfat yogurt (see page 229 for a
> thicker dip)
> 2 garlic cloves, peeled and halved
> ¼ teaspoon salt
> ¼ cup chopped fresh mint or dill
> Fresh lemon juice to taste

1. Place the yogurt in a bowl.
2. Pound the garlic and salt together into a paste in a mortar and pestle. Stir into the yogurt along with the mint or dill and the lemon juice.

Other Dipping Sauces for Artichokes

Low-Fat Lemon-Yogurt or Buttermilk Vinaigrette (page 125)
Vinaigrette (page 56)

Get out the following equipment: measuring cup; paring knife; mortar and pestle; measuring spoons; chef's knife and cutting board or scissors

Advance preparation: This can be held for a few hours in the refrigerator, but the garlic will become more pungent.

PER ¼-CUP SERVING:
0 gm total fat
0 gm saturated fat
28 calories
4.5 gm carbohydrates
2.6 gm protein

Creamy Garlic Dip

This makes a great dip for other steamed vegetables, crudités, and artichokes. It also makes a good substitute for garlic mayonnaise. Use a food processor, mini-processor, or blender, or the cottage cheese won't smooth out properly.

2 garlic cloves, peeled and halved

¼ teaspoon salt or more to taste

½ cup nonfat cottage cheese

3 tablespoons plain nonfat yogurt

2 tablespoons mayonnaise, preferably Hellmann's or Best Foods

1. Pound the garlic and salt together into a paste in a mortar and pestle.
2. Blend the cottage cheese in a blender, mini-processor, or food processor fitted with the steel blade until fairly smooth. Add the yogurt and mayonnaise and continue to blend until very smooth. Add the garlic paste and combine well. Taste and adjust the salt.

Caponata

Makes 6 servings

Caponata is a Sicilian eggplant dish that combines eggplant, celery, capers, and olives in a sweet-and-sour tomato sauce. I haven't seen a recipe that also contains red peppers, but I think the peppers add beautiful (and necessary) color and sweet depth to the dish. This is really just another version of ratatouille, the Provençal vegetable stew on page 73, using other Mediterranean ingredients. It should be served at room temperature and benefits from a day or two in the refrigerator; a perfect do-ahead dish for a party. The best type of canned tomatoes to use for this are crushed tomatoes in puree—they are ready to go and don't require the added step of pureeing the tomatoes.

1 large eggplant (about 1½ pounds), cut in half lengthwise

1 tablespoon salt (for cooking water) plus about 1 teaspoon or more to your taste, for the caponata

3 celery ribs, cut into ½-inch-thick slices

2 tablespoons olive oil

1 medium-size onion, peeled and chopped

3 large garlic cloves, peeled and minced or pressed

2 medium-size red bell peppers, seeded and diced (about ½-inch cubes)

Get out the following equipment: measuring cup and measuring spoons; paring knife; mortar and pestle; minichop or food processor fitted with steel blade or blender; spatula

Advance preparation: This will keep in the refrigerator until the cottage cheese "sell by" date, but the garlic will become more pungent.

PER ¾-CUP SERVING:
5.5 gm total fat
0.8 gm saturated fat
78 calories
2.5 gm carbohydrates
4.5 gm protein

One 14-ounce can or half a 28-ounce can crushed tomatoes in puree

2 tablespoons plus ¼ teaspoon sugar

3 heaping tablespoons capers, rinsed and drained

¼ cup pitted green olives, coarsely chopped

¼ cup red wine vinegar or sherry vinegar

Freshly ground black pepper to taste

1. Preheat the oven to 450°F. Lightly oil a baking sheet with olive oil. Score the eggplant halves down to the skin but not through it. Place the eggplant on the baking sheet, cut side down, and bake until the eggplant collapses and the skin begins to shrivel, about 20 minutes. Remove from the oven, transfer cut side down to a bowl or a colander set in the sink, and allow to cool. The eggplant should lose a lot of water as it cools. This is bitter, and you should throw it out. When cool enough to handle, pull off the skin, scraping off any eggplant that adheres to it, and cut the eggplant into ½-inch pieces, discarding the skin. The eggplant will be soft and is not meant to hold its shape.

2. While the eggplant is roasting, bring a pot of water to a boil and add 1 tablespoon of the salt and the celery. Cook until just tender, about 5 minutes, then drain and rinse with cold water. Set aside.

3. Heat 1 tablespoon of the oil over medium heat in the skillet and add the onion. Cook, stirring, until tender but not browned, about 5 minutes, then add 2 of the garlic cloves. Cook together for a minute, until the garlic begins to smell fragrant, then add the red peppers and about ¼ teaspoon of salt. Cook, stirring, until the peppers are just about tender, about 8 minutes. Add the eggplant and stir together until all the vegetables are tender, another 5 minutes. The eggplant will fall apart, which is fine. Transfer to a bowl.

4. Add the remaining tablespoon olive oil and the remaining garlic to the skillet. Cook for about 30 seconds, just until the garlic begins to color, then add the tomatoes with about ¼ teaspoon salt and ¼ teaspoon of the sugar. Cook, stirring, until the tomatoes have cooked down somewhat—they should not be dry, however—and smell fragrant, 5 to 10 minutes. Return all of the vegetables to the skillet and stir together. Add the celery, capers, olives, the remaining 2 tablespoons sugar, and the vinegar. Reduce the heat to medium-low and cook, stirring often, until the vegetables are thoroughly tender and the mixture is quite thick, sweet, and fragrant, 15 to 30 minutes. Season with salt and pepper and remove from the heat. Allow to cool to room temperature. If possible, cover and chill overnight.

To serve, allow the caponata to come to room temperature. Taste it again to make sure the salt is right. Mound in a wide shallow bowl and surround with croutons, fennel sticks, and celery.

Get out the following equipment: chef's knife and cutting board; baking sheet; large, heavy nonstick skillet and long-handled wooden spoon; saucepan or pot; measuring spoons and measuring cups; 3-quart or larger saucepan or pot; large bowl

Advance preparation: This will keep for a week in the refrigerator and can be frozen for a few months.

PER SERVING:
5.7 gm total fat
0.8 gm saturated fat
128 calories
19.0 gm carbohydrates
2.8 gm protein

Preferred Cooking Methods for Vegetables

Vegetable	Steam	Bake/Roast	Blanch/Boil	Pan-Cook
Artichokes	30 to 45 minutes, depending on size (see page 220)			
Asparagus	5 to 10 minutes; trim by snapping off tough bottoms first			
Beans: Green, Yellow, Italian	5 to 8 minutes; remove strings and snap if directed first		2 to 5 minutes; remove strings and snap if directed first	
Beans, Fava			1 minute; remove from pods, boil 1 minute, rinse with cold water, and slip off shells (see page 231)	
Beets	30 to 40 minutes for whole; 15 to 30 minutes for wedges	425°F; 30 to 45 minutes (60 minutes for large beets); covered, 1/4 inch water in dish. (See page 238)		
Broccoli	5 to 8 minutes		2 to 5 minutes	
Brussels Sprouts	Steam 1 to 2 minutes; lift cover for 15 seconds; cover and steam for 5 to 12 minutes			
Cabbage	Steam 1 to 2 minutes; lift cover for 15 seconds; cover and steam 3 to 5 minutes for shredded cabbage; 5 to 10 minutes for wedges			Wilt shredded cabbage in a small amount of liquid or oil in nonstick pan; 5 to 10 minutes
Carrots	5 to 10 minutes for whole; 3 to 4 minutes for slices	350°F; 30 to 45 minutes, covered		
Cauliflower	Steam 1 to 2 minutes; lift cover for 15 seconds; cover and steam for 5 to 8 minutes for florets, 12 to 20 minutes for whole cauliflower			
Corn on the Cob	5 to 8 minutes		5 to 8 minutes	
Eggplant		450°F. Cut in half lengthwise, score, and bake 20 to 30 minutes, depending on the recipe. For a smoky flavor, grill or broil, turning every 10 minutes, until uniformly charred		

Vegetable	Steam	Bake/Roast	Blanch/Boil	Pan-Cook
Greens: Broccoli Raab, Collards, Kale, Dandelion Greens, Mustard Greens, Swiss Chard, Turnip Greens, Beet Greens, Spinach	"Steam" softer greens like spinach and Swiss chard in the water left on leaves after washing. Heat in a large nonstick skillet until the leaves wilt		The best method for most greens, particularly the tougher ones. Cook 3 to 5 minutes or longer to taste	Greens can be pan-cooked in olive oil with garlic and other seasonings. They should be blanched or steamed first. See page 23
Mushrooms				Pan-cook for 5 to 20 minutes (see recipe, page 233)
Parsnips	20 to 40 minutes for whole; 5 to 15 minutes for cut up	350°F for 30 to 60 minutes (whole, covered)		
Peas, Sugar Snap Peas, Snow Peas	Peas: 5 to 10 minutes; sugar snap peas: 2 to 5 minutes; snow peas: 2 to 3 minutes		1 to 5 minutes for sugar snap and shelled peas; 30 seconds to a minute for snow peas	
Sweet Peppers		400°F for 30 to 40 minutes (see recipe, page 131)		In olive or canola oil, depending on the recipe, for 8 to 10 minutes
Potatoes	10 minutes for diced, 20 to 40 minutes for whole	425°F for 45 to 60 minutes for russets (see recipe, page 236 for others)	Boil whole potatoes for 10 to 30 minutes, depending on the size	
Squash, Summer: Zucchini, golden, Zucchini, yellow, Crookneck, yellow, Straightneck, Patty Pan	3 to 5 minutes for diced or sliced; 10 to 12 minutes for whole			5 to 10 minutes, according to the recipe
Squash, Winter: Butternut, Pumpkin, Spaghetti, Acorn, Banana. Use a heavy knife or cleaver to cut in half, then scoop out seeds and fibers; peel after cooking unless directed	10 to 20 minutes for pieces, depending on the size	400°F; 30 to 60 minutes for large cut-up pieces, 40 to 60 minutes for large halves or whole squash. Covered, ¼ inch water in dish		
Sweet Potatoes		425°F; 30 to 60 minutes, depending on the size; pierce in a few places before baking		
Tomatoes		400°F for 20 minutes; 300°F for 2 hours; roast under broiler for 2 to 5 minutes, turn and repeat (see page 235)		Pan-cook for sauces
Turnips	20 to 25 minutes for whole medium; 5 to 15 minutes for cut-up or small	350°F; 30 to 45 minutes for quartered; covered		

Get out the following equipment: chef's knife and cutting board; garlic press or minichop if using; baking sheet; measuring spoons; large, heavy skillet and wooden spoon; 2- to 2½-quart baking or gratin dish; large measuring cup; grater; food processor

Advance preparation: The gratin can be assembled up to 3 days before baking and kept, covered with plastic wrap, in the refrigerator. It can also be frozen for several months, before or after baking.

PER SERVING:
6.5 gm total fat
1.8 gm saturated fat
177 calories
24.5 gm carbohydrates
7.8 gm protein

Eggplant "Parmesan"

∎

Makes 6 servings

This heady gratin has everything I love about eggplant Parmesan, minus the fat. The eggplant is baked, rather than fried as it is in traditional similar dishes. Consequently it will not form neat slices, and your layers of eggplant might be rather amorphous. But that won't matter in the final dish. The gratin is even better if it sits for a day in the refrigerator, allowing the flavors to ripen. Assemble as directed, but do not bake until the day you are serving it.

3 pounds (3 medium-large) eggplant, cut in half lengthwise

4 teaspoons olive oil

3 large garlic cloves, peeled and minced or pressed

3 pounds (12 medium-size) firm, ripe tomatoes, peeled and seeded, or two 28-ounce cans tomatoes, drained and seeded, coarsely pureed in a food processor

¼ teaspoon sugar

Salt to taste

3 tablespoons slivered fresh basil leaves or 1 teaspoon dried oregano

Freshly ground black pepper to taste

1½ ounces Parmesan cheese, grated (⅓ cup)

¼ cup fresh or dry bread crumbs

1. Preheat the oven to 450°F. Cut the eggplants in half lengthwise, score them down the middle to the skin but not through it, and place on an oiled baking sheet cut side down. Bake until thoroughly tender, 30 to 35 minutes. Remove from the oven and allow to cool. When cool enough to handle, carefully peel away the skins or scoop the eggplant out from the skins and cut into ¼-inch-thick slices. Don't worry if the slices fall apart. Reduce the oven temperature to 425°F.

2. While the eggplants are baking, heat 1 teaspoon of the oil in the skillet over medium heat and add the garlic. When it begins to color, 30 seconds to a minute, add the tomatoes, sugar, salt, and basil or oregano. Cook, stirring often, until the tomatoes have cooked down and are beginning to stick to the skillet (the time varies with the juiciness and ripeness of the tomatoes), 15 to 30 minutes. Taste the sauce and adjust the salt. Season with pepper, then transfer to the measuring cup.

3. Oil the baking or gratin dish. Spoon a small amount of the tomato sauce over the bottom and place one third of the eggplant slices on top. Salt and pepper the eggplant lightly. Spoon one third of the remaining

tomato sauce over the eggplant. Make 2 more layers, seasoning each layer of eggplant and ending with tomato sauce. Mix together the cheese and bread crumbs and sprinkle over the top. Drizzle on the remaining tablespoon olive oil. Bake until the top is lightly browned and the gratin is bubbling, 30 to 40 minutes. Remove from the heat and serve hot or warm.

Cauliflower Gratin with Goat Cheese

Makes 6 servings

This rich-tasting gratin is quickly thrown together and is one of the most delicious cauliflower dishes I can think of.

1 large cauliflower, broken into florets and stems discarded
1 large garlic clove, peeled
½ pound (about 1 cup) nonfat cottage cheese
3 ounces (about ¾ cup) goat cheese
¼ cup skim milk or plain nonfat yogurt
2 teaspoons fresh thyme leaves or 1 teaspoon dried thyme
Freshly ground black pepper to taste
⅓ cup fresh or dry bread crumbs
1 tablespoon olive oil

1. Preheat the oven to 425°F. Oil the baking or gratin dish.
2. Bring an inch of water to a boil in the saucepan fitted with the steamer. Add the cauliflower, cover, and steam until tender, about 10 minutes. Drain and spread out in an even layer in the dish.
3. Turn on the food processor and drop in the garlic to chop. Add the cottage cheese and goat cheese and blend together until smooth. Add the milk or yogurt, thyme, and pepper and blend until the mixture is quite smooth.
4. Spread the goat cheese mixture over the cauliflower. Sprinkle on the bread crumbs. Drizzle on the olive oil. Place in the oven and bake until the bread crumbs are browned and the dish is bubbling, 15 to 20 minutes. Serve hot or warm.

Get out the following equipment: **chef's knife and cutting board; 2-quart baking or gratin dish; steamer large enough for steaming a head of cauliflower; measuring cups and measuring spoons; food processor fitted with steel blade**

Advance preparation: **The dish can be assembled up to a day ahead of baking and held in the refrigerator. Once the dish is ready, you can turn off the oven and leave it there until ready to serve, or for about an hour. It's most dramatic, however (if drama is what you're after), if you take it, sizzling, from the oven to the table.**

PER SERVING:
5.79 gm total fat
2.4 gm saturated fat
132 calories
11.3 gm carbohydrates
10.9 gm protein

Corn on the Cob

PER SERVING:
1.0 gm total fat
0.2 gm saturated fat
83 calories
19.3 gm carbohydrates
2.6 gm protein

Corn on the cob, in season, can be a meal in itself, or at least the highlight of the meal. Its success depends on the quality of the corn itself. It must be sweet and freshly picked. My advice is to buy local corn in season and to refrigerate it as soon as you get home; at room temperature corn loses its sugar six times faster than at 32°F and can lose up to half its sugar content in one day. Cook it as soon after buying it as possible. Leave it unhusked until you are ready to cook it. If you can't use the corn for a day or two, husk and parboil for 2 minutes, then store in the refrigerator in plastic bags. This stops the conversion of sugar to starch.

Once you have a good ear, the only other key is not to overcook it—4 or 7 minutes steaming or boiling is all it needs (the time variation is dependent on the maturity of the corn; most often I cook it for 5 minutes). And if you're cooking only one or two ears, there's nothing easier than the microwave.

When is corn done? To test for doneness, I pierce a kernel with my thumbnail. It should not resist, but it should still be moist, and the color should be deeper than that of the uncooked corn.

Steaming: Shuck the corn, removing the leaves and all of the silk. If the stem is so long that the corn won't fit into the steamer, cut or break it off. Bring 1 inch of water to a boil in the bottom of a steamer or a large pot and place the corn on the steaming rack. Cover and steam for 5 to 8 minutes. Remove from the heat, wrap in a clean kitchen towel, and serve on a platter or transfer directly to plates.

Boiling: Do not salt boiling water for corn because salt will toughen the corn. Bring a large pot of water to a rolling boil and add the corn. Boil for 5 to 8 minutes; or, when the water comes back to a boil, cover and turn off the heat and let sit for 5 minutes. Drain, wrap in a clean kitchen towel, and serve on a platter, or transfer directly to plates.

Microwaving: This is really convenient if you're cooking only one or two ears. Do not shuck the corn. Place one or two ears of corn on a plate with a tablespoon of water. Microwave at 100% power, 2 minutes for one ear, 5 minutes for two (or check your microwave manual). Remove from the heat, allow to cool until you can handle the ears, and shuck. Serve at once.

Grilling: Do not shuck the corn. About 1 hour before serving, place the corn, in their husks, in a large bowl or pot of water, or in a sink full of water, and weight down with heavy pans to keep the ears submerged.

Prepare your grill with the grill about 4 inches from the coals. When the coals are medium-hot, the grill is ready for the corn. If you are using a gas grill, set it between medium and medium-high. Twenty to 30 minutes before serving, lay the corn on the grill. Turn the corn after 10 minutes and grill until the outer leaves are blackened, another 10 minutes (it should cook for about 20 minutes altogether; some of the kernels should be lightly browned). Remove from the grill and let sit until you can handle it, then remove the leaves and silk. Wrap in a clean kitchen towel to keep warm and serve.

What to Serve on Corn? Butter is traditional, but it's not a light alternative. I find salt and pepper sufficient for really sweet corn. You could brush the corn with a bit of olive oil or serve with one of the creamy sauces that follow.

Thickened Yogurt with Garlic

Makes ½ cup

1 cup plain nonfat yogurt

1 or 2 large garlic cloves, to your taste, peeled

¼ teaspoon salt

1 tablespoon chopped fresh herbs, such as flat-leaf parsley, thyme, chives, sage, and/or tarragon

2 teaspoons olive oil (optional)

1 to 2 teaspoons fresh lemon juice (optional), to your taste

1. Drain the yogurt: place in a cheesecloth-lined strainer set over a bowl and let drain in the refrigerator for a couple of hours.

2. Mash the garlic and salt together into a paste in a mortar and pestle. Mix with the yogurt and herbs. Add the olive oil and lemon juice if desired and mix well.

Creamy Chipotle Dip

Makes 1½ cups

This dip, from my book *Mexican Light*, is one of my all-time favorite corn condiments. Naturally it's the perfect match when the meal has Mexican overtones. Chipotle chiles are smoked jalapeños. They are canned in a barbecuelike sauce called *adobo* and available wherever Mexican products are sold. This dip is also wonderful with shrimp and with steamed vegetables and crudités.

Get out the following equipment: **medium-size strainer lined with cheesecloth; medium bowl; measuring cup; measuring spoons; mortar and pestle; whisk or fork**

Advance preparation: **This will keep for a few hours in the refrigerator, but the garlic will become more pungent.**

PER **2**-TABLESPOON SERVING:
2.47 gm total fat
0.4 gm saturated fat
54 calories
4.9 gm carbohydrates
3.47 gm protein

Get out the following equipment: **measuring cups and measuring spoons; mortar and pestle; food processor fitted with steel blade; spatula**

Grains, Beans, Vegetables, and Tofu

229

continued

Other Simple Condiments for Corn

- Salt and ground cumin, mixed
- Pure ground chile powder or cayenne pepper
- Salt and curry powder, mixed
- Red or green salsa

Get out the following equipment: 2-quart baking or gratin dish; large, heavy nonstick skillet and wooden spoon; chef's knife and cutting board; measuring spoons; measuring cup; blender or food processor fitted with steel blade; cheese grater

Advance preparation:
This is nice served warm, so bake it an hour ahead and let sit on the stove or reheat in a low oven. Assemble the gratin several hours before baking and refrigerate. Take it out a half hour before you bake and stir before putting it into the oven.

2 large garlic cloves, peeled and cut in half lengthwise

½ teaspoon salt

2 canned chipotle chiles in adobo, rinsed and seeded

1 cup nonfat cottage cheese

¼ cup plain nonfat yogurt

¼ cup Hellmann's or Best Foods mayonnaise

1. Place the garlic cloves in a mortar with ¼ teaspoon of the salt and pound and mash together with the pestle until the mixture is smooth. Add the chipotles and continue to pound and mash to a paste with the garlic.

2. Place the cottage cheese in the food processor and blend until smooth. Add the yogurt and mayonnaise and continue to blend until the mixture is very smooth; the cottage cheese should not be grainy at all. Add the chipotle paste and blend in. Taste and adjust the salt. Refrigerate in a covered container until ready to use.

Note: If you want to make the dip without using a mortar, before adding the cottage cheese to the food processor, turn on and drop in the garlic and chipotles with the machine running. Stop the machine, scrape down the sides, add salt, and proceed with step 2.

Southwestern Corn and Pepper Gratin

Makes 4 to 6 servings

The sweetness of corn contrasts beautifully here with the spice of fresh chiles and cumin. This gratin tastes luxuriously rich due to the custard mixture of pureed corn, milk, and eggs. It's as beautiful to look at as it is delicious.

Kernels from 4 ears of corn (3 to 4 cups, depending on their size)

1 tablespoon olive or canola oil

1 medium-size white onion, peeled and chopped

1 medium-size green bell pepper, seeded and diced (about 1 cup)

1 medium-size red bell pepper, seeded and diced (about 1 cup)

Salt to taste

2 serrano or 1 jalapeño chile, seeded for a milder gratin and finely chopped

1 teaspoon cumin seeds, crushed in a mortar and pestle

Freshly ground black pepper to taste

1½ ounces Monterey Jack or mild white cheddar cheese, grated (⅓ cup)

3 large eggs

½ cup skim milk

1. Preheat the oven to 425°F. Separate ¾ cup of the corn kernels from the remaining kernels. Oil the baking or gratin dish.

2. Heat the oil in the skillet over medium heat. Add the onion and cook, stirring often, until tender, about 5 minutes. Add the green and red peppers and ¼ teaspoon salt. Continue to cook, stirring, for 5 minutes. Add the chiles, all the corn kernels but the ¾ cup you set aside, and the cumin. Cook, stirring often, until the vegetables are just tender, about 5 minutes. Remove from the heat and season with salt and pepper. Toss with the grated cheese. Transfer to the baking dish.

3. In the blender or food processor, blend together the eggs, milk, the reserved corn kernels, and about ½ teaspoon salt until fairly smooth.

4. Pour the milk mixture over the corn-and-pepper mixture in the baking dish. Give the mixture a stir. Place in the oven and bake until set, firm, and golden brown, 30 to 40 minutes. Serve hot or warm.

PER SERVING:
11.7 gm total fat
3.8 gm saturated fat
253 calories
28.3 gm carbohydrates
12.4 gm protein

Fava Beans with Swiss Chard

Makes 4 to 6 servings

This is inspired by a classic dish from Apulia in southern Italy that is made with a bitter green called *chicory*—what we call curly endive. Swiss chard also pairs beautifully with the fresh fava beans. A cross between a soup and a stew, the greens and beans are served in their broth over garlicky bruschetta. I make the dish in the spring, when favas come into my farmers' markets in abundance. Fava beans, a Mediterranean staple, are relatively new on the American vegetable scene and are available mostly at farmers' markets and vegetable stands. They are large flat green beans that come in a thick pod. They require a bit of work, because once you remove them from the pods, you have to peel them, since each bean is wrapped in a very tough shell. This is easy to do—you just blanch for 1 minute, rinse with cold water, and pop the shells off—but it does take time. For me, the time is well spent, because I love the beans so much. Favas also come in dried form. When they are dry, their hull is brown and the beans yellow; but often the dried beans are sold already hulled. In Italy this dish is made with dried beans in winter, but this is the springtime version. If you can't find fava beans, try this dish with fresh peas. Substitute 2 pounds peas (unshelled weight), shelled, and omit step 1.

The Parmesan rind, that hard end of the Parmesan chunk that you pay for and then throw away, adds a cheesy flavor without cheese, so fat remains low. I use Parmesan rind to flavor some of my soups as well (see page 153).

Get out the following equipment: **chef's knife and cutting board; garlic press or minichop if using; large, heavy casserole or soup pot; strainer, skimmer, or slotted spoon; bowl of ice water; measuring spoons; grater; medium-size bowl; wooden spoon**

Advance preparation: **The beans and Swiss chard can be cooked a few hours ahead of time and reheated. All of the vegetables can be prepared hours ahead of making the dish.**

Grains, Beans, Vegetables, and Tofu

continued

PER SERVING:
7.8 gm total fat
1.9 gm saturated fat
467 calories
78.2 gm carbohydrates
25.9 gm protein

4 pounds fresh fava beans, shelled

1 pound Swiss chard leaves (about 2 pounds with stems)

Salt

2 tablespoons olive oil

2 medium-size onions, 1 peeled and chopped, and 1 (optional), grated or
  finely chopped and rinsed with cold water, for garnish

6 large garlic cloves, peeled and minced or pressed

5 cups water

1 Parmesan rind (optional)

Freshly ground black pepper to taste

4 to 6 thick slices country bread

1 garlic clove, cut in half lengthwise

1 ounce Parmesan cheese, grated (about ¼ cup)

1. Fill the casserole with water, bring to a boil, and drop in the fava beans. Boil for 1 minute, then remove the beans from the water with a skimmer, strainer, or slotted spoon; transfer them immediately to the ice water. Let sit for 1 minute, then drain. Remove the tough outer skins from the beans. They should pop off easily if you break them open at the sprout end and squeeze gently.

2. After removing the chard leaves from the stems and discarding the stems, wash the leaves thoroughly in cold water to remove sand. Bring the casserole of water back to a rolling boil, then add 2 teaspoons salt and the chard. Boil for 2 minutes and transfer, using a skimmer or slotted spoon, to a bowl of ice water. Drain, squeeze dry, and chop coarsely. Set aside. Drain the casserole and wipe dry.

3. Heat 1 tablespoon of the olive oil in the casserole or soup pot over medium heat and add the chopped onion. Cook, stirring, until tender, about 5 minutes. Add half the chopped garlic, stir together for about 30 seconds, and add the fava beans, water, and optional Parmesan rind. Bring to a boil. Add the remaining chopped garlic, season with salt, reduce the heat to low, cover, and simmer for 20 minutes. Remove the Parmesan rind. Stir in the chopped chard leaves. Taste, adjust the salt, and season with pepper. Keep hot while you prepare the bruschetta.

4. Warm 4 wide soup bowls. Toast the bread lightly on both sides. Rub with the halved garlic and brush with the remaining tablespoon olive oil. Place a slice in each bowl. Ladle in the beans and chard with a bit of broth. Serve, passing the grated or chopped onion and the Parmesan at the table for those who wish to sprinkle some over the top.

Variation: If you want a richer broth, cook 1 ounce chopped trimmed pancetta or unsmoked bacon (about ¼ cup) with the onion and proceed with the recipe.

Pan-Cooked Mushrooms

Makes 4 generous servings

Mushrooms cooked with a little wine, garlic, and herbs make a savory, satisfying dish, really a wonderful dinner. Serve them with pasta or grains, as a topping on bruschetta or pizza, as an omelet filling, or as a side with meat or fish. I particularly like to make this dish with oyster mushrooms, a wild mushroom that is actually cultivated today and not too hard to find. But regular mushrooms are cheaper and easier to come by, so you have the choice. You could also use a combination of the two.

1½ pounds oyster mushrooms, large regular mushrooms, or portobello
    mushrooms (or a mixture of cultivated and wild mushrooms)
½ teaspoon salt, or to your taste
½ cup dry white or red wine
1½ teaspoons fresh thyme leaves or ¾ teaspoon dried thyme
1½ teaspoons chopped fresh rosemary leaves or ¾ teaspoon crumbled dried
1½ tablespoons olive oil
2 to 4 large garlic cloves, to your taste, peeled and minced or pressed
Freshly ground black pepper to taste
3 tablespoons chopped fresh flat-leaf parsley leaves

1. Trim away the tough stems of oyster mushrooms or remove them from the portobellos; for regular mushrooms just cut the very ends of the stems away. Rinse briefly in cold water to remove sand and shake or wipe dry with paper towels. Cut into thick slices. With oyster mushrooms I just tear them in half with my hands. If they are in big clumps, cut away the bottom of the stem and separate them.

2. Heat the skillet over medium-high heat and add the mushrooms and salt. The mushrooms will very soon begin to release liquid. Stir and cook until the liquid has evaporated, which can be anywhere from 5 to 15 minutes, depending on the moisture and type of the mushrooms. Stir in the wine, thyme, and rosemary. Reduce the heat to medium and cook, stirring, until the wine has evaporated, 5 to 10 minutes. Add the olive oil and garlic. Cook, stirring, until the garlic begins to color and the dish smells very

Get out the following equipment: **chef's knife and cutting board; measuring spoons and measuring cup; garlic press or minichop if using; large, heavy nonstick skillet and wooden spoon**

Advance preparation: **This can be cooked several hours ahead of time and reheated.**

PER SERVING:
5.9 gm total fat
0.8 gm saturated fat
114 calories
9.6 gm carbohydrates
3.9 gm protein

fragrant, about 5 minutes. Season with pepper, stir in the parsley, taste, and add salt as necessary. Remove from the heat and serve.

Pan-Cooked Summer Squash

∎

Makes 4 servings

Summer squash is a beautiful vegetable to buy when it's in season. There are so many different shapes and colors. This easy dish is to my mind the simplest and most delicious way to work with the vegetable. See also the tacos with summer squash, corn, and beans on page 330.

1 tablespoon olive oil

2 garlic cloves, peeled and minced or pressed

1 pound summer squash (a mixture of colors is nice), sliced about ¼ inch
    thick (if you are working with very large zucchini, cut them lengthwise
    into halves or quarters, then slice)

Salt and freshly ground black pepper to taste

Chopped fresh herbs as desired, such as flat-leaf parsley, thyme, or chives
    (optional)

Heat the olive oil in the skillet over medium heat and add the garlic. Cook for about 30 seconds, just until it begins to smell fragrant, then add the squash and about ¼ teaspoon salt, or to taste. Cook, stirring often, until the squash is tender and translucent, 5 to 10 minutes. Add lots of freshly ground pepper, sprinkle with herbs if you wish, and remove from the heat.

Zucchini and Feta Gratin

∎

Makes 4 servings

This gratin is assembled quickly and can be eaten hot or cold. The combination of mint and feta gives it the most refreshing flavor. It can serve as a main or side dish.

1½ pounds zucchini, sliced about ¼ inch thick

Salt and freshly ground black pepper to taste

4 large eggs

3 ounces feta cheese, crumbled

1½ tablespoons chopped fresh mint leaves or 2 teaspoons crumbled dried

Pinch of freshly grated nutmeg

1. Preheat the oven to 375°F. Oil the gratin or baking dish with olive oil.
2. Bring an inch of water to a boil in the saucepan. Place the zucchini in the steamer, cover, and steam for 5 minutes. Plunge into cold water to stop the cooking and drain on paper towels. Transfer to the gratin dish and toss with salt and pepper.
3. Blend together the eggs and cheese in a bowl with a whisk or fork or in the food processor or blender until fairly smooth. Add the mint and nutmeg and a scant ¼ teaspoon salt. Pour over the zucchini. Bake until set and just beginning to brown on top, 30 to 40 minutes. Serve hot, warm, or at room temperature.

Advance preparation: **Since this is good at room temperature, it can be prepared hours ahead of serving.**

PER SERVING:
9.8 gm total fat
4.8 gm saturated fat
155 calories
6.5 gm carbohydrates
11.3 gm protein

Baked Tomatoes, Fast or Slow

Makes 4 servings

When tomatoes are baked, they become even sweeter, especially when slow-baked for 2 hours, which caramelizes them. Baking is a particularly good idea if your tomatoes are slightly green. Serve baked tomatoes as a side dish with chicken or fish or cut them up and toss with pasta.

> 4 medium-size or large firm, ripe tomatoes, cut in half crosswise
> Salt and freshly ground black pepper to taste
> 2 tablespoons olive oil
> 2 tablespoons chopped fresh herbs, such as flat-leaf parsley, basil, or
> marjoram, or 1 teaspoon dried thyme or oregano

Quick-Baked

Preheat the oven to 400°F. Lightly oil the baking dish. Place the tomatoes in it cut side up. Sprinkle with salt and pepper and drizzle with the olive oil. Sprinkle on the herbs. Bake until they are bubbling and beginning to brown on top, about 20 minutes. Serve as a side dish or cut them up in the baking dish and toss, with their juices, with hot cooked pasta.

Slow-Baked

Preheat the oven to 300°F. Prepare the tomatoes as directed, but don't add the herbs. Bake for 1½ hours. Sprinkle on the herbs and bake for another 30 minutes. The tomatoes will be shriveled and very sweet. Serve as directed.

Get out the following equipment: **chef's knife or serrated knife and cutting board; baking dish large enough for the tomatoes; measuring spoons**

Advance preparation: **These can be baked ahead and reheated or served at room temperature, but you'll lose some of the juices.**

PER SERVING:
7.4 gm total fat
0.9 gm saturated fat
98 calories
6.5 gm carbohydrates
1.7 gm protein

- **Drained yogurt (page 40), plain or mixed with chopped chives or other herbs**
- **Toppings for corn on the cob, pages 229–230**

PER SERVING:
0.2 gm total fat
.04 gm saturated fat
145 calories
33.6 gm carbohydrates
3 gm protein

Get out the following equipment: **chef's knife and cutting board; baking sheet**

Advance preparation: **I have made these an hour before serving and kept them warm in the oven (I just turn off the oven when they're done and leave them in there).**

PER SERVING:
0.2 gm total fat
0 gm saturated fat
192 calories
44.5 gm carbohydrates
4.0 gm protein

Get out the following equipment: **potato peeler if using; measuring cup and measuring spoons; 2- or 3-quart saucepan; small saucepan; potato masher or fork**

Baked Russet Potatoes

You can make a meal of a baked potato and a salad, and you probably have done so many times. The Idaho russet is the best potato for baking. There's nothing to it.

1. Preheat the oven to 425°F. Scrub the potatoes and pierce in a few places with a sharp knife or fork (this keeps them from exploding in the oven).
2. Bake in the preheated oven until tender, about 1 hour. Remove from the heat and slice down the middle, then across.

Dry-Roasted Potatoes

Makes 4 servings

These incredibly hassle-free potatoes were a revelation to me when a friend first made them for me, in France. The potatoes are cut in half, then sprinkled with salt and pepper, herbs if you like, and roasted at 400°F until they puff and brown. They need no oil and taste so good that you won't wonder where the butter or sour cream is. Don't use russets—the normal baking potatoes—for these; they're too dry. Use a waxy or semiwaxy potato, like Yukon Gold, white creamers, or White Rose.

> **1½ to 2 pounds medium-size potatoes, scrubbed and cut in half lengthwise**
> **Salt, preferably coarse sea salt, and freshly ground black pepper to taste**
> **Dried thyme to taste (optional)**

1. Preheat the oven to 400°F. Put the potatoes cut side up on the baking sheet. Sprinkle on salt, pepper, and the optional thyme.
2. Bake until the tops are puffed and brown and the potatoes tender, 30 to 40 minutes. Remove from the heat and serve or turn off the oven and leave in until ready to serve.

Mashed Potatoes

Makes 4 to 6 servings

Although there's a restaurant vogue now for hyper-rich mashed potatoes, oozing with butter or olive oil, sometimes pungent with garlic, you can make absolutely delicious mashed potatoes with no butter at all, and if you do want a bit, then a tablespoon will do. If you use waxy potatoes or semi-waxy potatoes like Yukon Gold, they won't beg for butter or oil; milk will do just fine for moistening. I love these mashed potatoes, a comforting dish at any time and always on our Christmas table. Do not try to mash these in a food processor or electric mixer; they will become gummy if you do.

> 2 pounds waxy potatoes, peeled if desired (or some peeled, some just scrubbed)
> 1 teaspoon salt, plus more to your taste
> About 1 cup 1% milk
> 1 tablespoon unsalted butter (optional)
> Freshly ground black pepper to taste

1. Combine the potatoes, water to cover, and salt in the 2- or 3-quart saucepan and bring to a boil. Boil until tender, about 30 minutes. Drain, and if not eating right away, cover the pot to keep the potatoes warm. Meanwhile, warm a serving dish.
2. Heat the milk in the small saucepan until just trembling. Remove from the heat.
3. Mash the potatoes in their warm saucepan, using a potato masher or a fork. Add the optional butter and gradually add the milk, mashing and stirring, until the mixture is moistened to your taste. Add salt to taste and lots of pepper. Transfer to the warm serving dish and serve.

Advance preparation:
The potatoes can be peeled hours ahead of time and kept in a bowl of cold water. They can be cooked and held in the warm saucepan, in a small amount of the cooking water if holding for over an hour, for a few hours as well. Once mashed, they should be served quickly.

PER SERVING:
0.8 gm total fat
0.56 gm saturated fat
203 calories
44.2 gm carbohydrates
5.5 gm protein

Baked Sweet Potatoes

Makes 4 servings

During the fall and winter I crave sweet potatoes. I bake several at a time and eat them for lunch. When you bake sweet potatoes, they caramelize and ooze sweetness. They're a marvelous food and need little embellishment.

> 4 medium-size or 2 large sweet potatoes, scrubbed
> 4 teaspoons unsalted butter (optional) or 2 limes, quartered

1. Preheat the oven to 425°F. Cover the baking sheet with foil. Pierce the sweet potatoes in several places with a sharp knife and cut off the ends if shriveled. Place on the baking sheet and bake until soft and oozing, 1 to 1½ hours for large sweet potatoes, about 40 minutes for smaller potatoes. Remove from the heat.
2. Cut large potatoes in half lengthwise and divide among plates. Slit smaller potatoes down the middle. Top with a teaspoon of butter or a squeeze of lime.

Get out the following equipment: baking sheet and aluminum foil; paring knife

Advance preparation:
Sweet potatoes benefit from sitting for several hours or overnight. You can place in the refrigerator in a covered dish and reheat in the microwave or in a 350°F oven.

PER SERVING:
0.1 gm total fat
0 gm saturated fat
117 calories
27.7 gm carbohydrates
2.0 gm protein

Grains, Beans,
Vegetables, and Tofu

Sweet Potato and Apple Puree

Makes 6 servings

Try this next year for Thanksgiving. You'll never want candied sweet potatoes again.

2 pounds sweet potatoes

2 tart apples, such as Granny Smith or Gravenstein

Juice of 1 lime (about 3 tablespoons)

¼ cup plain low-fat yogurt

1 tablespoon unsalted butter

1 tablespoon mild-flavored honey such as clover or acacia

Salt to taste

1. Preheat the oven to 425°F. Line the baking sheet with foil. Pierce the sweet potatoes and apples in several places with a sharp knife. Place on the baking sheet and bake until tender and beginning to ooze. After 30 minutes, the apples should be softened. Remove from the heat. The sweet potatoes should take another 30 minutes to soften thoroughly. Test by piercing with a knife or skewer. Remove from the heat and allow to cool until you can handle them.
2. Remove the skins from the baked sweet potatoes. Peel and core the apples, scraping all the flesh you can from the inside of the skins. Cut everything into large pieces.
3. Lower the oven to 350°F. Puree the sweet potatoes and apples in the food processor until smooth. Add the remaining ingredients and blend together well. Transfer to a lightly buttered baking dish. Heat the puree in the oven until steaming, 20 to 30 minutes. Serve hot.

Roasted Beets

Makes 2 to 4 servings

I think the easiest way to work with beets is to roast them in their skins. This method also results in particularly sweet, tender beets. There's more than one way to do it; this is the method I always use, with great results.

1 to 2 bunches beets

Get out the following equipment: baking sheet; aluminum foil; paring knife; lemon press; food processor fitted with steel blade; measuring spoons; 2-quart baking dish

Advance preparation: The sweet potatoes and apples can be baked a few days ahead of serving, and the entire dish will hold for a day or two in the refrigerator before being baked.

PER SERVING:
2.7 gm total fat
1.4 gm saturated fat
184 calories
39.2 gm carbohydrates
2.6 gm protein

Get out the following equipment: vegetable brush; lidded baking dish large enough to accommodate the beets or a baking dish and aluminum foil; knife

Preheat the oven to 425°F. Cut away the greens from the beets and set aside for another purpose (such as Pan-Cooked Greens, page 241). Trim the roots (cut off the long, pointed strand at the end of the bulb). Scrub the beets under warm water with a vegetable brush. Place in the baking dish and add about ¼ inch of water. Cover with a lid or foil and bake for 30 minutes to an hour, depending on size. Medium-size beets take about 40 minutes, large beets 50 to 60 minutes, and small ones take about 30 minutes. Test for doneness by sticking a knife into the beet. It should slide right through. Remove from the heat and allow to cool. If there is time, leave the lid on while the beets cool; they continue to steam, and it's even easier to slip the skins off. Slip off the skins, holding the beets in a towel if they're hot. Cut into wedges and serve or serve whole if very small.

Advance preparation: **Roasted beets, peeled or unpeeled, will keep for several days in the refrigerator and can be reheated in a microwave or by dipping them in a pot of simmering water.**

PER SERVING:
0.4 9 gm total fat
0.1 gm saturated fat
98 calories
21.7 gm carbohydrates
3.6 gm protein

■ Two Recipes for Parsnips ■

Parsnips are an overlooked vegetable in this country, which is a pity, because they taste wonderful. They're closely related to carrots and have a very sweet, somewhat carrotlike flavor. They are good roasted or mashed, steamed or glazed. We often roast them right alongside chicken or serve them mashed. The roots have a fibrous core that must be removed before cooking.

Roasted Parsnips

■

Makes 4 servings

1 pound parsnips, peeled, quartered lengthwise, and cored
1 tablespoon butter
Salt and freshly ground black pepper to taste

Preheat the oven to 350°F. Place the parsnips in the baking dish and add about ¼ inch of water. Cover and bake until tender, 30 to 40 minutes. If any water remains in the dish, pour it off. Add the butter and toss with salt and pepper. Serve hot.

Get out the following equipment: **lidded baking dish large enough to accommodate the parsnips or baking dish and aluminum foil; vegetable peeler; chef's knife and cutting board**

Advance preparation: **Roasted parsnips will keep for a few days in the refrigerator and can be reheated in the oven or microwave.**

PER SERVING:
3.4 gm total fat
2.0 gm saturated fat
122 calories
22.9 gm carbohydrates
1.6 gm protein

Get out the following
equipment: vegetable
peeler; chef's knife and
cutting board; measur-
ing cup; 3-quart
saucepan and steamer;
1-quart saucepan;
potato masher or fork

Advance preparation:
**The parsnips and pota-
toes can be cooked a
day ahead. Mash with
the hot milk and heat
through over low heat
shortly before serving.**

PER SERVING:
0.9 gm total fat
0.3 gm saturated fat
183 calories
41.9 gm carbohydrates
4.2 gm protein

Mashed Parsnips

Makes 4 servings

1¼ pounds parsnips, peeled, cut into lengthwise quarters, cored, and cut
  into 1-inch pieces
½ pound boiling potatoes, peeled and quartered
½ to ¾ cup 1% milk, heated
Salt and freshly ground black pepper to taste
2 teaspoons unsalted butter (optional)

1. Bring an inch of water to a boil in the 3-quart saucepan fitted with the
   steamer. Add the parsnips and potatoes, cover, and steam until tender,
   about 15 minutes. Remove from the heat and pour the water from the
   pan.
2. Mash the cooked parsnips and potatoes in the pan with a potato masher
   or fork. Add hot milk to taste and salt and pepper, stir in the optional
   butter, and blend together well. Serve hot.

▪ Cooked Greens ▪

Greens are nutrient-dense and taste wonderful. I love them plain,
blanched and seasoned with a little salt, pepper, and lemon juice (I like them
this way both hot and cold). And they make a wonderful dish when pan-
fried with garlic and doused with lemon juice.

Greens vary in strength and bitterness, spinach and Swiss chard being the
mildest, collards and kale being the strongest. Once you cook greens, their
volume diminishes greatly. One big bunch, ¾ pound to a pound, will feed
two. If you buy beets by the bunch, when you get home cut off the greens
and cook them as directed here.

Cooked Greens with Lemon

Makes 2 servings

1 bunch greens
1 tablespoon salt, plus more to taste
Freshly ground black pepper to taste
Fresh lemon juice to taste

Get out the following
equipment: large pot
like a pasta pot; large
bowl or salad spinner;
slotted spoon or deep-
fry skimmer; chef's
knife and cutting board
or kitchen scissors;
colander

1. Fill the pot with water and bring to a boil over high heat while you stem and wash your greens. Pull the leaves away from the stems and discard the stems. Place the leaves in a large bowl of cold water or in the bottom of your salad spinner and swish around to remove sand. Lift from the water, change the water, and repeat.

2. When the water comes to a boil, add the salt and greens. Meanwhile, fill the bowl you used for cleaning the greens with cold water and place it next to the pot with the greens. Cook the greens until tender, 2 to 5 minutes (depending on the type of green), and transfer with a slotted spoon or deep-fry skimmer to the bowl of cold water. Drain and gently squeeze out the water (you don't have to squeeze them completely dry).

3. Chop the greens coarsely with a knife or scissors. Season with salt, pepper, and lemon juice. Serve hot or cold.

PER SERVING:
0.8 gm total fat
0.1 gm saturated fat
50 calories
7.9 gm carbohydrates
6.5 gm protein

Pan-Cooked Greens with Garlic and Lemon

Makes 4 servings

2 large bunches (1½ to 2 pounds) greens, such as Swiss chard, beet greens, turnip greens, or kale
1 tablespoon salt, plus more to taste
1 tablespoon olive oil
2 garlic cloves, peeled and minced or pressed
Freshly ground black pepper to taste
1 lemon, cut into wedges

1. Fill the pot with water and put over high heat to bring to a boil while you stem and wash your greens. Pull the leaves away from the stems and discard the stems. Place the leaves in a large bowl of cold water or the bottom of your salad spinner, and swish around to remove sand. Lift from the water, change the water, and repeat.

2. When the water on the stove comes to a boil, add the tablespoon of salt and greens. Meanwhile, fill the bowl you used for cleaning the greens with cold water and place it next to the pot with the greens. Cook the greens until tender, 2 to 5 minutes (depending on the type of green), and transfer with a slotted spoon or deep-fry skimmer to the bowl of cold water. Drain and gently squeeze out the water (you don't have to squeeze them completely dry). Chop the greens coarsely with a knife or scissors.

3. Heat the oil in the skillet over medium heat. Add the garlic and cook just until it begins to color, 30 seconds to a minute. Stir in the greens and stir until nicely seasoned with the oil and garlic, a couple of minutes. Season

Get out the following equipment: **large pot like a pasta pot; large bowl or salad spinner; slotted spoon or deep-fry skimmer; chef's knife and cutting board or kitchen scissors; colander; large, heavy nonstick skillet and wooden spoon; measuring spoons; garlic press or minichop if using**

Advance preparation: **The greens can be blanched and held in the refrigerator for 3 to 4 days in a plastic bag, then seasoned or cooked with the garlic just before serving.**

PER SERVING:
3.9 gm total fat
0.5 gm saturated fat
173 calories
29.7 gm carbohydrates
13.3 gm protein

with salt and pepper and remove from the heat. Serve with meat, fish, or grains, passing the lemon wedges for people to squeeze over their greens.

Broccoli Rabe with Garlic and Hot Red Pepper

Makes 4 servings

Broccoli rabe, also called *cima di rapa* or *rapini*, is becoming increasingly more available in supermarkets. It's a delicious vegetable, sort of a cross between broccoli and greens. I usually cook it with pasta, but here I've left it alone, with garlic and hot pepper, to serve as a delicious classic Italian side dish. You could also toss this with pasta. This recipe is based on one by Faith Willinger, from her excellent book *Red, White & Greens* (HarperCollins, 1996).

1½ pounds broccoli rabe

1 tablespoon salt, plus more to taste

2 tablespoons olive oil

2 to 3 garlic cloves, to your taste, peeled and minced or pressed

1 dried chile, seeded and crumbled, or ¼ teaspoon red pepper flakes

1. Fill the pot with water and bring to a boil over high heat while you prepare the other ingredients.
2. Wash the broccoli rabe and break or cut off the tough stem ends. When the water comes to a boil, add the salt and broccoli rabe. Boil until the stems are tender, about 5 minutes. Remove ½ cup of the water from the pot and drain the broccoli rabe.
3. Heat the oil in the skillet over medium heat. Add the garlic and chile or red pepper flakes and cook, stirring, for about 30 seconds, until the garlic begins to color. Stir in the broccoli rabe and the reserved water and cook, stirring, until the water evaporates. Add salt and taste. Do you need to add more? Could it use more garlic? Adjust the seasonings, remove from the heat, and serve.

Get out the following equipment: **large pot like a pasta pot; garlic press, minichop, or chef's knife and cutting board; measuring spoons and measuring cup; large, heavy non-stick skillet and wooden spoon**

Advance preparation: **This can be made several hours ahead of time and reheated gently. The broccoli rabe can be boiled and held in the refrigerator in a plastic bag for a few days.**

PER SERVING:
6.8 gm total fat
0.9 gm saturated fat
78 calories
3.7 gm carbohydrates
2.1 gm protein

Pasta, Pizza, and Bruschetta

■

The first dinner I learned to cook was spaghetti with meat sauce. Even back in the sixties, before pasta became the rage, spaghetti was one of the dishes a beginning cook learned, although the beginner's pasta sauce I teach in this book (see page 43) is a far cry from the beef-based sauce that I learned way back when.

All of the pastas in this chapter are made with dried pasta made from semolina flour and water, or, in the case of Asian pastas, buckwheat pasta (soba) may be used. The pasta sauces here are light, vegetable-based or non-fat dairy-based sauces whose rich flavors come from the vegetables themselves and their seasonings. Pasta makes such a great vehicle for practically any vegetable—greens, beans, peas, broccoli, tomatoes (raw or cooked, fresh or canned), squash. You can impulse buy at a farmers' market and be sure that the vegetable you've bought can find a home as a pasta topping or sauce.

Pasta is also convenience food; many of the sauces here are pantry sauces, made with canned goods like tomatoes, beans, and tuna. If your pantry is well stocked, you could live on pasta for a week and never go to the store.

Mostly, we associate pasta with the Mediterranean. But Asia has always produced myriad noodle recipes, and you'll find a few simple dishes here with Asian flavors. I've included bruschetta—thick, garlicky slices of toasted country bread—and a few pizza recipes in this chapter as well. Bruschetta and pizza, like pasta, are low-fat vehicles for any number of healthy vegetable-based toppings. Many of the sauces that top pasta also work beautifully for bruschetta and for pizza.

■ Light Pasta Basics ■

Types of Pasta

It's a good idea to have a few different shapes of pasta on hand. In these recipes I'm usually not dictatorial about the type of pasta you should use, but some shapes are particularly suited to specific sauces. For example, tubular pasta is nice with vegetables like peas and green beans, which find their way into the hollows when you toss the pasta; ridged and squiggly pastas are good with chunky sauces, which lodge in the ridges and squiggles. Smooth spaghettis and flat noodles carry smooth, creamy sauces nicely.

Long Pastas

Capelli d'angelo (angel hair): These are very thin strands of spaghetti-like pasta that cook very quickly. Italians never serve this with sauce but with broth. However, I think it's nice with thin Asian sauces and toppings (pages 267–269).

Spaghettini (thin spaghetti): Nice with light-textured sauces.

Spaghetti: Everyone knows spaghetti. These sturdy strands are very versatile and can accompany both smooth and chunky sauces.

Linguine: Flat, thin noodles that go well with smooth sauces and pestos.

Bucatini, perciatelli: Sturdy, long, hollow spaghetti-shaped strands. They pair well with rustic sauces.

Fusilli lunghi ("long springs"): Long, corkscrew-shaped strands that go well with chunky sauces that lodge in the curls.

Ribbons

Tagliatelle: Bolognese ribbons, about ⅓ inch wide.

Fettuccine (also called *trenette*): The most widely used of ribbon pastas, fettuccine is narrower than tagliatelle and is usually served with creamy or smooth sauces.

Pappardelle: Noodles about ¾ inch wide that can have a straight or ridged edge. Nice with creamy sauces, tomato sauces, and vegetables.

Lasagne: Very wide, flat noodles used for layered pasta dishes. The edges can be ridged or straight.

Tagliolini: Very thin ribbons. Suitable for light sauces.

Tubes

Penne: Medium-size tubes with pointed ends ("quills"). They come in smooth (*lisce*) and ridged (*rigate*) varieties. They go well with both chunky and creamy sauces.

Maccheroni: Tubular pasta, either smooth or ridged, with straight ends. *Maccheroni* comes in several lengths and also refers to curved tubes, "elbow macaroni" or *chifferi*. Goes with a variety of sauces and is also used in soups and casseroles (e.g., macaroni and cheese).

Rigatoni: Large, chewy, ridged tubes. They go beautifully with chunky pasta sauces and sauces with vegetables like beans or peas that can get lodged in the hollows. Also good with creamy sauces and meat sauces.

Other Shapes

Conchiglie (shells): They come in many sizes, from very big to very small. The big ones are generally stuffed. The small shells are excellent in pasta and bean soups.

Fusilli (springs): Short spiral-shaped pasta. I use it quite often. They go especially well with textured tomato sauces, which lodge in the springs.

Farfalle (bow ties): These bow-tie or butterfly-shaped noodles go well with textured and smooth sauces. They are especially nice with vegetables.

Orecchiette ("little ears"): A specialty of Apulia in southern Italy, these small domed disks are traditionally served with a broccoli rabe sauce. Good with greens and pestos.

Orzo: Rice-shaped pasta; good in soups and with simple creamy herb sauces.

Rotelle, ruote de carro (cartwheels): A specialty of Sicily, these are good with chunky sauces, which lodge in the spokes. Also good in soups.

How to Cook Pasta

See page 48.

These five pastas prove my maxim: if you have a well-equipped pantry, you have dinner. They're all southern Italian sauces with a tomato base. If you wish, you can substitute 1½ cups bottled tomato sauce, but it won't be as good as the tomato sauce you prepare yourself.

Note: All of the sauces that follow are adequate for saucing ¾ to 1 pound of pasta. For four people, use ¾ pound, and if another dinner guest or two arrive, use the same sauce quantities and increase the pasta to 1 pound.

Equipment needed for all five of the pastas: **chef's knife and cutting board; garlic press or minichop if using; measuring spoons and measuring cup; food processor if necessary for tomatoes; large, heavy nonstick skillet and wooden spoon; large pot and colander or pasta pot; wide pasta serving bowl and servers if not tossing the pasta directly in the pan**

Advance preparation: **All of these sauces will keep for 3 to 5 days in the refrigerator.**

PER SERVING:
4.8 gm total fat
0.7 gm saturated fat
400 calories
72.6 gm carbohydrates
13.1 gm protein

Penne with Spicy Tomato Sauce

▪

Makes 4 servings

Called *penne all'arrabbiata* in Italian, this recipe has several interpretations. Some include diced pancetta for a richer, meatier flavor; some have more or less garlic or more or less parsley. What they all have, and what makes this "angry pasta," is hot red pepper. Traditionally this dish is not served with Parmesan, but you have the option here.

1 tablespoon olive oil
3 to 4 large garlic cloves, to your taste, peeled and minced or pressed
One 28-ounce can whole or chopped tomatoes, drained, peeled, seeded, and
    crushed (you can do this in a food processor), or one 28-ounce can
    crushed tomatoes in puree
½ to ¾ teaspoon salt, to your taste, plus at least 1 tablespoon for the water
¼ to ½ teaspoon crushed dried red chiles or red pepper flakes, to your taste
1 teaspoon dried oregano, 2 tablespoons slivered fresh basil leaves, or ¼ cup
    chopped fresh flat-leaf parsley leaves
¾ pound (for 4) to 1 pound (for 5 or 6) penne
¼ cup freshly grated Parmesan cheese (optional)

1. Begin heating a large pot of water (4 to 6 quarts) for the pasta while you make your sauce.
2. Heat the oil in the skillet over medium heat and add the garlic. When the garlic begins to color, add the tomatoes, salt, chiles or red pepper flakes, and oregano if using. Cook, stirring often, until the tomatoes are cooked

down and just beginning to stick to the skillet, 15 to 25 minutes. Taste. Is there enough salt, garlic, and seasoning? Adjust the flavors as desired. Keep warm while cooking the pasta.

3. When the water comes to a rolling boil, add the tablespoon salt (or more) and gradually add the pasta. Stir to ensure that the pasta doesn't stick. Cook until the pasta is al dente, firm to the bite, about 10 minutes. To test it, remove a piece of pasta with tongs or a spoon, run it under cold water, and taste it. It should be cooked through but not at all mushy. Drain and toss at once with the sauce and the basil or parsley if using, either in the skillet with the sauce or in a warm wide pasta bowl, and serve, passing the Parmesan in a separate bowl.

Spaghetti with Olives, Capers, Hot Peppers, and Anchovies

Makes 4 servings

The Italian name for this dish is *spaghetti alla puttanesca*, which means "whore's pasta." Whether it got that name because southern Italian prostitutes used it to seduce customers or for the more likely reason that it is quickly made with local ingredients (making it the perfect dish to prepare and eat between clients) remains open to question. What is certain, though, is that this pasta is addictive. Even if you think you don't like anchovies, try it. They act more as a seasoning than as a strong extra flavor; they dissolve as they cook, lending a robust touch to the tomato sauce.

2 tablespoons olive oil

4 anchovy fillets, well rinsed and chopped

3 large garlic cloves, peeled and minced or pressed

1 small dried red chile, crumbled, or ¼ to ½ teaspoon red pepper flakes, to your taste

One 28-ounce can whole or chopped tomatoes, drained, peeled, seeded, and crushed (you can do this in a food processor), or one 28-ounce can crushed tomatoes in puree

½ teaspoon dried oregano

2 tablespoons drained capers, rinsed

8 imported black olives, such as Italian Gaeta, Greek Amphissa or Kalamata, or French Nyons, pitted and quartered

Salt to taste, plus at least 1 tablespoon for the water

¾ pound (for 4) to 1 pound (for 5 or 6) spaghetti

¼ cup chopped fresh flat-leaf parsley leaves

PER SERVING:
10 gm total fat
1.4 gm saturated fat
442 calories
74.2 gm carbohydrates
14.3 gm protein

continued

1. Begin heating a large pot of water (4 to 6 quarts) for the pasta while you make your sauce.
2. Put the olive oil and anchovies in the skillet and heat over medium-low heat until the anchovies begin to sizzle. Cook, stirring and crushing with a wooden spoon, until the anchovies fall apart, dissolving into the olive oil. Add the garlic and crumbled chile or red pepper flakes and cook, stirring, until the garlic begins to color ever so slightly and to smell fragrant, 30 seconds to a minute. Stir in the tomatoes and increase the heat to medium. Cook, stirring often, until the tomatoes have cooked down a bit, about 10 minutes. Add the oregano, capers, and olives and continue to cook, stirring often, until the tomatoes are cooked down and just beginning to stick to the skillet, 5 to 15 minutes. Taste and add salt or red pepper flakes as desired. The anchovies contribute a fair amount of salt, but you'll probably want to add a bit more. Keep warm while cooking the pasta.
3. When the water comes to a rolling boil, add the tablespoon salt (or more) and gradually add the pasta. Stir to ensure that the pasta doesn't stick. Cook until the pasta is al dente, firm to the bite, about 10 minutes. To test it, remove a piece of pasta with tongs or a spoon, run it under cold water, and taste it. It should be cooked through but not at all mushy. Drain and toss at once with the sauce and parsley, either in the skillet or in a warm wide pasta bowl, and serve.

Pasta with Anchovies, Tomatoes, and Hot Peppers

Omit the capers and olives for an even simpler, easily accomplished dish.

Pasta with Tomato Sauce and Chickpeas or White Beans

■

Makes 4 to 6 servings

Pasta and beans make another frequent quick meal in our house. It's a high-protein dish with a marvelous contrast of textures.

1 tablespoon olive oil

2 to 3 large garlic cloves, to your taste, peeled and minced or pressed

One 28-ounce can whole or chopped tomatoes, drained, peeled, seeded, and crushed (you can do this in a food processor), or one 28-ounce can crushed tomatoes in puree

1 dried red chile, crumbled, or ¼ to ½ teaspoon red pepper flakes (optional), to your taste

PER SERVING:
8.1 gm total fat
1.7 gm saturated fat
516 calories
91.3 gm carbohydrates
19.6 gm protein

⅛ teaspoon sugar

1 teaspoon dried oregano, 2 tablespoons slivered fresh basil leaves, or ¼ cup
chopped fresh parsley leaves (preferably chopped with scissors)

½ to ¾ teaspoon salt, to your taste, plus at least 1 tablespoon for the water

One 15-ounce can chickpeas or white beans, drained and rinsed

Freshly ground black pepper to taste (omit if using the red chile)

¾ pound (for 4) to 1 pound (for 5 or 6) pasta, such as fusilli, shells, penne,
farfalle, or rigatoni

¼ cup freshly grated Parmesan cheese

1. Begin heating a large pot of water (4 to 6 quarts) for the pasta while you
   make your sauce.

2. Heat the oil in the skillet over medium heat. Add the garlic and cook until it begins to color, about 30 seconds. Add the tomatoes, optional dried
   red chile, sugar, oregano if using, and salt. Cook, stirring often, until the
   tomatoes are cooked down and beginning to stick to the skillet, 10 to 20
   minutes. Stir in the chickpeas or white beans and pepper and heat
   through. Taste. Is there enough salt? Garlic? Adjust the seasonings as desired. Keep warm while cooking the pasta.

3. When the water comes to a rolling boil, add the 1 tablespoon salt (or
   more) and gradually add the pasta. Stir to ensure that the pasta doesn't
   stick. Cook until the pasta is al dente, firm to the bite, about 10 minutes.
   To test it, remove a piece of pasta with tongs or a spoon, run it under cold
   water, and taste it. It should be cooked through but not at all mushy.
   Drain and toss with the sauce, in either the skillet or a warm pasta bowl,
   add the basil or parsley if using, and serve, passing the Parmesan in a separate bowl.

Pasta with Tuna and Tomato Sauce

■

Makes 4 to 6 servings

My father-in-law has a version of this dish every night for dinner. "It's so
easy," he said when I asked him if he didn't get tired of eating the same thing
night after night, "and I don't have to worry about what I'm going to eat because I always have the ingredients in the cupboard—and it's good." Point
taken.

PER SERVING:
6.3 gm total fat
1.0 gm saturated fat
473 calories
79.5 gm carbohydrates
24.3 gm protein

continued

1 tablespoon olive oil

2 to 3 large garlic cloves, to your taste, peeled and minced or pressed

One 28-ounce can whole or chopped tomatoes, drained, peeled, seeded, and crushed (you can do this in a food processor), or one 28-ounce can crushed tomatoes in puree

⅛ teaspoon sugar

1 teaspoon dried oregano, ½ teaspoon dried thyme, 1 tablespoon chopped fresh sage leaves, or ¼ cup chopped fresh flat-leaf parsley leaves

½ to ¾ teaspoon salt, to your taste, plus at least 1 tablespoon for the water

One 6-ounce can water-packed tuna, drained

Freshly ground black pepper to taste

¾ pound (for 4) to 1 pound (for 5 or 6) pasta, such as fusilli, spaghetti, penne, farfalle, or rigatoni

1 Begin heating a large pot of water (4 to 6 quarts) for the pasta while you make your sauce.

2. Heat the oil in the skillet over medium heat. Add the garlic and cook until it begins to color, about 30 seconds. Add the tomatoes, sugar, oregano or thyme if using, and salt. Cook, stirring often, until the tomatoes are cooked down and beginning to stick to the skillet, 10 to 25 minutes. Break up the tuna with a fork, stir it in, season with pepper, and heat through. Taste. Is there enough salt? Garlic? Adjust the seasonings as desired. Keep warm while cooking the pasta.

3. When the water comes to a rolling boil, add the tablespoon salt (or more) and gradually add the pasta. Stir to ensure that the pasta doesn't stick. Cook until the pasta is al dente, firm to the bite, about 10 minutes. To test it, remove a piece of pasta with tongs or a spoon, run it under cold water, and taste it. It should be cooked through but not at all mushy. Drain and toss with the sauce and sage or parsley if using, in either the skillet or a warm pasta bowl, and serve.

Note: My father-in-law adds a small onion, chopped, and a few sliced mushrooms to this recipe. Cook them in the olive oil until tender, 5 to 10 minutes, then add the garlic and proceed as directed.

Pasta with Dried Mushrooms and Tomato Sauce

PER SERVING:
6.8 gm total fat
1.7 gm saturated fat
434 calories
78.6 gm carbohydrates
15.6 gm protein

Makes 4 to 6 servings

Earthy and rich-tasting, porcini add meaty depth to a sauce or stew. Keep them around for this impromptu dish.

1 ounce (about 1 cup) dried porcini mushrooms (cèpes)

1 tablespoon olive oil

2 to 3 large garlic cloves, to your taste, peeled and minced or pressed

½ to ¾ teaspoon salt, plus at least 1 tablespoon for the water

½ teaspoon dried thyme or 1 teaspoon fresh thyme leaves

½ teaspoon crumbled dried rosemary or 1 teaspoon chopped fresh rosemary leaves

One 28-ounce can whole or chopped tomatoes, drained, peeled, seeded, and crushed, or one 28-ounce can crushed tomatoes in puree

Freshly ground black pepper to taste

¾ pound (for 4) to 1 pound (for 5 or 6) pasta, such as fusilli, spaghetti, fettuccine, or penne

¼ cup chopped fresh flat-leaf parsley leaves (optional)

¼ cup freshly grated Parmesan cheese

1. Place the mushrooms in a bowl and cover with hot water. Let soak for 15 to 30 minutes. Drain through a strainer lined with cheesecloth or a paper towel set over a bowl. Reserve the strained soaking water. Squeeze the mushrooms over the strainer and rinse in several changes of water, until there is no more trace of sand. Meanwhile, begin heating a large pot of water (4 to 6 quarts) for the pasta.

2. Heat the oil in the skillet over medium heat. Add the garlic and cook until it begins to color, about 30 seconds. Add the mushrooms, salt, thyme, and rosemary. Stir together for a minute or two, until the mushrooms are coated with oil and beginning to smell fragrant. Add the tomatoes and cook, stirring often, until the tomatoes have cooked down and are beginning to stick to the skillet, 10 to 20 minutes. Add ¼ cup of the reserved mushroom-soaking water and cook, stirring often, until the mixture is no longer watery, another 10 minutes. Season with pepper. Taste. Is there enough salt? Garlic? Adjust the seasonings as desired. Keep warm while cooking the pasta.

3. When the water comes to a rolling boil, add the tablespoon salt (or more) and gradually add the pasta. Stir to ensure that the pasta doesn't stick. Cook until the pasta is al dente, firm to the bite, about 10 minutes. To

test it, remove a piece of pasta with tongs or a spoon, run it under cold water, and taste it. It should be cooked through but not at all mushy. Drain and toss with the sauce and parsley if using, in either the skillet or a warm pasta bowl, and serve, passing the Parmesan in a separate bowl.

Pasta with Fresh Mushrooms and Tomato Sauce

This isn't a pantry pasta, since you have to buy the fresh mushrooms; but if you can't find dried porcini or they're not within your budget, try this dish instead.

Substitute ½ pound portobello mushrooms, cleaned, stems trimmed away, and tops cut in half, then sliced, or ½ pound regular mushrooms, cleaned, trimmed, and sliced, for the dried mushrooms.

Bring a large pot of water to a boil for the pasta while you make the sauce. Heat the mushrooms with about 1/4 teaspoon salt in a large, heavy nonstick skillet over medium heat until they begin to release water. Stir until most of the liquid in the skillet has evaporated and add the olive oil and garlic, as in step 2. Proceed with the recipe.

▪ And More Pasta ▪

Pasta with Tomato Sauce, Goat Cheese, and Green Beans

▪

Makes 4 servings

Goat cheese adds a deep new flavor dimension to a tomato sauce and gives this pasta dish a creamy texture and rich taste. This dish can be made with broccoli when sweet fresh green beans are out of season.

1 tablespoon olive oil

2 to 3 large garlic cloves, to your taste, peeled and minced or pressed

One 28-ounce can chopped or whole tomatoes, drained, seeded, and diced or crushed (you can do this in a food processor), or 1¾ pounds firm, ripe tomatoes, peeled, seeded, and diced or pureed

⅛ teaspoon sugar

½ to ¾ teaspoon salt, plus at least 1 tablespoon for the water

½ to 1 teaspoon dried or fresh thyme, oregano, rosemary, or a mixture, or 1 tablespoon chopped or slivered fresh basil leaves

Freshly ground black pepper to taste

Get out the following equipment: chef's knife and cutting board; garlic press or minichop if using; measuring spoons; pasta pot; large, heavy nonstick skillet and wooden spoon

Advance preparation: The sauce, before the goat cheese is added, will keep for 3 days in the refrigerator and can be frozen for several months. Reheat and stir in the goat cheese.

2 ounces goat cheese, crumbled (about ¼ cup)

¾ pound fusilli or other pasta, such as penne, shells, or rotelle

¾ pound green beans, trimmed and broken in half

PER SERVING:
8.0 gm total fat
2.8 gm saturated fat
461 calories
80.0 gm carbohydrates
17.0 gm protein

1. Bring a large pot of water (4 to 6 quarts) to a boil while you make the tomato sauce.
2. Heat the olive oil in the skillet over medium-low heat. Add the garlic and cook, stirring, just until it begins to color, 30 seconds to a minute. Add the tomatoes, sugar, salt, and dried (but not fresh) herbs. Increase the heat to medium, bring to a simmer, and cook, stirring often, until the tomatoes have cooked down, smell fragrant, and are just beginning to stick to the skillet, 10 to 20 minutes. Remove from the heat and stir in the fresh herbs if using, pepper, and goat cheese. Taste and adjust the salt.
3. When the water comes to a rolling boil, add the tablespoon salt (or more) and gradually add the pasta. Stir to ensure that the pasta doesn't stick. Cook until the pasta is al dente, firm to the bite, about 10 minutes. To test it, remove a piece of pasta with tongs or a spoon, run it under cold water, and taste it. It should be cooked through but not at all mushy. Five minutes before the pasta is done, drop the green beans into the pasta water. Drain the pasta with the green beans when the pasta is done and toss with the tomato sauce in the skillet or a warm pasta bowl. Serve at once on warm plates.

Variation with Broccoli: Substitute 1 pound broccoli, broken into florets, stems peeled and chopped, for the green beans. Proceed as directed.

Pasta with Tomatoes, Green Beans, and Garlic Bread Crumbs

Makes 4 servings

When you are comfortable with cooking and have essential foods on hand, practically anything can inspire dinner. Take this recipe—it was inspired by leftover toast. Not one to throw anything away that can be recycled, one Sunday afternoon, aware of the ever-hardening pieces of toasted whole-wheat country bread from my breakfast, I sat down and wrote this recipe. Bread crumbs are used in Sicilian pasta dishes. They have the most wonderful quality, since they soak up anything with flavor, which is everything here. This pasta, with its uncooked tomato sauce, is good hot or at room temperature. If you don't have green beans on hand, try a cup of thawed frozen peas.

Get out the following equipment: **chef's knife and cutting board; garlic press or minichop if using; measuring spoons; large pot and colander or pasta pot; small nonstick skillet and wooden spoon or spatula; small bowl; pasta bowl and servers**

Pasta, Pizza, and Bruschetta

continued

253

Advance preparation:
The bread crumbs can
be prepared hours
ahead of time and
stored at room temper-
ature in a small bowl.
The tomato mixture
will also hold for sev-
eral hours at room tem-
perature.

PER SERVING:
7.2 gm total fat
1.7 gm saturated fat
445 calories
78.2 gm carbohydrates
16.2 gm protein

1 tablespoon olive oil

¼ cup dry plain bread crumbs

2 to 3 large garlic cloves, to your taste, minced or pressed

2 tablespoons chopped fresh flat-leaf parsley leaves

1 pound firm, ripe tomatoes, peeled and seeded if desired and finely
  chopped

1 to 2 teaspoons balsamic vinegar (optional), to your taste

2 tablespoons slivered fresh basil leaves

¼ to ¾ teaspoon salt, plus at least 1 tablespoon for the water

Freshly ground black pepper to taste

¾ pound tubular pasta, such as rigatoni or penne

½ pound green beans, trimmed and broken into 2-inch lengths

¼ cup freshly grated Parmesan cheese

1. Begin heating a large pot of water (4 to 6 quarts) for the pasta. Meanwhile, heat the oil in the medium skillet over medium heat. Add the
   bread crumbs and 1 clove of the minced garlic. Cook, stirring, until the
   bread crumbs have absorbed the oil and the mixture is toasty and fragrant, about 1½ minutes. Stir in the parsley and remove from the heat.
   Transfer at once to a small bowl.

2. If the tomatoes are not supersweet vine-ripened tomatoes, toss them with
   the balsamic vinegar in a pasta bowl. Add the remaining garlic, the basil,
   salt, and pepper.

3. When the water comes to a rolling boil, add the tablespoon salt (or more)
   and the pasta and cook for 5 minutes. Add the green beans and cook until the pasta is al dente, firm to the bite, about another 5 minutes. To test
   it, remove a piece of pasta with tongs or a spoon, run it under cold water,
   and taste it. It should be cooked through but not at all mushy. Drain, toss
   them with the tomatoes and bread crumbs in the pasta bowl, and serve,
   passing the Parmesan at the table.

Pasta with Uncooked Tomato Sauce

Makes 4 servings

We eat this luscious tomato sauce throughout the summer and early fall tomato harvest. You can serve the pasta and tomato sauce with no further additions or add other fresh vegetables in season. This is particularly beautiful if you use a selection of different-colored tomatoes from the farmers' market.

2 pounds (about 8 medium-size) firm, ripe tomatoes, peeled if desired, seeded, and chopped

2 to 3 large garlic cloves, to your taste, peeled and minced or pressed

2 to 3 teaspoons balsamic vinegar, to your taste

½ teaspoon salt, or more to your taste

Freshly ground black pepper to taste

1 tablespoon olive oil

2 to 4 tablespoons chopped or slivered fresh basil leaves, to your taste

¾ pound fusilli

1 cup fresh peas, ½ pound green beans, trimmed and cut in half, or ½ pound asparagus, bottoms trimmed and cut into 1-inch pieces (optional)

¼ cup freshly grated Parmesan cheese

1. Toss together the tomatoes, garlic, vinegar, salt, pepper, and olive oil in the serving bowl. Add the basil and let sit for 15 to 30 minutes. Taste and adjust the seasonings.
2. Meanwhile, bring a large pot of water (4 to 6 quarts) to a boil and add the tablespoon salt (or more) and the pasta. Cook until al dente, firm to the bite, about 10 minutes. To test it, remove a piece of pasta with tongs or a spoon, run it under cold water, and taste it. It should be cooked through but not at all mushy. Four to 5 minutes before the end of cooking, add the green vegetables if using to the pot and continue to boil with the pasta. Drain and toss with the tomato sauce in the bowl. Serve hot or at room temperature. Serve with the Parmesan on the side.

Get out the following equipment: pasta serving bowl; chef's knife and cutting board; pasta pot; measuring spoons; garlic press or minichop if using; salad servers or pasta tongs

Advance preparation: The tomato sauce will hold for a few hours, preferably out of the refrigerator. The pasta should not sit in the sauce for very long, however, or it will become soggy.

PER SERVING:
7.2 gm total fat
1.6 gm saturated fat
455 calories
79.0 gm carbohydrates
17.3 gm protein

Get out the following
equipment: baking
sheet; aluminum foil;
chef's knife and cutting
board; bowl and
strainer; measuring
spoons; garlic press or
minichop if using;
large, heavy nonstick
skillet and wooden
spoon; large pot and
colander or pasta pot;
pasta bowl; food
processor fitted with
steel blade, blender, or
food mill

Advance preparation:
The tomato sauce will
keep for several days in
the refrigerator.

PER SERVING:
6.7 gm total fat
.9 gm saturated fat
494.4 calories
79.6 gm carbohydrates
27.3 gm protein

Pasta with Roasted Tomatoes, Tuna, and a Green Vegetable

Makes 4 servings

This is a delicious take on pasta with tuna and tomato sauce. The tomatoes are roasted, which gives the sauce a rich grilled flavor. It's nice with sugar snap peas, or regular peas, green beans, broccoli, or snow peas.

1½ pounds (6 medium-size) firm, ripe tomatoes

1 tablespoon olive oil

2 to 4 garlic cloves, to your taste, peeled and minced or pressed

1 dried red chile, seeded and crumbled, or ½ teaspoon red pepper flakes

½ to ¾ teaspoon salt, plus at least 1 tablespoon for the water

One 6-ounce can water-packed tuna, drained

2 tablespoons slivered fresh basil leaves, 6 fresh sage leaves, slivered, or a
    combination

Freshly ground black pepper to taste

¾ pound pasta, such as fusilli or penne

1 pound sugar snap peas, trimmed; peas (1 cup shelled); green beans,
    trimmed and broken in half; or broccoli florets

1. Preheat the broiler. Line the baking sheet with foil and broil the tomatoes until charred on one side, 2 to 5 minutes. Flip them over and broil on the other side until charred. Remove from the oven and transfer to a bowl with any juices that may be on the baking sheet. Allow to cool (this takes some time). When cool enough to handle, core and peel. Cut in half, gently squeeze out the seeds into a strainer set over a bowl, and chop or puree the tomatoes.

2. Heat the oil in the skillet over medium heat. Add the garlic and crumbled chile and cook, stirring, until the garlic begins to color, about 30 seconds. Stir in the tomatoes and their juice and the salt. Bring to a simmer and simmer until the tomatoes cook down somewhat, about 5 minutes. Add the tuna, break it up with the back of your spoon, and cook, stirring often, for another 5 minutes. Stir in the herbs, season with pepper, and taste. Does the sauce need salt?

3. Bring a large pot of water (4 to 6 quarts) to a boil. Add the tablespoon of salt (or more) and the pasta. Cook for 5 minutes and add the green vegetables. Boil until the pasta is cooked al dente, firm to the bite, about another 5 minutes. To test it, remove a piece of pasta with tongs, run it under cold water, and taste it. It should be cooked through but not at all mushy. Drain and toss with the tomato-and-tuna mixture and serve.

Pasta with Tomato-Mint Sauce and Shrimp

Makes 4 servings

The same tomato-mint vinaigrette that tops a piece of fish so nicely (page 292) also makes a delicious summer pasta sauce. I like to add green vegetables—peas or beans—to the mixture and top the pasta with a few plump cooked shrimp.

1 pound (4 medium-size) firm, ripe tomatoes, peeled and seeded

1 large garlic clove, or more to taste, peeled and cut in half

2 to 3 teaspoons balsamic vinegar, to your taste

1 tablespoon red wine vinegar

1 tablespoon olive oil

2 tablespoons chopped fresh mint leaves

1/2 to 3/4 teaspoon salt, plus at least 1 tablespoon for the water

Freshly ground black pepper to taste

Zest of 1/2 orange, finely minced

3/4 pound pasta, preferably spaghetti or fettuccine

1 cup peas or 1 1/2 cups trimmed green beans, broken into 1- to 1 1/2-inch pieces

20 medium-size shrimp, uncooked or cooked (if uncooked, shelled and
  deveined)

1. Bring a large pot of water (4 to 6 quarts) to a boil while you make the sauce. Blend together the tomatoes, garlic, vinegars, olive oil, mint leaves, salt, and pepper until smooth (see Note). Stir in the orange zest. Taste. Is there enough salt? Garlic? Adjust the seasonings. Transfer to the pasta bowl.

2. When the pasta water reaches a boil, add the tablespoon salt (or more) and the pasta a handful at a time. Give the pasta a stir so it doesn't stick to the pot. Boil for 5 minutes, then add the peas or beans. Continue to cook until the pasta is al dente, firm to the bite, usually another 5 minutes. To test it, remove a piece of pasta with tongs or a spoon, run it under cold water, and taste it. It should be cooked through but not at all mushy. If you are cooking the shrimp, you can throw them in with the pasta 2 to 3 minutes before the end of the cooking time. If the shrimp is already cooked, throw it into the pot just before you drain to heat. Drain and toss with the sauce.

Note: If using a food processor, turn on and drop in the garlic first. Then pulse the tomatoes until they're pureed. Add the remaining ingredients and blend until smooth.

Get out the following equipment: **large pot and colander or pasta pot; chef's knife and cutting board; measuring spoons; food processor fitted with steel blade or blender; paring knife if deveining; pasta serving bowl and servers or tongs**

Advance preparation: **The sauce will keep for a day in the refrigerator. The shrimp can be cooked a day ahead of time and refrigerated as well.**

PER SERVING:
5.9 gm total fat
0.8 gm saturated fat
445 calories
75.2 gm carbohydrates
21.2 gm protein

Pasta with Anchovies, Greens, and Garlic

■

Makes 4 servings

When this recipe is made with arugula, it is typical of the southern Italian region of Apulia, the heel of the boot. It works well, however, with other greens, and it's one of my favorite ways to use the tops of the beets I buy at the farmers' markets in winter in Los Angeles. Roast the beets for a salad (page 134) and use the greens for this dish.

1 tablespoon salt, or more to taste

¾ pound pasta, such as orecchiette, fusilli, or farfalle

2 pounds greens (arugula, beet greens, chard, spinach, turnip greens),
    stemmed, well washed, and chopped

2 tablespoons olive oil

4 anchovy fillets, well rinsed

2 large garlic cloves, minced or pressed

¼ cup grated pecorino cheese (optional)

1. Bring a large pot of water (4 to 6 quarts) to a rolling boil. Add the salt and pasta and cook for 5 minutes, then add the greens.

2. Meanwhile, combine the olive oil and anchovy fillets in the skillet and warm over medium-low heat. Cook, stirring and mashing the anchovies with the back of a wooden spoon, until they break down (in cooking terms, the anchovies "melt"), about 1 minute. Add the garlic and cook, stirring, until it just begins to color, 30 seconds to a minute. Taste and add salt if necessary: if you used salted anchovies and rinsed off the salt, you might be surprised to find that you need some.

3. Remove ½ cup cooking water from the pasta and greens. Cook the pasta until al dente, firm to the bite, about 8 to 10 minutes. To test it, remove a piece of pasta with tongs or a spoon, run it under cold water, and taste it. It should be cooked through but not at all mushy. Drain and toss with the anchovy mixture and reserved cooking liquid in the serving bowl. Sprinkle on the cheese. Serve at once.

Get out the following equipment: **large pot and colander or pasta pot; large bowl or salad spinner for washing greens; chef's knife and cutting board; garlic press or minichop if using; small nonstick skillet; serving bowl and spoons or servers**

Advance preparation: **The garlic-and-anchovy mixture can sit on top of the stove for a few hours and be reheated; however, it takes no time at all to prepare the mixture while the pasta water is heating. You can prepare the greens hours ahead of time.**

PER SERVING:
10 gm total fat
1.2 gm saturated fat
444 calories
72.5 gm carbohydrates
18.0 gm protein

Pasta with Sugar Snap Peas and Cottage Cheese "Pesto"

Makes 4 servings

If you want a creamy pasta sauce with no cream, this cottage cheese–based sauce is a real winner. While the water is coming to a boil for the pasta, throw the ingredients for the sauce into a food processor. Cook the sugar snap peas right in the water with the pasta for a one-pot meal. I particularly like this combination because the sugar snap peas are so sweet and contrast beautifully with the savory garlicky sauce. Rigatoni is a nice pasta to use because of the way the sugar snap peas (or peas or beans) find their way inside the wide cylinders of pasta. The basil here is chopped rather than pureed as it would be in a real pesto. Make sure you dry the leaves thoroughly and handle them gently and that you add them to the food processor after processing the cottage cheese. If you bruise the leaves, the sauce will not be a pretty color.

2 large garlic cloves, peeled
1 cup nonfat cottage cheese
Salt to taste, plus at least 1 tablespoon for the water
2 tablespoons plain nonfat yogurt
1 tablespoon olive oil
Freshly ground black pepper to taste
¼ cup freshly grated Parmesan cheese
1 cup fresh basil leaves, rinsed and thoroughly dried
¾ pound rigatoni, penne, or fusilli
¾ pound sugar snap peas (about 3 cups), trimmed

1. Bring a large pot of water (4 to 6 quarts) to a boil while you make the sauce. Turn on the food processor, drop in the garlic, and process until finely chopped. Scrape down the sides of the bowl. Add the cottage cheese and process until fairly smooth. Scrape down the sides of the bowl again. Add the salt, yogurt, olive oil, pepper, and Parmesan and process until completely smooth. Add the basil and process until finely chopped. Transfer to the pasta bowl.
2. When your water comes to a rolling boil, add the tablespoon salt (or more) and the pasta. Boil for 5 minutes and drop in the sugar snap peas. Ladle out 2 tablespoons of the cooking water and stir it into the cottage cheese mixture. Continue to cook the pasta until al dente, firm to the bite, 5 to 8 more minutes. To test it, remove a piece of pasta with tongs or

Get out the following equipment: large pot and colander or pasta pot; food processor fitted with steel blade; measuring spoons and measuring cups; cheese grater; pasta bowl and servers

Advance preparation: You can make the sauce and prepare the sugar snap peas hours or even a day before serving. You can keep the sauce on hand in the refrigerator for several days for quick meals. However, the surface will discolor because of the basil, so stir before serving or skim off the top surface.

PER SERVING:
6.5 gm total fat
1.6 gm saturated fat
454 calories
73.9 gm carbohydrates
23.6 gm protein

a spoon, run it under cold water, and taste it. It should be cooked through but not at all mushy. Drain and toss at once with the sauce. Serve hot.

Variations: Other vegetables can be substituted for the sugar snap peas:
- 1 to 1½ pounds broccoli (1 head), broken into florets, stems peeled and chopped
- 2 cups fresh or thawed frozen peas
- 1 pound green beans, trimmed and broken in half

If fresh basil is difficult to find, use ½ cup chopped fresh flat-leaf parsley leaves instead.

Pasta with Mushrooms and Broccoli

Makes 4 servings

The topping for this pasta isn't saucy and thick, the way you might expect a pasta topping to be. Rather, it's vegetable rich and savory. When you toss the cooked pasta and broccoli with the mushrooms cooked with white wine and broth, the noodles become infused with the piquant flavors of the mushrooms. You can use more broth if you want a wetter pasta. As for the type of pasta, I like a broad, flat noodle with this, something like pappardelle or fettuccine, but any pasta will work. A good way to heat your pasta bowl is to ladle some of the pasta cooking water into it while the pasta is cooking; drain the water just before you toss the pasta.

½ pound mushrooms, cleaned and stems trimmed

½ to ¾ teaspoon salt, plus at least 1 tablespoon for the water

1 tablespoon olive oil

3 to 4 large garlic cloves, to your taste, peeled and minced or pressed

1 teaspoon chopped fresh rosemary or ½ teaspoon crumbled dried

½ teaspoon fresh thyme leaves or ¼ teaspoon dried thyme

½ cup dry white wine

1½ cups defatted chicken stock (page 155), vegetable stock (page 156), or canned broth; more as needed

Freshly ground black pepper to taste

¾ pound pasta such as pappardelle, but any shape will do

1 pound broccoli

¼ cup freshly grated Parmesan cheese

Get out the following equipment: **large pot and colander or pasta pot; chef's knife and cutting board; garlic press or minichop if using; measuring spoons; large, heavy nonstick skillet and wooden spoon; serving bowl if using**

Advance preparation: **You can cook the mushrooms hours ahead of time and reheat. However, they continue to absorb moisture, so you will probably have to add more stock or, if you've run out of stock, a bit of the pasta-cooking water.**

PER SERVING:
6.9 gm total fat
1.7 gm saturated fat
451 calories
73.4 gm carbohydrates
20.0 gm protein

1. If the mushrooms are large, cut them into thick slices. If they're small, quarter them.
2. Fill a large pasta pot with water (4 to 6 quarts) and bring to a boil while you prepare the topping.
3. Heat the mushrooms and salt together in the skillet over medium heat. In a couple of minutes they'll be sizzling and moist; they're releasing their own water, which will mostly evaporate. When most of the liquid has evaporated, add the olive oil, garlic, and herbs. Stir together for about half a minute, until you smell the garlic cooking. Add the wine and cook, stirring, until most of it has evaporated. Add 1¼ cups of the stock, reduce the heat to low, and simmer for 10 minutes. Taste. Is there enough flavor? Add salt or garlic if there isn't. Grind in some pepper and toss. The mushrooms should be glazed, and the mixture shouldn't be watery; cook for a few more minutes if it is. On the other hand, if it seems dry, add more stock. Keep warm or at a very slow simmer while you cook the pasta.
4. When your water comes to a rolling boil, add the tablespoon salt (or more) and the pasta. Give the pasta a stir to keep it from sticking. Cook for about 5 minutes while you prepare the broccoli.
5. Cut the florets off the broccoli stems and, if they are quite large, cut them into smaller pieces. Drop them into the boiling water with the pasta. Cook until the pasta is al dente, firm to the bite, 3 to 5 more minutes for most pastas. To test it, remove a piece of pasta with tongs or a spoon, run it under cold water, and taste it. It should be cooked through but not at all mushy.
6. Carefully drain the pasta and broccoli, toss thoroughly with the mushroom mixture, either in the skillet or in a large warm pasta bowl, and serve at once. Sprinkle a tablespoon of Parmesan over each serving.

Pasta with Summer Squash Stew

■

Makes 4 servings

Inspired by the multicolored summer squash I find in August at my farmers' market, the stew that tops this mixture could actually stand alone or be served with other grains, with fish, or with chicken. The lemon zest here is a wonderful touch.

1 tablespoon olive oil

1 small sweet red onion, peeled and sliced

4 large garlic cloves, peeled and minced or pressed

1 pound summer squash, such as pattypan, zucchini, round green squash, or yellow squash (or a mixture), cut into 1- by ¼-inch strips (julienne)

½ to ¾ teaspoon salt, plus at least 1 tablespoon for the water

1 teaspoon fresh thyme leaves or ½ teaspoon dried

1 pound firm, ripe tomatoes, peeled, seeded, and chopped

Freshly ground black pepper to taste

2 tablespoons slivered fresh basil leaves

½ to 1 teaspoon finely chopped lemon zest, to your taste

¾ pound farfalle

2 ounces feta cheese, crumbled

1. Begin heating a large pot of water (4 to 6 quarts) for the pasta while you make your sauce.

2. Heat the oil in the skillet over medium heat. Add the onion and cook, stirring, until tender, 3 to 5 minutes. Add the garlic and stir together until it begins to smell fragrant, 30 seconds to a minute. Stir in the squash and salt and cook, stirring often, until the squash juices flow and the squash has softened and become translucent, 5 to 7 minutes. Add the thyme and tomatoes and continue to cook, stirring often, for another 5 to 10 minutes. The tomatoes should cook down and render their juices, but the juices shouldn't evaporate. Stir in the pepper, basil, and lemon zest. Taste. Do you need to add more salt? (You probably do.) Adjust the seasonings, remove from the heat, and set aside.

3. When the water comes to a rolling boil, add the tablespoon salt (or more) and gradually add the pasta. Stir to ensure that the pasta doesn't stick. Cook until the pasta is al dente, firm to the bite, about 10 minutes. To test it, remove a piece of pasta with tongs or a spoon, run it under cold water, and taste it. It should be cooked through but not at all mushy. Drain and toss with the zucchini mixture and feta, in either the skillet or a warm pasta bowl, and serve.

Get out the following equipment: chef's knife and cutting board; garlic press or minichop if using; saucepan for blanching; measuring spoons; zester; large, heavy nonstick skillet and wooden spoon; large pot and colander or pasta pot; pasta bowl and servers if using

Advance preparation: The zucchini stew can be made a few hours to a day ahead and reheated, but don't add the basil until you reheat it.

PER SERVING:
8.6 gm total fat
2.8 gm saturated fat
448 calories
76.9 gm carbohydrates
15.6 gm protein

Pasta e Fagioli
Pasta and Bean Soup

Makes 4 to 6 servings

A hearty parsley-flecked soup rather than a pasta, this has been a favorite dish of mine since the first time I ate it over twenty years ago.

1 pound (2¼ cups) dried white beans, cranberry beans, pinto beans, or chickpeas, washed and picked over

1 piece Parmesan rind

1 bay leaf

1 small dried red chile

1 tablespoon olive oil

1 medium-size onion, peeled and chopped

1 medium-size carrot, peeled and finely chopped

1 celery rib, finely chopped

4 large garlic cloves, peeled and minced or pressed

1½ to 1¾ pounds (3 large or 7 medium-size) firm, ripe tomatoes or one 28-ounce can tomatoes, drained, peeled, seeded, and chopped or coarsely pureed

7 to 8 cups water, as needed

2 to 3 teaspoons salt, or more to your taste

1 teaspoon dried oregano

1 teaspoon fresh thyme leaves or ½ teaspoon dried thyme

¼ teaspoon dried rosemary or ½ teaspoon chopped fresh

6 ounces macaroni shells or fusilli

Freshly ground black pepper to taste

½ cup chopped fresh flat-leaf parsley leaves

¼ cup freshly grated Parmesan cheese

1. Soak the beans in the bowl in three times their volume of water for 6 hours or overnight. Drain. Tie the rind, bay leaf, and dried chile together with kitchen string to facilitate removing at the end of cooking.
2. Heat the oil in the soup pot or Dutch oven over medium heat. Add the onion, carrot, and celery and cook, stirring, until tender, 5 to 8 minutes. Add half the garlic and cook, stirring, until the garlic begins to color, 30 seconds to a minute. Add the tomatoes, bring to a simmer, and cook, stirring often, until they cook down a bit and smell fragrant, about 10 minutes.

Get out the following equipment: large bowl; chef's knife and cutting board; garlic press or minichop if using; kitchen string; measuring spoons and measuring cup; large heavy soup pot or Dutch oven; wooden spoon; blender or food processor fitted with steel blade; small saucepan

Advance preparation: This will keep for 3 days in the refrigerator without the addition of the pasta (bring the soup back to a boil and add the pasta close to serving time). The flavors get better overnight. It freezes well for several months without the pasta.

PER SERVING:
7.5 gm total fat
1.8 gm saturated fat
664 calories
115.0 gm carbohydrates
37.0 gm protein

continued

3. Add the beans, 7 cups of the water, the Parmesan rind, bay leaf, and chile and bring to a boil. Reduce the heat to low, cover, and simmer gently for 1 hour. Season with salt, add the remaining garlic, the oregano, thyme, and rosemary, and simmer, covered, until the beans are tender, another 30 minutes to an hour. Taste. Is there enough salt? Garlic? Adjust the seasonings. Remove the Parmesan rind, bay leaf, and chile.

4. Remove 2 cups of the beans with a bit of broth and puree in the blender or food processor. Return to the pot and stir together.

5. Bring the remaining cup of water to a simmer in the small saucepan. Turn up the heat so that the soup is at a gentle boil and add the pasta to the soup. If the soup seems too thick, stir in the simmering water. Cook, stirring, until the pasta is al dente, firm to the bite, 10 to 15 minutes. To test it, remove a piece of pasta with tongs or a spoon, run it under cold water, and taste it. If should be cooked through but not at all mushy. Remove from the heat. Add lots of pepper. Taste and adjust the salt again. Stir in the parsley. Serve hot or warm, with the grated Parmesan.

Pasta e Fagioli Made with Canned Beans

Substitute two 15-ounce cans white beans or chickpeas, drained and rinsed, for the dried beans, and reduce the water to 1 quart (4 cups). Start with step 2. In step 3, add the water, the Parmesan rind, bay leaf, and chile and bring to a boil. Reduce the heat to low, cover, and simmer, uncovered, for 30 minutes. Season with salt (about 1½ teaspoons), add the remaining garlic, the beans, oregano, thyme, and rosemary, and simmer, covered, for another 15 minutes. Proceed with the rest of the recipe.

■ Lasagne ■

Lasagne has always been one of my dinner party standbys; everybody loves it. But making lasagne was always a time-consuming affair, a dish I'd make on weekends. I'd usually make my own pasta because the commercial brands weren't thin enough for my taste. Now I've discovered the no-boil noodles, very thin sheets of pasta that require no cooking when used in baked dishes. The combination of the moisture from the sauce and the steam produced when they bake is enough to cook them to a beautiful al dente texture. Made from semolina and water, with no fat at all, the noodles have a wonderful flavor, and they've changed my lasagne-making life. Now I can throw together a beautiful lasagne dinner very quickly.

Spinach and Tomato Lasagne

∎

Makes 6 servings

This savory lasagne is packed with spinach (other greens, such as chard or kale, could be used in conjunction with spinach). Nonfat cottage cheese, blended with the greens, replaces the more traditional high-fat ricotta and mozzarella.

FOR THE TOMATO SAUCE:

1 tablespoon olive oil

1 small onion, peeled and chopped

3 large garlic cloves, peeled and minced or pressed

3 pounds firm, ripe tomatoes, peeled, seeded, and chopped, or two 28-ounce cans chopped tomatoes, lightly drained

Pinch of sugar

1 teaspoon dried oregano

½ teaspoon dried thyme, or more to taste

About 1 teaspoon salt, or more to your taste

Freshly ground black pepper to taste

2 tablespoons chopped or slivered fresh basil leaves, if available

FOR THE LASAGNE:

1 bunch (¾ to 1 pound) fresh spinach, a combination of spinach and other greens such as Swiss chard or kale, or one 10-ounce box frozen chopped spinach, thawed

1½ cups nonfat cottage cheese

½ pound no-boil lasagne noodles

⅔ cup freshly grated Parmesan cheese (about 2½ ounces)

3 tablespoons dry or fresh bread crumbs (white or whole wheat)

1 tablespoon olive oil

1. Make the tomato sauce. Heat the olive oil in one of the skillets over medium heat. Add the onion and cook, stirring, until tender, about 5 minutes. Add half the minced garlic and cook, stirring, until the garlic begins to color, another minute. Add the tomatoes, remaining garlic, sugar, oregano, thyme, and salt. Stir together and simmer, uncovered, over medium-low heat, stirring often, until the tomatoes are cooked down and fragrant, 20 to 30 minutes. The sauce should not stick to the skillet; it should retain some liquid. Season with pepper, add the basil, reduce the

Get out the following equipment: **chef's knife and cutting board; garlic press or minichop if using; measuring spoons and cups; 2 large, heavy nonstick skillets and wooden spoon; food processor fitted with steel blade or blender; 3-quart baking or gratin dish, preferably rectangular**

Advance preparation: The lasagne, either version, can be assembled a day ahead of time, in plastic wrap, and refrigerated overnight. Add 5 minutes to the covered baking time if chilled. The assembled lasagne can also be wrapped in plastic, then foil, and frozen for a month.

PER SERVING:
9.1 gm total fat
2.5 gm saturated fat
350 calories
46.2 gm carbohydrates
20.9 gm protein

heat to low, and continue to cook, stirring often, for another 5 to 10 minutes. Remove from the heat, taste, and adjust the seasonings.

2. While the tomato sauce is simmering, stem and wash the spinach or spinach and greens, and wilt, in batches, in the other skillet in the liquid left on their leaves after washing. This should take a couple of minutes once the water on the leaves begins to boil. Alternatively, blanch in a large pot of boiling salted water (see page 23). Drain and rinse with cold water, then squeeze dry with your hands, or wrap in a kitchen towel and squeeze. Chop coarsely. If using thawed frozen spinach, squeeze dry in a towel.

3. In the food processor or in a blender, blend the cottage cheese until fairly smooth. Add ½ cup of the tomato sauce and blend again until smooth. Add the spinach and briefly blend until the spinach is mixed in with the cottage cheese mixture (do not puree).

4. Assemble the lasagne. Oil the baking or gratin dish. Preheat the oven to 375°F. Have all of your ingredients within reach. Spoon about ½ cup sauce into the baking dish and spread over the bottom of the dish. Make a layer of lasagne noodles over the sauce. Break noodles if necessary to make a layer that covers the surface of the dish. Dot the noodles with spoonfuls of the cottage cheese/spinach mixture and gently spread over the noodles. Top with a layer of sauce, then a thin layer of Parmesan (about 1½ tablespoons). Repeat the layers—pasta, cottage cheese and spinach, sauce, Parmesan—2 or 3 more times, depending on the shape of your dish. Make sure you end up with a layer of tomato sauce topped with Parmesan. Sprinkle on the bread crumbs. Drizzle on the oil.

5. Brush or spray the dull side of a piece of aluminum foil cut to cover the dish. Cover the lasagne oiled side down. Bake for 25 minutes. Uncover and bake until the top is beginning to brown, about another 15 minutes. Serve hot.

Quick Spinach and Tomato Lasagne

Makes 6 servings

This lasagne, made with prepared tomato sauce and frozen spinach, is almost as delicious as the previous one, and it takes 10 to 15 minutes to assemble. The spinach can be thawed in the microwave, following the instructions on the package. Be sure to check labels in the supermarket for a low-fat sauce.

1½ cups nonfat cottage cheese

One 26-ounce jar prepared tomato sauce

One 10-ounce package frozen spinach, thawed and squeezed dry

Get out the following equipment: **measuring cups and measuring spoons; 3-quart baking or gratin dish; food processor fitted with steel blade or blender; aluminum foil**

PER SERVING:
11.5 gm total fat
2.9 gm saturated fat
390 calories
52.3 gm carbohydrates
19.8 gm protein

½ pound no-boil lasagne noodles

⅔ cup freshly grated Parmesan cheese (about 2½ ounces)

3 tablespoons fresh or dry bread crumbs

1 tablespoon olive oil

1. Oil or butter the baking or gratin dish. Preheat the oven to 375°F. In the food processor or blender, blend the cottage cheese until fairly smooth. Add ½ cup of the tomato sauce and blend until smooth. Add the spinach and blend briefly until the spinach is mixed in with the cottage cheese mixture (do not puree).

2. Assemble the lasagne. Have all of your ingredients within reach. Spoon about ½ cup of sauce into the baking dish and spread over the bottom. Make a layer of lasagne noodles over the sauce. Break noodles if necessary to make a layer that covers the surface of the dish. Dot the noodles with spoonfuls of the cottage cheese/spinach mixture and gently spread over the noodles. Top with a layer of sauce, then a thin layer of Parmesan (about 1½ tablespoons). Repeat the layers—pasta, cottage cheese and spinach, sauce, Parmesan—2 or 3 more times, depending on the shape of your dish. Make sure you end up with a layer of tomato sauce topped with Parmesan. Sprinkle on the bread crumbs. Drizzle on the oil.

3. Brush or spray the dull side of a piece of foil cut to cover the dish. Cover the lasagne oiled side down and bake for 25 minutes. Uncover and bake until the top is beginning to brown, about another 15 minutes. Serve hot.

▪ Pasta with Asian Flavors ▪

Since my culinary focus has centered mostly around the Mediterranean and Mexico, my pasta recipes usually mean Italian-inspired pasta. But every country in Asia has its noodle dishes as well, with exciting, gingery flavors. Many require long lists of ingredients, which might keep you from making them. So I've distilled some of my favorite Asian flavors here into a few simple pasta dishes. Make them with soba (buckwheat pasta) or with spaghettini or angel hair pasta.

Get out the following
equipment: large pot
and colander or pasta
pot; chef's knife and
cutting board; garlic
press or minichop if us-
ing; large, heavy non-
stick skillet; long-
handled wooden spoon;
pasta bowl if using and
servers

Advance preparation:
The chicken mixture
can be cooked up to a
day ahead and refrig-
erated. Reheat and
proceed with the recipe.

PER SERVING:
9.1 gm total fat
1.3 gm saturated fat
463 calories
71.3 gm carbohydrates
29.2 gm protein

Pasta with Chicken and Snow Peas or Sugar Snap Peas

Makes 4 servings

2 boneless, skinless chicken breast halves, about ¼ pound each

1 tablespoon canola oil or peanut oil

2 teaspoons peeled and finely chopped or grated fresh ginger

2 garlic cloves, peeled and minced or pressed

1 tablespoon soy sauce

1 cup defatted chicken stock (page 155) or vegetable stock (page 156) or
bouillon, or canned low-sodium broth

1 tablespoon salt for the water, plus more to taste

¾ pound snow peas or sugar snap peas, strings removed

¾ pound buckwheat pasta (soba) or angel hair pasta

1 tablespoon dark sesame oil

¼ cup chopped fresh cilantro leaves

1. Begin heating a large pot of water (4 to 6 quarts) for the pasta while you make your sauce.

2. Cut the chicken breasts into ¼-inch-thick slices, then cut the slices into ¼-inch-wide strips.

3. Heat the oil in the skillet over medium-high heat and add the ginger and garlic. Cook, stirring, for a few seconds after the ginger and garlic sizzle, then add the chicken strips and cook, stirring, until the chicken is cooked through, about 5 minutes. Stir in the soy sauce, toss together, and add the stock or bouillon. Bring to a simmer and simmer for a couple of minutes. Taste and adjust the salt. Keep warm while you cook the pasta.

4. When the water comes to a rolling boil, add the tablespoon of salt and gradually add the snow peas or sugar snap peas and pasta. Stir to ensure that the pasta doesn't stick. Cook until the pasta is al dente, firm to the bite, which may be as little as 3 to 5 minutes for soba or angel hair (check often), and drain. To test it, remove a piece of pasta with tongs or a spoon, run it under cold water, and taste it. It should be cooked through but not at all mushy. Toss with the chicken mixture, sesame oil, and cilantro, in either the skillet or a warm pasta bowl, and serve.

Asian Pasta with Broccoli and Mushrooms

Makes 4 servings

As in the preceding dish, you can use soba or angel hair pasta for this delicious vegetarian pasta. I particularly like soba.

Salt to taste, plus at least 1 tablespoon for the water

½ pound shiitake, oyster, or regular mushrooms, cleaned, trimmed, and thickly sliced

2 tablespoons dry white wine or sherry

1 tablespoon canola oil or peanut oil

2 garlic cloves, peeled and minced or pressed

2 teaspoons peeled and finely chopped or grated fresh ginger

2 teaspoons soy sauce

1 cup defatted chicken stock (page 155), vegetable stock (page 156), or bouillon, or canned low-sodium broth

¾ pound buckwheat pasta (soba) or angel hair pasta

1 pound broccoli, broken into florets and stems peeled and chopped

1 tablespoon dark sesame oil

¼ cup chopped fresh cilantro leaves

1. Begin heating a large pot of water (4 to 6 quarts) for the pasta while you make your sauce.
2. Salt the mushrooms and heat in the skillet over medium-high heat. They should begin to release liquid after a few minutes. Add the wine and cook, shaking the skillet or stirring from time to time, until most of the liquid has evaporated. Add the oil, garlic, and ginger and cook, stirring, until the garlic and ginger begin to color. Add the soy sauce and stir together, then add the stock or bouillon and bring to a simmer. Simmer gently while you cook the pasta.
3. When the water comes to a rolling boil, add the tablespoon salt (or more) and gradually add the pasta and broccoli. Stir to ensure that the pasta doesn't stick. Cook until the pasta is al dente, firm to the bite, which may be as little as 3 to 5 minutes for soba or angel hair (check often). To test it, remove a piece of pasta with tongs or a spoon, run it under cold water, and taste it. It should be cooked through but not at all mushy. Drain. Toss with the mushroom mixture, sesame oil, and cilantro, in either the skillet or a warm pasta bowl, and serve.

Get out the following equipment: chef's knife and cutting board; garlic press or minichop if using; large pot and colander or pasta pot; large, heavy nonstick skillet; long-handled wooden spoon; pasta bowl if using and servers

Advance preparation: The mushroom mixture can be made up to a day ahead of time and reheated gently.

PER SERVING:
8.1 gm total fat
0.9 gm saturated fat
410 calories
73.3 gm carbohydrates
18.7 gm protein

▪ Pizza ▪

I am assuming that you do not intend to come home from work or school and begin making pizza dough for a very late dinner. But if you have a crust in the freezer, a perfectly marvelous, easy pizza dinner is a possibility. The suggestions here are for pizzas made with prepared or homemade crusts. For those of you who do wish to try your hand at pizza dough, see the recipe that follows.

American pizzas, even California pizzas, are highly caloric. They usually contain a lot of cheese, and they're huge. But pizzas don't require cheese, and those that have it don't require vast quantities. Many classic Italian pizzas contain no cheese at all or just a sprinkling. Classic Neapolitan pizzas (Naples is the home of the pizza) are topped simply, and the topping is a thin film of tomatoes seasoned with garlic in the case of *pizza napoletana*; of tomatoes, mozzarella, and a bit of parsley, oregano, or basil for *pizza Margherita*; and of tomatoes and anchovies (and sometimes olives) in the case of *pizza alla marinara*. What serves one or two people in the United States serves four in Italy; this is the sensible way to eat pizza.

To ensure pizza success, your oven should be very hot and preferably should have a pizza stone in it. This is a round ceramic stone that you can get at cookware stores. Place the pizza or pizza pan directly on top of the preheated stone.

Pizza Dough

▪

Makes two 12- to 14-inch pizza crusts; 12 servings

This dough handles very easily and can be baked either in pizza pans or directly on a hot baking stone. The dough can be refrigerated for a day or two, or frozen for several months, before or after being rolled out. If you do not roll it out before refrigerating or freezing, let the dough come to room temperature before rolling it out. If you have rolled out the dough, do not thaw, but top and bake directly.

> 2 teaspoons active dry yeast
> 1½ cups lukewarm water
> 2 teaspoons salt
> 1 cup whole-wheat flour
> 3 cups unbleached all-purpose flour, plus up to ½ cup as needed for
>   kneading
> Olive oil

Get out the following equipment: large bowl and large wooden spoon or electric mixer with paddle and dough hook attachments; spatula or dough scraper; liquid and dry measuring cups; measuring spoons; pizza pans; rolling pin

Before You Begin: A Kneading Lesson

This may be the first time you have ever made anything resembling bread, so I should tell you how to knead. Dough must be kneaded to develop the long strands of protein in the dough (gluten) that expand as the yeast in the dough multiplies, giving the dough its volume and elasticity. When you knead, air is incorporated into the dough and the dough is warmed; it needs both air and warmth to rise properly.

The recipe will tell you to scrape the dough out onto a lightly floured kneading surface when it can be scraped out in one piece. It helps to have a pastry scraper for this, but a wooden spoon and your hands will do. The dough is still sticky at this stage, so I advise you to remove your rings and to keep your hands dusted with flour. Fold the mass of dough in half toward you (using a pastry scraper if you have one) and, making sure your hands are floured, gently lean into the dough, pressing your weight from the heels of your palms out through your fingertips and pushing the dough away from you rather than into the work surface. Turn the dough a quarter turn and repeat. Continue with this "fold, lean, turn" rhythm. The dough will go from annoyingly sticky to workable after a few turns (add flour to the work surface as necessary). You have to knead for at least 10 minutes to develop the gluten properly. After about 5 minutes the dough will stiffen up and won't be difficult to work with.

When the dough is fairly smooth and elastic—it will spring back when you stick a finger into it—shape it into a ball. To do this, fold the dough over itself, toward you, but don't lean into it; instead turn it and repeat. Do this all the way around, then pinch the dough together at the bottom.

Note: In the piecrust recipes on pages 308, 309, and 352, you are instructed to knead the dough gently. *This is because you* don't *want to develop the gluten too much. When instructed to knead gently, fold and lean gently into the dough and turn it just a few times, until it is smooth and amalgamated.*

To Make the Pizza Dough

1. Dissolve the yeast in the lukewarm water in the mixing bowl or the bowl of your electric mixer and let sit until creamy, about 5 minutes.
2. *Kneading the dough by hand:* Mix together the salt and the whole-wheat flour and stir into the yeast water. Fold in the all-purpose flour ½ cup at a time, until the dough can be scraped out of the bowl in one piece. Add ½ cup all-purpose flour to your kneading surface and knead, adding more flour as necessary, for at least 10 minutes. The dough will be sticky at first but will become very elastic. To test that the dough has been kneaded

Advance preparation: **This dough freezes well for a few months and can be refrigerated for a couple of days. I recommend freezing over chilling, however, to prevent too much rising. You can freeze it right in the pans, or after punching down, shape into a ball and freeze in a plastic bag. Allow to thaw and come to room temperature before rolling out.**

PER SERVING:
0.6 gm total fat
0 gm saturated fat
156 calories
32.3 gm carbohydrates
5.4 gm protein

enough, stick a finger into the dough: the dough should spring back slowly.

Using an electric mixer: Combine the salt, whole-wheat flour, and 2½ cups of the all-purpose flour and add all at once to the bowl. Mix together with the paddle, then change to the dough hook. Mix at low speed for 2 minutes, then at medium speed for 8 to 10 minutes. Add more all-purpose flour as necessary if the dough seems very wet and sticky. Scrape out the dough onto a lightly floured surface and knead for a minute or so by hand. Shape into a ball.

3. Rinse out your bowl, dry, and brush lightly with olive oil. Place the dough in the bowl, rounded side down first, then rounded side up, until entirely coated with oil. Cover with plastic wrap and a kitchen towel and set in a warm, draft-free place to rise until the dough has doubled in size, about 1½ hours. If you are going to refrigerate or freeze the dough at this point, punch it down, divide it in half, and shape into balls. Seal the balls in plastic bags and refrigerate or freeze. You can also roll out the dough and refrigerate or freeze directly on the pizza pans.

4. Preheat the oven, with a baking stone or baking tiles in it, to 450°F for 30 minutes. If you are using pizza pans, which I recommend, oil the pans lightly and sprinkle with cornmeal or semolina. Punch down the dough (literally, stick your fist into it to deflate it) and divide into 2 or 3 pieces. Cover the portions you aren't working with with plastic wrap or a damp paper or kitchen towel and roll out each piece. Rolling out takes a bit of patience, because the dough is springy and elastic and will at first shrink back each time you roll it. But persevere, turning the dough over from time to time, and you'll get it rolled out thin and to the size you desire. Dust your work surface and the dough regularly with light sprinklings of flour to prevent sticking. You can use your hands to press out the dough if you prefer this to a rolling pin.

5. Line two 12- or 14-inch pizza pans or place smaller crusts on a baking sheet or, if baking directly on the stone, place on a cornmeal- or semolina-dusted baking peel (a wooden board with a handle) or a cornmeal- or semolina-dusted baking sheet. The dough should be rolled no thicker than ¼ inch, thinner if possible. Whether you are using pizza pans or not, roll the edges of the pizza dough in and pinch an attractive lip all the way around. Top with the garnishes of your choice and either gently slide from the peel or baking sheet onto the hot baking stone or place pans on top of the baking stone. Bake for 15 to 25 minutes or as directed in the recipe.

Pizza Napoletana
Pizza with Tomatoes and Garlic

Makes one 12- to 14-inch pizza; 6 servings

2 tablespoons olive oil

1 to 1½ pounds firm, ripe tomatoes, peeled, seeded, and chopped, or one
  14-ounce can tomatoes, drained and chopped if not chopped already

2 to 3 large garlic cloves, to your taste, peeled and minced or pressed

1½ teaspoons dried oregano or 1 tablespoon slivered fresh basil leaves

¾ teaspoon salt, or more to your taste

Freshly ground black pepper to taste

1 pizza crust ready for the oven (page 270)

Brush the pizza dough with 1 tablespoon of the oil. Mix together the tomatoes, garlic, oregano or basil, salt, and pepper and spread over the pizza.
Drizzle on the remaining tablespoon oil. Bake at 450°F, as instructed on
page 272, until the crust is brown, 15 to 30 minutes.

Additions to Pizza Napoletana:

- 2 or more red, yellow, or green bell peppers, seeded and thinly sliced
- 1 to 2 onions, peeled and thinly sliced
- ½ pound mushrooms, cleaned, bottoms trimmed, and thinly sliced
- ¼ cup imported black olives, pitted if desired
- 2 to 4 tablespoons drained capers, to your taste, rinsed
- 4 canned artichoke hearts, drained, rinsed, and thinly sliced
- 2 ounces mozzarella or smoked mozzarella cheese, very thinly sliced

Scatter any or all of the above, with the exception of the cheese, over the
tomato sauce before drizzling on the final tablespoon of oil. Bake as directed. For the cheese, bake the pizza for 15 minutes, then arrange the
cheese on top and bake until it melts and begins to bubble, another 5 to 10
minutes.

*Get out the following
equipment:* **chef's knife
and cutting board; gar-
lic press or minichop if
using; measuring
spoons; pastry brush**

PER SERVING:
*5.5 gm total fat
0.6 gm saturated fat
220 calories
36.6 gm carbohydrates
6.4 gm protein*

Pizza alla Marinara
Pizza with Tomatoes, Garlic, and Anchovies

Makes one 12- to 14-inch pizza; 6 servings

2 tablespoons olive oil

1 to 1½ pounds firm, ripe tomatoes, peeled, seeded, and chopped, or one
     14-ounce can tomatoes, drained and chopped if not chopped already

2 to 3 large garlic cloves, to your taste, peeled and minced or pressed

1 teaspoon dried oregano

½ teaspoon salt

1 pizza crust ready for the oven (page 270)

3 to 4 anchovy fillets, to your taste, rinsed and cut into small pieces

Brush the pizza dough with 1 tablespoon of the oil. Mix together the tomatoes, garlic, oregano, and salt and spread over the pizza. Sprinkle on the anchovies. Drizzle on the remaining tablespoon oil. Bake at 450°F as directed
on page 272 until the crust is brown, 15 to 30 minutes.

Pizza Bianca
Herb and Garlic Pizza

Makes one 12- to 14-inch pizza; 6 servings

3 tablespoons olive oil

3 to 4 garlic cloves, to your taste, peeled and minced or pressed

1 pizza crust ready for the oven (page 270)

¼ cup chopped fresh rosemary, sage, or oregano leaves, or a mixture

1 ounce Parmesan cheese, grated (¼ cup)

1. Mix together the oil and garlic. Brush the crust generously with this mixture. Sprinkle with the chopped herbs and Parmesan.
2. Bake at 450°F as instructed on page 272 until the crust is crisp, browned,
   and fragrant, 15 to 25 minutes. Remove from the heat and serve hot or
   warm.

Pizza with Shrimp

Makes one 12- to 14-inch pizza; 6 servings

1 pizza crust ready for the oven (page 270)

2 tablespoons olive oil

1 to 1½ pounds firm, ripe tomatoes, peeled, seeded, and chopped, or one 14-ounce can tomatoes, drained and chopped if not chopped already

2 to 3 large garlic cloves, or to your taste, peeled and minced or pressed

1½ teaspoons dried oregano or 1 tablespoon slivered fresh basil leaves

¾ teaspoon salt, or more to your taste

½ teaspoon red pepper flakes, or more to your taste

½ pound cooked bay shrimp

1. Brush the pizza dough with 1 tablespoon of the olive oil. Mix together the tomatoes, garlic, oregano or basil, salt, and red pepper flakes and spread over the pizza. Drizzle on the remaining tablespoon olive oil.

2. Bake at 450°F as instructed on page 272 until the crust is brown, 15 to 30 minutes. Remove from the oven and scatter the shrimp over the top. Turn off the oven and return the pizza to it for 5 minutes to heat the shrimp.

Get out the following equipment: **chef's knife and cutting board; garlic press or minichop if using; measuring spoons; kitchen scissors if using for basil; pastry brush; mixing bowl**

PER SERVING:
5.9 gm total fat
0.8 gm saturated fat
257 calories
36.6 gm carbohydrates
14.3 gm protein

Toppings

Tomato sauces that top pasta or accompany fish can also top bruschetta. The tomato sauce for the basic pasta on page 43 is marvelous, with a little Parmesan sprinkled over the top. Other toppings include:

- Spicy tomato sauce (page 246)
- Puttanesca sauce (page 247)
- Dried mushrooms and tomato sauce (page 251)
- Tomato, caper, and mint sauce (page 291)
- Ratatouille (page 73)
- Caponata (page 222)

Advance preparation: Bruschette are best if toasted shortly before serving but can be kept warm in a 250°F oven for 30 minutes.

PER SERVING:
4.7 gm total fat
1.2 gm saturated fat
366 calories
67.5 gm carbohydrates
11.9 gm protein

◾ Bruschetta ◾

Bruschetta (pronounced brus-*ket*-ah) is a thick slice of lightly toasted country bread rubbed with garlic and brushed (or drizzled in a higher-fat environment) with olive oil, often with a topping. Bruschette are the Italian answer to the open-faced sandwich and make a marvelous, satisfying quick dinner.

Sometimes you want the taste of pasta sauce but not the pasta, or you just don't want to wait for a big pot of water to come to a boil. If you have good-quality crusty bread on hand, bruschette are a great alternative. They are a favorite late-night supper in our house. They also make a wonderful lunch and a perfect vehicle for leftovers. Virtually anything that you'd like on an open-faced sandwich can top bruschetta, so don't limit yourself to these suggestions.

Basic Bruschetta

◾

Makes 4 to 6 servings

Use a crusty, porous country bread for this. The only topping is garlic and olive oil. From here you can go on forever. I usually toast my bruschetta in a toaster oven, but you can grill or broil the bread as well.

8 to 12 thick slices country bread
1 to 2 large garlic cloves, as needed, sliced in half
1 to 2 tablespoons olive oil (optional), as needed

1. If you are not using a toaster or a toaster oven, prepare a grill or preheat the broiler. Lightly toast the bread or set the bread over hot coals or under the broiler 4 to 5 inches from the heat source. The bread should toast on both sides and remain soft inside. This goes very quickly under a broiler (a minute or less per side), so watch carefully to avoid burning the bread.

2. Remove from the heat and immediately rub both sides with the cut cloves of garlic. Brush with the olive oil. Cut into halves if your slices are wide.

Note: You may keep the bruschetta warm in a very low (250°F) oven.

Tomato Concassee Bruschetta

Makes 6 servings

1½ pounds firm, ripe tomatoes, seeded and chopped

Coarse sea salt and freshly ground black pepper to taste

1 to 2 large garlic cloves, to your taste, peeled and minced or pressed

2 to 3 teaspoons balsamic vinegar, to your taste

1 tablespoon olive oil

2 to 3 tablespoons slivered fresh basil leaves, to your taste

6 thick slices country bread

1 ounce Parmesan cheese, shaved into slivers

Small fresh basil leaves for garnish

1. Toss together the tomatoes, salt, pepper, garlic, vinegar, olive oil, and slivered basil. Let sit for 15 minutes or longer to let the flavors mingle.
2. Make the bruschetta as directed on page 276. Top with the tomato mixture and Parmesan slivers and serve each one with a basil leaf.

Get out the following equipment: chef's knife and cutting board; garlic press or minichop if using; medium-size bowl; measuring spoons

Advance preparation: The topping will keep in the refrigerator for a day, but the fresher it is, the better. The garlic becomes more pungent over time, so if making ahead, use the smaller amount.

PER SERVING:

7.2 gm total fat

2.0 gm saturated fat

314 calories

50.3 gm carbohydrates

11.1 gm protein

Sweet Red Pepper and Goat Cheese Bruschetta

Makes 6 servings

4 large red bell peppers

Coarse sea salt and freshly ground black pepper to taste

2 large garlic cloves, or more to taste, peeled and minced or pressed

1 tablespoon olive oil

2 tablespoons slivered fresh basil leaves

6 thick slices country bread

3 ounces goat cheese, crumbled

1. Roast the peppers in the oven following the directions on page 131.
2. Holding the peppers over the bowl, skin them and remove the seeds and membranes. Slice into thin strips. Strain the liquid into another bowl and toss with the sliced peppers, coarse salt, pepper, garlic, olive oil, and basil. Marinate for at least 30 minutes at room temperature.
3. Make the bruschetta as directed on page 276. Top with the peppers, sprinkle on the goat cheese, heat through if desired in a preheated 350°F oven for 10 minutes, and serve.

Get out the following equipment: 2 bowls large enough to hold the peppers; garlic press or minichop if using; baking sheet; chef's knife and cutting board; strainer; measuring spoons

Advance preparation: The roasted peppers in their marinade will keep for up to a week in the refrigerator. But don't add the garlic and basil until a few hours before serving.

PER SERVING:

8.9 gm total fat

3.1 gm saturated fat

354 calories

56.4 gm carbohydrates

13.6 gm protein

Wild Mushroom Bruschetta

■

Makes 6 servings

Get out the following equipment: small bowl or large measuring cup; strainer for dried mushrooms; cheesecloth or paper towels; chef's knife and cutting board; garlic press or minichop if using; measuring spoons; large, heavy nonstick skillet and wooden spoon

Advance preparation: The wild mushroom topping will keep for up to 3 days in the refrigerator.

PER SERVING:
5.8 gm total fat
1.1 gm saturated fat
294 calories
49.6 gm carbohydrates
9.7 gm protein

1 ounce (about 1 cup) dried porcini (cèpes) (optional)

Boiling water to cover

1 pound fresh wild mushrooms, such as oyster mushrooms, portobellos, morels, girolles, chanterelles, or a combination of wild and cultivated mushrooms, cleaned and trimmed

1 tablespoon olive oil

2 medium-size shallots, peeled and finely chopped

About ½ teaspoon salt, or more to taste

3 large garlic cloves, peeled, minced, or pressed

¼ cup dry white or red wine

1 teaspoon chopped fresh rosemary leaves or ½ teaspoon crumble dried rosemary

1 teaspoon fresh thyme leaves or ½ teaspoon dried thyme

Freshly ground black pepper to taste

2 tablespoons chopped fresh parsley leaves

6 thick slices country bread

1. Place the dried mushrooms in the bowl or measuring cup and pour on boiling water to cover. Let sit until thoroughly tender, 15 to 30 minutes. Place the strainer over the small bowl and line with cheesecloth or paper towels. Drain the mushrooms and squeeze dry over the strainer. Reserve this soaking water. Rinse the mushrooms thoroughly in several changes of water, until there is no sign of sand; squeeze dry and chop coarsely. Set aside.

2. If the fresh mushrooms are quite large, cut them in half, then slice about ¼ inch thick. Set aside.

3. Heat the oil in the skillet over medium heat and add the shallots. Cook, stirring, until tender and beginning to brown, about 5 minutes. Add the fresh mushrooms and a little salt. Cook, stirring, until the mushrooms begin to release water, then add the garlic and soaked dried mushrooms. Cook, stirring, for another couple of minutes. Add the wine, herbs, and pepper and continue to cook, stirring often, until the mushrooms are tender, about 10 minutes. Add 3 tablespoons of the reserved mushroom-soaking water from the dried mushrooms if you used them. Add more salt and pepper to taste. Stir together until the mushrooms are nicely glazed. Remove from the heat. Stir in the parsley. Taste and adjust the seasonings.

5. Make the bruschetta as directed on page 276. Warm the mushrooms, top the bread with them, and serve.

Fish and Shellfish

∎

Fish and shellfish are two of the most important sources of protein a health-conscious nonvegetarian can get. They're also one of the quickest-cooking foods; you could almost rank them as convenience food, because they need very little embellishment, provided they are impeccably fresh. For most fish and shellfish dishes you can prepare sauces and accompaniments ahead of time; then no more than 10 to 30 minutes (depending on the dish) will be required for cooking the fish. For this reason I serve fish or shellfish often for dinner parties.

∎ Light Fish Basics ∎

Success with fish begins at the market (as it does for all foods, but especially fish). Freshness is essential; most of the reasons that people don't like fish have to do with strong "fishy" smells and tastes. But these won't be part of the equation if the fish is fresh.

Buying Fish

Your best bet for quality fish is a good fish store, which may be the fish department in your supermarket. If you rely on one-stop shopping and want to include fish in your diet, choose a supermarket with a fish department. Packaged fish in the meat section is not good enough. You need to be able to look at the fish closely, to see if the flesh has a healthy, fresh sheen.

- The fish store or department should not smell "fishy"—briny, maybe, like the ocean, but not fishy. This is a sure sign that the fish isn't fresh.

- Look for moist, shiny, translucent color and firm flesh. These days nobody will let you touch the fish to see if the flesh is firm and springy, but that's the way it should be, so observe closely when the rubber-gloved clerk handles it. You have to rely on your eyes. Some fish clerks will let you smell if you ask. Steaks and fillets should not be sunken or graying or yellowing around the edges. Whole fish should have clear, shiny, slightly bulging eyes.

- If you can see lots of lines of white fat in salmon fillets and steaks, choose another type of fish. Some farmed salmon is so fatty that it doesn't taste good.

- Although I try to buy fresh fish, some fish has been flash-frozen on fishing boats and is sold as fresh. There is usually a label indicating if this is the case. These fish can be of good quality; use the same criteria you use for buying fresh fish and do not freeze it again.

- If you ever do buy fish or shellfish and discover, once you get it home, that it has an off taste, do not eat it. Take it back to the supermarket and report it to a manager.

- *Quantities:* I figure on 5 to 6 ounces of fish or shrimp per person. Precut fish steaks and fillets often weigh as much as a pound, but you can always get the fishmonger to cut pieces in half, or you can cut them down when you get home. When buying whole fish, figure on 10 to 12 ounces per person.

Storage

- Cook fish no more than one day after you buy it and preferably on the day you buy it. Lean fish keeps better than fatty fish (like salmon, bluefish, and mackerel), and whole fish keeps better than steaks or fillets.

- If you are cooking fish that day, simply put the package in the coldest part of your refrigerator. If you are waiting a day, unwrap and rinse the fish, wipe with paper towels, and seal in a clean plastic bag or in a plastic container. Or place on a plate and cover tightly with plastic wrap. Store in the coldest part of the refrigerator.

- If fish is to be marinated for more than 30 minutes before cooking, do not marinate at room temperature but place in the refrigerator.

Cooking Times

With the exception of microwaving, cooking times for fish are pretty much the same whether you steam, poach, bake, or grill (grilling may be a minute or two faster). I still use the Canadian Fisheries method I learned years ago, which recommends 10 minutes of cooking per inch of fish (measured at the thickest point). *However*, I rely on my eyes more than my timer, and for tuna, which I prefer rare, I cook for only 6 to 8 minutes per inch. Also, when fish is cooked in a sauce it can take 5 to 10 minutes longer to cook, and over a very hot grill it can take 8 minutes per inch. You just have to check.

When Is Fish Done? The color change is your best indication: It should go from translucent to just opaque, still perhaps ever so slightly shiny in the middle. Gently poke it at the thickest point with a fork or knife. If it flakes apart, you have cooked it too long and it will probably be dry. It should not resist but pull apart easily and hint at flaking.

Cooking Methods

I'll discuss only the methods that apply to low-fat cooking. Fish can also be pan-fried, deep-fried, and stir-fried, but these methods require more oil than I like to use.

Microwaving

I don't use a microwave for cooking very much, but it is very effective for cooking fish, particularly if you are cooking only one or two portions. Arrange fillets or steaks on a plate or microwaveable dish, with the thicker part on the outside. Top with a sauce or whatever ingredients your recipe calls for. Cover with plastic wrap and pierce the plastic in a few places with a sharp knife to vent. Timing varies according to the recipe, the cut of fish (steak or fillet) and the thickness of the cut, the number of pieces, and the size and power of your microwave. You should always check the fish a minute earlier than the recipe calls for, to make sure it isn't overdone. Zap it for another minute or two if it isn't. It should be opaque at the edges and still ever so slightly translucent at the thickest point. It will continue to cook as it stands once you remove it from the microwave. Generally speaking, two ¾-inch-thick steaks or 1-inch-thick fillets take 4 to 5 minutes. Two ½-inch-thick fillets take about 2½ minutes.

Baking

Baking in a tightly covered, lightly oiled or buttered baking dish works well for all types of fish, whether fatty or lean, fillet or steak, or whole. Lean fish require a small amount of liquid in the baking dish so that they don't dry out. This can be the sauce you are serving with the fish or a small amount of wine, broth, or water. Fish can also be wrapped in lettuce or spinach leaves to seal in moisture. I usually bake fish at fairly high heat, 400° to 425°F.

Baking en Papillote: Here fish is sealed into individual parchment paper or aluminum foil packets and baked. The lightly oiled or buttered parchment or foil is wrapped loosely around the fish, which might be topped with aromatics or a sauce, and tightly crimped. The fish steams inside the packet as it bakes, releasing juice that is delicious as a sauce. The packets can be cut open and served on each diner's plate, or the fish can be removed from the packet and the juice poured over it on the plate.

Broiling

Fish is cooked directly under a broiler, about 4 inches from the heat. Oilier fish such as salmon and mackerel, as well as sturdy steaks like tuna and swordfish, are the best broilers. But leaner types can be used too if they're ¾ inch thick (otherwise it's too easy to dry them out). Marinating leaner fish for about 30 minutes before cooking, and sturdier fish for 15 minutes, helps lock in moisture. I usually broil 1-inch-thick steaks about 4 minutes per side.

Grilling

Any fish that can be broiled can also be grilled. Make sure your grilling rack is well oiled, whether you are setting the fish directly on the grill or using a hinged fine-mesh grilling rack. Fillets and steaks should be marinated to lock in moisture. I usually reserve grilling for sturdy steaks and whole fish.

Pan-Grilling

Pan-grilling on top of the stove in a ridged pan gives you the nice seared taste of a grill, although you don't get the wood smoke flavor. It's a method I use frequently for the same types of fish (sturdy steaks and fillets) that I choose for grilling. You should be sure to have a well-vented stove, however, before you pan-grill fish, because you will definitely smell the fish when you cook it this way. Heat a lightly oiled nonstick ridged pan until water sizzles away immediately on contact. Cook the fish for 8 to 10 minutes per inch of thickness, turning halfway through and shifting the fish around from time to time to get crosshatch grill marks on the surface.

Poaching

Poaching means to cook in barely simmering liquid, which can be a sauce, a fish stock, a mixture of water, wine, or lemon juice and aromatics, a mixture of water and milk, or a light stock. When you cook fish in a fish soup, you are poaching it. Firm-fleshed fish such sea bass and sole are good candidates, whereas very thin fillets like flounder tend to fall apart, as do oily fish like bluefish. Whole salmon is a traditional poacher. For poaching a large whole fish you need a poacher or roasting pan fitted with a rack. For fillets, steaks, and small whole fish you can use a large skillet or a casserole, and you don't need a rack. The fish should be just covered with the liquid. Bring the stock or sauce to a simmer and add the fish. Reduce the heat until there are only the gentlest of bubbles, cover, and simmer until the flesh turns opaque. If serving the fish cold, decrease the cooking time by a few minutes and allow it to cool in the poaching liquid.

Steaming

Here fish is cooked above simmering liquid, with moist, tender results. Any fish that can be poached can be steamed. Cook the fish with aromatics like ginger, garlic, and herbs and place herbs in the steaming water as well. You can steam vegetables along with the fish. Use a lightly oiled fold-up steamer set in a wok or saucepan, a lightly oiled tiered steamer, or place the fish on a heatproof plate and place on a wire rack in a saucepan, covered skillet, wok, or casserole. Bring 1 to 2 inches of water to a boil, set the fish over it, cover, and steam the fish until opaque, 10 minutes per inch.

Fish Pure and Simple

One of the things I love about dining in seaside villages, whether in the United States, Mexico, or Europe, is the abundance of fresh, unadorned seafood. A truly fresh piece of fish, while it can be enhanced marvelously by a sauce or topping, actually needs nothing more than salt, pepper, and perhaps a drizzle of olive oil and/or lemon juice. Before you get into the adorned recipes in this chapter, you might want to experiment with cooking plain fresh fish. It's a good way to learn which fish you like best of the fresh varieties available to you.

The fish chart that follows is by no means exhaustive, but it covers most of the types of fish you are likely to find in local supermarkets and fish stores, their flavors and textures, and the best cooking methods. Again, frying methods are not included because they require more oil than I use in my low-fat cuisine. All fish may be cooked in the microwave.

Good Accompaniments To Fish Dishes

- Rice or other grains
- Steamed potatoes (page 52)
- Baked potatoes (page 236)
- Baked tomatoes (page 235)
- Steamed green vegetables
- Roasted root vegetables, such as beets and parsnips (pages 238–239)
- Cooked greens (page 240)

Fish	Taste/Texture	Best Cooking Methods
Arctic char*	Related to salmon and trout but fattier; mild, firm, rosy flesh	Bake, broil, grill, pan-grill, poach
Bluefish*	Strong taste, soft flesh	Bake, broil, grill, pan-grill
Chilean sea bass	Rich, full-flavored, firm, large flake	Stew, broil, grill, bake
Cod	Mild taste, firm but flaky texture	Bake, broil, poach, steam
Flounder	Delicate taste, soft, flaky texture	Bake, pan-grill, steam
Halibut	Delicate taste, firm texture	Bake, broil, grill, pan-grill, steam
Mackerel*	Strong taste, firm texture	Bake, broil, grill, pan-grill, poach
Mahimahi	Rich taste, firm texture	Bake, broil, grill, pan-grill, steam
Monkfish	Mild taste, very firm texture	Stew, bake, broil, poach, steam
Mullet	Nutty flavor, firm texture	Bake, broil, grill, pan-grill, poach
Orange roughy	Mild taste, firm but flaky texture	Bake, broil, poach, steam
Salmon*	Strong flavor, firm texture	Bake, broil, grill, pan-grill, poach
Sea bass	Mild flavor, firm texture	Bake, broil, grill, pan-grill, poach, steam
Shad*	Medium-strong flavor, firm texture	Bake, broil, grill, pan-grill, poach
Shark	Mild flavor, firm texture	Stew, bake, broil, grill, pan-grill
Snapper, red snapper	Mild flavor, firm but flaky texture	Bake, broil, poach, steam
Sole	Delicate taste, fine texture	Bake, broil, steam, poach
Spiny dogfish	Resembles shark but fattier; rich, large flake	Stew, bake, grill
Striped bass	Medium-strong taste, firm texture	Bake, broil, grill, pan-grill, steam
Swordfish	Strong taste, steaklike, firm texture	Bake, broil, grill, pan-grill
Tilefish	Mild taste, firm but flaky texture	Bake, broil, poach, steam
Trout*	Strong flavor, firm texture	Bake, broil, grill, pan-grill, poach
Tuna	Strong flavor, steaklike, firm texture	Bake, broil, grill, pan-grill
Whiting	Mild flavor, firm but flaky texture	Bake, broil, poach, steam

*High in fat but also in cholesterol-lowering omega-3 fatty acids

Grilled Fish Steaks with Asian Flavors

Makes 4 servings

Here's a gingery marinade that works well with all different types of fish. It stands up to the strong flavor of salmon or tuna, yet it doesn't overwhelm milder fish like halibut. I think my favorite is tuna. Rice wine vinegar, mirin, and sesame oil can be found on the imported foods shelf of your supermarket.

Four 1-inch-thick fish steaks, such as tuna, salmon, swordfish, or halibut
  (about 6 ounces each; see Note)
1 tablespoon fresh lime juice
1 tablespoon rice wine vinegar
1 tablespoon mirin or semidry sherry
½ teaspoon sugar (if using the sherry)
2 teaspoons grated or finely chopped fresh ginger
2 garlic cloves, peeled and minced or pressed
2 teaspoons dark sesame oil
Lime wedges for serving
Hoisin or plum sauce for serving (optional)

1. Rinse the fish steaks and pat dry with paper towels. Place in the baking dish or bowl. Mix together the remaining ingredients and pour over the fish. Turn the steaks over so that they are coated on both sides. Cover the dish with plastic wrap. If you are going to cook the fish within 30 minutes, leave at room temperature. You can also marinate the steaks for up to a few hours in the refrigerator, turning them several times.

2. Prepare a grill (medium heat for a gas grill), preheat the broiler with the rack about 4 inches from the heat, or heat a grill pan over medium-high heat. Place the steaks on a broiler pan if broiling or on the grill or grill pan and cook for 3 to 5 minutes (if you like tuna steak rare in the middle, cook for only 3 to 4 minutes per side). Carefully turn them over, using tongs or a spatula. Cook for another 4 to 5 minutes. The fish should still be slightly pink inside. Be careful not to overcook. Remove from the heat and serve with lime wedges and/or hoisin or plum sauce if desired.

Note: You will probably have to cut the huge steaks they sell at the grocery store yourself. Note the weight on the package and cut accordingly.

Get out the following equipment: **flat glass, ceramic, or stainless-steel baking dish or wide bowl; measuring spoons and measuring cup; citrus press; garlic press or minichop if using; grater if using; chef's knife and cutting board; small knife; grill pan, grill, or broiler pan; tongs or wide spatula**

Advance preparation: **The marinade can be made up to a day ahead of time.**

PER SERVING:
2.1 gm total fat
0.5 gm saturated fat
187 calories
0.4 gm carbohydrates
38.7 gm protein

Grilled Marinated Swordfish

Makes 4 servings

I love this succulent grilled swordfish. The marinade has Greek accents—lemon, olive oil, yogurt, and mint. You can substitute other Mediterranean herbs—oregano, rosemary—if you don't have those called for on hand. The marinade is quickly thrown together, so marinate the fish while you prepare the rest of your dinner and you'll sit down to a delicious meal very quickly. This goes well with rice, potatoes, and/or simply steamed or roasted vegetables.

Four 6-ounce swordfish steaks (see Note on page 285)
2 tablespoons olive oil
¼ cup plain nonfat yogurt
½ cup fresh lemon juice
1 tablespoon chopped fresh dill
2 tablespoons chopped fresh mint leaves
2 garlic cloves, peeled and minced or pressed
½ teaspoon salt
Freshly ground black pepper to taste
Chopped fresh mint leaves for garnish

1. Rinse the steaks and pat dry with paper towels. Place in the baking dish or bowl.
2. Mix together the olive oil, yogurt, lemon juice, dill, mint, garlic, salt, and pepper and pour over the fish. Turn the steaks over so they are coated on both sides. Cover with plastic wrap. Marinate for 30 minutes at room temperature or up to a few hours in the refrigerator.
3. Heat a grill pan over medium-high heat or prepare an outdoor grill (if you are using a gas grill, preheat for 15 minutes at medium). Remove the fish from the marinade and grill on one side for 5 minutes. Turn and grill on the other side for 5 minutes. Remove from the heat, garnish with mint, and serve.

Swordfish Kebabs

Makes 6 servings

The marinade in this recipe is Turkish, which is marvelous with fish or meat. The onions have a tenderizing effect, and it all tastes wonderful. The seasoned thickened yogurt makes a delicious nonfat accompaniment. This

Get out the following equipment: knife; citrus press; garlic press or minichop if using; measuring spoons and measuring cup; glass, ceramic, or stainless-steel baking dish or wide bowl; grill pan or grill; spatula; pastry brush

Advance preparation: The marinade will keep for a day in the refrigerator, but it's best freshly made.

PER SERVING:
8.5 gm total fat
2.1 gm saturated fat
226 calories
1.1 gm carbohydrates
33.9 gm protein

makes an easy summer dinner party meal. Serve with the roasted potatoes on page 236 or with rice.

FOR THE MARINADE:

2 medium-size onions, peeled

2 teaspoons salt

¼ cup fresh lemon juice

2 tablespoons olive oil

8 bay leaves, crumbled

FOR THE FISH AND VEGETABLES:

1½ pounds swordfish steaks, skin removed and cut into 1-inch pieces

2 large red bell peppers, seeded and cut into 1-inch pieces

2 medium-size red onions, peeled, cut into eighths, and separated into layers

FOR THE SAUCE:

¾ cup drained plain nonfat yogurt (1½ cups unthickened; see page 40)

2 to 4 tablespoons fresh lemon juice, to your taste

2 garlic cloves, peeled and crushed into a paste in a mortar and pestle with ¼ teaspoon salt or pressed

3 tablespoons chopped fresh dill or mint leaves

Salt and freshly ground black pepper to taste

1. Make the marinade. Place the onions and salt in the food processor and process until smooth. Let sit for 10 to 15 minutes in the strainer set over a bowl. (Squeeze over a bowl in a double thickness of cheesecloth or a clean kitchen towel if your strainer doesn't have a fine mesh.) Measure out ½ cup of the onion juice. Mix with the other marinade ingredients and toss with the fish and vegetables in the baking dish or bowl. Cover with plastic wrap and refrigerate for at least 1 to 2 hours, tossing every now and again to redistribute the marinade. Meanwhile, if using wooden skewers, soak for 30 minutes in a bowl of cold water.

2. Mix together the ingredients for the sauce, seasoning with salt and pepper.

3. Prepare a charcoal grill or preheat the broiler with the rack about 4 inches from the flame. Thread the fish and vegetables onto the skewers. Grill or broil for 4 to 5 minutes, then turn and grill for another 4 to 5 minutes. Serve at once with the sauce on the side.

Get out the following equipment: **chef's knife and cutting board; food processor fitted with the steel blade; medium-size fine-mesh strainer; medium-size bowl; measuring spoons and measuring cup; large bowl; glass, ceramic, or stainless-steel baking dish or wide bowl; bowl for the sauce; mortar and pestle or garlic press; grill or broiler pan; skewers**

Advance preparation: **The fish and vegetables can marinate in the refrigerator for up to a day.**

PER SERVING:

6.1 gm total fat

1.5 gm saturated fat

224 calories

14.4 gm carbohydrates

27.7 gm protein

Get out the following equipment: chef's knife and cutting board; garlic press or minichop if using; measuring spoons; 3-quart bowl; grill or grill pan; spatula or tongs

Advance preparation: **The sauce will hold for several hours.**

PER SERVING:
5.4 gm total fat
0.8 gm saturated fat
232 calories
6.7 gm carbohydrates
37.1 gm protein

Grilled Tuna with Uncooked Summer Tomato Sauce

Makes 6 servings

Here's one reason to keep this uncooked tomato sauce on hand once fresh tomatoes begin to hit the farmers' market. It's great not only with grilled fish of all kinds but also with pasta, on pizza, or as a topping for bruschetta.

I hardly cook the tuna, so that it's pink in the middle. Feel free to grill for a minute longer on each side if you prefer it more well done. But don't overcook, or it will become cottony.

2 pounds (8 medium-size) ripe tomatoes, peeled, seeded, and finely chopped

2 to 3 large garlic cloves, to your taste, peeled and minced or pressed

2 to 3 teaspoons balsamic vinegar, to your taste

Salt to taste

3 tablespoons slivered fresh basil leaves

1½ tablespoons olive oil

6 tuna steaks, ¾ to 1 inch thick and 5 to 6 ounces each (see Note on page 285)

Freshly ground black pepper to taste

Fresh basil sprigs for garnish

1. Mix together the tomatoes, garlic, vinegar, salt, basil, and 1 tablespoon of the olive oil in the bowl. Taste. Does it taste vivid? Garlicky and sweet? Is there enough salt? Adjust the seasonings.
2. Heat a grill, either an outside grill or a top-of-the-stove nonstick grilling pan. Brush the fish steaks with the remaining ½ tablespoon olive oil and salt and pepper lightly. Cook over high heat for 3 to 4 minutes on each side (longer if desired) and transfer to a platter or individual plates.
3. Serve with the sauce spooned partially on top of the fish, partially on the side. Garnish with basil.

Broiled or Grilled Salmon with Wilted Spinach

Makes 4 servings

I always delight in eating in French bistros, where it's possible to get a plain grilled piece of fish with steamed potatoes and perhaps spinach on the side. When I lived in Paris, this was the dish I ordered regularly at my neighborhood restaurant. The simplest dishes are often the best—sometimes you don't want other flavors, just the pure taste of the fish, especially a strong fish like salmon.

2 pounds fresh spinach, stemmed and well washed
Salt and freshly ground black pepper to taste
Four 6-ounce salmon steaks or fillets (see Note on page 285)
2 teaspoons olive oil
2 lemons, cut in half or into wedges

1. Make sure the spinach has been cleaned of all sand. Heat the skillet over medium-high heat. Add the spinach and wilt in the water left on the leaves after washing. This will take 3 or 4 minutes once the water begins to bubble. Stir until wilted and remove from the heat. Season with salt and pepper. Keep warm while you cook the fish.

2. Preheat the broiler with the broiler pan about 4 inches from the heat and cover a baking sheet with lightly oiled aluminum foil, heat a grill pan over medium-high heat, or prepare a grill. Rinse the salmon and pat dry with paper towels. Lightly salt and pepper the salmon and brush with the oil. Measure the fish at the thickest point. Cook 10 minutes per inch of thickness, turning halfway through. Remove from the heat and serve with the spinach and lemon halves or wedges (the lemon is good on the fish and on the spinach).

Salmon Fillet Cooked in a Microwave

Makes 2 servings

This dinner is practically instant. Microwaving is a perfect method for salmon, resulting in moist fish and no pans to wash. Serve with the roasted potatoes on page 236 for a terrific no-fuss meal.

Two 6-ounce salmon fillets (see Note on page 285)
Salt and freshly ground black pepper to taste
Juice of ½ lemon
2 fresh tarragon sprigs (optional)
1 firm, ripe tomato, sliced
Pinch of dried thyme or a sprinkling of fresh chopped herbs, such as basil, dill, and/or tarragon

Get out the following equipment: large bowl or salad spinner for washing spinach; large, heavy nonstick skillet; colander; broiling pan or grill pan; baking sheet; measuring spoons; tongs or spatula

Advance preparation: Spinach can be cooked hours or even a day before serving. You can reheat it by dipping it into simmering water for a few seconds or in the microwave. I keep cooked spinach in zippered plastic bags in the refrigerator.

PER SERVING:
13.6 gm total fat
2.0 gm saturated fat
305 calories
7.9 gm carbohydrates
39.3 gm protein

Get out the following equipment: chef's knife and cutting board; microwaveable plate or baking dish large enough for the salmon fillets

Advance preparation: The fish can be prepared on the plate with its topping, covered, and refrigerated up to an hour before you microwave it.

continued

PER SERVING:
10.7 gm total fat
1.5 gm saturated fat
252 calories
3.5 gm carbohydrates
33.5 gm protein

1. Rinse the salmon fillets and pat dry with paper towels. Place side by side on the plate or baking dish. Sprinkle with salt, pepper, and lemon juice. Lay a sprig of tarragon over each fillet and top with the tomato slices. Salt and pepper the tomato slices, sprinkle with the thyme or other herbs, and cover the dish tightly with microwaveable plastic wrap.

2. Pierce the plastic in a few places and microwave for 4½ minutes, just until the salmon is opaque all the way through. Let sit for a minute, then check to see if the salmon is done. Return to the microwave for another 30 seconds to a minute if necessary. Place on 2 plates, pour any juices that have collected on the cooking plate over the fish, and serve.

Fish Steaks or Fillets with Tomatoes, Capers, and Mint

Makes 4 to 6 servings

This robust Mediterranean sauce can accompany practically any type of fish, with the exception of very delicate fillets of sole or petrale sole. In Mediterranean countries it most often accompanies grilled swordfish or tuna. But I've served it time and again with simply baked or steamed white-fleshed fish fillets, and it always pleases.

Get out the following equipment: chef's knife and cutting board; measuring spoons; garlic press or minichop if using; large, heavy nonstick skillet; wooden spoon; grill or nonstick grill pan; tongs or spatula; steamer or baking dish if using

Advance preparation: The sauce will keep for a few days in the refrigerator and can be frozen. However, you may want to add the mint when you reheat the sauce.

PER SERVING:
14.4 gm total fat
3.0 gm saturated fat
393 calories
18.9 gm carbohydrates
44.4 gm protein

1½ tablespoons olive oil (1 tablespoon if baking or steaming)

1 small or ½ medium-size onion, peeled and chopped

3 to 4 large garlic cloves, to your taste, peeled and minced or pressed

¼ cup drained capers, rinsed

1¾ pounds (7 medium-size) ripe tomatoes, peeled, seeded, and chopped, or one 28-ounce can, drained, seeded, and chopped (if not chopped already)

⅛ to ¼ teaspoon sugar, to your taste

Salt and freshly ground black pepper to taste

2 tablespoons slivered fresh mint leaves

Four to six 1-inch-thick swordfish or tuna steaks or fish fillets, such as red snapper, cod, mahimahi, halibut, or orange roughy (4 to 6 ounces each)

3 tablespoons water or dry white wine if baking or steaming

Fresh mint sprigs and lemon wedges for garnish

1. Heat 1 tablespoon of the oil in the skillet over medium heat and add the onion. Cook, stirring, until softened, about 5 minutes, then add the garlic and capers. Cook, stirring, until the garlic begins to smell fragrant, 30 seconds to a minute. Add the tomatoes, sugar, salt, and pepper, and bring to a simmer. Cook, stirring often, until the tomatoes cook down

and smell fragrant, 15 to 30 minutes. Stir in the mint. Taste. Is it tangy and robust? Does it have enough garlic and salt? Do you taste the mint? Adjust the seasoning and remove from the heat.

2. Cook the fish:

For steaks: Prepare a grill or heat a nonstick grill pan over medium-high heat (medium for a gas grill) until a drop of water evaporates immediately on contact. Brush the fish with the remaining ½ tablespoon oil and salt and pepper lightly. Grill the steaks for 3 to 5 minutes per side, to taste. The fish should be slightly pink in the middle (tuna can be rare in the middle).

For fillets: Either bake or steam. If baking, preheat the oven to 425°F. Place the fillets in an oiled baking dish. Add the water or wine and cover tightly with aluminum foil. Bake for 10 minutes per inch of thickness measured at the thickest point. The fish should be opaque all the way through and pull apart when poked with a fork. Remove from the heat. If steaming, place in a steamer above 1 inch of boiling water and cover. Steam for 8 to 10 minutes per inch of thickness. Remove from the heat and uncover.

If you bake or steam the fillets, you can pull out the pinbones easily once the fish is cooked.

3. Serve the fish with some of the sauce spooned over and some on the side. Garnish with mint sprigs and lemon wedges.

Cold Fish Fillets with Tomatoes, Capers, and Mint Sauce

Use fish fillets and steam as directed. Remove from the heat and transfer to a lightly oiled platter. Cover with plastic wrap and refrigerate until 30 minutes before you wish to serve. Serve as described, garnished with mint sprigs.

Another Variation

Substitute slivered fresh basil for the mint.

Hot or Cold Steamed Fillets with Tomato-Mint Vinaigrette

Makes 4 servings

One of the advantages to this summer dish is that both the sauce and the fish can be prepared hours ahead of time. You can arrange the fillets on a platter and top with the sauce or serve them on individual plates. It's a wonderful dish for a buffet but requires fresh, sweet tomatoes in season. The sauce is nice with delicate fillets like sole, but any white-fleshed fish will do.

1 large garlic clove, or more to taste, peeled and cut in half lengthwise

1 pound (4 medium-size) firm, ripe tomatoes, peeled, seeded, and cut into pieces

1 tablespoon balsamic vinegar

1 tablespoon red wine vinegar

1 tablespoon olive oil

2 tablespoons chopped fresh mint leaves, plus a few sprigs for the steaming water and for garnish

Salt and freshly ground black pepper to taste

Four 5 - to 6-ounce white-fleshed fish fillets, such as sole, snapper, cod, or orange roughy

½ lemon

Finely grated zest of ½ orange (optional)

1. Turn the food processor on and drop in the garlic. Then add the tomatoes and pulse until they're smooth. Then add the vinegars, olive oil, chopped mint, salt, and pepper and blend until smooth. Taste. Is there enough salt? Garlic? Adjust the flavors. Refrigerate until ready to serve.

2. Put a few mint sprigs in an inch of water in the bottom of the steamer and bring to a boil. Lightly oil the steaming rack and place the fillets on it after measuring at the thickest point to gauge cooking time. Cover and turn the heat to medium. Steam the fish (10 minutes per inch of thickness) until it is opaque and pulls apart when tested with a fork, 5 to 7 minutes. Remove from the heat and transfer to a plate. If any bones are visible, pull them out; they'll come out easily now. Salt and pepper lightly, sprinkle lightly with lemon juice squeezed from the lemon half, and spoon on a very small amount of the vinaigrette to prevent the fish from drying out. Cover the fish tightly with plastic wrap if not serving right away and refrigerate until 30 minutes before serving.

Get out the following equipment: **chef's knife and cutting board; measuring spoons; food processor fitted with steel blade or blender; steamer large enough to hold the fish (if you don't have one big enough, cook the fish in 2 batches); serving plate or platter**

Advance preparation: **The sauce and the fish can be made hours before serving and refrigerated. Let sit at room temperature for 15 to 30 minutes before serving.**

PER SERVING:
**5.5 gm total fat
0.9 gm saturated fat
192 calories
6.5 gm carbohydrates
28.0 gm protein**

3. If using the orange zest, stir into the vinaigrette. Serve the fish hot or chilled, topped with the vinaigrette.

Note: You can also cook the fish in the microwave. Four fillets will take about 5 minutes (check and zap longer if necessary).

Red Snapper Fillets with Garlic and Rosemary Baked in Foil

Makes 4 servings

This dish is quickly thrown together. The robust flavor of the rosemary contrasts nicely with the mild fish. The important thing is not to overcook the fish, because snapper dries out quickly, even with the moisture that it will release in the foil packet.

4 red snapper fillets (5 to 6 ounces each)
Salt and freshly ground black pepper to taste
2 teaspoons olive oil
2 large garlic cloves, peeled and thinly sliced
4 fresh rosemary sprigs or 1 teaspoon crumbled dried rosemary
Lemon wedges for serving

1. Preheat the oven to 450°F. Cut 4 sheets of heavy-duty foil or 8 sheets of lighter foil (for double thickness) into squares that are at least 2 inches longer than the length of your fillets. Brush the dull sides with olive oil.
2. Measure the snapper at the thickest point to gauge the cooking time, which will be 10 minutes per inch of thickness. Lay each fillet on a square of foil. Salt and pepper lightly and drizzle with ½ teaspoon of the olive oil. Sprinkle with the slices of garlic and lay a sprig of rosemary over each one (or sprinkle each with ¼ teaspoon dried rosemary).
3. Fold the foil up loosely over the snapper and crimp the edges together tightly. Place the packets on the baking sheet and bake for 5 to 10 minutes, depending on the thickness. Remove from the heat, open, and test one (it should be opaque and come apart easily when tested with a fork). Cut the packets open across the top. Serve in the foil packets or transfer to plates and pour the juices from the packets over the fish. Serve with lemon wedges.

Get out the following equipment: aluminum foil; baking sheet; chef's knife and cutting board

Advance preparation: The packets can be assembled hours before cooking and held in the refrigerator. Remove from the refrigerator 15 to 30 minutes before cooking.

PER SERVING:
4.4 gm total fat
0.8 gm saturated fat
179 calories
0.9 gm carbohydrates
32.1 gm protein

Red Snapper with Ratatouille and Olives

Makes 6 servings

There are so many ways to use ratatouille. This recipe came about as a result of having leftovers. It turns out that ratatouille makes a marvelous sauce for fish. You don't have to limit this to snapper. Any firm white-fleshed fish will work, and so will salmon.

1 recipe ratatouille (page 73), preferably made a day or two before to bring
    out the most flavor
1 whole red snapper (about 3 pounds), cleaned, or six 6-ounce fillets red
    snapper, orange roughy, mahimahi, Chilean sea bass, or cod
Juice of 1 lemon
1 tablespoon olive oil
Salt and freshly ground black pepper to taste
¼ cup imported black olives, preferably Niçoise, pitted if desired
Slivered fresh basil or chopped fresh flat-leaf parsley leaves for garnish

1. Prepare the ratatouille.
2. Preheat the oven to 450°F. Oil the baking dish with olive oil. Rinse the fish or fish fillets, pat dry with paper towels, and place in the dish. Sprinkle with the lemon juice and olive oil and toss gently. Salt and pepper both sides. Mix half the ratatouille with the olives and spoon over and around the fish. Oil the dull side of a large piece of aluminum foil with olive oil and cover the baking dish tightly, oiled side down. Place in the oven and bake for 30 minutes for a large whole snapper, 10 to 15 minutes for fillets.
3. While the fish is baking, heat the remaining ratatouille in the saucepan or skillet on top of the stove over medium heat.
4. Check the fish. The fillets should break apart when poked with a fork. Stick the tines of the fork into the widest part of a whole fish. The flesh should come apart easily and be opaque. Remove from the heat and serve with some of the ratatouille from the baking dish and more from the saucepan on the side. Garnish with the basil or parsley.

Note: To serve a whole fish: Using a chef's knife or fish filleting knife, make a slit along the length of the back and the belly, from head to tail. Lift off and discard the skin. Now make a cut down the length of the center of the fish, through to the bones. Using a spatula or the knife, ease the top half of the fish away from the bones. Cut this long fillet into serving portions. Ease the bottom half away from the bones and cut into serving portions. Now lift the tail and bend up toward the head, bringing the skeleton with it, and ease away from the bottom half of the fish. Divide into serving portions and serve.

Get out the following equipment: large baking dish (large enough for fish or fillets); lemon press; measuring spoons; sharp chef's knife or filleting knife for whole fish; spatula; medium-size saucepan or skillet and wooden spoon

Advance preparation: The ratatouille can be made several days ahead. The fish can be prepared and the baking dish assembled with the ratatouille hours before you bake the fish. Refrigerate, but remove from the refrigerator 15 to 30 minutes before baking.

PER SERVING:
12.1 gm total fat
1.7 gm saturated fat
393 calories
31.7 gm carbohydrates
41.5 gm protein

Whole Trout Baked in Foil

Makes 4 servings

These days most supermarket fish counters sell small farmed trout, either white fleshed or the lovely pink-fleshed salmon trout. The fish are very easy to cook in aluminum foil and need little in the way of embellishment. They are often sold already boned.

2 teaspoons unsalted butter or olive oil, plus additional for the foil

4 small trout (8 to 10 ounces each), cleaned (if boned, they may weigh about 6 ounces)

Salt and freshly ground black pepper to taste

2 lemons, sliced

FOR SEASONING, CHOOSE ONE:

8 fresh tarragon or dill sprigs

¼ cup chopped fresh flat-leaf parsley leaves

2 teaspoons crushed fennel seeds

2 teaspoons chopped fresh or crumbled dried rosemary or thyme

Get out the following equipment: aluminum foil; baking sheet; mortar and pestle or spice mill if using fennel seeds; small knife and cutting board if using chopped herbs

Advance preparation: The foil packets can be assembled hours before cooking the trout and kept in the refrigerator. Remove from the refrigerator 15 to 30 minutes before cooking.

PER SERVING:
7.8 gm total fat
2.4 gm saturated fat
222 calories
0.2 gm carbohydrates
35.2 gm protein

1. Preheat the oven to 450°F. Cut 4 sheets of heavy-duty aluminum foil or 8 sheets of lighter foil (for double thickness) into squares that are 2 inches longer than the length of your fish. Butter or oil the dull sides.

2. Measure the trout at the thickest point to gauge the cooking time, which will be 10 minutes per inch of thickness. Rinse the trout inside and out and pat dry with paper towels. Salt and pepper lightly. Place ½ teaspoon of the butter or oil in the cavity of each trout. If using dill or tarragon, place 1 sprig in each cavity. If using seeds or chopped herbs, place half in the cavity of each fish and sprinkle the other half over the outside.

3. Lay each trout on a square of foil and place a few slices of lemon on each one. Fold the foil up loosely over the trout and crimp the edges together tightly. Place the packets on the baking sheet and bake for 10 to 15 minutes. Open one packet after 10 minutes to test. The flesh should be opaque and pull apart easily when tested with a fork.

4. To serve, cut each packet across the top and open it out. Serve the fish in the packets or transfer them to plates and pour the juices in the packet over.

Fish, Potato, and Spinach Gratin

Makes 4 servings

This is an easy, comforting casserole, a sort of modern-day version of the old tuna-noodle casserole that was popular in the fifties and sixties. Cod would be my first choice for the fish.

FOR THE BÉCHAMEL:

1½ cups 1% milk

1 tablespoon olive oil

1 heaping tablespoon all-purpose flour

Salt and freshly ground black pepper to taste

Pinch of freshly grated nutmeg

FOR THE CASSEROLE:

2 bunches fresh spinach, stemmed and cleaned, or two 10-ounce packages
   frozen spinach, thawed

1 pound cod or snapper fillets

1 pound waxy potatoes, such as Yukon Gold or White Rose, scrubbed

Salt

½ cup skim or 1% milk, heated

Freshly ground black pepper to taste

1 garlic clove (optional), peeled and minced or pressed

¼ cup dry or fresh bread crumbs

1 tablespoon olive oil

1. Preheat the oven to 400°F. Oil the gratin or baking dish. Make the béchamel: Heat the milk in the 1-quart saucepan until the top just trembles. Meanwhile, heat the oil in the 2-quart saucepan over medium heat and add the flour. Stir together into a smooth paste with a wooden spoon and continue to stir as the mixture bubbles for 2 to 3 minutes. It should not brown. Whisk in the hot milk. Whisk over medium heat until the mixture comes to a simmer and begins to thicken. Be sure to whisk the sides and edges of the saucepan so that the sauce doesn't stick and burn. Reduce the heat to very low and simmer, whisking often, until there is no trace of a raw flour taste, about 10 minutes. Remove from the heat and season with salt, pepper, and the nutmeg.

2. Wilt the spinach in the skillet over high heat in the water left on the leaves after washing. Refresh with cold water, squeeze out the excess water, and chop. Squeeze the excess water out of the thawed spinach if using frozen.

3. To microwave the fish, place on a microwaveable plate and cover with plastic wrap. Pierce the plastic in a few places. Microwave until opaque, 3 to 4 minutes at 100% heat. Alternatively, steam the fish until opaque, about 7 minutes (see page 283). Remove from the heat. Remove any small bones and flake.

4. Boil or steam the potatoes until tender. To boil, cover with water in a 2-quart saucepan and add 1 teaspoon salt. Bring to a boil and boil until tender. Drain. If steaming, bring 1 inch of water to a boil in a 2-quart saucepan under the steamer. Place the potatoes in the steamer, reduce the heat to medium, and cover. Steam until tender, 20 to 30 minutes. Peel if desired and mash coarsely with the milk. Season with salt and pepper. Stir in the fish. Layer in the oiled gratin dish.

5. Mix together the béchamel and spinach. Stir in the optional garlic. Taste and adjust the seasonings. Spread in an even layer over the potatoes and fish. Sprinkle on the bread crumbs. Drizzle on the oil. Bake until the top browns, about 20 minutes. Serve hot or warm.

Mediterranean Fish Stew: A Simple Recipe

Makes 4 to 6 servings

I love serving fish stews and soups for big dinner parties, because everything up to the adding of the fish can be done a day or a few days ahead of time. This master recipe, quickly made and as easy as can be, does not require a fish broth as many classic fish soups and stews do. A fish broth is easy enough to make, provided you find fish heads and bones. And these, I have found, are not so easy to come by unless you live near a Mexican or Asian market where whole fish is sold on the bone. But a good fish stew can be made without a fish broth if you begin with a gutsy tomato base. Looking through Colman Andrews's excellent *Flavors of the Riviera* (Bantam Books, 1996), I find two excellent Italian fish soups that begin with just such a base, as do my own Mexican fish soups. The one here is based on his recipes. The key is the anchovies: they add the depth of flavor that makes this broth taste as if you went to the trouble to make a fish stock, so don't leave them out even if you think you don't like anchovies.

Get out the following equipment: **chef's knife and cutting board; garlic press or minichop if using; measuring spoons and measuring cup; strainer and bowl; large, heavy soup pot; wooden spoon**

continued

Advance preparation:
You can make the soup base days ahead of time and refrigerate or freeze it. Bring back to a simmer and add the orange zest, fish, and parsley shortly before serving.

PER SERVING:
13.4 gm total fat
1.8 gm saturated fat
479 calories
21.0 gm carbohydrates
52.2 gm protein

2 tablespoons olive oil

2 medium-size onions, peeled and chopped

1 celery rib, chopped

1 large or 2 medium-size carrots, peeled and chopped

4 large garlic cloves, peeled and minced or pressed

Leaves from 4 fresh flat-leaf parsley sprigs, minced

4 anchovy fillets, rinsed and chopped

2 pounds (4 large or 8 medium-size) firm, ripe tomatoes, peeled, seeded, and chopped, or one 28-ounce can with juice (see Note), seeded and chopped

1½ cups dry white wine

3 cups water (less if using canned tomatoes; see Note)

Salt to taste

2 wide strips orange zest

2 pounds firm white-fleshed fish fillets, such as halibut, hake, mahimahi, shark, cod, or monkfish, or a combination, cut into 2-inch pieces

Freshly ground black pepper

¼ cup chopped fresh flat-leaf parsley or slivered basil leaves for garnish

1. Heat the oil in the soup pot over medium-low heat. Add the onions, celery, and carrot and cook, stirring, until thoroughly tender, 10 to 15 minutes. Add the garlic and parsley and cook for another few minutes, until the garlic is fragrant and has colored slightly. Stir in the anchovies and tomatoes. Cook, stirring often, until the tomatoes have cooked down somewhat and the mixture is aromatic, about 10 minutes.

2. Stir in the wine, increase the heat to high, and bring to a boil. Boil for 5 minutes, stirring often. Add the water (or water and tomato juice) and bring to a simmer. Season with salt, reduce the heat to low, and simmer, uncovered, for another 15 minutes, stirring often. Taste. Does the mixture taste aromatic? Is there enough salt and garlic? Imagine it with the fish, which will add more depth. Adjust the seasonings.

3. Stir in the orange zest and fish and simmer, uncovered, for about 15 minutes. Make sure the stew isn't boiling: it should be at a slow simmer. The fish should be cooked through and the broth aromatic. Season with pepper, taste and adjust the salt, and stir in the parsley or basil. Remove the orange zest. Remove from the heat and serve with crusty bread or garlic croutons (page 39).

Note: If using canned tomatoes, drain into a strainer set over a bowl. Measure the liquid in a 1-quart measuring cup and add water to equal 3 cups.

Variations: You can vary the fish and add shellfish such as shrimp or clams or squid; do *not,* however, use strong-flavored fish like salmon or tuna, because these fish will overpower the soup. You can also add cooked vegetables, such as blanched or steamed green beans, peas, or zucchini, or steamed pumpkin to the mixture. Use about ½ pound vegetables. Blanch or steam until tender, 5 to 8 minutes, ahead of time and add to the pot to heat through just before serving. This makes a hearty and complete meal.

Mexican Fish Stew

Add a couple of minced jalapeño or serrano chiles when cooking the onion. Garnish with 3 to 4 tablespoons chopped fresh cilantro leaves instead of parsley or basil and serve with halved limes for people to squeeze into their stew.

◾ How to Prepare Unshelled Shrimp ◾

Most shrimp recipes call for "fresh shrimp, shelled and deveined." This means you must remove the shells and the little intestinal vein that runs down the back of the shrimp. It's easy. Pull the shells off by loosening them with your thumb and just pulling them away. You can pull off the tail part or leave it on; recipes often specify leaving it on, because it's pretty. Then, with a sharp paring knife, with the tip of a potato peeler, or with a special tool for deveining shrimp, cut a slit no deeper than ⅛ inch down the back—i.e., the outside curve—of the shrimp. You'll usually, but not always, see a little vein in there. Lift it out with the tip of your knife and discard. Some people don't devein shrimp unless they actually see the vein. I leave the choice to you, although the recipes that following instruct you to devein.

Cooking Shrimp

Whether boiled, grilled, or pan-cooked, shrimp cook in minutes. Add to simmering or boiling liquid or to a hot skillet with a little oil or butter and cook until the shrimp turns pink, 2 to 4 minutes. Remove from the heat.

Garlic Shrimp

■

Makes 4 servings

If you like garlic and shrimp, you'll love this dish. Serve the shrimp with rice or pasta and plenty of crusty bread for sopping up the sauce.

1½ pounds medium-size shrimp, shelled and deveined
Sea salt or kosher salt to taste
2 tablespoons olive oil
8 garlic cloves, peeled and coarsely chopped or thinly sliced
1 dried red chile, seeded and crumbled
3 tablespoons minced fresh flat-leaf parsley leaves

1. In the bowl, sprinkle the shrimp with salt, toss, and let sit for 15 minutes or longer.
2. Heat the oil in the skillet over medium heat and add the garlic and chile. Cook, stirring, until the garlic begins to color, about 1 minute. Increase the heat to medium-high and add the shrimp. Cook, stirring, until the shrimp turns pink and is cooked through, 2 to 4 minutes. Remove from the heat, sprinkle with the parsley, and serve.

Curried Shrimp

■

Makes 4 servings

The preparation here is almost exactly the same as in Garlic Shrimp (preceding recipe), but the flavors are different because of the curry and cilantro. I think shrimp and curry make a wonderful marriage. Curry powder is not authentic curry, which is a complex mixture of spices, but I think it works very nicely here. Serve this dish with basmati or regular rice.

1½ pounds medium-size shrimp, shelled and deveined
Sea salt or kosher salt to taste
3 tablespoons fresh lime juice
1½ tablespoons canola oil
6 garlic cloves, peeled and coarsely chopped or thinly sliced
1½ teaspoons curry powder
1 dried red chile, seeded and crumbled
2 tablespoons chopped fresh cilantro leaves

Get out the following equipment: **small knife for deveining; medium-size bowl; chef's knife and cutting board or minichop; large, heavy nonstick skillet; wooden spoon**

Advance preparation: **You can clean the shrimp and salt it hours ahead of making the dish. Keep in a covered dish in the refrigerator.**

PER SERVING:
9.0 gm total fat
1.3 gm saturated fat
206 calories
3.6 gm carbohydrates
26.4 gm protein

Get out the following equipment: **small knife for deveining; medium-size bowl; chef's knife and cutting board or minichop; large heavy nonstick skillet; wooden spoon**

Advance preparation: **You can clean the shrimp and toss it with the salt and lime juice hours ahead. Keep in a covered dish in the refrigerator.**

PER SERVING:
7.5 gm total fat
0.8 gm saturated fat
195 calories
4.6 gm carbohydrates
26.4 gm protein

1. In the bowl, sprinkle the shrimp with salt and the lime juice, toss, and let sit for 15 minutes or longer.
2. Heat the oil in the skillet over medium heat and add the garlic, curry powder, and chile. Cook, stirring, until the garlic begins to color, about 1 minute. Increase the heat to medium-high and add the shrimp with its marinade. Cook, stirring, until the shrimp turns pink and is cooked through, 2 to 4 minutes. Remove from the heat, sprinkle with the cilantro, and serve.

Hot-and-Sour Shrimp and Rice Soup with Dried Mushrooms

Makes 4 servings

This recipe combines flavors from a classic Thai hot-and-sour soup and a Vietnamese shrimp-and-rice soup. It makes a marvelous meal-in-a-bowl. The Southeast Asian flavors are due in great part to the lemongrass and fish sauce. Both are available at Asian markets.

1 pound medium-size shrimp

8 dried Chinese mushrooms

1 tablespoon canola or peanut oil

5 cups water

One 15-ounce can or 1½ cups defatted chicken stock (page 155)

2 stalks lemongrass, outer leaves discarded, coarsely chopped

3 large garlic cloves, peeled and finely minced or pounded to a paste with a little salt in a mortar and pestle

1 teaspoon slivered lime zest

2 green serrano or Thai chiles, seeded for a milder soup and thinly sliced

Salt to taste

¾ cup long-grain jasmine, basmati, or long-grain white rice

3 to 4 tablespoons lime juice (from 2 limes), to your taste

1 tablespoon Thai or Vietnamese fish sauce (nuoc nam, available at Asian groceries)

½ cup chopped fresh cilantro leaves

2 red serrano or Thai chiles, seeded if desired and finely chopped

1. Peel and devein the shrimp, rinsing and retaining the shells. Soak the mushrooms in hot water to cover until softened, about 15 minutes. Drain through a cheesecloth-lined strainer if sandy and cut away the stems, then slice thinly. Set aside.

Get out the following equipment: chef's knife and cutting board; mini-chop or mortar and pestle if using; medium-size and large bowls; measuring spoons and measuring cups; strainer lined with cheesecloth; large, heavy soup pot and long-handled spoon

Advance preparation: The recipe can be made through step 2 several hours ahead. Keep the shrimp in the refrigerator.

PER SERVING:
5.4 gm total fat
0.6 gm saturated fat
304 calories
38.6 gm carbohydrates
24.0 gm protein

continued

2. Heat the oil in the soup pot and add the shrimp shells. Cook, stirring, until they turn pink, then add the water, chicken stock, lemongrass, garlic, lime zest, and sliced chiles. Bring to a boil, skim off any foam, reduce the heat to medium-low, cover, and simmer for 20 minutes. Strain the mixture through a cheesecloth-lined strainer and return to the pot.

3. Bring back to a simmer, season with salt, and add the rice and mushroom slivers. Simmer until the rice is tender, about 15 minutes. Add the shrimp and cook until just cooked through and pink, 2 to 4 minutes. Turn off the heat and stir in the lime juice and fish sauce. Taste and adjust the salt. Stir in the cilantro and serve, passing the chopped chiles for people to add as desired.

■ How to Clean Mussels and Clams ■

It is *extremely important* to examine each mussel or clam before you begin, to determine if there are any broken shells or dead mollusks. If the shell is broken, the mussel or clam has died, inviting the growth of indigestible bacteria, and it must be discarded. If the shell is open, and doesn't close when you tap it, the mollusk is dead as well and must be discarded.

With the water in your sink running, rinse each mussel or clam and discard any with cracked shells. If you are working with mussels, pull out the beards—the tuft of fibrous strands that hangs out of the shells—as you inspect them. If they are very sandy, brush with a toothbrush. Place in a large bowl. When all the mussels or clams have been duly inspected and rinsed, fill the bowl with cold water and rinse several times by pouring out the water and refilling it. Now place the mussels or clams in your sink or a bowl large enough so that they can be covered with water. Add 3 tablespoons salt or vinegar and fill with water. Let sit for 15 minutes. The salt or vinegar will help purge the mollusks of sand as they expel the nasty-tasting water when they imbibe it, along with sand in their shells. Rinse thoroughly and repeat. Rinse thoroughly again. If not cooking right away, place in a bowl, cover with a damp towel, and refrigerate.

Mussels or Clams Steamed in White Wine

Makes 4 to 6 servings

This is the classic way to prepare mussels and clams. The time-consuming part is the cleaning; the cooking takes only 5 minutes. I choose the smallest clams I can find for this dish, and I prefer the smaller black mussels to the huge New Zealand mussels.

4 pounds mussels or small clams, or 12 to 16 per person

2 cups dry white wine

1 small onion or 4 shallots, peeled and minced

2 to 3 garlic cloves, to your taste, peeled and crushed

4 fresh flat-leaf parsley sprigs

1 small bay leaf

6 black peppercorns

½ teaspoon dried thyme or 1 teaspoon fresh thyme leaves

3 tablespoons finely chopped fresh flat-leaf parsley leaves

1. Clean the mussels or clams as described on page 302.
2. Combine the wine, onion or shallots, garlic, parsley sprigs, bay leaf, peppercorns, and thyme in the large pot (or you can do this in batches, using the same wine mixture for each batch). Bring to a boil and boil for 2 minutes. Add the mussels or clams and cover tightly. Set your timer for 5 minutes. Grab the pot with two hands and shake it vigorously after 2 minutes. If the pot is too heavy for this, give the mollusks a stir with a long-handled spoon. The mussels or clams are ready when their shells have opened, which usually takes about 5 minutes.
3. Spoon the mollusks into wide soup bowls, discarding any that have not opened up. (If they don't open up, that means they weren't alive and should not be eaten.) Strain the broth from the pot through a fine-mesh strainer set over a bowl and preferably lined with cheesecloth and spoon it over the mussels or clams. Sprinkle with the parsley and serve.

Get out the following equipment: **large bowl and brush (such as a toothbrush); measuring spoons and measuring cup; chef's knife and cutting board; large pot with lid that will hold all of the mussels or clams; fine-mesh strainer and cheesecloth**

Advance preparation: **The mussels or clams can be cleaned and held in the refrigerator hours before cooking.**

PER SERVING:
3.8 gm total fat
0.7 gm saturated fat
228 calories
7.4 gm carbohydrates
20.5 gm protein

Mediterranean Mussels or Clams

■

Makes 4 to 6 servings

In this gutsy dish the mollusks are cooked in a slightly piquant tomato-wine sauce. There are two ways to make the dish. The first is to prepare the mussels or clams exactly as instructed in the previous recipe and to add to the wine 1 cup prepared tomato sauce or a few tablespoons tomato paste diluted with an equal amount of water, as well as dried red chile. Or you can begin from scratch:

4 pounds mussels or small clams, or 12 to 16 per person

1 tablespoon olive oil

1 small onion or 3 shallots, peeled and minced

2 to 3 large garlic cloves, to your taste, peeled and minced or pressed

1¾ pounds (7 medium-size) firm, ripe tomatoes or one 28-ounce can, drained, peeled, seeded, and crushed in a food processor

⅛ teaspoon sugar

Salt to taste

¾ teaspoon dried thyme

1 small dried red chile or a pinch of cayenne pepper

2 cups dry white wine

3 tablespoons finely chopped fresh flat-leaf parsley leaves

1. Clean the mussels or clams as described on page 302.
2. Heat the oil in the large pot over medium heat (or you can do this in batches, using the same wine mixture for each batch) and add the onion or shallots. Cook, stirring, until tender, about 5 minutes. Add the garlic and cook until the garlic begins to color, about 30 seconds. Add the tomatoes, sugar, salt, thyme, and cayenne. Cook, stirring often, until the tomatoes are cooked down and beginning to stick to the pan, 15 to 25 minutes. Stir in the wine and bring to a simmer. Simmer for 2 minutes.
3. Add the mussels or clams to the pot and cover tightly. Set your timer for 5 minutes. Grab the pot with two hands and shake it vigorously after 2 minutes. If the pot is too heavy for this, give the mollusks a stir with a long-handled spoon. The mussels or clams are ready when their shells have opened, which usually takes about 5 minutes.
4. Spoon the mollusks into wide soup bowls, discarding any that have not opened up. (If they don't open up, that means they weren't alive and should not be eaten.) Spoon the sauce in the pot over the mussels or clams, sprinkle with the parsley, and serve.

Get out the following equipment: **large bowl and brush (such as a toothbrush); measuring spoons and measuring cup; chef's knife and cutting board; garlic press or minichop if using; large pot with lid that will hold all the mussels or clams; wooden spoon**

Advance preparation: **You can prepare the tomato sauce through step 2 hours or even a day before cooking the mussels or clams. Bring back to a simmer, stir, and proceed with the recipe. The mussels or clams can be cleaned and held in the refrigerator hours before cooking.**

PER SERVING:
8.0 gm total fat
1.2 gm saturated fat
315 calories
17.9 gm carbohydrates
22.9 gm protein

Main-Dish Tarts

You may think that quiches and tarts have no place in a low-fat diet, but they do, and they make an exceptionally pretty and appealing main dish, as well as hors d'oeuvre or starter, especially for vegetarians. The only thing that must go out the window are traditional butter-rich crusts and a portion of the eggs and cheese called for in the old recipes. Cream and whole milk are easily replaced by low-fat milk enriched with nonfat dry milk, and with the intense flavors of the fillings here, there is just no need for extra cheese. *The important thing is to use good-quality imported Gruyère and Parmesan* whenever called for. The taste of the cheese will then be vivid enough so that only a few ounces are required.

There are plenty of delicious crusts that don't require butter, and they have the added advantage of being easier to roll out than short pastries. In fact, the earliest French quiches were made with bread dough, which later came to be replaced by short pastries and layered butter pastries. The ones I have adapted come from the Mediterranean, where butter gives way to olive oil, and not much olive oil at that. You have a choice here of the quick Greek Baking Powder Piecrust, which can be made with unbleached white flour or with half whole-wheat flour, and the Yeasted Olive Oil Pastry, from Provence. This one is like a pizza crust but thinner, and the dough is not nearly as stiff and elastic. Both require only 3 tablespoons of oil for two crusts. They are not soft and crumbly like a short pastry; rather, the edges become very crisp (dare I say hard?) when they bake, while the thin part of the crust that encloses the filling is slightly bready without being the least bit soggy. In this way both crusts resemble pizza crusts more than traditional piecrusts. You'll find them very easy to work with.

The other type of crust I use is made from Greek or Middle Eastern filo dough. These are thin, paperlike sheets of pastry that are layered in a pie dish or tart pan and wrapped around a filling. Each sheet must be brushed with olive oil (or butter), but you can be sparing with the brush. The baked result is beautiful to look at and has a marvelous crisp texture.

Quiche or Tart?

The traditional French quiche (or quiche Lorraine, named after its place of origin) is a tart with a custard filling made with eggs, crème fraîche, cheese, and bacon. Eventually *quiche* came to refer to all tarts bound with this egg, cream, and cheese custard; they could contain onions or ham, mussels or salmon, or vegetables. So, in that sense, all of the tarts here, because they're bound with milk and eggs, are quiches. However, I think of a quiche as a tart in which the custard filling is the main feature, with other additions, such as onions, bacon, or smoked salmon, as flavorings. When the vegetable filling really packs the crust, and the eggs, cheese, and milk serve as binder and flavoring, to me that's a tart. So in this chapter there's a basic quiche and an asparagus quiche, but most of the others, brimming as they are with luscious and healthy vegetables, are tarts. It's really a matter of semantics.

What's important is practically anything that tastes good can serve as a filling for a tart. If you have leftover ratatouille, for example, you could mix it up with eggs, a bit of cheese, and milk, and bake it in a crust for a marvelous reincarnation of the original dish (see recipe, page 73). Frozen spinach makes a very convenient filling, and a tart makes an exceptional vehicle for this vegetable; my cousin got her kids to eat their spinach the entire time they were growing up by baking it into quiches.

■ Light Tart Basics ■

■ Use one of the olive oil crusts I provide to cut way back on fats. The finished crusts are stiff around the edges, so use a serrated bread knife or pizza cutter to slice them. (The crust is not hard underneath the filling.) Always prebake the crust according to recipe directions; this keeps it from getting soggy.

■ Measuring flour: When measuring flour for the crusts, stir the flour first, then spoon it into the measuring cup until it is higher than the rim of the cup. Then level it off by running a knife flush against the edge of the cup. (If you scoop the flour directly out of the bin or bag, the flour will be

- Instead of using whole-fat milk or cream, use 1% milk (or skim milk) and enrich by mixing it with nonfat dry milk, usually 2 tablespoons per cup of milk.
- Use high-quality imported Gruyère and Parmesan when called for. The flavors are so good that you need very little for them to come through. With some of the rich, savory vegetable fillings such as ratatouille tart on page 319 or mushroom tart on page 312, you could eliminate the cheese altogether.
- The quiches and tarts in this chapter call for three whole eggs; you can alternatively use two whole eggs and two egg whites.
- Always cook the vegetables that go into a tart or quiche first, following recipe instructions.
- Crusts can be frozen and transferred directly from the freezer to the oven for prebaking. Tarts can all be made a day ahead and reheated.

Serving Tarts as Hors d'Oeuvres

These make very convenient and impressive party fare. Allow the tarts to cool slightly, then cut them into small (about 1½-inch) diamond shapes. To do this, cut 1½-inch-wide strips, then cut 1½-inch-wide strips on the diagonal across your original cuts. Transfer to a platter or serve from the pan. To serve as a first course, cut the tarts into 10 small wedges.

▪ Crustless Tarts ▪
(Gratins, Custards, and Timbales)

A tart without a crust becomes a gratin and a quiche becomes a custard or *timbale*. The tarts that are thick with vegetables, such as cabbage and onion tart with cumin (page 313), mushroom tart (page 312), Greek spinach and leek pie (page 321), and ratatouille tart (page 319), could be baked in a baking or gratin dish, thus becoming a gratin. Oil the bottom and sides of the dish well and bake as directed. The quiches, if made without crusts, can be made in the tart pan or a gratin, baking, or soufflé dish or in individual ramekins. The dish, however, must be placed in a pan of water (called a *bain-marie*, or water bath) for baking to ensure even cooking of the custard. You can serve it directly from the dish or unmold individual custards onto plates.

Greek Baking Powder Piecrust

Makes two 10-inch crusts; 12 servings

Get out the following equipment: dry and liquid measuring cups; measuring spoons; mixing bowl and fork or electric mixer fitted with the paddle attachment or food processor fitted with steel blade; heavy rolling pin; two 10-inch tart pans or pie dishes

Advance preparation: **The dough will keep for 3 days in the refrigerator and can be frozen. Remove from the freezer very shortly before prebaking.**

PER SERVING:
3.7 gm total fat
0.5 gm saturated fat
120 calories
18.6 gm carbohydrates
2.8 gm protein

This crust is used widely in Greece for any number of marvelous vegetable pies. It's the easiest crust I've ever worked with and has the added virtue of being very low in fat. It's a crisp piecrust rather than a crumbly one; be warned that the edges will be quite hard, so you will need a serrated knife or a pizza cutter to slice the tart. But the crust underneath the filling will have a somewhat bready, thin pizza-crust quality. It works equally well with unbleached white flour, half unbleached and half whole wheat, or whole-wheat pastry flour. The whole-wheat version has a nuttier flavor.

> 2¼ cups unbleached white flour or 1¼ cups unbleached white and 1 cup whole-wheat or whole-wheat pastry flour, plus unbleached flour as necessary for rolling out the dough
>
> ½ teaspoon salt
>
> 2 teaspoons baking powder
>
> ¾ cup water
>
> 3 tablespoons olive oil

1. In a bowl or in the bowl of an electric mixer, mix together the flour, salt, and baking powder. Make a well in the center and add the water and olive oil. Mix together with a fork or, in the mixer, with the paddle attachment until the ingredients are thoroughly combined. You can also do this in a food processor.

2. Turn the dough out onto a lightly floured surface and knead until smooth (see page 271 for more on how to knead), not more than a minute. Divide the dough in half. Press each half into a circle about 4 inches in diameter. Dust with flour if the dough is sticky. Wrap tightly in plastic wrap and seal in a plastic bag. Refrigerate for 15 minutes or up to 3 days (the dough can also be frozen for up to a month).

3. Roll out each piece of chilled dough on a lightly floured surface into a thin 12-inch round, dust both sides with unbleached white flour as necessary to keep it from sticking.

4. Spray or brush the tart pans with olive or vegetable oil. Line the pans with the dough and pinch an attractive edge around the rim. Wrap in plastic wrap and aluminum foil (to secure the plastic) and refrigerate or freeze until ready to use. Proceed as instructed in the individual recipes.

Yeasted Olive Oil Pastry

Makes two 10-inch piecrusts; 12 servings

This crust is very light compared to a butter pastry and extremely easy to work with. The important thing to remember is to roll the dough very thin so that it won't be too bready.

1½ teaspoons active dry yeast
½ cup lukewarm water
¼ teaspoon sugar
1 large egg, at room temperature
3 tablespoons olive oil
2 to 2½ cups unbleached flour
¾ teaspoon salt

1. Dissolve the yeast in the water, add the sugar, and let sit until creamy, 5 to 10 minutes. Beat in the egg and olive oil. Combine 2 cups of the flour and the salt and stir into the yeast mixture (this can be done in the mixer or food processor fitted with the steel blade; combine the ingredients using the paddle, then switch to the dough hook). Work the dough until it comes together in a coherent mass, adding flour as necessary if it is very moist and sticky, then turn out onto a lightly floured surface. Knead for a few minutes (see page 271 for more on how to knead), adding flour as necessary, until the dough is smooth, then shape the dough into a ball. Do not overwork. Place in a lightly oiled bowl, cover the bowl tightly with plastic wrap, and let rise in a warm draft-free spot until doubled in size, about 1 hour.

2. When the pastry has risen and softened, punch it down gently and shape into a ball. Cut into 2 equal pieces and shape each piece into a ball. Cover each ball loosely with plastic wrap and let rest for 10 minutes.

3. Butter or oil the tart or pie pans. Roll out each ball of dough on a lightly floured surface until about ⅛ inch thick, dusting both sides with flour if necessary to keep it from sticking. It should be about 1 inch bigger than the circumference of your pans. Line the pans with the dough. An easy way to do this is to fold the dough in half, then set over one half of the pan and unfold. Press the dough gently into the pans (this is often called "easing" the dough into the pans). You should have a bit of overhang around the edges of the pan. Roll the dough in and pinch an attractive lip around the edge of the pan. Cover loosely with a kitchen towel and let rest for 20 to 30 minutes if you are baking right away. If you are not bak-

Get out the following equipment: liquid and dry measuring cups and measuring spoons; large bowl or electric mixer and the paddle and dough hook attachments or food processor; heavy rolling pin; two 10-inch pie or tart pans

Advance preparation: This will keep for several months in the freezer.

PER SERVING:
4.1 gm total fat
0.6 gm saturated fat
128 calories
18.9 gm carbohydrates
3.5 gm protein

ing right away, cover with plastic wrap and place in the freezer to keep the dough from rising and becoming too bready. Remove from the freezer very shortly before prebaking. Bake as directed.

Plain Old-Fashioned Quiche

Makes one 10-inch quiche; 6 servings

This is a basic savory, light quiche, just milk, egg, a little cheese, and onion. An authentic quiche would be richer, with cream and ham. This one tastes richer than it is, because the milk is fortified with powdered skim milk. Use imported Gruyère cheese; the quality counts here—you'll see that a little goes a long way. Once you master this, try the variations that follow.

3 large eggs, or 2 large eggs and 2 large egg whites, at room temperature
1 Greek baking powder piecrust (page 308) or yeasted olive oil pastry
    (page 309)
1 tablespoon unsalted butter or olive oil
½ cup minced onion (½ medium-size onion)
1 cup 1% milk
2 tablespoons nonfat dry milk
½ teaspoon salt
Freshly ground black pepper to taste
Dash of Worcestershire sauce (optional)
2 ounces Gruyère cheese, grated (½ cup tightly packed)
1 ounce Parmesan cheese, grated (¼ cup tightly packed)

1. Preheat the oven to 375°F. Beat the eggs (or eggs and egg whites) together and brush the surface of the piecrust fitted into the pan lightly with some of it. Prebake for 7 minutes and remove from the oven. Cool on a wire rack.
2. Heat the butter or oil in the skillet over medium heat. Add the onion and cook, stirring, until tender, about 5 minutes. Remove from the heat.
3. In a blender or bowl with a whisk, blend together the liquid and dry milk. Add the salt, beaten eggs, pepper, and Worcestershire and blend together well. Stir in the onion and cheeses. Pour into the prebaked piecrust.
4. Bake until the custard is set and the top is just beginning to brown, 30 to 40 minutes. Remove from the heat and cool on a wire rack if not serving right away. Serve hot or warm.

Get out the following equipment: **chef's knife and cutting board; measuring spoons and measuring cup; small, heavy nonstick skillet and wooden spoon; blender if using; medium-size bowl and whisk or fork; grater; 10-inch pie or tart pan; pastry brush**

Advance preparation: **This can be made a day ahead and reheated gently or served at room temperature. The crust will remain crisp.**

PER SERVING:
13.1 gm total fat
5.5 gm saturated fat
263 calories
22.9 gm carbohydrates
12.7 gm protein

Quiche with Bacon, Smoked Turkey, or Smoked Ham

Add 1 to 2 ounces lean bacon, smoked turkey, or smoked ham. Cook and crumble the bacon; cut the smoked turkey or ham into small dice. Stir into the filling. Bake as directed.

Quiche with Smoked Salmon or Smoked Trout

Add 1 to 2 ounces diced smoked salmon or crumbled smoked trout to the filling. Bake as directed.

Asparagus Quiche

Makes one 10-inch quiche; 6 servings

This custardy tart tastes like spring itself. It's light and pretty and very quick to throw together.

> 3 large eggs, or 2 large eggs and 2 large egg whites
>
> 1 Greek baking powder piecrust (page 308)
>
> 1 pound asparagus bottoms, trimmed and cut into ¾-inch pieces
>
> 2 ounces Gruyère cheese, grated (½ cup tightly packed)
>
> 1 ounce Parmesan cheese, grated (¼ cup tightly packed)
>
> 1 cup 1% milk
>
> 2 tablespoons nonfat dry milk
>
> ½ teaspoon salt
>
> Freshly ground black pepper to taste
>
> ¼ cup chopped fresh chives
>
> 1 teaspoon fresh thyme leaves

1. Preheat the oven to 375°F. Beat the eggs (or eggs and egg whites) together and brush the surface of the piecrust fitted into the pan lightly with some of it. Prebake for 7 minutes and remove from the oven. Cool on a wire rack.

2. Bring an inch of water to a boil in the saucepan fitted with the steamer. Add the asparagus, cover, and steam until just tender, about 5 minutes. Remove from the heat, refresh under cold water, and drain. Transfer to a bowl and toss with the cheeses.

3. In a blender or bowl with a whisk, blend together the liquid and dry milk. Add the salt, pepper, and eggs, and blend together well. Stir in the herbs.

PER SERVING (BACON; TURKEY OR HAM):
14.1; 13.3 gm total fat
5.8; 5.5 gm saturated fat
274; 270 calories
22.8; 23.0 gm carbohydrates
13.3; 14.0 gm protein

PER SERVING:
13.4 gm total fat
5.5 gm saturated fat
271 calories
22.8 gm carbohydrates
14.0 gm protein

Get out the following equipment: chef's knife and cutting board; measuring spoons and measuring cup; steamer and lidded saucepan; pastry brush; blender if using; medium-size bowl and whisk or fork; grater; 10-inch pie or tart pan

Advance preparation: This can be made a day ahead and reheated gently or served at room temperature. The crust will remain crisp.

PER SERVING:
11.2 gm total fat
4.2 gm saturated fat
256 calories
24.8 gm carbohydrates
14.1 gm protein

Main-Dish Tarts
311

continued

4. Spread the asparagus and cheese in an even layer over the bottom of the crust. Pour in the milk mixture. Place in the oven and bake until the tart is firm and the top is just beginning to brown, 35 to 40 minutes. Remove from the oven and cool on a wire rack or serve hot.

PER SERVING:
11.4 gm total fat
4.2 gm saturated fat
263 calories
24.8 gm carbohydrates
15.5 gm protein

Get out the following equipment: **chef's knife and cutting board; measuring spoons and measuring cup; garlic press or minichop if using; large, heavy nonstick skillet and wooden spoon; pastry brush; blender if using; medium-size bowl and whisk or fork; grater; 10-inch pie or tart pan**

Advance preparation: **The mushroom mixture can be prepared a day or two before assembling the tart and kept in a covered dish in the refrigerator. Allow to come to room temperature before baking. The tart can be made a day ahead of time and reheated gently or served at room temperature.**

PER SERVING:
13.9 gm total fat
4.5 gm saturated fat
312 calories
31.0 gm carbohydrates
15.8 gm protein

Asparagus Tart with Smoked Salmon or Smoked Trout

Toss 1 to 2 ounces diced or flaked smoked salmon or trout with the cooked asparagus and cheeses. Proceed with the recipe.

Mushroom Tart

Makes one 10-inch tart; 6 servings

Positively meaty with mushrooms, this definitely rates as a tart rather than a quiche. The custard holds it together, but the savory mushrooms are the main event. One of the reasons they're so intense is that they cook for quite a while, until they are glazed with their own juices.

1 tablespoon olive oil

1 medium-size onion, peeled and chopped

2 pounds mushrooms or 1 pound wild mushrooms such as oyster mushrooms and 1 pound regular mushrooms, cleaned, stems trimmed, and quartered

3 large garlic cloves, peeled and minced or pressed

Salt to taste

¼ cup dry white wine

1 teaspoon soy sauce

½ teaspoon dried thyme

1 teaspoon chopped fresh rosemary leaves or ½ teaspoon crumbled dried rosemary

Freshly ground black pepper to taste

2 ounces Gruyère cheese, grated (½ cup tightly packed)

1 ounce Parmesan cheese, grated (¼ cup tightly packed)

3 tablespoons chopped fresh flat-leaf parsley leaves

1 Greek baking powder piecrust (page 308) or yeasted olive oil pastry (page 309)

3 large eggs, or 2 large eggs and 2 large egg whites, beaten

⅔ cup 1% milk

2 tablespoons nonfat dry milk

1. Heat the oil in the skillet over medium heat. Add the onion and cook, stirring, until tender and beginning to brown, about 8 minutes. Add the mushrooms, garlic, and about ¼ teaspoon salt and continue to cook, stirring often, until the mushrooms have released their liquid and the liquid has just about evaporated (the mushrooms shouldn't be dry, but they shouldn't be swimming in liquid either), 10 to 15 minutes. If there is still a lot of liquid in the skillet after this time, increase the heat to medium-high so that it cooks off more rapidly. Stir in the wine, soy sauce, thyme, and rosemary and cook, stirring, until the liquid has thickened and glazed the mushrooms. Season with salt and pepper and remove from the heat. Transfer to a bowl and toss with the cheeses and parsley.

2. Preheat the oven to 375°F. Brush the surface of the crust fitted into the pan lightly with some of the beaten egg and prebake for 7 minutes. Remove from the oven and cool on a wire rack.

3. In a blender or a mixing bowl with a whisk, beat together the liquid and dry milks and ½ teaspoon salt. Beat in the eggs and season with pepper.

4. Spread the mushrooms and cheeses over the bottom of the prebaked crust in an even layer. Pour on the milk mixture. Bake until the custard is set and the top is beginning to brown, 30 to 40 minutes. Remove from the oven and cool on a wire rack if not serving right away. Serve hot or warm.

Cabbage and Onion Tart with Cumin

Makes one 10-inch tart; 6 servings

When cabbage and onions are cooked together for a while, they become sweet, and the flavors meld together in a delicious way. Cumin adds another dimension to this tart.

1 Greek baking powder piecrust (page 308) or yeasted olive oil pastry (page 309)

3 large eggs, or 2 large eggs and 2 large egg whites, beaten

1 tablespoon olive oil or canola oil

2 medium-size onions, peeled and finely chopped

2 pounds (about 1 medium-size head) Savoy cabbage (the dark crinkly kind), cored and shredded (about 8 cups)

Salt to taste

½ cup water, or more as needed

1 teaspoon cumin seeds, slightly crushed

Freshly ground black pepper to taste

2 ounces Gruyère cheese, grated (½ cup tightly packed)

1 cup 1% milk

2 tablespoons nonfat dry milk

Get out the following equipment: **chef's knife and cutting board; measuring spoons and measuring cup; pastry brush; large, heavy non-stick skillet and wooden spoon; blender if using; medium-size bowl and whisk or fork; mortar and pestle; grater; 10-inch pie or tart pan**

Advance preparation: **This can be made a day ahead and reheated gently or served at room temperature. The crust will remain crisp. The cabbage mixture will hold for a few days in the refrigerator if you want to work ahead.**

continued

PER SERVING:
12.2 gm total fat
3.6 gm saturated fat
296 calories
34.4 gm carbohydrates
14.1 gm protein

1. Preheat the oven to 375°F. Brush the surface of the crust fitted into the pan with a bit of the beaten egg and prebake for 7 minutes. Remove from the oven and cool on a wire rack.

2. Heat the oil in the skillet over medium heat. Add the onions and cook, stirring, until tender and beginning to brown around the edges, about 8 minutes. Add the shredded cabbage and about ¼ teaspoon salt and stir together until the cabbage begins to wilt, a few minutes. Stir in the water and cumin seeds and cook, stirring often, until the cabbage is tender, the onions are slightly colored, and the water has evaporated, about 15 minutes. Season with pepper, taste, add salt if the mixture seems bland, and remove from the heat. Transfer to a bowl and toss with the Gruyère. Spread over the bottom of the prebaked crust in an even layer.

3. In a blender or bowl with a whisk, blend together the liquid and dry milk. Add ½ teaspoon salt, the eggs (or eggs and egg whites), and some pepper and blend together well. Pour over the cabbage mixture.

4. Bake the tart until set and slightly browned on the top, 30 to 40 minutes. Remove from the oven and cool on a wire rack if not serving right away. Serve hot or warm.

Summer Squash, Sweet Onion, and Red Pepper Tart

Makes one 10-inch tart; 6 servings

This gorgeous tart is studded with chopped red pepper and diced or julienned zucchini. The onion and red pepper add a sweet depth of flavor, all held together by the light custard.

Get out the following equipment: **chef's knife and cutting board; measuring spoons and measuring cup; garlic press or minichop if using; large, heavy nonstick skillet and wooden spoon; large bowl; blender if using; medium-size bowl and whisk or fork; grater; 10-inch pie or tart pan; pastry brush**

Advance preparation: **The squash mixture can be prepared a day ahead of assembling the tart and refrigerated. The tart can be made a day ahead of time and reheated gently or served at room temperature.**

1 tablespoon olive oil

1 large onion (Torpedo or Vidalia is the sweetest, but a large yellow onion is fine), peeled and chopped

Salt to taste

1 large red bell pepper, seeded and chopped (about 2 cups)

1 pound zucchini or summer squash, diced or cut into julienne (about 4 cups)

2 large garlic cloves, peeled and minced or pressed

1 teaspoon fresh thyme leaves or ½ teaspoon dried thyme

Freshly ground black pepper to taste

1 ounce Parmesan cheese, grated (¼ cup tightly packed)

1 ounce Gruyère cheese, grated (¼ cup tightly packed)

3 large eggs, or 2 large eggs and 2 large egg whites

1 Greek baking powder piecrust (page 308) or yeasted olive oil pastry (page 309)

⅔ cup 1% milk

2 tablespoons nonfat dry milk

PER SERVING:
11.9 gm total fat
3.5 gm saturated fat
273 calories
29.3 gm carbohydrates
12.7 gm protein

1. Preheat the oven to 375°F. Heat the oil in the skillet over medium-low heat. Add the onion and cook, stirring often, until the onion is tender and just beginning to brown, 5 to 8 minutes. Add a bit of salt (about ¼ teaspoon) and stir in the bell pepper. Continue to cook, stirring often, for about 5 minutes. Add the squash and garlic and cook, stirring often, until the squash is tender but still bright and the vegetables taste sweet and fragrant, about 10 minutes. (The vegetables shouldn't stick to the pan if you add salt, which brings out their juices; but if they do, add a tablespoon or two of water.) Stir in the thyme and black pepper, taste, and adjust the salt. Remove from the heat. Transfer to a bowl and toss with the cheeses.

2. Beat the eggs or the eggs and egg whites together and lightly brush the surface of the piecrust fitted into the pan with some of it. Prebake for 7 minutes. Remove from the oven and cool on a wire rack.

3. In a blender or bowl with a whisk, blend together the liquid and dry milks. Add ½ teaspoon salt, the beaten eggs, and black pepper to taste.

4. Line the prebaked piecrust with the squash mixture. Pour on the milk mixture. Place in the oven and bake until set and just beginning to brown, about 45 minutes. Cool on a wire rack if not serving right away. Serve hot, warm, or room temperature.

Herb and Scallion Quiche

■

Makes one 10-inch quiche; 6 servings

This is an herb garden in a crust. I love a mixture of sweet and savory herbs here—tarragon or basil, parsley, chives, and thyme, or dill, marjoram, chives, and parsley.

1 Greek baking powder piecrust (page 308) or yeasted olive oil pastry
   (page 309)

3 large eggs, or 2 large eggs and 2 large egg whites, beaten

1 tablespoon olive oil

2 bunches scallions, both white and green parts, chopped

2 large garlic cloves, peeled and minced or pressed

1 cup 1% milk

2 tablespoons nonfat dry milk

½ teaspoon salt

Freshly ground black pepper to taste

1 cup mixed stemmed fresh herbs, such as parsley, tarragon, dill, thyme,
   marjoram, chives, and/or basil (use at least 2 and not more than 4 types),
   chopped (½ cup chopped)

2 ounces Gruyère cheese, grated (½ cup tightly packed)

1 ounce Parmesan cheese, grated (¼ cup tightly packed)

1. Preheat the oven to 375°F. Brush the bottom of the piecrust fitted into the pan with a little bit of the beaten egg. Prebake for 7 minutes and remove from the oven. Cool on a wire rack

2. Heat the oil in the skillet over medium heat. Add the scallions and cook, stirring, until tender, 3 to 5 minutes. Stir in the garlic and cook, stirring, until the garlic begins to color and smell fragrant, another minute. Remove from the heat.

3. In a blender or bowl with a whisk, blend together the liquid and dry milks. Add the salt, beaten eggs, and pepper and blend together well. Stir in the cooked scallion mixture and chopped fresh herbs. Add the cheeses and mix together well. Pour this into the prebaked crust.

4. Bake until the top is just beginning to brown and the custard has set, 30 to 40 minutes. Remove from the oven and allow to cool on a wire rack before cutting.

Get out the following equipment: **chef's knife and cutting board; garlic press or minichop if using; measuring spoons and measuring cup; scissors; large, heavy nonstick skillet and wooden spoon; blender if using; medium-size bowl and whisk or fork; grater; 10-inch pie or tart pan; pastry brush**

Advance preparation: **This can be made a day ahead and reheated gently or served at room temperature. The crust will remain crisp.**

PER SERVING:
13.4 gm total fat
4.5 gm saturated fat
269 calories
23.7 gm carbohydrates
13.1 gm protein

Potato and Leek Tart or Gratin with Cumin

Makes one 10-inch tart; 6 servings

This is great in a crust or baked without one in a gratin dish. Potatoes and leeks always make a great combination, and the cumin gives the dish a Middle Eastern flavor.

1½ pounds (6 medium-size) new or waxy potatoes, scrubbed and sliced about ¼ or ⅓ inch thick

1 Greek baking powder piecrust (page 308) or yeasted olive oil pastry (page 309) (optional)

3 large eggs, or 2 large eggs and 2 large egg whites, beaten

1 tablespoon unsalted butter or olive oil

2 large or 3 medium-size leeks, white part only, well washed and thinly sliced

1 teaspoon cumin seeds, slightly crushed

Pinch of cayenne pepper

Salt and freshly ground black pepper to taste

2 ounces Gruyère cheese, grated (½ cup tightly packed)

⅔ cup 1% milk

2 tablespoons nonfat dry milk

1. Bring an inch of water to a boil in the saucepan fitted with the steamer. Add the potatoes, cover, and reduce the heat to medium. Steam until just tender, 10 to 15 minutes. Remove from the heat and set aside.

2. Preheat the oven to 375°F. Brush the surface of the piecrust fitted into the pan with a bit of the beaten egg and prebake for 7 minutes. Remove from the oven and cool on a wire rack. If not using a crust, brush the baking or gratin dish with olive oil.

3. Heat the butter or oil in the skillet over medium heat. Add the leeks and cook, stirring often, until tender, about 5 minutes. Stir in the cumin seeds, cayenne, potatoes, and a little salt and black pepper. Toss together gently for about a minute and remove from the heat. Transfer to a bowl and toss with the Gruyère. Turn into the crust or dish and spread evenly.

4. In a blender or bowl with a whisk, blend together the liquid and dry milks. Add ½ teaspoon salt, the beaten eggs, and black pepper to taste. Mix together well and pour over the potato mixture. Bake until firm and the top is beginning to brown, 30 to 40 minutes. Remove from the heat and cool on a wire rack if not serving right away.

Get out the following equipment: chef's knife and cutting board; measuring spoons and measuring cup; 3-quart saucepan and steamer basket; blender or bowl and whisk; large, heavy nonstick skillet and wooden spoon; 10-inch pie or tart pan or 2-quart baking or gratin dish; pastry brush if using crust

Advance preparation: This can be made a day ahead and reheated in a medium oven.

PER SERVING:
12.0 gm total fat
4.5 gm saturated fat
433 calories
67.9 gm carbohydrates
14.4 gm protein

Get out the following equipment: chef's knife and cutting board; measuring spoons and measuring cup; large, heavy nonstick skillet and wooden spoon; garlic press or mini-chop if using; blender if using; medium-size bowl and whisk or fork; grater; 10-inch pie or tart pan; pastry brush

Advance preparation: The tomato sauce can be made up to 3 days before assembling the tart and refrigerated. The tart can be made a day ahead of time and reheated gently or served at room temperature.

PER SERVING:
12.3 gm total fat
3.5 gm saturated fat
276 calories
28.5 gm carbohydrates
12.5 gm protein

Garlicky Tomato Tart

Makes one 10-inch tart; 6 servings

This rich-tasting, savory tart is like a custard-topped pizza. You can use canned tomatoes in winter. In that case, omit the sliced tomatoes that line the tart. It will still be wonderful.

3 large eggs, or 2 large eggs and 2 large egg whites

1 Greek baking powder piecrust (page 308) or yeasted olive oil pastry (page 309)

1 tablespoon olive oil

4 large garlic cloves, peeled and minced or pressed

1 pound fresh or canned tomatoes, peeled, seeded, and chopped

1 tablespoon tomato paste

⅛ teaspoon sugar

½ teaspoon salt, or more to your taste

1 teaspoon fresh thyme leaves or ¼ to ½ teaspoon dried thyme, to your taste

1 tablespoon chopped fresh basil leaves, if available

Freshly ground black pepper to taste

⅔ cup 1% milk

2 tablespoons nonfat dry milk

1 ounce Gruyère cheese, grated (¼ cup tightly packed)

1 ounce Parmesan cheese, grated (¼ cup tightly packed)

2 large firm, ripe tomatoes, sliced crosswise about ¼ inch thick

1. Preheat the oven to 375°F. Beat the eggs or eggs and egg whites together and brush the bottom of the crust fitted into the pan lightly with some of it. Prebake for 7 minutes. Remove from the oven and let cool on a wire rack.

2. Heat the olive oil in the skillet over medium-low heat. Add half the garlic and cook, stirring, until fragrant and beginning to color, 30 seconds to a minute. Add the chopped (not the sliced) tomatoes, tomato paste, sugar, the remaining garlic, and salt (at least ¼ teaspoon) and increase the heat to medium. Cook, stirring, until the tomatoes have cooked down to a paste and are beginning to stick to the skillet, 15 to 20 minutes. Stir in the thyme, basil, and pepper; taste and adjust the salt. Remove from the heat.

3. In a blender or bowl with a whisk, blend together the liquid and dry milks. Add ¼ teaspoon salt, the beaten eggs, and some pepper. Transfer to a bowl and stir in the tomato sauce and cheeses.

4. Line the bottom of the crust with the sliced tomatoes. Pour in the tomato mixture. (If using canned tomatoes, pour the tomato mixture directly into the crust.) Bake until a knife inserted in the middle comes out clean, about 45 minutes. Let sit on a wire rack for 15 to 20 minutes before serving. This can also be served at room temperature.

Ratatouille Tart

Makes one 10-inch tart; 6 servings

You might not want to make ratatouille just for this luscious tart, but if you happen to have leftovers, this is one of the many things that leftover ratatouille is good for.

1 Greek baking powder piecrust (page 308) or yeasted olive oil pastry (page 309)

3 large eggs, or 2 large eggs and 2 large egg whites, beaten

3 cups ratatouille (½ recipe, page 73)

½ ounce Gruyère cheese, grated (2 tablespoons tightly packed)

1 ounce Parmesan cheese, grated (¼ cup tightly packed)

½ cup 1% milk

¼ teaspoon salt

1. Preheat the oven to 375°F. Brush the surface of the piecrust fitted into the pan with a bit of the beaten egg and prebake for 7 minutes. Remove from the oven and cool on a wire rack.

2. Toss together the ratatouille and cheeses. Beat together the milk, salt, and eggs and stir into the ratatouille mixture. Turn into the prebaked crust and spread in an even layer. Bake until firm and lightly browned on the top, 40 to 45 minutes. Remove from the heat and cool on a wire rack if not serving right away.

Get out the following equipment: **measuring spoons and measuring cup; medium-size bowl and whisk or fork; grater; 10-inch pie or tart pan; pastry brush**

Advance preparation: **The ratatouille will keep for 3 or 4 days in the refrigerator and can be frozen for several months. The tart can be made a day ahead and reheated gently or served at room temperature.**

PER SERVING:
11.8 gm total fat
3.1 gm saturated fat
292 calories
35.1 gm carbohydrates
12.5 gm protein

Spinach Quiche (or Tart)

■

Makes one 10-inch quiche; 6 servings

This is so thick with spinach it might more accurately be called a tart. It's a great way to eat your leafy greens. If you use frozen spinach, this is quickly assembled.

1 Greek baking powder pie crust (page 308) or yeasted olive oil pastry
(page 309)

3 large eggs, or 2 large eggs and 2 large egg whites, beaten

1½ pounds fresh spinach, stemmed and washed, or two 10-ounce packages
frozen chopped spinach, thawed

1 tablespoon olive oil or unsalted butter

1 medium-size onion, peeled and chopped

1 cup 1% milk

2 tablespoons nonfat dry milk

½ teaspoon salt

Freshly ground black pepper to taste

Pinch of freshly grated nutmeg

2 ounces Gruyère cheese, grated (½ cup tightly packed)

1 ounce Parmesan cheese, grated (¼ cup tightly packed)

1. Preheat the oven to 375°F. Brush the surface of the piecrust fitted into the pan with a little bit of the beaten egg. Bake for 7 minutes and remove from the oven. Allow to cool on a wire rack.

2. Blanch the fresh spinach in a large pot of boiling salted water for 1 minute or wilt in the skillet over high heat in the water left on its leaves after washing. Drain and rinse at once with cold water. Squeeze dry in a kitchen towel and chop. (If using thawed frozen spinach, squeeze dry in a towel.)

3. Heat the olive oil or butter in the skillet (wiped dry if you used it to wilt the spinach) over medium heat. Add the onion and cook, stirring, until tender, about 5 minutes. Add the chopped spinach and stir together for about 30 seconds, then remove from the heat.

4. In a blender or bowl with a whisk, beat together the liquid and dry milks. Add the salt, beaten eggs, pepper, and nutmeg and blend together well. Stir in the spinach, onion, and cheeses. Turn into the crust, spread evenly, and place in the oven. Bake until the top is just beginning to brown and the custard has set, 30 to 40 minutes. Remove from the heat and allow to cool slightly on a wire rack before cutting.

Get out the following equipment: chef's knife and cutting board; measuring spoons and measuring cup; pot for blanching the spinach if using; colander; large, heavy nonstick skillet and wooden spoon; blender if using; medium-size bowl and whisk or fork; grater; 10-inch pie or tart pan; pastry brush

Advance preparation: This can be made a day ahead and reheated gently or served at room temperature. The crust will remain crisp.

PER SERVING:
13.7 gm total fat
4.6 gm saturated fat
292 calories
27.4 gm carbohydrates
16.0 gm protein

Greek Spinach and Leek Pie

Makes one 10-or 12-inch pie; 6 servings

This beautiful Greek pie, made with filo (phyllo) dough, is best made with fresh spinach since the spinach is its defining ingredient. Frozen will work, however, if you just don't feel like cleaning 2 pounds of spinach (it goes pretty quickly if you fill your kitchen sink with water and put all the spinach in it, then stem the leaves). Filo dough can be found at many supermarkets (look in the freezer department) and any Middle Eastern store. Freeze what you don't use.

Working with filo dough: The sheets are paper-thin, dusted with cornstarch so they don't stick to each other. They're easy to manipulate. The main risk is their drying out and becoming brittle while you work with them. Here's how to avoid that: Take the filo from the package and unfold it. Remove the nine sheets you will need and refold and rewrap the remaining filo right away. Lay the sheets out under a slightly damp kitchen towel and work quickly.

> 2 to 2½ pounds (3 bunches) fresh spinach, stemmed and washed, or three 10-ounce packages frozen chopped spinach, thawed
> ¼ cup olive oil
> 3 large leeks, white part only, well washed and thinly sliced
> 3 large eggs, or 2 large eggs and 2 large egg whites
> 3 ounces feta cheese, crumbled (about ⅔ cup)
> ¼ cup chopped fresh dill
> Salt and freshly ground black pepper to taste
> Pinch of freshly grated nutmeg
> 9 sheets filo dough
> 1 large egg white, lightly beaten

1. If using fresh spinach, wilt in the skillet over high heat in the water left on its leaves after washing. This will take a couple of minutes once the water begins to boil. Alternatively, blanch the spinach for 1 minute in a large pot of salted boiling water (see page 23). Transfer to a colander, rinse with cold water, and press out as much water as possible. When the spinach is cool enough to handle, wrap it in a kitchen towel and squeeze out more water. Chop finely (you can do this in a food processor) and set aside. For thawed frozen spinach, squeeze out the excess water in a towel.

2. Preheat the oven to 375°F. Heat 1 tablespoon olive oil in the skillet (wiping it dry first if you used it to wilt the spinach) over medium heat. Add the leeks and cook, stirring often, until softened and just beginning to brown, 5 to 10 minutes. Remove from the heat.

continued

Get out the following equipment: **large, heavy nonstick skillet and wooden spoon; colander; chef's knife and cutting board; measuring spoons; 10- or 12-inch pie or tart pan; pastry brush; food processor fitted with steel blade if using; medium-size bowl**

Advance preparation: **This can be assembled a day ahead of time and refrigerated, covered with plastic wrap. Bake on the day you are serving it. It will hold, once baked, for a few hours, but the crust may need crisping in a warm oven (300°–325°) for 10 to 15 minutes.**

PER SERVING:
17.1 gm total fat
4.5 gm saturated fat
336 calories
35.0 gm carbohydrates
14.0 gm protein

3. Beat the eggs or eggs and egg whites together. Crumble in the feta. Stir in the leeks, dill, spinach, salt, pepper, and nutmeg. Taste and adjust the seasonings, keeping in mind that the feta is very salty and will season the pie as it bakes.

4. Brush the tart or pie pan lightly with olive oil. Layer in 4 sheets of filo dough, placing them not quite evenly on top of each other so that the edges overlap the sides of the pan all the way around. Brush each sheet lightly with some of the remaining 3 tablespoons olive oil before adding the next. Top with the spinach mixture. Fold the edges of the dough over the spinach mixture and brush them with olive oil. Layer 5 more sheets of dough over the top, brushing each sheet lightly with olive oil, and crimp the edges into the sides of the pan. Brush the top with the beaten egg white. Pierce the top of the pie in several places with a sharp knife. Bake until the top is golden brown and the filo crisp, 45 to 50 minutes. Serve hot or at room temperature.

Broccoli Timbale

Makes 4 to 6 servings

A timbale is a molded custard, a sort of crustless quiche, baked in a soufflé dish set in a baking dish or pan filled with water. The water regulates the cooking temperature of the custard. The timbale can be unmolded but is just as nice served from the dish if you don't want to bother with unmolding.

1 pound broccoli crowns
4 large eggs
1½ cups 1% milk
2 tablespoons nonfat dry milk
¾ teaspoon salt
Freshly ground black pepper to taste
2 ounces Parmesan or Gruyère cheese, grated (½ cup tightly packed)
2 tablespoons chopped fresh flat-leaf parsley (optional)
1 cup prepared or homemade tomato sauce (page 43) for serving (optional)

1. Preheat the oven to 350°F. Oil or butter the soufflé dish.

2. Bring an inch of water to a boil in the saucepan fitted with the steamer and add the broccoli. Cover and steam until just about tender, 5 minutes. Drain and rinse with cold water. Chop the broccoli finely, using the chef's knife or food processor.

Get out the following equipment: 2-quart soufflé dish; large saucepan fitted with a steamer; chef's knife and cutting board or food processor fitted with steel blade; medium-size bowl and whisk; small saucepan; grater; measuring spoons and measuring cup; pan that the soufflé dish can sit in

Advance preparation: The ingredients can be prepared hours before assembling and baking the timbale, but it's best served hot or warm.

PER SERVING:
10.7 gm total fat
4.9 gm saturated fat
216.7 calories
12.6 gm carbohydrates
19.3 gm protein

3. Beat the eggs in the bowl. Heat the 1% milk in the small saucepan until the surface begins to tremble (do not boil) and whisk it into the eggs. Add the nonfat milk, salt, pepper, Parmesan, and optional parsley, then stir in the broccoli. Pour into the prepared dish.

4. Set the dish in a pan of hot water and place in the oven. Bake until set and just beginning to brown, 50 to 60 minutes. It should also be pulling away from the sides of the dish. Test after 50 minutes by sticking a sharp knife in the center; it should come out clean. Remove from the oven and let sit for 10 minutes before unmolding onto a large plate or platter, or serve from the dish. To unmold, first run a dinner knife around the edge of the soufflé dish. Place the plate or platter over the top of the dish. Hold it tightly against the dish. Lift up the dish, using a pot holder to protect your hand (it will still be hot), and invert the dish and plate. The timbale should slide right out onto the plate. Surround with tomato sauce if desired. If serving with the sauce, spoon sauce onto the plate first, then top with a wedge of timbale.

Tacos, Quesadillas, and Salsas

■

The role that Mexican, Tex-Mex, or California Mexican food plays in your life probably depends on where you live. If you live in California or the Southwest, quesadillas and tacos may be quick meals you grew up with. The wonderful flavors of Mexico came into my life when I lived in Texas during the seventies, and I have pursued Mexican cooking ever since. Now that we have Mexican-American populations all over the United States, the food has become more widespread, but many of you may not know how easy, delicious, and healthy Mexican food can be.

Many think of Mexican food as fattening, filling food, but authentic Mexican food is not. It's a cuisine that relies on the sparkling flavors of fresh produce, chiles, herbs, and spices as much as those of heavier ingredients. What passes as Mexican food in this country is often fat-laden, but it needn't be. I've lightened it further, with a minimum of cheese called for in nonetheless cheesy quesadillas.

The *Light Basics* tacos and quesadillas here are made with corn tortillas and aren't fried. In fact, this is a more authentic way to prepare these dishes than the more familiar Tex-Mex way. In Mexico, tacos are often served on a hot, soft corn tortilla or on a toasted one and virtually never on a deep-fried moon-shaped one. Quesadillas may be made with flour tortillas in the north of Mexico, but farther south corn tortillas are the norm. The reason I opt for corn tortillas is that they are virtually fat-free and taste great, whereas flour tortillas contain quite a bit of shortening (and the fat-free brands have a tough, cardboard texture when heated).

Keep corn tortillas on hand in the freezer and salsa in the pantry or refrigerator. You can top a hot corn tortilla with just about anything. The selections here combine chicken, shrimp, or vegetables with salsas and chiles. But beyond these recipes, think about recycling leftovers into a Mexican meal. You'll find that a dinner of quesadillas filled with a small amount of cheese or my high-protein low-fat quesadilla filling and vegetables or salsa can be very quickly thrown together. Hopefully Mexican food will become not only a family favorite but the cook's favorite, too, because it's so convenient.

Salsa Fresca
Fresh Tomato Salsa

Makes about 2 cups

This is sometimes referred to as *pico de gallo*. It's a simple, vibrant salsa that requires little more than quality tomatoes and about 10 minutes of your time. Serve it with tacos and quesadillas, with grilled fish and chicken breasts, or as a dip for chips.

1 to 1¼ pounds (4 medium-size or 2 large) firm, ripe tomatoes, finely chopped

½ small red onion, peeled, minced, and rinsed with cold water

2 to 3 jalapeño or serrano chiles, to your taste, seeded for a milder salsa and minced

¼ cup chopped fresh cilantro leaves, or more to taste

1 to 2 teaspoons balsamic vinegar, rice wine vinegar, or fresh lime juice (optional), to your taste

Salt to taste

Mix together all the ingredients. Let sit for about 15 minutes before serving.

Salsa Fresca with Avocado

Add 1 small avocado, pitted, peeled, and finely diced, to the salsa.

Get out the following equipment: **chef's knife and cutting board; rubber gloves for handling the chiles; bowl; measuring spoons**

Advance preparation: **This should be made on the day you wish to serve it, but it will hold for several hours in the refrigerator. The salt will draw juice out of the tomatoes, so it will be more watery, but this doesn't bother me.**

PER ¼-CUP SERVING:
0.53 gm total fat
0 gm saturated fat
36.8 calories
6.4 gm carbohydrates
1.5 gm protein

Cooked Tomato Salsa
Salsa Ranchera

Makes about 2 cups

This classic cooked tomato-chile sauce is terrific with just about anything—eggs (like poached huevos rancheros, page 188), fish, chicken, tacos, or chips. If your tomatoes are very pulpy, thin them out with water.

(page 188)

2 pounds (8 medium-size or 4 large) firm, ripe tomatoes, roasted, peeled, and cored (see Note)

2 to 3 serrano or 1 to 2 jalapeño chiles, to your taste, seeded for a milder sauce and chopped

¼ to ½ small onion, to your taste, peeled, coarsely chopped (2 to 4 tablespoons), and rinsed with cold water

2 garlic cloves, peeled and minced or pressed

1 tablespoon canola oil

Salt to taste

1. Place the tomatoes, along with any liquid that has accumulated in the bowl in which they cooled, the chiles, onion, and garlic in the blender or food processor and puree, retaining a bit of texture.

2. Heat the oil in the skillet over medium heat. Drop a bit of puree into the skillet, and if it sizzles loudly, add the rest (wait another minute or two if it doesn't). Cook, stirring, until the sauce darkens, thickens, and begins to stick to the skillet, 10 to 15 minutes. Season with salt and thin out with water as necessary. Remove from the heat. Serve hot or at room temperature.

Note: To roast tomatoes: *Preheat the broiler. Line a baking sheet with foil and top with the tomatoes. Place under the broiler 2 to 3 inches from the heat (at the highest rack setting). Turn after 2 or 3 minutes, when the tomatoes have charred on one side (this may take longer in an electric oven), and repeat on the other side. Remove from the heat and transfer to a bowl. When the tomatoes are cool enough to handle, peel and core.*

Smoky Cooked Tomato Salsa

For a smoky, hot taste, add 1 or 2 canned chipotle chiles in adobo and simmer with the tomatoes. Remove them from the sauce when it is cooked.

Get out the following equipment: baking sheet and aluminum foil; large, heavy nonstick skillet and wooden spoon; chef's knife, paring knife, and cutting board; rubber gloves for handling chiles; blender or food processor fitted with steel blade; measuring spoons; bowl

Advance preparation: This will keep for 4 to 5 days in the refrigerator. It can be frozen for 3 months.

PER ¼-CUP SERVING:
2.1 gm total fat
0.1 gm saturated fat
43 calories
4.9 gm carbohydrates
1.2 gm protein

Fresh Tomatillo Salsa
Salsa Verde Fresca

Makes 2½ cups

This classic, lively, bright green salsa is made with either fresh or canned tomatillos, the little paper-husked green tomatoes that really aren't tomatoes at all. It is easy to prepare and makes a great sauce for any kind of quesadilla or taco, as well as for fish, chicken, potatoes, or plain old tortilla chips. You can find tomatillos at any supermarket that sells Mexican ingredients.

1 pound fresh tomatillos, husked and washed, or two 13-ounce cans tomatillos, drained

2 to 5 jalapeño or serrano chiles, to your taste, seeded for a milder salsa and coarsely chopped

½ small or medium-size onion, peeled, roughly chopped, and rinsed with cold water

2 large garlic cloves (optional), peeled and roughly chopped

Salt to taste

8 fresh cilantro sprigs, or more to taste

¼ to ½ cup water, as needed

If using fresh tomatillos, simmer them in water to cover in the saucepan until drab, about 10 minutes. Flip them over halfway through the cooking time or weight with a lightweight lid so they stay submerged. Whether using fresh or canned, drain and place in the blender or a food processor. Add the chiles, onion, garlic, salt, and cilantro and process to a coarse puree. Transfer to a bowl and thin out as desired with the water. Taste and adjust the seasoning. Let stand for 30 minutes or longer, to allow the flavors to develop, before serving.

Tomatillo and Cilantro Salsa

For an emerald-green sauce that rings with the flavor of cilantro, use 2 whole bunches of cilantro, washed and stems trimmed. You should have about 2 cups tightly packed cilantro leaves. Add it to the blender to process with everything.

Get out the following equipment: **chef's knife and cutting board; 3-quart saucepan if using; rubber gloves for handling the chiles; blender or food processor fitted with steel blade; measuring spoons and measuring cup; bowl**

Advance preparation: **This will hold for a few days in the refrigerator, but the fresher it is, the more vivid the flavors. It thickens with time but can be thinned out as desired with water.**

PER SERVING:
4.7 gm total fat
0 gm saturated fat
171 calories
30.7 gm carbohydrates
4.9 gm protein

Tomatillo and Chipotle Salsa

Substitute 1 to 3 canned chipotle chiles in adobo, to your taste, rinsed, seeded, and chopped, or 1 to 3 dried chipotles, to your taste, soaked in boiling water until soft, then seeded and stemmed, and coarsely chopped, for the green chiles.

Mango Salsa

Makes 1 cup

This tropical salsa is as evocative of Southeast Asia as it is of the Southwest or Mexico. Serve it with grilled or steamed halibut, swordfish, snapper, or sea bass, or with grilled chicken breasts.

> 1 large ripe mango
> 2 serrano chiles, seeded for a milder salsa if desired and minced
> 1 tablespoon chopped fresh cilantro leaves
> Juice of 1 medium-size lime
> Salt to taste

Peel and finely chop the mango (see page 32) for more detailed directions on how to do this). If it is very ripe, the mixture may have more of a pureed than diced consistency, which is fine. Toss with the remaining ingredients. Let sit for at least 1 hour in or out of the refrigerator before serving. Serve at room temperature.

Peach Salsa

Makes 1 cup

Another salsa with a tropical taste, this is good with grilled fish, shrimp, or chicken.

> 2 large ripe peaches
> 1 slice red onion (optional), peeled, minced, and rinsed with cold water
> 2 serrano chiles, seeded for a milder salsa if desired and minced
> 1 tablespoon chopped fresh cilantro leaves
> 1 tablespoon chopped fresh mint leaves
> Juice of 1 medium-size lime
> Salt to taste

Get out the following equipment: chef's knife, paring knife, and cutting board; rubber gloves for handling chiles; bowl; measuring spoons

Advance preparation: This can be made a few hours before serving and held in the refrigerator.

PER ¼-CUP SERVING:
0.3 gm total fat
0.1 gm saturated fat
60 calories
15.7 gm carbohydrates
0.8 gm protein

Get out the following equipment: 2-quart saucepan and bowl; chef's knife and cutting board; rubber gloves for handling chiles; measuring spoons; citrus press

Advance preparation: This can be made a few hours before serving and held in the refrigerator.

Peel the peaches by dropping them into a saucepan of boiling water for 30 seconds (1 minute if they are very hard), then rinsing with cold water; the skins should slip off. Cut in half, remove the pits, and finely dice. Toss with the remaining ingredients. Let sit for at least 1 hour before serving, in or out of the refrigerator.

PER ¼-CUP SERVING:
0.1 gm total fat
0 gm saturated fat
38 calories
9.8 gm carbohydrates
0.9 gm protein

Peach-Chipotle Salsa

Substitute 1 canned chipotle chile in adobo, rinsed, seeded, and minced, for the serranos.

Tacos with Chicken and Tomatillo and Chipotle Salsa

Makes 4 servings

This taco always gets raves. Everybody loves the flavor contrasts of the shredded chicken bathed with tangy-smoky tomatillo and chipotle salsa. The ingredients for the topping keep well in the refrigerator, so you can have this topping made up in advance for quick after-work meals.

> 1 large whole chicken breast or 2 boneless, skinless breasts, poached
>   (page 97) and shredded (1¾ to 2 cups)
> 1 cup Tomatillo and Chipotle Salsa (page 328)
> Salt to taste
> 2 to 3 tablespoons chopped fresh cilantro leaves, to your taste
> 8 to 10 corn tortillas
> ⅓ cup drained yogurt (see Note on page 40)
> 2 limes, cut into wedges

1. Poach and shred the chicken
2. Make the salsa. Toss 1 cup of it with the shredded chicken. Season with salt and sprinkle with the cilantro.
3. Heat the tortillas (see Note on page 332). Place 2 warm tortillas on each plate, top with the chicken mixture, add a spoonful of the yogurt, and serve, passing lime wedges for people to squeeze on as desired. People can fold the tortillas over and eat these with their hands or use a fork.

Get out the following equipment: chef's knife and cutting board; measuring spoons and measuring cup; saucepan for poaching chicken

Advance preparation: Both the salsa and the cooked chicken breasts, shredded or whole, will keep for 4 days in the refrigerator. The filling can be mixed and held for an hour or two in the refrigerator.

PER SERVING:
4.3 gm total fat
0.9 gm saturated fat
271 calories
32.5 gm carbohydrates
26.0 gm protein

Get out the following equipment: citrus zester and juicer; chef's knife and cutting board; measuring spoons; skillet for heating the cumin and tortillas (or a steamer or baking sheet if using); mortar and pestle

Advance preparation: The topping will keep for a few hours in the refrigerator.

PER SERVING:
3.0 gm total fat
0.5 gm saturated fat
274 calories
34.3 gm carbohydrates
27.6 gm protein

Quick Shrimp and Lime Tacos

Makes 4 to 5 servings

This is a great taco to throw together after work. Just stop at the supermarket and pick up limes, salsa, and some cooked shrimp—I recommend the little bay shrimp, which demand no work at all, and you have a lively, fresh, light dinner in minutes.

1 pound cooked, shelled medium-size shrimp (page 299, or buy already
    cooked), coarsely chopped, or cooked bay shrimp, rinsed
¼ cup fresh lime juice
Finely minced zest of 2 limes (2 teaspoons)
¼ cup chopped fresh cilantro leaves
1 teaspoon cumin seeds, or more to taste
Salt to taste
10 corn tortillas
½ to 1 cup red or green salsa, homemade or store-bought, to your taste
Cilantro sprigs for garnish

1. Toss together the shrimp, lime juice and zest, and cilantro.
2. Heat the cumin seeds in a dry skillet over medium heat until they begin to pop and smell toasty. Remove from the heat at once. Lightly crush in the mortar with the pestle and stir into the shrimp mixture. Taste and add salt as desired.
3. Heat the tortillas (see Note on page 332). Place 2 tortillas on a plate and top with the shrimp mixture. Add a spoonful of salsa. Garnish with cilantro sprigs and serve.

Soft Tacos with Corn, Squash, and Beans

Makes 6 servings

This is a lovely vegetarian taco topped with a classic Mexican combination—squash, corn, and beans.

1 tablespoon canola or olive oil
1 medium-size red onion, peeled and chopped
2 medium-size zucchini, cut into ¼-inch dice
2 ears of corn, kernels removed (about 2 cups)
½ teaspoon salt, plus more to taste

Get out the following equipment: chef's knife and cutting board; measuring spoons and measuring cups; large, heavy nonstick skillet

Advance preparation: The topping will hold for a few hours on top of the stove and can be reheated. Stir in the cilantro when you reheat.

2 small to medium-size or 1 large firm, ripe tomato, seeded and diced

2 serrano chiles, seeded for a milder filling if desired and minced

One 15-ounce can black beans, drained and rinsed

3 tablespoons chopped fresh cilantro leaves

12 corn tortillas

⅓ cup crumbled Mexican or feta cheese (optional)

PER SERVING:
4.3 gm total fat
0.4 gm saturated fat
222 calories
42.7 gm carbohydrates
8.0 gm protein

1. Heat the oil in the skillet over medium heat. Add the onion and cook, stirring, until just about tender, about 3 minutes. Add the zucchini and corn kernels, sprinkle on the salt, and cook, stirring, until the zucchini is translucent and the corn kernels are tender, 5 to 10 minutes. Stir in the tomatoes and chiles and stir together for another minute. Stir in the beans and heat through. Remove from the heat, taste, and add more salt as desired. Stir in the cilantro.

2. Heat the tortillas (see Note on page 332). Place 2 tortillas on a plate and top with the squash mixture. Sprinkle with cheese if desired and serve.

Potato and Egg Tacos

Makes 4 servings

Comforting and filling, these are great for breakfast as well as dinner. The authentic version would feature fried potatoes, but this light steamed potato rendition is excellent.

8 corn tortillas

1 pound (4 medium-size) waxy potatoes, scrubbed and cut into ½-inch dice

3 large eggs, or 2 large eggs and 2 large egg whites, beaten

Salt and freshly ground black pepper to taste

1 tablespoon canola or olive oil

1 small onion, peeled and thinly sliced or chopped

Green or red salsa, homemade or store-bought

1. Preheat the oven to 350°F. Wrap the tortillas in aluminum foil and heat in the oven for 10 minutes while you prepare the filling.

2. Bring an inch of water to a boil in the saucepan fitted with the steamer. Add the potatoes, cover, and reduce the heat to medium. Steam the potatoes until tender, about 10 minutes. Remove from the heat and set aside. Beat the eggs in a bowl and season with salt and pepper.

3. Heat the oil in the skillet over medium heat. Add the onion and cook, stirring, until tender, about 5 minutes. Stir in the potatoes, add a bit of

Get out the following equipment: **chef's knife and cutting board; steamer and saucepan with lid; bowl and whisk or fork; large, heavy nonstick skillet and wooden spoon**

Advance preparation: **You can cook the onions and potatoes several hours ahead, but the eggs are a last-minute addition.**

PER SERVING:
8.6 gm total fat
1.6 gm saturated fat
330 calories
54.4 gm carbohydrates
10.4 gm protein

salt and pepper, and stir together for a couple of minutes, until the potatoes begin to brown lightly. Stir in the beaten eggs and cook, stirring constantly, until they set. Remove from the heat. Place 2 warm tortillas on a plate, top with the filling, and serve at once, with salsa.

Classic Quesadillas

Makes 1 serving

Made in minutes, quesadillas are the ultimate homemade fast food. Corn tortillas have virtually no fat, whereas flour tortillas are a high-fat item, and the ones that boast no fat will have the texture of cardboard when you heat them. Each quesadilla is made with barely ½ ounce of cheese, which doesn't make them exceptionally high in fat—unless you eat more than three. Use either Monterey Jack cheese or mild or sharp cheddar. Monterey Jack is blander, but it's also more like classically Mexican melting cheeses, and you can add salsa or other ingredients for added flavor.

FOR EACH QUESADILLA:
1 corn tortilla
½ ounce cheddar or Monterey Jack cheese, grated (about 2 tablespoons)
Salsa, homemade or commercial

Heat the tortilla in the dry skillet over medium-high heat. Turn it over and sprinkle the grated cheese over its surface. When the cheese begins to melt, fold the tortilla over with the help of the spatula. Heat for about 30 seconds, then flip it over and continue to heat until the tortilla is lightly browned in places. Remove from the heat and serve with salsa.

Note: You can use a cast-iron skillet for this too, but the nonstick skillet is particularly convenient for cleaning off bits of cheese that escape the tortilla and melt on the pan.

Layered Quesadillas This method might keep the amount of cheese down, since you double the number of tortillas in each quesadilla without doubling the amount of cheese, so one layered quesadilla might be enough for a serving, whereas one Classic Quesadilla is skimpy. Add one more tortilla to the recipe. Heat the first tortilla as directed above. Flip it over and sprinkle on the cheese. When the cheese begins to melt, top with the other tortilla. When the bottom tortilla begins to brown in spots, flip over the layered quesadilla and heat until the other tortilla is lightly browned and the cheese melted. Remove from the heat, cut into quarters, and serve, with salsa.

Get out the following equipment: grater; nonstick skillet (see Note); spatula

Advance preparation: **Quesadillas should be made to order. However, if you're making a bunch of them and need to keep the first ones warm, transfer them from the skillet to a heatproof platter and place in a 300° oven while you make the rest. Your cheese can be grated hours or days ahead for ultra-quick quesadilla dinners.**

PER SERVING:
5.3 gm total fat
3.1 gm saturated fat
113 calories
11.9 gm carbohydrates
5.0 gm protein

High-Protein, Low-Fat Quesadillas

Makes 4 servings

The problem with the Classic Quesadilla for those who are keeping their fats down is that it's difficult to eat just one. So I developed this quesadilla, filled with a mixture of nonfat cottage cheese and a small amount of melting cheese (Monterey Jack or cheddar) to give it the right texture. The cottage cheese is blended in a food processor until smooth, then mixed with the other cheese and spooned onto the hot tortillas. The quesadillas are made like the classic ones in the preceding recipe. The filling is runnier than the classic cheese filling, so these quesadillas are more easily handled when cut in half, if you're eating them with your hands. You can also eat them with knife and fork.

1 cup nonfat cottage cheese
1½ ounces Monterey Jack, mild or sharp white cheddar, or Parmesan cheese
    (or combine 2 parts Monterey Jack with 1 part Parmesan for a good
    flavor/texture mix), grated (⅓ cup)
8 corn tortillas
Green or red salsa, homemade or store-bought, for serving

1. Blend together the cottage cheese and grated cheese in the food processor until completely smooth.
2. Heat the tortillas, 1 to 3 at a time, in the dry skillet over medium-high heat until flexible. Turn over and top each tortilla with 2 tablespoons of the cheese mixture. Fold the tortilla over. Heat through, turning the folded tortilla over from time to time, until the cheese melts and the tortilla browns in spots. Don't worry if some of the cheese runs out onto the skillet (it probably will). Transfer to plates and serve hot, passing salsa to spoon over the top.

Microwaved or Baked Quesadillas

These methods can be convenient if you're making a lot of quesadillas, but the flavor results are best when they're made in the pan.

Using a Microwave

Wrap 4 tortillas in microwaveable plastic wrap, a dampened paper towel, or wax paper and heat for 30 seconds to 1 minute in the microwave, until flexible. Spread 2 tablespoons of the cheese mixture on each tortilla and fold the

Get out the following equipment: **measuring cups; food processor fitted with steel blade; spatula; nonstick skillet**

Advance preparation: **The cheese mixture will keep in the refrigerator until the "sell by" date on the cottage cheese. The quesadillas are assembled and heated through just before serving.**

PER SERVING:
4.5 gm total fat
2.2 gm saturated fat
191 calories
25.5 gm carbohydrates
13.0 gm protein

Classic Quesadillas With:

Sprinkle your choice of the following ingredients over the cheese as it begins to melt:
- **1 slice ripe tomato, finely chopped**
- **Spoonful or two of salsa**
- **1 slice avocado, peeled, diced, and sprinkled with a bit of salt**
- **Leftover shredded chicken**
- **Heaping tablespoon or two of cooked black beans (rinsed if canned)**
- **Chopped fresh cilantro leaves**

tortilla over. Place on a plate or plates and cover with plastic wrap, a paper towel, or wax paper. Repeat with the next 4 tortillas. Heat through in the microwave for 2 minutes, uncover, and serve hot, passing salsa to spoon over the top.

Using the Oven

Preheat the oven to 400°F. Heat the tortillas, one at a time, turning in a dry skillet over medium-high heat until flexible; or wrap in microwaveable plastic wrap, wax paper, or a paper towel and heat for 30 seconds to a minute in the microwave, until flexible. Spread 2 tablespoons of the cheese mixture over each tortilla and fold the tortilla over. Place on an unoiled baking sheet. Heat, fill, and fold all of the tortillas in this way. Heat through in the hot oven until the cheese melts and the tortillas just begin to crisp and curl up slightly on top, about 10 minutes. Transfer to plates and serve hot, passing salsa to spoon over the top.

■ More Quesadilla Fillings ■

All of the following fillings can also be used with Classic Quesadillas on page 332.

Avocado and Green Salsa Quesadillas

Makes 4 servings

High-Protein, Low-Fat Cheese Filling (page 333)

8 corn tortillas

1 large ripe avocado, pitted, peeled, and thinly sliced

Salt to taste (optional)

½ cup Fresh Tomatillo Salsa or Fresh Tomatillo Salsa with Chipotles
(pages 327 and 328), or store-bought green salsa

Additional equipment:
chef's knife and cutting board

See *advance preparation* for High-Protein, Low-Fat Quesadillas, page 333, and for salsas, pages 327 and 328.

PER SERVING:
16.8 gm total fat
2.2 gm saturated fat
306 calories
27.2 gm carbohydrates
14.8 gm protein

1. Prepare the cottage cheese filling.
2. Heat the tortillas, 1 to 3 at a time, in the dry skillet over medium-high heat until flexible. Turn over and top each tortilla with 2 tablespoons of the cheese mixture. Top with a few slices of avocado (salt lightly if desired) and a generous spoonful of salsa. Fold the tortilla over. Heat through, turning the folded tortilla over from time to time, until the cheese melts and the tortilla browns in spots. Don't worry if some of the

cheese runs out onto the skillet (it probably will). Transfer to plates and serve hot, passing additional salsa to spoon over the top.

Black Bean Quesadillas

Makes 4 servings

3 cups cooked black beans (page 204), with some liquid, or two 15-ounce cans black beans, drained and rinsed

High-Protein Low-Fat Cheese Filling (page 333)

8 corn tortillas

1 cup Salsa Fresca (page 325), Cooked Tomato Salsa (page 326), or store-bought salsa

1. Heat the beans in a nonstick skillet and mash with a bean masher or potato masher or coarsely puree in a food processor. Moisten with a bit of water if they seem dry.
2. Prepare the cottage cheese filling as instructed.
3. Heat the tortillas, 1 to 3 at a time, in a dry nonstick skillet over medium-high heat until flexible. Turn over and top each tortilla with 2 tablespoons of the cheese mixture. Top with 2 tablespoons of the black beans and a spoonful of salsa. Fold the tortilla over. Heat through, turning the folded tortilla over from time to time, until the cheese melts and the tortilla browns in spots. Don't worry if some of the cheese runs out onto the skillet (it probably will). Transfer to plates and serve hot, passing additional salsa to spoon over the top.

Additional equipment: another nonstick skillet; bean masher or potato masher

Advance preparation: The black beans will keep for 4 days in the refrigerator. See *advance preparation* for High-Protein, Low-Fat filling and for salsas, pages 333, 325, and 326.

PER SERVING:
5.4 gm total fat
2.4 gm saturated fat
379 calories
59.2 gm carbohydrates
25.1 gm protein

Spinach Quesadillas

Makes 4 servings

1 bunch fresh spinach (10 to 12 ounces), stemmed and washed, or one 10-ounce package frozen chopped spinach, thawed

1 tablespoon olive oil

1 to 2 garlic cloves, to your taste, peeled and minced or pressed

Salt and freshly ground black pepper to taste

High-Protein, Low-Fat Cheese Filling (page 333)

8 corn tortillas

Green or red salsa, homemade or store-bought, for serving

Additional equipment: large bowl or salad spinner for fresh spinach, large pot or nonstick skillet for fresh spinach; chef's knife and cutting board; garlic press or minichop if using; measuring spoons

Tacos, Quesadillas, and Salsas

continued

1. If using fresh spinach, wilt in a large nonstick skillet over high heat in the water left on the leaves after washing or blanch for 1 to 2 minutes in a large pot of boiling salted water. Drain, rinse with cold water, and squeeze dry in a kitchen towel. Chop coarsely. If using frozen spinach, squeeze dry in a kitchen towel.

2. Heat the oil in the large, heavy nonstick skillet over medium heat. Add the garlic and cook until it begins to color, 30 seconds to a minute. Stir in the spinach. Stir together for a minute and remove from the heat. Season to taste with salt and pepper.

3. Prepare the cottage cheese filling.

4. Heat the tortillas, 1 to 3 at a time, in a dry nonstick skillet over medium-high heat until flexible. Turn over and top each tortilla with 2 tablespoons of the cheese mixture. Top with 2 tablespoons of the spinach. Fold the tortilla over. Heat through, turning the folded tortilla over from time to time, until the cheese melts and the tortilla browns in spots. Don't worry if some of the cheese runs out onto the skillet (it probably will). Transfer to plates and serve hot, passing salsa to spoon over the top.

Note: Other greens such as Swiss chard, beet greens, or kale can be substituted for the spinach.

Mushroom Quesadillas

Makes 4 servings

1 pound mushrooms, cleaned, stems trimmed, and sliced

¼ teaspoon salt

1 tablespoon olive or canola oil

1 to 2 garlic cloves, to your taste, peeled and minced or pressed

1 serrano chile, seeded for a milder flavor if desired and finely chopped, or
   1 canned chipotle in adobe, rinsed, seeded, and chopped, or more to taste

2 tablespoons chopped fresh cilantro or flat-leaf parsley leaves

High-Protein, Low-Fat Cheese Filling (page 333)

8 corn tortillas

Green or red salsa, homemade or store-bought, for serving

1. Heat the mushrooms with the salt in the large, heavy nonstick skillet over medium heat until they begin to release water. Cook, stirring, until the

mushrooms have softened and the liquid has just about evaporated. Add the oil, garlic, and chile and cook, stirring, until the garlic and mushrooms are fragrant, a couple of minutes. Stir in the cilantro or parsley and remove from the heat. Taste and adjust salt.

2. Prepare the cottage cheese filling.

3. Heat the tortillas, 1 to 3 at a time, in a dry nonstick skillet over medium-high heat until flexible. Turn over and top each tortilla with 2 tablespoons of the cheese mixture. Top with 2 tablespoons of the mushrooms. Fold the tortilla over. Heat through, turning the folded tortilla over from time to time, until the cheese melts and the tortilla browns in spots. Don't worry if some of the cheese runs out onto the skillet (it probably will). Transfer to plates and serve hot, passing salsa to spoon over the top.

Quesadillas with Roasted Red or Poblano Peppers

Makes 4 servings

2 large red bell peppers or 3 poblano chiles, roasted (page 131), peeled, seeded, and cut into thin strips

Salt to taste

High-Protein, Low-Fat Cheese Filling (page 333)

8 corn tortillas

Green or red salsa, homemade or store-bought, for serving

1. Season the strips of peppers with a bit of salt.

2. Prepare the cottage cheese filling.

3. Heat the tortillas, 1 to 3 at a time, in a dry nonstick skillet over medium-high heat until flexible. Turn over and top each tortilla with 2 tablespoons of the cheese mixture. Top with strips of pepper. Fold the tortilla over. Heat through, turning the folded tortilla over from time to time, until the cheese melts and the tortilla browns in spots. Don't worry if some of the cheese runs out onto the skillet (it probably will). Transfer to plates and serve hot, passing salsa to spoon over the top.

Additional equipment: baking sheet and medium bowl; plastic gloves; chef's knife and cutting board

Advance preparation: The pepper strips will keep for 4–5 days in the refrigerator. See page 333 for High Protein, Low-Fat Filling.

PER SERVING:
4.8 gm total fat
2.2 gm saturated fat
228 calories
33.5 gm carbohydrates
15.2 gm protein

Swiss Chard and Goat Cheese Quesadillas

Makes 4 servings

These luscious quesadillas are a variation of High-Protein, Low-Fat Quesadillas (page 333), with goat cheese replacing the grated cheese in the cottage cheese mixture. The flavor is distinctive, and the quesadillas taste rich.

1 pound red or green Swiss chard (1 large bunch)
2 teaspoons salt, plus more to taste
1 tablespoon olive oil
½ medium-size or 1 small onion, peeled and chopped
2 large garlic cloves, peeled and minced or pressed
Freshly ground black pepper to taste
1 cup nonfat cottage cheese
2 ounces goat cheese, crumbled (about ¼ cup)
8 corn tortillas
Salsa, homemade or store-bought, for serving

1. Bring a large pot of water to a boil. Meanwhile, tear the chard leaves from the stems and discard the stems. Wash the leaves thoroughly. When the water comes to a rolling boil, add the salt and chard. Cook for 3 minutes, then drain and rinse with cold water. Squeeze out the water and chop the chard.

2. Heat the oil in the skillet over medium heat. Add the onion and cook, stirring, until tender, 3 to 5 minutes. Add the garlic and cook, stirring, until the garlic begins to color, about 1 minute. Stir in the chard and stir together for about 1 minute, then remove from the heat. Season with salt and pepper. Set aside.

3. Blend the cottage cheese and goat cheese together in the food processor until completely smooth, stopping the machine once to scrape down the sides.

4. Heat the tortillas, 2 or 3 at a time, in a dry nonstick skillet over medium-high heat until flexible. Spread 2 tablespoons of the cheese mixture over each tortilla. Place a heaping tablespoon of the chard mixture down the center of the cheese and fold the tortilla over. Heat through, turning the folded tortilla over from time to time, until the cheese melts and the tortillas brown in spots, 5 to 8 minutes. Don't worry if some of the cheese runs out onto the skillet (it probably will). Transfer to plates and serve hot, passing salsa to spoon over the top.

Soft Tacos with
Chicken, Salsa Fresca, and Avocado

Makes 4 servings

This is the kind of meal you can throw together if you have corn tortillas and chicken breasts in your freezer and salsa in the pantry. But I must say, it's best made with fresh salsa. Serve these tacos on a hot summer night, with corn on the cob.

1 large whole chicken breast or 2 boneless, skinless breasts, poached
   (page 97) and shredded (1¾ to 2 cups)

2 large or 4 medium-size firm, ripe tomatoes (¾ to 1 pound), chopped

2 serrano or 1 to 2 jalapeño chiles, to your taste, seeded for a milder filling if
   desired and minced

¼ cup chopped fresh cilantro leaves

½ small red or white onion, peeled, minced, and rinsed with cold water

Salt to taste

1 small avocado, pitted, peeled, and cut into small dice

1 tablespoon fresh lime juice, or more to taste

8 to 10 corn tortillas

⅓ cup crumbled queso fresco or feta cheese (optional)

1. Poach and shred the chicken.
2. Combine the tomatoes, chiles, cilantro, onion, and salt in a bowl. Stir in the avocado and lime juice. Taste and adjust the salt. Toss with the shredded chicken.
3. Heat the tortillas (see Note on page 332). Place 2 warm tortillas on each plate, top with the chicken mixture, sprinkle on a dusting of cheese if desired, and serve. People can fold the tortillas over and eat these with their hands or use a fork.

Quick Version, Using Prepared Salsa: You can make the tacos with prepared salsa—either red or green. Use 1½ to 2 cups salsa, to your taste. Toss with the chicken and proceed as instructed.

Get out the following equipment: **chef's knife and cutting board; measuring spoons; bowl and wooden spoons**

Advance preparation: **The cooked chicken breasts, shredded or whole, will keep for 4 days in the refrigerator. The filling can be mixed and held for an hour or two in the refrigerator.**

PER SERVING:
10.2 gm total fat
0.8 gm saturated fat
313 calories
31.5 gm carbohydrates
25.2 gm protein

Desserts

■

For me, the ultimate dessert is a perfectly ripe piece of fruit in season. In the fall and winter I love seedless tangerines, muscat grapes, tart crisp apples, and ripe, buttery pears. In the late spring and early summer cherries come in for their short season, and then the summer fruits begin to roll in—melons and peaches, apricots and plums, nectarines and berries and figs. Strawberries from Mexico always seem to be available, but they don't taste anything like the fresh local ones that appear in spring and last through the summer.

But when guests come for dinner, I usually make a dessert (although a large bowl of fruit passed after an impromptu dinner party is always appreciated). Desserts are not something most of us tend to make every day, but we do make them for dinner parties. My desserts are virtually all fruit-based, the simplest being fruit salads, which are sometimes spiked with a liqueur or seasoned with fresh mint. The trick to a successful fruit salad is in the combination and the garnish. Not all fruits go together well, but certain fruits in combination—oranges and pomegranate; apricots and peaches with currants; peaches and blueberries; strawberries and mango—can embellish each other.

Fruit can also be poached or baked. Simple baked apples are about as easy and pleasing a winter dessert as I can think of; we often forget about this possibility when searching for a dish. There are all sorts of possibilities here for poaching fruit in wine or syrup. Not only fresh fruits but dried lend themselves to this method of cooking. The results are often called compotes, and they make great, easy winter and summer desserts.

As for baked desserts, I'm not a total ascetic here. I love crumbles, which require a buttery topping but feed a lot of people. You'll find a few tarts here too, but the crust is a yeasted one, containing very little butter and more bready like a coffee cake than crumbly like a traditional flaky crust. If you've made all the dishes in the "Warm-up Exercises" chapter, you'll have discovered the wonders of the clafoutis, that easy French dessert that is somewhat like a cross between a flan and a pancake.

A small cookie or biscotti served with a fruit salad or poached fruit adds a special touch to a dessert. Meringues and biscotti are not high-fat cookies, and they're easy to make or to find at the supermarket. Biscotti are particularly nice for dipping into marinades and syrups.

Note on nonreactive saucepans: These are esssentially nonaluminum saucepans. They won't react with the acidity in fruits and should be used where specified.

Fresh Fruit Combos

Making dessert can be as simple as the act of cutting up fruit and arranging it in an attractive serving bowl. You'll be appreciated for your minimal effort. Cut-up fruit has a lot going for it: it's pretty, fragrant, and juicy. Here are some combinations that look and taste especially good together.

- Oranges and pomegranate
- Oranges or blood oranges and strawberries (quarter the strawberries)
- Mixed citrus fruits and dates
- Oranges and fresh mint
- Strawberries in fresh orange juice, with fresh mint
- Strawberries doused with fresh lemon or lime juice and a little sugar, garnished with fresh mint
- Pineapple and fresh mint; pineapple, strawberries, and mint
- Mangoes and berries (strawberries, blueberries, or raspberries)
- Apricots and strawberries
- Apricots, peaches, or nectarines and strawberries
- Peaches or nectarines and blueberries
- Papaya and blueberries
- Pears and currants
- Melon (cantaloupe, honeydew) and strawberries or blueberries (or both)
- Watermelon and fresh mint
- Mixed melon balls and fresh mint

- Fresh lime juice and optional sugar: with strawberries, melon, mango, and papaya
- Fresh lemon juice and optional sugar: with peaches, nectarines, strawberries, apricots, pears, and apples
- Fresh mint: with berries, melon, oranges, tangerines, pineapple, mango, and kiwi
- Orange liqueur (like Grand Marnier, Cointreau, Triple Sec): citrus fruits, strawberries
- Kirsch (a cherry liqueur): cherries, pears, and plums

Oranges with Cointreau and Mint

Makes 4 servings

I love this combination and serve it as often for a planned dinner party as I do when people drop by unexpectedly. I always have the ingredients on hand (it helps to have a pot of mint at the ready). Refreshing, thirst quenching, and light, this dessert is always appreciated.

4 navel oranges
2 to 3 tablespoons Cointreau or Triple Sec, to your taste
3 tablespoons slivered fresh mint leaves
Fresh mint sprigs for garnish

1. Peel and pith the oranges as directed on page 32. Slice crosswise and toss in an attractive bowl with the liqueur. Chill until ready to serve.
2. Just before serving, toss with the slivered mint. Garnish with mint sprigs and serve.

Orange and Pomegranate Salad in Pomegranate Juice

Makes 4 servings

Pomegranates are widely available at farmers' markets and many supermarket in the autumn. Their hard outer skin should be red and leathery. Inside, they'll be packed with juicy red seeds.

Get out the following equipment: chef's knife and cutting board; paring knife; attractive serving bowl

Advance preparation: The oranges can be tossed with the Cointreau a few hours before serving, but add the mint just before serving.

PER SERVING:
0.2 gm total fat
0 gm saturated fat
93 calories
19.2 gm carbohydrates
1.3 gm protein

Get out the following equipment: chef's knife and cutting board; paring knife; measuring spoons and measuring cup; medium-size bowl or citrus press; small saucepan; strainer and bowl; pestle or wooden spoon

4 navel oranges

1½ ripe pomegranates

¼ cup water

1 tablespoon sugar

Zest of 1 orange, finely minced if desired

Fresh mint leaves for garnish

1. Peel and pith the oranges as directed on page 32. Slice crosswise and transfer to an attractive bowl.

2. Cut the pomegranates in half crosswise, across their equator. Juice one of the pomegranates, either by placing it in a bowl cut side down and pressing hard on it with the palm of your hand or by pressing over a citrus juicer. Strain the juice. Now take all of the seeds, some of which haven't been fully extracted of their juice, and place in a strainer set over a bowl. Using a pestle or a wooden spoon, press the seeds to extract the remaining juice. Discard the pulp and add the pomegranate juice to the bowl with the oranges. Remove the pomegranate seeds from the remaining pomegranate half and toss them with the oranges.

3. Combine the water and sugar in a small saucepan and bring to a boil. Add the orange zest, reduce the heat to low, and simmer for 10 minutes. Strain this sugar syrup into the oranges and pomegranate. Chill until ready to serve. Serve garnished with mint leaves.

Variation: Substitute 1 pink grapefruit for one of the oranges.

Blood Orange and Tangerine Salad

Makes 4 servings

Blood oranges have the most wonderful tart-sweet taste, and their color is unbelievable. Winter oranges, they are available for a few months a year, the same months that sweet, seedless tangerines are around.

4 blood oranges

6 seedless tangerines, peeled

3 tablespoons Grand Marnier or Cointreau

2 tablespoons slivered fresh mint leaves

Fresh mint sprigs for garnish

Advance preparation: These salads will hold for a couple of hours in the refrigerator, but they're best when not made too far ahead of time, because the orange juice will become more acidic.

PER SERVING:
0.3 gm total fat
0 gm saturated fat
116 calories
29.2 gm carbohydrates
1.8 gm protein

Get out the following equipment: chef's knife and cutting board; paring knife; measuring spoons; attractive serving bowl

Advance preparation: This will hold for a couple of hours in the refrigerator but is best not made too far ahead of time, because the citrus juice will become more acidic.

continued

PER SERVING:
0.4 gm total fat
0 gm saturated fat
154 calories
33.9 gm carbohydrates
2.1 gm protein

1. Peel and pith the oranges as directed on page 32. Slice crosswise and transfer to the serving bowl. Remove any pithy strings from the sides of the peeled tangerines and slice crosswise. Add to the oranges and toss with the liqueur. Refrigerate until ready to serve.
2. Just before serving, toss with the slivered mint. Serve, garnishing each dish with a mint sprig.

Peach and Apricot Salad

Makes 4 servings

This is a perfect summer dessert for that short period of time when the California apricots are juicy and sweet. You could substitute a high-quality brand of canned or jarred apricots if you can't find good fresh ones—that is, if the fresh apricots are mealy.

Get out the following equipment: **chef's knife and cutting board; paring knife; measuring spoons; attractive serving bowl**

Advance preparation: **This will hold for several hours in the refrigerator.**

PER SERVING:
0.3 gm total fat
0 gm saturated fat
83 calories
21.0 gm carbohydrates
1.5 gm protein

2 tablespoons fresh lemon juice

1 tablespoon sugar

4 firm, ripe peaches, pitted and sliced

6 ripe apricots, pitted and sliced

1 tablespoon currants

Combine the lemon juice and sugar in the serving bowl. Add the fruit and toss well. For best results, chill for an hour or more before serving. Toss again just before serving.

Variation: Substitute ½ cup fresh raspberries for the currants.

Rhubarb and Strawberry Compote

Makes 4 to 6 servings

Rhubarb is a marvelous fruit that can be eaten only if it is cooked and sweetened. It has a tart flavor that complements strawberries and oranges.

Get out the following equipment: **chef's knife and cutting board; citrus press; measuring cups; paring knife; 3-quart nonreactive saucepan**

Advance preparation: **This will keep for 4 or 5 days in the refrigerator.**

2 pounds rhubarb, washed, trimmed (leaves discarded), and stems sliced about ½ inch thick

½ cup water

⅓ cup mild-flavored honey, such as clover or acacia, or sugar, or more to taste

1½ cups fresh orange juice, or blood orange juice if in season

1 pint fresh strawberries, hulled and cut in half
Fresh mint leaves for garnish

PER SERVING:
0.9 gm total fat
0 gm saturated fat
196 calories
48.1 gm carbohydrates
3.2 gm protein

Combine the rhubarb, water, and honey or sugar in the saucepan and bring to a simmer. Simmer until the rhubarb has softened, about 8 minutes. Add the orange juice and strawberries and simmer for another 5 minutes. Remove from the heat and allow to cool slightly. Serve warm or chilled, garnished with mint.

Dried Fruit Compote with Apples or Pears

Makes 6 servings

Dried fruit compotes make a versatile, soothing winter dessert. You can use a range of different dried fruits or just a few. Fresh apples or pears are added to this one, for a nice contrast of textures. The compote gets sweeter by the day, and I love to eat leftovers for breakfast with yogurt.

½ pound mixed dried fruit, such as pitted cherries, apricots, figs, prunes,
   and/or raisins
2 tablespoons fresh lemon juice
3 wide strips lemon zest
One 2-inch cinnamon stick
5 tablespoons sugar
3 large apples such as Granny Smith, Pippin, or Pink Ladies, or firm ripe
   pears
1 vanilla bean (optional), cut in half lengthwise

Get out the following equipment: 2 medium-size bowls; strainer; 3-quart nonreactive saucepan; measuring cup; chef's knife and cutting board; paring knife; attractive serving dish

Advance preparation: This will keep for several weeks in the refrigerator. The dried fruit will lose some flavor, but the syrup will become sweeter.

PER SERVING:
0.6 gm total fat
0.1 gm saturated fat
203 calories
53.1 gm carbohydrates
1.4 gm protein

1. Place the dried fruit in the bowl and cover with hot water. Let sit for 4 hours or overnight. Drain through a strainer set over a bowl.
2. Measure the soaking water from the dried fruit and add water to make 1 quart. Combine with the lemon juice, lemon zest, cinnamon stick, and sugar in the saucepan and bring to a simmer. Peel, core, and slice the apples or pears and drop immediately into the saucepan. Add the dried fruit. Simmer until the fresh fruit is translucent, 15 to 30 minutes. Pears will cook faster than apples (in 15 to 20 minutes, depending on how ripe they are). Strain over a bowl and transfer the fruit to the serving dish. Discard the cinnamon stick and lemon zest.
3. Return the syrup to the pan and scrape in the seeds from the optional vanilla bean. Bring to a boil and boil until the syrup is thick and reduced by about a third. Pour over the fruit. Serve hot or cold.

Prunes Poached in Red Wine

Makes 6 servings

Prunes are really an underrated fruit. They take beautifully to poaching, as they are here in red wine. Keep prunes and red wine on hand so you can easily throw this popular French bistro dessert together.

1 pound pitted prunes
Boiling water to cover
2 cups (about ⅔ bottle) fruity red wine, such as a Côtes-du-Rhône,
    Zinfandel, Merlot, or Beaujolais
¼ cup sugar or 3 tablespoons mild-flavored honey such as acacia or clover
Juice of ½ lemon
3 wide strips orange zest

1. Place the prunes in the bowl and pour on boiling water to cover. Let sit for 1 to 2 hours. Drain.
2. Combine the prunes with the remaining ingredients in the saucepan and bring to a boil. Boil for 2 minutes and remove from the heat. Remove the strips of orange zest. Transfer to the serving dish and allow to cool. Chill if desired.

Peaches Poached in Red Wine

Makes 4 to 8 servings

A gorgeous summer dish, this has enough syrup here for eight, but you can poach only enough peaches for four and reuse the syrup as a topping for other fresh fruit (or low-fat ice cream).

4 to 8 medium-size or 4 large peaches
1 bottle fruity red wine, such as Côtes-du-Rhône, Zindandel, Merlot, or
    Beaujolais
½ cup sugar
Fresh mint sprigs for garnish

1. Fill the saucepan with water, bring to a boil, and plunge the peaches into the water for 30 seconds (if the peaches are very hard, boil for 1 minute). Drain and cool at once with cold water. Peel off the skins (they should slip off easily).

Get out the following equipment: medium-size bowl; strainer; 2-quart nonreactive saucepan; measuring cup and measuring spoons; paring knife or zester; serving dish

Advance preparation: This will keep for several days in the refrigerator.

PER SERVING:
0.6 gm total fat
0 gm saturated fat
346 calories
77.7 gm carbohydrates
3.0 gm protein

Get out the following equipment: 3-quart nonreactive saucepan; large wooden spoon; measuring cups; bowl large enough for the peaches and poaching liquid; individual serving bowls

Advance preparation: This needs several hours of chilling time. It is fine the next day, but the peaches turn darker the longer they sit in the syrup, so it might not be as pretty.

2. Combine the wine and sugar in the saucepan and stir over low heat until the sugar is dissolved. Add the peaches and bring to a gentle simmer. Cook, flipping the peaches over with a wooden spoon from time to time, for 8 minutes for small peaches, 10 minutes for larger ones. The peaches should be just tender when pierced with a needle or the tip of a knife. Remove the peaches with a slotted spoon and transfer to the bowl. Allow to cool. If the peaches are large, cut them in half and discard the pit.

3. Turn up the heat and reduce the wine mixture until it reaches a syrupy consistency, coating the front and back of your spoon (the bubbling will make a thick slurping sound in the pot). This will take anywhere from 10 to 20 minutes. Remove from the heat and pour the syrup over the peaches. Allow to cool, then cover and refrigerate, turning the peaches in the syrup from time to time, until shortly before serving.

4. Serve in bowls, with the syrup and a mint sprig.

PER SERVING:
0.1 gm total fat
0 gm saturated fat
153 calories
23.8 gm carbohydrates
0.8 gm protein

Pears Poached in Ginger-Honey Syrup

Makes 4 servings

Ginger infusions are wonderful for poaching fruit. They're also a soothing winter beverage, thought to be good for colds and sore throats.

2 tablespoons peeled and grated or finely chopped fresh ginger
3 cups boiling water
3 tablespoons mild-flavored honey such as clover or acacia
4 firm, ripe pears, peeled, cored, and cut into thick wedges and tossed with 1 tablespoon fresh lemon juice
2 tablespoons dried currants

1. Place the ginger in the bowl or measuring cup and pour on the boiling water. Cover and steep for 15 minutes. Strain into the saucepan and add the honey. Bring to a boil and boil until reduced by about a third. Turn the heat down to a simmer.

2. Add the pears and lemon juice to the simmering ginger syrup along with the currants. Simmer until translucent, about 10 minutes. Remove from the heat. Transfer the pears to the serving bowl and return the ginger syrup to the heat. Bring to a boil again and boil until the syrup thickens slightly, 3 to 5 minutes. Remove from the heat, pour over the pears, and allow to cool. Serve cold or at room temperature.

Get out the following equipment: **grater, mini-chop, or chef's knife and cutting board; medium-size bowl or large measuring cup; 2- or 3-quart nonreactive saucepan; measuring spoons; paring knife or potato peeler; strainer; serving bowl**

Advance preparation: **This can be made a day or two ahead of time.**

PER SERVING:
0.7 gm total fat
0 gm saturated fat
162 calories
42.2 gm carbohydrates
1.0 gm protein

Pears Poached in Beaujolais Nouveau

Makes 6 servings

Beaujolais Nouveau is a fruity French wine that appears on the market in mid-November. These poached pears make a nice Thanksgiving dessert. Serve biscotti on the side; it's nice to dip the hard cookies into the wine.

Get out the following equipment: potato peeler or paring knife; large bowl; large nonreactive saucepan or soup pot; piece of cheesecloth or tea ball; measuring cups and measuring spoons; serving dish

Advance preparation: The poached pears will keep for a few days in the refrigerator, but they will become more saturated with the wine. For best results, serve no more than a day after poaching.

PER SERVING:
1.0 gm total fat
0.1 saturated fat
279 calories
50.8 gm carbohydrates
1.2 gm protein

1 tablespoon black peppercorns
6 large, ripe, firm pears
A bowl of water mixed with the juice of 1 large lemon
1 bottle Beaujolais Nouveau
⅓ cup sugar
Fresh mint sprigs for garnish

1. Tie the peppercorns into a cheesecloth bag or place in the tea ball.
2. Leaving the stem on, peel the pears and drop them immediately into the bowl of acidulated water.
3. In the saucepan or soup pot, combine the Beaujolais, sugar, and peppercorns and bring to a simmer. Stir until the sugar dissolves, reduce the heat to medium-low and simmer gently for 10 minutes. Carefully drop in the pears. Simmer, without letting the wine boil, for another 10 minutes. Remove from the heat and allow the pears to cool in the liquid.
4. Discard the peppercorns. Carefully transfer the pears to the serving dish (glass is nice). Heat the wine to a boil and reduce by about one third. Pour over the pears and refrigerate for several hours.
5. Serve the pears in wide bowls, ladling some of the wine on top. Garnish each pear with a sprig of mint.

Baked Apples

Makes 4 servings

Get out the following equipment: paring knife or potato peeler; small baking dish that will hold the apples; measuring cup; citrus zester

Advance preparation: Baked apples can be made a day ahead and reheated or served at room temperature.

Baked apples are one of the simplest and most satisfying desserts, particularly in the fall and winter. I prefer a tart or moderately tart apple here, a Pippin, Pink lady, Braeburn, Fuji, or Granny Smith. The lemony apple juice moistens the apples as they bake, then makes a lovely syrup for spooning over.

4 tart, firm apples
½ lemon for rubbing the peeled apples
½ cup apple juice
Zest of 1 lemon

1. Preheat the oven to 350°F. Peel the top quarter of the apples. Core by cutting a cone out of the stem end, using either a paring knife or the tip of your peeler. Rub the peeled parts with the cut lemon half. Place the apples, standing up, in the baking dish. Pour the apple juice over the apples and into the dish, pouring some of it into the cores to moisten them. Add the lemon zest to the apple juice in the dish. Cover with aluminum foil or a lid if the dish is deep.

2. Bake until the apples are tender, 30 to 40 minutes. Remove from the heat and serve hot or warm, spooning the apple juice over the apples.

PER SERVING:
0.5 gm total fat
0.1 gm saturated fat
96 calories
24.6 gm carbohydrates
0.3 gm protein

Dessert Couscous with Oranges and Dates

Makes 6 to 8 servings

When I was in Tunisia, some of the most delightful dishes we were served were desserts made with couscous. Sweetened with a sugar syrup and delicately flavored with orange flower water and spices, these sweet couscous dishes were not only served at evening meals but often found their way to the breakfast table. Mine are less sweet than typical North African couscous and don't contain a fraction of the butter that would normally be used. Orange flower water is widely used in North African and Middle Eastern cooking. It has a perfumed, subtle flavor. You can find it at Middle Eastern groceries. If you can't get hold of it, the dessert will still be good, so do make it.

2¼ cups water

¼ cup sugar

2 tablespoons orange flower water, if available

1 tablespoon unsalted butter

1½ cups instant couscous

¼ cup dried currants or golden raisins

1 teaspoon ground cinnamon

Generous pinch of salt

2 tablespoons finely chopped orange zest (from 2 oranges)

3 seedless navel oranges

10 dates, quartered lengthwise and seeds removed

1. Combine the water and sugar in the saucepan and bring to a boil. Reduce the heat to medium and boil slowly until the mixture thickens slightly,

Get out the following equipment: 2-quart saucepan; large bowl; measuring cups and measuring spoons; wooden spoon; paring knife; steamer, strainer or colander and pot, or couscoussière; serving bowl or platter

Advance preparation: **This can be made several hours ahead and held at room temperature or chilled. You can make it through step 3 a day or two before and refrigerate. Allow to come to room temperature and proceed with step 4 a few hours or shortly before serving.**

PER SERVING:
2.5 gm total fat
1.3 gm saturated fat
314 calories
67.5 gm carbohydrates
7.2 gm protein

about 10 minutes. Stir in the orange flower water and remove from the heat. Stir in the butter and allow it to melt.

2. Place the couscous in the bowl. Stir in the currants or raisins, cinnamon, salt, and orange zest. Pour the syrup over. Let sit for 20 minutes, stirring from time to time with a wooden spoon to break up any lumps.

3. Line a steamer, the top part of a couscoussière, a strainer, or a colander with a clean kitchen towel and place the couscous on top of the towel. Cover and steam for 15 minutes above boiling water, making sure that the water is well below the couscous. Turn into a bowl.

4. Peel the oranges, holding the orange above the couscous so that any juice that escapes will go into the couscous. Remove the skin and pith at the same time by holding the knife against the orange at a slight angle and turning the orange against the knife, so that the skin comes off in a spiral. Squeeze the skin over the couscous to obtain any juice from the pulp that you may have cut off with the skin. Cut 2 of the oranges in half crosswise, then into small sections. Section the third orange for decorating the top of the couscous. Toss the steamed couscous with the chopped oranges. Transfer to the serving dish and shape the couscous into a cone-shaped mound. Decorate the top with the remaining orange slices and the dates. Serve warm or at room temperature.

Dessert Couscous with Pomegranate

Substitute the seeds of 1 large pomegranate for one of the oranges. Toss the steamed couscous with the dates and 2 oranges and decorate the top with the pomegranate seeds.

Pear Clafoutis

Makes 8 servings

If you've worked your way through all of the "Warm-up Exercises," you'll know how much I love clafoutis, an easy and elegant dessert that is sort of a cross between a flan and a pancake. I make the Cherry Clafoutis on page 87 during the short cherry season; the pear season is longer, and this popular dessert is one I make frequently.

2 to 2¼ pounds firm, ripe pears (about 6 medium-size pears)

3 tablespoons kirsch or pear eau-de-vie or liqueur

6 tablespoons sugar

3 large eggs

1 vanilla bean or ½ teaspoon pure vanilla extract

Get out the following equipment: **chef's knife and cutting board; paring knife; measuring spoons; whisk or electric mixer; large bowl and medium-size bowl; 10-inch ceramic or glass baking dish or tart pan; measuring cups; sifter or strainer; wire rack for cooling**

Pinch of salt

⅔ cup sifted unbleached flour

¾ cup plain nonfat yogurt

1. Peel, core, and slice the pears. Toss at once with the kirsch or eau-de-vie and 2 tablespoons of the sugar in the large bowl and let sit for 30 minutes. Meanwhile, preheat the oven to 400°F. Butter the tart pan or baking dish.

2. Beat the eggs with the seeds from the vanilla bean or the vanilla extract with an electric mixer or a whisk until smooth. Strain the liquid from the pears into the eggs and add the remaining 4 tablespoons sugar and the salt. Beat together. Slowly beat in the flour. Add the yogurt and mix together well.

3. Arrange the pears over the bottom of the baking dish. Pour in the batter. Bake until the top is browned and the clafoutis firm, 25 to 30 minutes. Press gently on the top to see if it's firm. If it isn't, return to the oven for 2 to 5 minutes. Remove from the oven and cool on a wire rack. Serve warm or at room temperature.

Moist Apple Cake

Makes one 10- to 12-inch cake; 10 to 12 servings

Cakes have never been my strong point, and most cakes don't fit too well into the low-fat profile. But this one, which is sort of like a coffee cake, is mostly fruit, bathed in a moist, not-too-sweet batter. It's a great winter cake, for dessert or tea.

1 tablespoon unsalted butter

4 pounds Golden Delicious apples

3 large eggs

⅓ cup sugar

¼ cup canola oil

2 tablespoons 1% or skim milk

1 teaspoon pure vanilla extract

2 tablespoons rum or whiskey

½ cup plus 2 heaping tablespoons sifted unbleached flour

1 tablespoon baking powder

1 teaspoon baking soda

Pinch of salt

Advance preparation: **The dish will hold for several hours at room temperature.**

PER SERVING:
2.5 gm total fat
0.6 gm saturated fat
206 calories
39.9 gm carbohydrates
5.3 gm protein

Get out the following equipment: **potato peeler or paring knife; large and small knives and cutting board; measuring spoons and measuring cups; large bowl; 2 medium-size bowls and whisk or electric mixer; rubber spatula; 10- to 12-inch round cake pan or 10-inch springform pan; wire rack for cooling**

continued

FOR THE TOPPING:

1 large egg

2 tablespoons unsalted butter, melted

2 tablespoons firmly packed dark brown sugar

½ teaspoon ground cinnamon

1. Preheat the oven to 425°F. Generously grease the cake pan or springform pan with the butter.

2. Peel and core the apples, then cut them into eighths. Place in the large bowl.

3. In the medium bowl, with an electric mixer or whisk, whisk together the eggs, sugar, oil, milk, vanilla, and rum or whiskey. In another bowl, sift together the flour, baking powder, baking soda, and salt and gradually add to the egg mixture (at medium speed with an electric mixer). Stir until blended. Pour over the apples and toss together so that all of them are coated.

4. Turn the apple mixture into the prepared pan, scraping every last bit of batter out of the bowl. Bake for 30 minutes. Meanwhile, mix together the ingredients for the topping. Pour over the cake after it has baked for 30 minutes and return it to the oven. Bake until the topping has caramelized, another 10 minutes. Remove from the oven and cool in the pan on a wire rack. Serve warm or at room temperature.

Yeasted Dessert Pastry

Makes two 10-inch piecrusts; 16 servings

If you want pies and tarts in your dessert repertoire, and you want to keep it light, this is a delicious alternative to the classic short pastry, which relies on a great deal more butter. This crust has a bready texture rather than the crisp, flaky texture of a traditional crust. I like the flavor, and to me the texture is somewhat like that of a thinly rolled coffee cake or sweet bread, which can be very nice unless you're expecting it to be like a short pastry. Because it's a yeasted pastry, when you prebake it in a tart pan the fluted edges can rise and collapse inward, causing the sides of the tart to be low. This is all right; it still ends up looking like a tart. But you might want to experiment with making a free-form galette on a baking sheet, rather than using a tart pan; you have the option.

1½ teaspoons active dry yeast

½ cup lukewarm water

2 tablespoons plus ¼ teaspoon sugar

1 large egg, at room temperature

2 to 2½ cups all-purpose flour

½ teaspoon salt

¼ cup (½ stick) unsalted butter, softened

Advance preparation:
This will keep for several months in the freezer. You can freeze the dough before rolling out as well; allow to thaw, then roll out. You can also keep the dough, before rolling out, in the refrigerator for a day. You will need to dust it generously with flour when you roll it out. You can transfer the dough directly from the freezer to the oven for baking.

PER SERVING:
3.4 gm total fat
1.9 gm saturated fat
105 calories
15.7 gm carbohydrates
2.7 gm protein

1. Dissolve the yeast in the water, add ¼ teaspoon of the sugar, and let sit until creamy, 5 to 10 minutes. Beat in the egg. Combine 2 cups of the flour, the remaining 2 tablespoons sugar, and the salt. Stir 1 cup of the flour mixture into the yeast mixture. Add the butter and stir in (this can be done in an electric mixer; combine the ingredients using the paddle, then switch to the dough hook). Add the remaining cup flour mixture. Work the dough until it comes together in a coherent mass, adding more of the remaining flour as necessary if it is very moist and sticky, then turn out onto a lightly floured surface. Knead gently, adding flour as necessary, just until the dough is smooth, and shape the dough into a ball. Do not overwork. Place in a lightly oiled or buttered bowl, cover the bowl tightly with plastic wrap, and let rise in a warm draft-free spot until doubled in size, about 1 hour.

2. When the pastry has risen and softened, punch it down gently and shape into a ball. Cut into 2 equal pieces and shape each piece into a ball. Cover each ball loosely with plastic wrap and let rest for 10 minutes. Butter or oil the tart or pie pans or baking sheets. Roll out each ball of dough on a lightly floured surface, dusting each side of the dough with flour so that it doesn't stick to your rolling pin or the table. Roll the dough very thin, about ⅛ inch thick. It should be about 1 inch bigger than the circumference of your pans.

   If using pans: Line the pans with the dough. An easy way to do this is to fold the dough in half, then place on one half of the pan and unfold. Press gently into the pans (this is often called "easing" the dough into the pans). You should have a bit of overhang around the edges of the pan. Roll the dough in and pinch an attractive lip around the edge of the pan.

   If making a free-form crust: Roll out as instructed into large circles, about ⅛ inch thick. Transfer to the baking sheet. Roll in the edges to form an attractive lip, as you would for a pizza.

   Cover loosely with a kitchen towel and let rest for 20 to 30 minutes if baking right away. If not, cover with plastic wrap and place in the freezer to keep the dough from rising and becoming too bready. Remove from the freezer very shortly before prebaking (it doesn't need to thaw). Bake as directed in the individual recipes.

Fresh Fig Tart

∎

Makes one 10-inch tart; 8 servings

Fresh figs are a luxury, but so worth indulging in. Serve this voluptuous tart
for dessert at a late summer dinner party. Nobody will forget it.

1 Yeasted Dessert Pastry crust (page 352)
1 large egg white, beaten
1½ pounds fresh figs, cut in half lengthwise
¼ cup mild-flavored honey such as clover or acacia
Finely minced zest of 1 orange

1. Preheat the oven to 375°F. Brush the surface of the piecrust with the egg
   white and prebake for 10 minutes. Remove from the oven and cool for 5
   to 10 minutes on a wire rack.
2. Arrange the fig halves over the crust. Heat the honey and orange zest together in a saucepan, just until it pours easily. Drizzle over the figs.
3. Bake until the crust is browned, 25 to 30 minutes. Remove from the oven
   and cool on a wire rack before serving.

Peach or Peach and Blueberry Pie

∎

Makes one 10-inch pie; 8 servings

I don't know anyone who doesn't love a peach pie. We have such a long
peach season in Los Angeles—it seems that somebody at the farmers' market
is always bringing in a new crop of late-variety peaches, right up until the
end of October—that I can indulge in this for several months of the year. Remember that the yeasted dessert crust has a bready rather than crumbly-flaky
texture, giving this tart the nature of something between a cobbler and a tart.

1 recipe Yeasted Dessert Pastry (page 352)
3 pounds ripe peaches
2 tablespoons fresh lemon juice
¼ cup firmly packed light brown sugar or 2 tablespoons mild-flavored honey
   such as clover or acacia
½ teaspoon ground cinnamon
1 tablespoon cornstarch
1 pint fresh blueberries (optional), rinsed and picked over

1 large egg white, beaten

1 tablespoon milk for glaze

2 teaspoons granulated sugar for glaze

1. Preheat the oven to 375°F with the rack in the middle. Butter the pie or tart pan. Divide the dough into 2 slightly unequal pieces. Roll out the larger piece, dusting your work surface with flour as necessary, and line the pan with it, pinching an attractive rim around the edge. Set the other piece of dough aside.

2. Bring a pot of water to a boil and drop in the peaches. Boil for 30 seconds (1 minute if very hard) and transfer to a bowl of cold water.

3. Combine the lemon juice, brown sugar or honey, cinnamon, and cornstarch in the large bowl. Peel the peaches, cut into wedges, and toss at once with this mixture. Add the blueberries if using and toss together.

4. Brush the crust fitted into the pan with the beaten egg white and prebake for 7 minutes. Remove from the oven. Spoon the fruit into the crust and scrape all of the juice in the bowl over it. Roll out the remaining pie dough about ⅛ inch thick and cut into ½-inch-wide strips. Lay the strips across the peaches. Turn the dish and lay strips across the strips, at right angles or on the diagonal, for a lattice. Carefully pinch the ends of the strips against the sides of the bottom crust. Trim off any excess. Brush with the milk and sprinkle with the granulated sugar.

5. Place a piece of aluminum foil on your rack to catch any juices that might bubble over. Place the pie on top of the foil. Bake until the crust is golden brown and the fruit bubbling, about 45 minutes. Remove from the heat and cool on a wire rack before serving.

▪ Crumbles or Crisps: ▪ Dessert Indulgences

I call them *crumbles*; you may call them *crisps*. To me they are one and the same. These are higher in fat than the other desserts here, but every once in a while you need an indulgence, particularly when you're giving a dinner party. Since the menus here are low in fat, a little butter on the dessert table shouldn't be too harmful. These are always appreciated, always showstoppers. And they're easy.

Advance preparation: **Crumbles can be baked a few hours ahead, but they're best served warm and baked not too far in advance, to ensure a crisp topping. You can reheat them in a warm oven to recrisp the top. The yogurt-and-honey topping will keep for a few days in the refrigerator. Leftovers with yogurt are a popular breakfast in my house.**

Crumble Topping

∎

Makes 6 to 8 servings

¼ cup shelled pecans

¾ cup rolled oats (old-fashioned, not instant)

½ cup whole-wheat pastry flour or all-purpose flour

¼ cup firmly packed light brown sugar, preferably unrefined turbinado sugar

¼ teaspoon salt

¼ teaspoon freshly grated nutmeg

1 teaspoon finely minced orange zest

6 tablespoons (¾ stick) cold unsalted butter

1. Heat the pecans in the dry skillet over medium heat, shaking it or stirring, until they begin to smell toasty. Remove from the skillet at once and
   chop coarsely.
2. Mix together the oats, flour, sugar, salt, nutmeg, and orange zest.
3. Cut the butter into small pieces and work it into the flour mixture, either
   by taking up the mixture in handfuls and rubbing it briskly between your
   fingers and thumbs or by using the pulse action in a food processor. The
   mixture should have a crumbly consistency. Stir in the pecans.

Honeyed Yogurt Topping

∎

Makes about 1 cup

This makes a delicious low-fat topping for any crumble.

1 cup plain nonfat yogurt

1 to 2 tablespoons mild-flavored honey such as clover or acacia, to your taste

Drain off any water sitting on the yogurt. Stir in the honey and mix well. Refrigerate until ready to use.

Plum Crumble

Makes 6 to 8 servings

2½ pounds plums, pitted and quartered if small or cut into smaller wedges if
   large

¼ cup sugar or 3 tablespoons mild-flavored honey such as clover or acacia

½ teaspoon pure vanilla extract

1 tablespoon plum brandy or kirsch

Crumble Topping (page 356)

Honeyed Yogurt Topping (page 356)

1. Preheat the oven to 375°F. Butter the baking or gratin dish. Toss together the
   plums, sugar or honey, vanilla, and brandy in the bowl. Turn into the dish.

2. Spoon the crumble over the filling in an even layer. Bake until browned,
   about 45 minutes. If you wish, finish very briefly under the broiler, being
   careful not to burn. Serve warm with the honeyed yogurt.

Pear Crumble

Makes 6 to 8 servings

3 tablespoons dried currants

2 tablespoons pear liqueur or eau-de-vie, kirsch, or brandy

2 tablespoons fresh lemon juice

2 tablespoons sugar

½ teaspoon ground ginger

1 tablespoon cornstarch or 1 teaspoon arrowroot

2½ pounds firm, ripe pears

Crumble Topping (page 356)

Honeyed Yogurt Topping (page 356)

1. Preheat the oven to 375°F. Butter the baking or gratin dish. Place the
   currants in the small bowl and toss with the liqueur, kirsch, or brandy.
   Let sit.

2. Combine the lemon juice, sugar, ginger, and cornstarch or arrowroot.
   Peel, core, and slice the pears and toss at once with the lemon juice mixture. Stir in the currants and any liqueur remaining in the bowl.

3. Turn into the prepared dish. Spread the crumble topping over the filling
   in an even layer. Bake until the top is crisp and brown, about 45 minutes.
   If you wish, finish browning the top briefly under the broiler, taking care
   not to burn it. Serve warm, with the honeyed yogurt.

*For all the crumbles, get
out the following equip-
ment: measuring
spoons; paring knife
and cutting board;
small and large bowls,
2-to 2½-quart baking
or gratin dish; paring
knife if needed*

PER SERVING:
*22.7 gm total fat
10.8 gm saturated fat
509 calories
72.9 gm carbohydrates
8.3 gm protein*

PER SERVING:
*22.3 gm total fat
10.7 gm saturated fat
527 calories
78.9 gm carbohydrates
7.8 gm protein*

Apple Crisp

Makes 6 to 8 servings

PER SERVING:
22.1 gm total fat
10.8 gm saturated fat
478 calories
68.8 gm carbohydrates
7.1 gm protein

2½ pounds tart apples, such as Pippin, Granny Smith, or Braeburn

2 tablespoons fresh lemon juice

2 tablespoons firmly packed light or dark brown sugar or unrefined
   turbinado brown sugar

¾ teaspoon ground cinnamon

Pinch of ground cloves (about 4 cloves)

¼ teaspoon freshly grated nutmeg

Crumble Topping (page 356)

Honeyed Yogurt Topping (page 356)

1. Preheat the oven to 375°F. Butter the baking or gratin dish. Peel, core, and thinly slice the apples. Toss with the remaining ingredients (except the crumble and yogurt toppings).

2. Turn into the buttered dish. Spread the crumble topping over the top in an even layer, making sure the apples are covered. Bake until the top is crisp and brown, about 45 minutes. If you wish, finish browning the top briefly under the broiler, taking care not to burn. Serve warm, with the honeyed yogurt.

Rhubarb-Strawberry Crumble

Makes 6 to 8 servings

PER SERVING:
22.0 gm total fat
10.7 gm saturated fat
498 calories
73.2 gm carbohydrates
8.6 gm protein

2 pounds rhubarb, trimmed, leaves discarded, and stalks sliced into ½-inch
   pieces; cut the stalks in half lengthwise first if wide

1 pint fresh strawberries, hulled and quartered

½ cup mild-flavored honey such as clover or acacia or ½ cup sugar

Finely chopped zest of 1 orange

½ teaspoon ground cinnamon

Crumble Topping (page 356)

Honeyed Yogurt Topping (page 356)

1. Preheat the oven to 375°F. Butter the baking or gratin dish. Toss together the rhubarb, strawberries, honey or sugar, orange zest, and cinnamon in the bowl.

2. Turn into the buttered dish. Spread the crumble topping over the top in an even layer. Bake until the top is crisp and brown, about 45 minutes. If you wish, finish browning the top briefly under the broiler, taking care not to burn it. Serve warm, with the honeyed yogurt.

Peach Crumble

Makes 6 to 8 servings

PER SERVING:
21.7 gm total fat
10.7 gm saturated fat
473 calories
67.2 gm carbohydrates
8.2 gm protein

2½ pounds firm, ripe peaches, pitted and sliced

3 tablespoons firmly packed light brown sugar

Seeds from 4 cardamom pods, ground (scant ¼ teaspoon) or ½ teaspoon ground cinnamon

½ teaspoon pure vanilla extract

1 tablespoon fresh lemon juice.

Crumble Topping (page 356)

Honeyed Yogurt Topping (page 356)

1. Preheat the oven to 375°F. Butter the baking or gratin dish. Toss together the peaches, sugar, cardamom, vanilla, and lemon juice in the bowl.
2. Turn into the buttered dish. Spread the crumble topping over the top in an even layer. Bake until the top is crisp and brown, about 45 minutes. If you wish, finish browning the top briefly under the broiler, taking care not to burn it. Serve warm, with the honeyed yogurt.

Two Meringue Cookies

Makes about 70 little cookies

Meringues are easy to make and light as a feather. The trick is to bake them long enough so that they'll be crisp. Serve them with fresh fruit desserts. Your guests will adore you.

4 large egg whites

¼ teaspoon cream of tartar

Pinch of salt

½ teaspoon pure vanilla extract

½ cup sugar

FOR LEMON MERINGUE COOKIES:

2 tablespoons finely chopped lemon zest (from 2 large lemons)

Get out the following equipment: **electric mixer fitted with the whisk attachment, or hand mixer and large bowl; measuring cups and measuring spoons; 2 baking sheets; parchment or wax paper; pastry bag fitted with the star tip if you have one; bowls for separating the eggs; wire rack for cooling; spatula**

Advance preparation: **If you can resist eating them, the cookies will keep for at least a week if well sealed.**

continued

PER SERVING:
0 gm total fat
0 gm saturated fat
7 calories
1.5 gm carbohydrates
0.2 gm protein

PER COOKIE
(LEMON; CHOCOLATE):
0; 0 gm total fat
0; 0 gm saturated fat
6.7; 7 calories
1.4; 1.6 gm carbohy-drates
0.2; 0.3 gm protein

FOR CHOCOLATE MERINGUE COOKIES:

¼ cup unsweetened cocoa powder

1. Preheat the oven to 300°F. Butter the baking sheets and cover with buttered parchment or wax paper.

2. Beat the egg whites in the large bowl until they begin to foam. Add the cream of tartar and the salt and continue to beat until the egg whites form stiff peaks. (Egg whites form stiff peaks if they stand up straight and don't lean over when you lift them into a little mound with a spatula. They should be shiny, and they shouldn't be so dry that they break apart, which will happen if you overbeat them.) Continue to beat on medium speed while you add the vanilla and gradually add the sugar, a tablespoon at a time.

3. *For lemon meringue cookies,* add the lemon zest, still beating to distribute it evenly through the meringue.

    For chocolate meringue cookies, gradually add the cocoa powder, still beating. You may have to stop the beaters a couple of times to stir down the sides of the bowl with a spatula, because some of the powder may stick to the sides.

    When all of the ingredients have been added, you should have a shiny meringue.

4. Spoon or pipe teaspoonsful of the meringue onto the prepared baking sheets and place in the oven. Bake until the cookies have browned and feel stiff, 25 to 30 minutes. Remove from the heat and let sit on the baking sheets for 5 minutes. If they were slightly soft, they should stiffen when they cool. If they are still soft after sitting on the baking sheet for 5 minutes, return to the oven and check again every 5 minutes. Let sit on the baking sheets for 5 minutes, then remove with a spatula and cool on wire racks. Keep in a covered container.

Almond Biscotti

Makes about 60 thin biscotti

These small, thin biscotti are much more delicate than the large, thick biscotti we usually find in stores.

⅔ cup unblanched almonds

2 large eggs

¼ cup granulated sugar

¼ cup firmly packed light brown sugar

1 teaspoon baking soda

¼ teaspoon salt

1¾ to 2 cups sifted unbleached flour, or a combination of unbleached and whole-wheat pastry flour, plus more as necessary for kneading

1 large egg white

Get out the following equipment: a baking sheet; chef's knife and cutting board; serrated knife; large bowl, food processor fitted with the steel blade, or electric mixer fitted with the paddle attachment; measuring cups and measuring spoons

Advance preparation: These will keep for weeks in a covered container.

PER BISCOTTI:
1.0 gm total fat
0.1 gm saturated fat
34 calories
5.2 gm carbohydrates
1.0 gm protein

1. Preheat the oven to 375°F. Place the almonds on the baking sheet and roast until golden brown and toasty, about 10 minutes. Remove from the oven and chop medium-fine with a knife (don't use the food processor; it will either grind them or leave big chunks).

2. Butter and flour the wiped-clean baking sheet

3. In a mixer or food processor, blend together the whole eggs and sugars. Add the baking soda and salt. Gradually add the flour. Use the pulse action to work in if using a food processor. When the dough is no longer sticky (it should come together on the blades of a food processor), gradually add the chopped almonds and work in using the pulse action. (If you are using a mixer, it will be easier to scrape the dough out onto a lightly floured work surface, press out the dough, and scatter the almonds over the top. Fold the dough over the almonds and knead gently until the almonds are distributed evenly through the dough.) Add a little more flour if the dough is sticky.

4. Divide the dough in half. Shape into 2 long logs about 1 inch wide and ¾ inch high. Place on the prepared baking sheet, not too close together. Beat the egg white until foamy and brush it over the logs. Bake until golden brown and shiny, 20 minutes. Remove from the oven and reduce the oven temperature to 275°F.

5. Using the serrated knife, cut the logs into diagonal slices about ¼ inch thick. Place on the baking sheet and bake again until dry, hard, and lightly browned, 25 to 40 minutes. Remove from the oven and cool. Store in a covered container.

Ginger Biscotti

Add 2 teaspoons ground ginger to the whole eggs and sugar when you beat them together.

Honey Biscotti

Substitute ½ cup mild-flavored honey such as clover or acacia for the granulated and brown sugars. Add up to another ¾ cup flour to get a workable dough.

Entertaining

■

Now that you can cook, you can give a dinner party. Don't panic! There is a trick to entertaining and enjoying it: it's all about choosing the menu. The menu shouldn't involve too much work, and it should include dishes that can be done, at least partially, ahead of time.

What's the difference, anyway, between a menu we would select for a dinner party and a meal we'd make for everyday dining? Usually a menu for company involves more courses—a starter, a main dish, perhaps a side dish, and a dessert. When we dine informally, we might serve the main dish and salad all at once, maybe eat a piece of fruit for dessert if we eat dessert at all, and that's dinner. For guests, we compose a meal, with beginning, middle, and end. And we usually offer a nibble beforehand with drinks, although that can be as simple as a dish of olives or radishes set out on the coffee table.

Light Basics Cookbook menus for entertaining are designed to please and satisfy guests without overdoing it. Too often we pull out rich dishes for company, when our friends and family don't necessarily want to be eating that way. It's quite possible to strike a balance between a copious, generous meal and one that is excessive. There might be a special, slightly rich dessert like a crumble, but if the rest of the meal is moderate, this will be an appropriate indulgence.

If you want to enjoy your party, organization is the key. Getting a little bit done on the days leading up to the party will make all the difference between panic and calm. Make lists and calendars for your work schedule: you can shop days before a dinner for everything except fresh fish and some lettuces; the table can be set the night before. Use the "advance preparation" notes ac-

362

companying the recipes to determine what can be made ahead of time. Prepare ingredients ahead and refrigerate them; this is usually the most time-consuming part of cooking, so the more you can get out of the way in that department, the better.

Setting the Table

A beautiful table, all ready for guests, is a reassuring sight, for both the host and the guests. When you put a little care into the look of the table, it shows, and even before people sit down to eat, it's clear that you've done something special for them. This doesn't require fancy dishes and stemware, just a bit of thought. Set a tablecloth or pretty mats under the plates, use cloth napkins if you have them; have flowers on the table, but make sure the arrangement is low enough so that diners can see each other. Just a few daisies or wildflowers in a little vase add a warm, cared-for look. Candles, too, are always on my dinner table. Even when you are planning to place the food on the plates in the kitchen or serve from a buffet, if you are having a sit-down dinner party the plates should be on the table when the guests arrive. You can clear them away when you get ready to serve. If you are serving wine and water, make sure there is a glass for each.

I find it very soothing to get table setting out of the way the night before my dinner parties, or at least before I begin cooking that day. You can get out all the dishes you'll need for each course, as well as serving dishes and utensils. Having this done makes me feel ready for my guests, even if I still have a number of things to do in the kitchen when they arrive.

Menus and Lists

The first thing you need to do when you're planning a dinner party (once you have your guest list) is choose the menu. If you have invited guests who are vegetarians, you need to think about a vegetarian menu or one that will include enough meatless fare so that those guests won't go hungry. Consider the weather; if it's hot, serve lighter food. In winter, stews and soups are welcome. Also consider the food that's in season. Don't plan a winter meal that requires peaches or sweet, ripe tomatoes (however, if canned tomatoes are indicated in the recipe, that's fine). My meals usually include a starter course—which can be a salad or a soup—a main dish, and a dessert. If the main dish is a stew or a main-dish soup, then side dishes aren't required (unless the stew is served with rice or other grains). If it is a fish, chicken, or vegetarian main dish, then a nice side dish will be much appreciated. This can be something like a gratin or a simple cooked vegetable, like corn on the cob, oven-roasted potatoes, or steamed green beans.

Once you've got your menu, go through each recipe and make a shopping list. First, ascertain whether you have to multiply ingredients in recipes. Most of the recipes here serve four people, although some serve six and a few serve eight. If you've got six at your table, you'll have to multiply ingredients for a salad for four by 1.5, or double them if you like having leftovers. Multiples of up to three work fine for all of these recipes. Check to make sure that all the staples on the list, items like vinegars and olive oil, even salt and pepper, are on hand. Also on the shopping list should be beverages and goods like candles and flowers, and a nice loaf of bread, if your city or town has a good bakery—which may be in a supermarket or organic food store.

Now make a work schedule. Read through each recipe to see what needs to be done and what can be done ahead of time. I usually begin my list on the day of the party and work backward. What are the things that have to be done at the last minute? What can be made ahead? How many days ahead? How far ahead can I shop? If you can get a little done each day on the three days leading up to your dinner party, you will have a much easier time as a host.

Here are some suggested seasonal dinner party menus and buffets. Some are vegetarian; others include chicken or fish. You can substitute unadorned fresh fruit for any of the desserts.

Arugula Salad with Beets
Mediterranean Fish Stew
Pear or Plum Crumble

■

Yellow Pepper Soup with Thyme
Chicken with Two Heads of Garlic
Steamed green vegetable
Tossed green salad
Blood Orange and Tangerine Salad
Meringues or Biscotti (optional)

■

Cold Turkish-Style Cucumber and Yogurt Soup
Swordfish Kebabs
Pilaf-Style Rice
Tossed green salad
Peach and Apricot Salad
Meringues or Biscotti (optional)

■

Wild Mushroom Bruschetta
Asparagus and Saffron Risotto
Tossed Green Salad
Cherry Clafoutis

■

Baby Spinach and Salad with Mushrooms
Hot or Cold Steamed Fish Fillets with Tomato-Mint Vinaigrette
Corn on the Cob
Steamed Green Vegetable or Pan-Cooked Greens with Garlic and Lemon
Peaches Poached in Red Wine
Biscotti (optional)

■

Arugula Salad with Beets
Spinach and Tomato Lasagne
(you can substitute greens from the beets for some or all of the spinach)
Pan-Cooked Mushrooms
Pears Poached in Ginger-Honey Syrup

■

Moroccan Carrot Salad
Winter Vegetable Couscous
Pear Clafoutis

Buffet Menus

Caponata
Chicken with Mediterranean Flavors or Tunisian Chicken with Olives, with
Couscous
Tossed Green Salad
Fresh Fig Tart

■

Caponata
Summer Squash, Sweet Onion, and Red Pepper Tart
Quiche with Smoked Salmon
White Bean and Pesto Salad
Rhubarb and Strawberry Compote
Fresh fruit

■

Asparagus (and Smoked Salmon or Smoked Trout) Frittata
Frittata with Sweet Red Pepper and Peas
Asian Noodle and Snow Pea Salad
Greek Salad
Mushroom Tart
Fresh fruit combos

The second and third buffet menus are particularly nice for brunch.

■ Sample Dinner Party Lists and ■ Work Schedules

Tuesday Dinner Party for Six

Arugula Salad with Beets
Mediterranean Fish Stew
Pear Crumble

Shopping List

SALAD (MULTIPLY INGREDIENTS BY 1.5):

2 bunches beets

9 ounces arugula

Small block of Parmesan

STEW:

2 onions

Celery

1 large or 2 medium-size carrots

Garlic

1 bunch flat-leaf parsley

Anchovies

1 28-ounce can tomatoes

Dry white wine (sauvignon blanc)

2 pounds fish fillets (such as halibut,
    mahimahi, shark, cod, or monkfish)

CRUMBLE:

Dried currants

Pear eau-de-vie or brandy

2½ pounds pears

2 lemons

1 orange

Pecans

Oats

Unsalted butter

Yogurt

Wine, water, bread

CHECK STAPLES:

Balsamic vinegar

Sherry vinegar

Salt, pepper

Olive oil

Dijon mustard

Granulated sugar

Brown sugar and turbinado sugar

Honey

Nutmeg

Flour

Candles

Work Schedule

SUNDAY:
All marketing except fish, bread, and
    arugula
Roast and peel beets
Make stew base (can also do on
    Monday)

MONDAY:
Buy and arrange flowers (can also do
    this on Tuesday)
Check wine and water supply; buy if
    necessary
Set table
Sweetened yogurt for dessert

TUESDAY:
Buy fish, cut it up, and finish soup
    just before serving
Buy arugula; wash and dry it
Buy bread
Make salad dressing
Make crumble

DISHES:
Dinner plates
Salad plates
Wide soup bowls
Dessert plates (can recycle salad
    plates)
Forks, knives, soupspoons, dessert
    forks or spoons
Wine and water glasses

Saturday Dinner Party for Six

Yellow Pepper Soup with Thyme
Chicken with Two Heads of Garlic
Green vegetable (broccoli)
Tossed Green Salad
Blood Orange and Tangerine Salad
Biscotti (make or buy)

Shopping List

SOUP:
1 onion
1 carrot
Garlic
2 pounds yellow bell peppers
½ pound potatoes
Chicken stock or bouillon
1 baguette
Fresh thyme

CHICKEN (MULTIPLY RECIPE BY 1.5
    OR DOUBLE AND ENJOY LEFT-
    OVERS; THIS LIST IS FOR 1.5):
1 chicken plus 2 legs and thighs, cut
    up and skinned
3 heads garlic
1 bottle sauvignon blanc
Fresh or dried thyme
Fresh or dried rosemary
1 bunch flat-leaf parsley
1 loaf country bread
1½ pounds broccoli

SALAD (MULTIPLY BY 1.5):
¾ pound lettuce or salad greens
Fresh herbs
5 to 6 mushrooms
1 lemon

DESSERT (MULTIPLY BY 1.5):
6 blood oranges
9 seedless tangerines
Grand Marnier or Cointreau
Fresh mint
Biscotti if buying

BISCOTTI (IF MAKING):
¾ cup almonds
Eggs (3)
Whole-wheat pastry flour and/or
    all-purpose flour

CHECK STAPLES:
Olive oil
Vinegar
Dijon mustard
Salt, pepper
Flour
Granulated sugar
Light brown sugar
Baking soda
Candles

Work Schedule

WEEKEND BEFORE:
Make shopping list
Make Biscotti if not buying

THURSDAY:
Marketing except lettuce and breads
    (buy on Friday or Saturday)

FRIDAY:
Buy lettuce and breads (or buy on
    Saturday)
Make soup
Prepare broccoli
Set table
Buy and arrange flowers

SATURDAY:
Prepare salad
Make salad dressing
Make all croutons (for soup and
    chicken)
Make Orange and Tangerine Salad
Make chicken
Steam broccoli

DISHES:
Soup bowls
Dinner plates
Salad plates
Dessert bowls
Bowl for fruit salad
Salad bowl
Soupspoons, forks (salad forks
    optional), knives, dessert spoons
Wine and water glasses

Index